THE URBAN ENVIRONMENT

THE URBAN ENVIRONMENT

Samuel E. Wallace
The University of Tennessee

1980

THE DORSEY PRESS   Homewood, Illinois 60430
Irwin-Dorsey Limited   Georgetown, Ontario   L7G 4B3

Cover: Photo by Harold M. Lambert.

ISBN 0-256-02218-6
Library of Congress Catalog Card No. 79–56087
Printed in the United States of America

1 2 3 4 5 6 7 8 9 0 ML 7 6 5 4 3 2 1 0

to
John T. Wallace
Everett C. Hughes
William E. Cole
Horace L. Mervin

PREFACE

The Urban Environment attempts to answer many of the questions students ask in basic urban courses. Answers to their questions are important first of all for the increased self- and social awareness the answers may bring about. To better understand themselves, students need to know what the consequences are, for them, of living in the midst of hundreds of millions of others. Are they suffering from sensory overload, from too high an intake of media? Is their salvation to be found in a rural commune or in the heart of the inner city?

Self-awareness is the necessary first step to social awareness. If we can understand ourselves and some of the conditions which have shaped us into what we have become, we can then begin to change the conditions that create problems. If we are indeed suffering from overcrowding, for example, then we ought to hasten the exodus from the inner cities and accelerate the sprawl now consuming the metropolitan hinterland. If, on the other hand, our understanding of the urban environment suggests our problems stem from other sources, different solutions will be in order. Whatever the issue confronted, the basic point is that understanding must come first.

Students of the urban environment are fortunate in having the scholarship of many different disciplines with their thousands of scholars on which to draw: archeology and anthropology, architecture, ecology, economics, geography, history, planning, political science, psychology, social psychology, sociology—and to this list some would add areas like housing, zoning, and perhaps community. In attempting to answer students' questions, *The Urban Environment* has drawn upon a wide variety of the available literature. Given this eclectic approach, it would have been inaccurate to refer to the literature as urban sociology, urban ecology, or by any other disciplinary designation. Therefore we have used the term *urbanology* to refer to the literature utilized and urbanologists to refer to those who study urban phenomena.

For the eclectic approach to be meaningful, however, the divergent and at times contradictory urban literature must be integrated into a unified framework. Ecology in the sense of interdependence has been the unifying perspective of *The Urban Environment*.

Professors have a wide variety of methods of study at their disposal. Some urbanologists have profitably used the statistical approach, entering the vast data banks of our urban civilization in search of the essential features of urbanization. Others have gone into the laboratory or have simulated laboratory conditions on city streets in the search for answers to questions about the urban environment. While using some of the principles derived from these and other approaches like them, *The Urban Environment* follows a different approach.

My first urban study project was of skid row. In 20 years of urban research since that first project, I have extended participant observation into many other areas within the urban environment. Although I have used other methods, including the statistical and especially the historical, I have been primarily a participant observer as I lived, worked, and studied such cities as San Juan, Puerto Rico; Marrackesh, Fez, Casablanca, and Rabat, in Morocco; Granada and Madrid in Spain; and Paris and Perouges in France. In the United States I have lived for extended periods in Kansas City, Minneapolis, New York, and Boston, in every case in the inner city itself. In addition I have studied firsthand for at least several weeks nearly all other major American metropolitan areas. Just as I experienced the reality of skid row as being different from the way in which it was (and is) often described, so my experience with many features of the urban environment has been found to differ from many views.

Having learned so much by going into the field, what better way to teach than by taking students into the field also—or even better, sending them out on their own when they would go? My own teaching has thus involved a heavy component of individual and class research projects, urbanology through participant observation. Extending that teaching practice, *The Urban Environment* attempts to teach by taking its readers into the field. Individual and class participant observation projects are also suggested at the end of some chapters.

Acknowledgments

Some of my students have gone on to become colleagues in urbanology and then to assist me. Thus former NYU student and now Professor Mark Kassop, a reviewer for The Dorsey Press, caught a major inconsistency in an early draft and made a number of other helpful suggestions as well. Jerry Harrison came with me to UT, and before leaving for New Mexico State University served as media coordinator in our continuing experimentation with audiovisual materials. Walter Robinson, now of Henderson State University, reviewed a draft of the manuscript.

Two of my former professors have continued to assist me in my own urban work, reviewing and commenting on this manuscript: Theodore Caplow of the University of Virginia, and Gregory Stone of the University of Minnesota.

Other colleagues from whom I have benefitted include Conrad Taeuber of Georgetown University and William E. Cole of the University of Tennessee.

My debt to many other scholars is also evident to those familiar with their work. However, among them acknowledgments must be paid to Walter Firey of the University of Texas at Austin. His publications on ecology and his review of the manuscript have been especially helpful.

Amy Bokerkamp typed most of the manuscript, in its numerous drafts, adding to it by her always excellent work. Loretta Reeves and Alan Ferguson assisted in the bibliographic work. Valerie Carr helped on the graphics. Christine Valentine and Anita Hardeman assisted me with their editing. Robin Williams, the editor for The Dorsey Press, by his wise counsel and thorough editing, helped save this struggling author from mistakes both large and small.

My daughter Michele, and my wife, Susan, continue to aid me in all my efforts, and to make them worthwhile.

February 1980   Samuel E. Wallace

CONTENTS

INTRODUCTION:
THE ORGANIZATION OF
THIS TEXT

The causes and consequences of urbanization is the topic of our inquiry. The topic includes such questions as why do cities arise and why do people flock to them? What impact does life in cities have on their inhabitants? What difference does the size of a city make? How does the urbanite survive in an urban world that is filled with strangers?

Urbanization is revolutionary; it accelerates change. Once the urban revolution began about 10,000 years ago, virtually every aspect of human life changed. The change is summarized in the word "civilization," which developed in cities. To be civilized is to be urban, if not urbane.

The urban revolution is a process. Through the study of countless scholars of the 10,000 years of urban history, we know that the process of urbanization has a different impact depending, in part, on location within it. To experience the city after reaching young adulthood on a farm is most revolutionary. But to move from a *world city* to a small town, or perhaps to a commune in a remote area, is also to experience the impact of urbanization—in reverse perhaps. When hundreds of thousands of people left the old urban heartland for the suburbs after World War II, the subsequent debate assumed that suburban location made a difference. Today a number of young people are moving into innercity neighborhoods. The question of the impact of this new location on them becomes germane.

Settlement size and the heterogeneity of the population also make a difference, along with the age of the settlement, the wealth of the people and how that wealth is distributed, the form of government, the technology available, and many other factors. Urbanization, we may conclude, has many dimensions.

The dimensions of urbanization are many and they are interrelated. Increasing the size of the population of a settlement increases its heterogeneity. Heterogeneous populations are more territorial. Territoriality reduces conflict. Reductions in conflict . . . and the interdependent chain of the many elements of the process of urbanization, goes on. While there are many different definitions of ecology, the sense in which we use the word is that of interdependence. Therefore we say that the process of urbanization is ecological.

Therefore we may conclude by saying that we will study the causes and consequences of urbanization. *Urbanization* is a multidimensional, revolutionary, ecological process.

Sources

The sources for the study of the causes and consequences of urbanization are as varied as its many dimensions. To understand the urban environment we need to draw upon virtually all the social sciences. To use such widely varied sources, however, may confuse the student more than it enlightens. How can we impose some unifying order on the potentially bewildering variety of relevant sources?

First, we will draw upon the work of those who have previously attempted to explain urbanization. Among the many such scholars to whom we are indebted is an urban sociologist named Otis Duncan. He identified four major components of the process of urbanization and gave them the acronym POET. We changed one of his components and added a fifth, this time drawing upon the work of another scholar, Walter Firey. A third student of urban life, Claude Fisher, classified theories of urbanization according to the major component stressed.

Approach

The multidimensional, revolutionary, ecological process of urbanization involves population (P), organization (O), economy (E), technology (T), and symbolism (S).

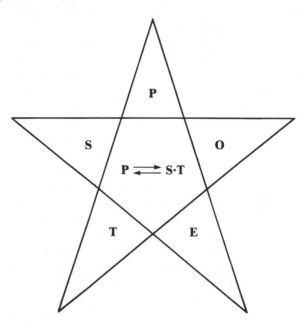

Theorists who stress the importance of population are called *compositionalists* (Fisher, 1976). Urban populations are liberal because they include so many young single adults, some compositionalists say. The composition of suburban populations, by contrast, is an overrepresentation of middle-aged and married adults with children. Therefore, suburban populations are conservative. In these and many other ways it is the composition of the population that is the most important, the compositionalists state. The disciplines on which they draw include demography, social psychology, and environmental psychology.

Those who stress the importance of organization (O) could be divided according to the type of organization deemed important: historical, geographic, political, or social organization. For our introductory purposes we will place all *organizationalists* into the same category. Generally they argue that it is the form of organization that is the most important factor in urbanization.

Economics (E) is of such major importance that some urban scholars think that it alone determines the causes and consequences of urbanization. The city in history arose around the market, they say. The distribution of wealth, systems of land tenure, the economics of housing supply, demand, and occupancy determine the nature of urbanization. These theorists are called *economic determinists*.

Without the invention of the wheel, the discovery of oil, the creation of jet propulsion, and today's existence of vast medical technologies, the process of urbanization would be far different. Technology (T) therefore is the fourth major component of urbanization. Those who believe that technology is the primary factor in urbanization are called *technological determinists*.

Symbolism (S) includes the values people hold. Some people may believe, for example, that to be urban is worth almost any sacrifice and may travel long distances to get to a city. Or some may believe that to be a Bostonian is to occupy a place in the very hub of the universe and therefore do anything to live there. Some people may value suburban communities, while others value old urban neighborhoods. The values that people hold are many and they are highly varied. Nevertheless, depending on their values, the nature of urbanization changes.

The values or symbolism of people also lead to interaction with some people but not with others. Because they value co-religionists, they interact more with them than with believers in other religions. Or perhaps because they value co-workers more than anyone else they interact mainly with other scientists, other artists, other actors, other law enforcement officers, or with other morticians. Those who stress the importance of interaction as it is structured by symbolism are termed *interactionalists*.

Earlier we observed that the components of the process of urbanization were ecological, that is, interdependent. Is there anything we can add about the nature of the interdependence of the components? It is our contention that the interdependency of the components is determined by the values of people. People's values about urban versus rural life determine their rates of migration. Values shape the forms of social and political organization which urbanites create. Values lead people to distribute the wealth or place it under the control of a few. And values lead people to embrace or reject technology—to welcome or oppose nuclear plants, for example.

The symbolic or value-determined nature of the ecology of the components of urbanization is thus the final element of our approach. We call our approach *symbolic ecology*.

Symbolic ecology is the approach we will use to study the multidimensional, revolutionary, ecological process of urbanization, which includes population (P), organization (O), economy (E), technology (T), and symbolism (S)—summarized by the acronym POETS.

Major sections

In Part One of this book we examine the three major forms of settlement that urbanization has thus far created: the city, the metropolis, and the urban environment.

Part Two examines the changes that urbanization makes in a population, including changes in birth and death rates. Variations in urbanization are then examined by region, economic activity, and nation.

The urban environment is organized into communities. Thus, Part Three studies ghettos, enclaves, clusters, and voluntary associations.

Part Four reviews the research on several areas of urban settlements: innercities, suburbs, urban frontiers, and new cities, new towns, and new communities.

Having examined progressively smaller units of the urban environment in previous sections, the text concludes in Part Five with the observation of the urbanite in public, in private, and in person.

Study Questions and Suggested Readings follow every chapter. Terms and concepts used are italicized in the text and reproduced at the end in the Glossary. Works cited in the text are given in the References, and our study is concluded with an index of subjects and authors.

VIDEOCASSETTES

Four videocassettes are available through the publisher for optional use with this text. The text can be used without the cassettes and the cassettes can be used without the text. However, because both print and nonprint materials were prepared by the author using the same approach, text and cassettes are integrated.

Use of the video materials stimulate interest, aid understanding of the written materials, and encourage further reading and discussion. A description of the four cassettes follows. Each cassette is in color, has monaural sound, and lasts about 30 minutes.

The following is a short description of each of the videocassettes:

1.   The Walled City

Description: Based on the author's studies of San Juan, Puerto Rico (with Theodore Caplow and Sheldon Stryker); Marrakesh, Morocco; and

Perouges, France. This cassette uses these three walled cities as examples of the settlement pattern of The City.

2. Boston: The Hub of New England

Description: Three years of systematic study of selected sections of Boston by the author comprise the data base for this cassette. Within the historical evolution of the urban environment, emphasis herein is upon the settlement form of The Metropolitan Area, the period of principal growth for Boston. The centralization of the metropolitan area, the segregation of land use and of people, and the ties between areas are concentrated upon.

3. Little Italy: An Ethnic Enclave

Description: Based on a 12-month field research project in Lower Manhattan's Little Italy, this cassette traces the rise of this enclave from 1880 through its decline following World War II. Access to Little Italy, first through the *padroni* and then by chain migration, structured internal space and defined its conditions of occupancy. Boundary formation in Little Italy is examined as a spatial expression of social divisions.

4. Plazas and Parks: Public Recreation

Description: Based on data collected over a year's study of parks in New York City, *the Plazas and Parks* cassette presents four types of public recreational space: unofficial and official local parks; a neighborhood park (Riverside); a community park (Washington Square); and a metropolitan park (New York Botanical). After indicating the importance of parks to urban dwellers, patterns of park usage and activity profiles are examined to supply information on a subject almost totally neglected by urbanologists.

STUDY QUESTIONS

1. Define the topic of study for this text.
2. Describe each major characteristic of the process of urbanization.
3. Name each of the five components of the process of urbanization, and describe some of the factors each component includes.
4. Briefly state the position taken on the causes and consequences of urbanization: by a compositionalist, by an organizationalist, by an economic determinist, by a technological determinist, by an interactionist.
5. Summarize the approach taken in this text.

SUGGESTED READINGS ────────────────────────────────────

Duncan, Otis D.   "Human Ecology and Population Studies." P. Hauser and O. Duncan, eds., pp. 678–715. *The Study of Population* (Chicago: University of Chicago Press, 1959).

Firey, Walter.   "Sentiment and Symbolism as Ecological Variables." *American Sociological Review,* vol. 10 (1945), pp. 137–146.

Fisher, Claude S.   *The Urban Experience* (New York: Harcourt Brace Jovanovich, 1976).

Schnore, Leo F.   "Social Morphology and Human Ecology," *American Journal of Sociology,* vol. 63 (1958), pp. 620–34.

PART ONE

Forms of urban
settlement

THE CITY

THE URBAN REVOLUTION

Evolution consists of gradual change over a long period; thus the evolution of the contemporary human species began millions of years ago. Man,[1] as the physical anthropologists call all of us, began to evolve from the apes (Leakey, 1979) more than 2 million years ago. One and a half million years elapsed before our distant relatives achieved erect posture. Another 300,000 years passed before *Homo sapiens* (man the wise) came into existence. Although Neanderthal man would not be classified by many physical anthropologists as *Homo sapiens,* he did have a larger brain than our own (1550 cc to our 1350 cc).

Although the Neanderthals appeared around 150,000 B.C., still another 120,000 years passed before what authorities call Modern Man appeared. Called the Cro-Magnons (for the place in France in which their remains were found), their bone structure was virtually identical to our own. They were nearly six feet tall, had a straight face, a high forehead, a strong jaw, and they made beautiful bone implements. Skillful as the Cro-Magnons were, however, at least a thousand generations passed—20,000 years— before the human species could grow grain and domesticate animals. After the domestication of plants and animals around 10,000 B.C., it was another 5,000 years before true cities came into existence.

With the appearance of cities all aspects of human life were transformed radically and the transformation took a comparatively short time. After the millions of years of evolution, the hundreds and thousands of years of slow and gradual change, what V. Gordon Childe (1950) aptly calls "The Urban Revolution" struck humankind. Just a thousand or so years after cities emerged, the human species could count, write, fire pottery, forge metals, organize activities by a calendar, move materials with the wheel, spin wool, build and sustain permanent homes, and organize nonkinship collectives. With urbanization, the same *Homo sapiens* who had been around for many hundreds of thousands of years created science, metallurgy, architecture, transportation, and irrigation systems in a relatively brief moment. Humankind then linked one city to another and forged chains of cities into vast empires and civilizations, in just two or three thousand years. The impact of the process of urbanization was indeed revolutionary.

Revolution as ecological process

Urbanization is a process, similar in a general way to the process of heating. With heating, for example, the specific consequences depend on what is being heated (a building or gasoline), when the action is taking

---

[1] Man (capitalized) refers collectively to the members of the human race.

place (after everything around it has been heated or as the first thing to be heated), and on other such critical considerations. The same applies to urbanization. The impact of the process of urbanization when it first appeared nearly 10,000 years ago differed enormously from its impact today in such places as South America, Southeast Asia, or Africa. Since urbanization is a process, we must always bear in mind the conditions within which it first began to operate. Remembering this will keep us from thinking that just because cities emerged in a certain way in the Near Eastern river valleys, then cities everywhere should resemble them. It will keep us from thinking that just because North American cities look a certain way, so should the cities now emerging in South America.

If in addition to remembering that urbanization is a process we also remember the interdependence of the components of the human ecosystem, then we can begin to trace the absorbing history of the emergence of the urban environment.

Life without cities

Prior to the emergence of cities, human life was spent in roving nomadic bands typically composed of 20 or 30 members. Our prehistoric ancestors roamed from site to site, following the seasons in search of food. Although such makeshift dwellings as caves and huts adjacent to a food source might have been used for refuge, competition with other groups of human beings and the depletion of available food necessitated constant movement.

In a world in which food surplus was virtually unknown, hunting and gathering food took most of the time of almost every member of the nomadic group. Both men and women, as well as children when able, engaged in most of life's activities—food preparation, the construction of shelter, and defense. As Sjoberg puts it: "The lack of a food surplus, itself a function of the little developed technology, permits a modicum of specialization of labor" (1960:9).

Human life under such circumstances was insecure, homogeneous, and short. Survival depended not only on skill and luck in finding food even during droughts or after the exhaustion of the available game, but also on the ability to fend off attacks by beasts and other groups of *Homo sapiens.*

In recent years much has been made of the aggressiveness of human beings by Lorenz (1966) and Ardsley (1961), but little attention has been given to the corollary of that presumed aggressiveness: namely, the need for defense in order to survive. Yet the survival of human life in the prehistoric period, as well as in periods for which there is written evidence, did depend in large part on the group's ability to defend itself, especially from the attacks of other human beings.

For most of the last million years, then, our species lived in groups that were small in size, undifferentiated by activity, and without permanent residence. Even if we restrict our consideration to our Cro-Magnon ancestors, human life from 30,000 B.C. to about 8000 B.C. was still insecure, uniform, and short. There were no cities.

The stabilization of environment

Between 8000 B.C. and 4500 B.C., our ancestors discovered that they could plant seeds to grow food instead of constantly having to search for it. Although scholars disagree about what made small settlements and villages turn into cities, there is no disagreement that the transition from hunting and gathering to agriculture made possible human settlement for a period of time longer than a season of the year.

Even though the sites of the small villages of this period had to be changed every 20 years or so as the soil became exhausted, the settlements were relatively permanent compared to those that preceded them. And even though they were sparsely scattered about wide expanses of territory, these relatively permanent settlements altered human existence by reducing the time spent in moving, searching for grain, and constructing shelter. Moreover, they began to produce the first food surplus.

Two hallmarks of urban existence were achieved in this period: a relatively stationary existence, and role differentiation. The food surplus meant that it was no longer necessary for everyone to engage in securing food. The domestication of animals also occurred during this period, called the Neolithic, or New Stone Age, and produced additional surpluses of food.

Although scholars also disagree about what role conquest played in the rise of cities, it is undeniable that human beings learned early that what could not be produced by one's own hands could just as well be taken from one's neighbors.

At the outset, the Neolithic villages were small and few in number. Whereas the populations of roving bands numbered in the lower tens, these small villages had populations in the lower hundreds. If we take into account all the human beings estimated to have been alive when these villages first emerged, we realize that the proportion of the total population living in such villages was less than a tenth of one percent.

Understanding that most of the population lived outside these first settled communities helps us to understand the dangers to which the first settlers were exposed. The foodstuffs to which the community owed its existence and continuing expansion inevitably proved to be a powerful incentive for external attack. Food was life, survival, and a surplus of it was almost unknown. Permanency in settlement site also made attack easy. Thus a number of villages succumbed to outsiders almost the moment they were born.

The transformation to walled settlement

Successful villages built the safest possible storage places for their grain surpluses, especially for the seed grain for the next year's crop, and then the granaries were expanded to provide safe havens for the animals. Fortifying the granary provided a small fort for refuge in time of attack. To the extent that such practices were successful, the village prospered.

Increased productivity in both agriculture and animal husbandry further increased surpluses, freeing additional labor for other pursuits. Labor was thus available to improve defense by the construction of a wall, first between two houses, and then to a third. Soon a wall ringed the village. If this wall should fall to invaders, the inner granary-fortress would become the second perimeter for defense. Now strong enough to discourage wanton attack, these small fortified villages expanded from the lower to the upper hundreds in population.

As these small fortified villages grew, a characteristic urban population arose. In addition to soldiers who guarded the walls and gates, there were priests, craftsmen, and laborers. There were farmers who tilled the soil outside city walls by day and slept within at night. Life within the walls, in contrast to that of nomadic hunters and gatherers, came to be defined less by kinship than by common residence. The walls also served to unite insiders and define outsiders.

To wall is to erect a boundary between those enclosed and those excluded, and therefore the city folk were separated from the country folk for the next nearly 10,000 years. As Marx observed: "The foundation of every division of labor that is well developed, and brought about the exchange of commodities, is the separation of town and country (1909:352).

Organization through sharing space

Interaction was intensified among those whom the walls enclosed. Whereas the precity small nomadic bands were made up of kin, contact between kin groups was necessary within the urban settlement. In becoming the first type of social collectivity to be organized on a nonkinship and purely residential basis, these fortified villages provided the bases on which larger associations could grow.

Interaction among those encircled by walls was also intensified by the undivided loyalty that the village could and did demand. Within the walls was the only known place of safety and security. Outside the walls survival was much less likely. The village could thus make powerful demands upon its members, enforcing these demands when necessary by banishment outside the walls. The undivided loyalty of the village's inhabitants was in this way assured, giving the group the power it needed over individuals to accomplish its own goals, even when these goals required the sacrifice of lives for the survival of the community.

Because space for the first time was enclosed, and therefore finite, rules governing its use had to be developed. Shared understandings in regulating the spatial order had reverberations in the social order, just as changes in the social order were reflected spatially. The need for agreements governing the use of space as well as relations with others added to the intensification of interaction which the walls had brought about.

There were other important consequences. Although individual residential compounds could be built at will, virtually anywhere in any way, the construction of communal fortifications required a heretofore unknown degree of common effort. Walls were either continuous, unbroken, or they were worthless. Whether directed by a powerful individual or developed by common consent, an overall plan was essential.

Walls had to have access points, gates, the location of which had to be decided in advance of actual construction. Whereas security considerations suggested limiting the number of access points, the convenience of movement of the population would be better served by a number of entry points. Even when the number of gates had been determined, additional decisions about who would have access to those gates had to be made. Again defense considerations worked in opposition to ease of access, with defense most often favored.

Whatever the process by which such decisions were made, outsiders were attracted to the emerging fortified settlements for the safety they promised. Some came because their labor was needed; others were compelled to serve as laborers for the settlements. Who and how many were to be enclosed by the planned defensive network? Every foot that the walls were extended required enormous investments of human energy. If too small a space were enclosed, growth might be severely inhibited, requiring rebuilding in a few years. If too large a space were enclosed, would there be enough people to defend the entire wall? Area enclosed and people protected had to be commensurate with the number needed to maintain the defenses.

Finally, the wall constituted not just a physical boundary but a social one as well. Based on residence rather than the ties of kinship, membership in the collective was simultaneously social and spatial. To be in the town was to be of it. The social, economic, political, administrative, and religious activities were all contained within the same spatial confines, their perfectly congruent boundaries coalescing with the walls to provide the shell within which cities could emerge.

The decisions reached in establishing the first spatial enclosure began a process requiring many other decisions as well. Who was to work in the fields, tend the flocks, patrol the hinterland? Agreements had to be reached, and rates of exchange for different kinds of labor had to be formulated. Each relationship established gave rise to the need for decisions in other spheres. A rudimentary division of labor and its component exchange of goods and services emerged.

The food surplus had first provided the economic base for permanent communal settlement and had also increased the need for defense. Releasing some persons from food procuring activities, though, allowed the construction of walls surrounding the people. The walls in turn intensified interaction and made coordination of human effort necessary on a larger scale. The process then multiplied and manifolded itself.

What started as a defensive measure soon became an offensive one as the village began to control the immediate area around it. Smaller and weaker settlements within the region were made subservient. Those entering the hinterland found themselves open to attack for the food they might have or for the labor their enslavement could provide.

As others were attracted to the villages that could successfully defend themselves, or as the settlement's hinterland expanded to incorporate others, the needs of the inhabitants diversified. Part-time specialists became full-time, accelerating development. For example, early workers in stone modified the already perfected techniques of the Paleolithic and Mesolithic periods with increased grinding and polishing. These developments laid the bases for the emergence of what most authorities regard as true urban settlements.

WHAT IS A CITY?

The process of urbanization began with the stabilization of settlement site made possible by the domestication of plants and animals. The need to protect the valuable food surplus led to the construction of walls, first around the granary and then surrounding the entire settlement. Spatial enclosure in turn intensified interaction within the community and produced new forms of social organization, including most importantly associations based on the sharing of space. As the food surplus expanded, additional persons were freed from food producing activities and were able to turn their attention to technological improvements, such as better implements with which to till the soil. Improved tools led to higher agricultural yields, which in turn increased the division of labor, and labor specialization then gave rise to new forms of social organization. One component influenced another—urbanization was an ecological process from its beginnings.

At what point in the process of urbanization should we say that cities emerged? Consideration of this question is not unlike the previous discussion regarding the evolution of the human species. At what point in the slow evolutionary process should we say that human beings like ourselves existed? Was it when our ancestors began to stand erect? Was it when their bone structure evolved to accomodate erect posture? Was it when forehead, jaw, and nose resembled our own? In that discussion we noted that different authorities used different criteria in attempting to answer the question.

Trying to pinpoint the emergence of cities also yields various answers. For convenience of discussion we can group the answers according to the criteria used by particular authorities. Criteria used can in turn be grouped into one of our five components; namely those of population, organization, economy, technology, and symbolism.

Population size is a widely used definition of a city, and so some argue that cities did not exist until a certain size of settlement was reached. Organization is used by others, but, since we only have fossils and ruins available to analyze, it is necessary to infer social and political organization from something else. Sjoberg, for example, states that urban centers "could never have arisen and been sustained were there not an elite to manage and control a relatively wide range of human activities" (1960:117). The importance of economy has also been stressed by many urbanologists. Max Weber begins his classic, *The City,* by saying: "The many definitions of the city have only one element in common: namely that the city consists of . . . a relatively closed settlement" (1958). But Weber goes on to argue that "where only the satisfaction of agricultural needs occurs within closed settlements . . . we shall speak of trade and commercial localities and of small market towns but not of 'cities'" (1958:8).

Technology, as seen in the construction of walls and fortresses, is taken by others to be the essence of cities.

"Typically, all or most of the preindustrial city is girdled by a wall . . . walled cities have been the generalized pattern throughout the Middle East from North Africa to Central Asia, and in India and China during much of their history. Even certain pre-Columbian cities of Meso-America conformed to this pattern" (Sjoberg, 1960:91).

The importance of walls is also suggested by the fact that the Latin word *urbs* means a walled city. Furthermore, in the earliest hieroglyphic script the ideogram meaning "city" is a cross enclosed in a circle. The cross represents the convergence of routes bringing in people, merchandise, and ideas; the circle is the moat or wall which physically binds the citizens together, emphasizing their distinctiveness (Pahl, 1968:3).

Authorities who acknowledge the importance of walls include some who stress the impact of enclosed space on a population and others who see the developing technology as an indication of social and political organization. Some of these authors, then, should more accurately be classified among the organizational than the technological determinists.

Those arguing from the standpoint of symbolism, the final component in our framework, would say that cities did not emerge until they were named; that is, until they were identified and recognized as a type. The appearance of the early pictographs would satisfy those who would define cities by their symbolism.

FIGURE 1–1
Walled city: Priene

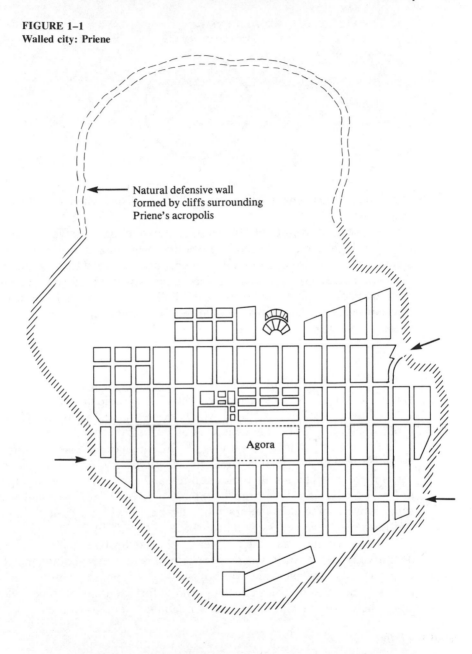

Natural defensive wall
formed by cliffs surrounding
Priene's acropolis

Agora

Such definitions have considerable merit. The difficulty in adopting any one of them to the exclusion of the others underscores the value of an ecological approach, in which all five components are not only necessary but must interact with each other if a city is to emerge. If, then, urbanization is accepted as a process involving the interaction of population, orga-

FIGURE 1-2
Pictograph for city

nization, environment, technology, and symbolism, when would we say cities emerged?

The construction of city walls is indicative of massive communal effort—a high degree of social and political organization. By enclosing space, walls also brought into interdependence all five of the components, POETS. The emergence of walled settlements will therefore be taken as the beginning of cities—what we shall call *incipient cities*. After several thousand years of interaction among the five components, *definitive cities* were to emerge.

Incipient cities

If we accept enclosing walls as the beginning of incipient cities, the earliest urban settlement uncovered thus far is Jericho, which is called "Pre-Pottery Neolithic A," and which existed about 8000 B.C. (Lampl, 1968:34). With a population estimated at about 2,000 people (de la Croix, 1972:13), Jericho's need to protect its growing, trade-based wealth resulted in the earliest-known stone fortifications. By 7500 B.C. the town "was surrounded by a wide rock-cut ditch and a massive stone wall that is preserved to a height of almost four meters. Built into this wall was a round tower, some eight meters in diameter . . . with a well-built interior staircase that gave access to its top" (de la Croix, 1972:13).

Settlements such as Jericho were eclipsed around 3500 B.C. when definitive cities arose. It was no later than this that Mesopotamian settlements added to the enclosing walls of the incipient phase the other characteristics that all authorities consider critical for a settlement to be called a city. Therefore, we call these later settlements definitive cities.

Definitive cities[2]

The vulnerability of the flat land of Mesopotamia, the proximity of cities due to the necessity of remaining close to rivers (the Euphrates and

---

[2] Marrakesh, Morocco, which was built in the 12th century; Perouges, France, which was built in the 14th century; and San Juan, Puerto Rico, which was built in the 16th century.

the Tigris), and the frequent power struggles among cities combined to turn walls into the very definition of a city. "The walls of ancient Ur are reputed to have had a thickness that varied between 25 and 34 meters" (de la Croix, 1972:15). The towers rose above the walls, with galleries built at arrowshot intervals apart, and provided the latest in defensive technology. A wide water-filled ditch often lay at the base of the walls, which were sometimes double, or even triple in their circuits. Internal walls were also present. During this time, it became the practice for the ruling monarch to design and plan his own city.

FIGURE 1–3
Incipient and definitive cities

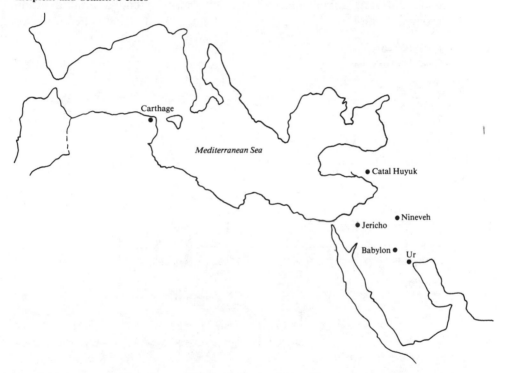

The classic form of urban settlement in Mesopotamia was the *citadel city*. Zincirli in Northern Syria, which dates from late in the second millennium, is a good example. "Forming an almost perfect circle, the double ring of outer walls is reinforced with 100 towers. Additional walls surround an ovaloid inner town, or citadel, that contained a palace and a temple" (de la Croix, 1972:16). The citadel city manifested spatially the

are used as living examples of the city form of settlement in the videocassette prepared for optional use with this text. Order from the publisher: *The Walled City.*

internal differentiation of the newly emergent city. As earlier presented, it probably grew initially from the fortified granary and the creation of the first encircling walls, and then through the expansion of both granary and walls. When later settlements were built, they incorporated the citadel spatial form. The citadel spatial form proved to be suited admirably to its control purposes and became a favorite type of construction wherever the military had dominance. Perhaps its best modern-day example is the Kremlin of Moscow.

    The inner walls surrounding the citadel were not the only interior walls of these early cities. The residential quarters of workers were sometimes walled off from the houses of the government officials and more wealthy merchants. At times interior partitions also extended around ethnic groups (Lampl, 1968:26, 31). Internal physical division reflects the in-

FIGURE 1–4
Citadel city: Peking

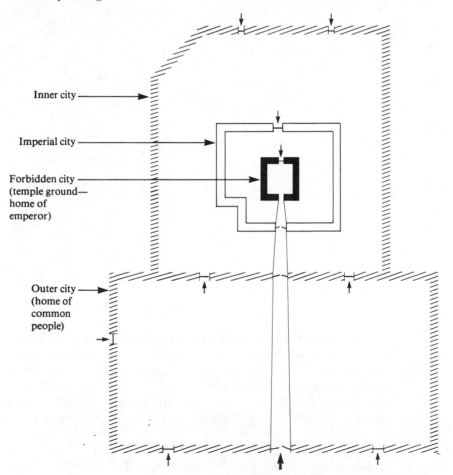

creasing social differentiation in the cities' populations. It is a truism that city life implies a stratified population. Social stratification and spatial segregation were features of the citadel city.

Food surplus had grown sufficiently to release many from agricultural work and to feed tens of thousands of urban inhabitants. Foodstuff inventories and distributions required the establishment of accounting methods. Writing, a calendar, and the basic sciences appeared. First copper, then bronze, and finally iron was discovered, and each in turn increased food production, releasing even more human energy for technological and cultural development.

The small, homogeneous, impoverished populations of settlements of the past were succeeded by settlements with populations perhaps exceeding 100,000. Wealthy landowners and merchants, money changers, priests and physicians, veterinarians, potters, metalworkers, tailors, and, of course, powerful rulers were to be found in these early cities. Nineveh, the capital of Assyria, had more than 12 miles of walls, complex hill citadels, palaces, and a variety of massive public buildings. Babylon's wealth and beauty was famed worldwide. Farther east in the Indus Valley, the streets of the ancient city of Mohenjo-Daro were laid out according to a gridiron plan and were lined with spacious two-story houses, served by brick-lined sewers.

As the city grew in size and wealth, its walls and fortifications also had to grow. Armies raised for defense were soon used to attack other cities. Wealth could be accumulated by sacking neighboring settlements, and the cities fell to fighting one another. In the race to conquer before being conquered, to increase power in order to maintain and extend boundaries and the area of the tributary hinterland, empires were built, flourished, and then succumbed to stronger forces.

The warfare often destroyed the agricultural base upon which the city had been founded, and the surviving population had to return to its nomadic hunting and gathering to survive. Systems of irrigation built up over centuries of peaceful occupation were destroyed, and with them the means of sustenance for the urban populations. Mohenjo-Daro fell, about 1500 B.C., possibly to the invading Aryans, never to arise again. Babylon was destroyed totally by the Assyrians in 689 B.C. Later rebuilt, it was destroyed again in 279 B.C. Throughout the second and first millennia, warfare succeeded so thoroughly in destroying the emergent urban civilization that cities largely ceased to exist in the regions of their origin.

The spread of cities

The definitive cities which had emerged around 3500 B.C. were destroyed totally time and time again, and with them their populations, organizations, economies, technologies, and symbolism. But the knowledge of the city held by residents and visitors never died. People took this knowledge with them and established cities wherever the five critical components could be forged into interaction.

In the second and first millennia B.C., the Phoenicians spread cities westward along the Mediterranean shores, to Carthage in North Africa (today Tunisia), to Sicily, and to Spain. Cities then spread through Persia, Afghanistan, Turkey, and into Central Asia and Asia Minor. South of Arabia, Mecca and Medina were founded. At times the knowledge of cities was spread by civilizations influenced by Mesopotamia and other early centers of urban settlements. In other places, such as China in 1200 B.C. and Meso-America about 1500 B.C., cities appear to have evolved independent of outside influence.

In the 8th century B.C. cities appeared throughout the Aegean and emerged slightly later in Italy in the settlements built by the Etruscans. In the 5th century B.C. the building of cities took place in England by the Romans, who also built settlements through Europe to the Rhine. Cities which survive today—such as York, London, Brussels, Utrecht, Granada, Seville, Cologne, Paris, Vienna, Zagreb, and Belgrade—were among those established during this early period.

Protection from attack remained essential for survival. With few exceptions, all cities were walled until the 18th century. The need for defense continued to dominate the site selection for cities, while the survival of older centers in large part depended on the population's ability to defend itself. Mountain plateaus, hilltops, peninsulas, and islands were therefore often chosen for settlement, even though their topographic features created problems for growth and access.

Just a few thousand years after their emergence, cities differentiated into many different types. There were colonial cities and capital cities; there were market cities which traded with foreign countries, others which serviced vast regions, and smaller market cities for local trade; there were cities which controlled their hinterlands, and others which were controlled by the rural gentry; there were university, monastery, and cathedral cities; there were centers of learning and cities of ignorance; and there were cities located on coasts, others in interiors, and still others on frontiers.

Only the barest historical outlines of the city's emergence has been given here. The process of urbanization touched many different places throughout the world, and each region had a different population, its own particular organization, and other variations in the other components. We continue this very condensed history by tracing the rates of urbanization to modern times, glancing briefly at urban life in colonial times, and then summarizing what we have learned about the city.

THE PROCESS OF URBANIZATION

The general drift of urbanization was north and east, moving from the Indus River in the modern state of India; from the Tigris, which is in the area we now call Iraq; and from the Euphrates, which flows through Turkey and Syria. Cities then began to take root around the Aegean and the Mediterranean.

From the beginning of Greek history to its climax in the 4th century B.C., the Greeks were organized politically in autonomous units known as city-states. Plato analyzed the constitutions of 158 city-states in his study of politics (1966). The word "polis" meant both city and city-state. Since city-states were autonomous, different states and the same state at different times ranged from absolute monarchy to complete participatory democracy.

The city continued to develop in Rome, whose population and political power exceeded those of the Greek city-states. At the crest of its imperial power the population of Rome may have reached the upper hundreds of thousands. And, unlike urban development among the autonomous city-states, Rome was a center supported by tribute and foodstuffs funneled through smaller cities in the far-flung Roman Empire.

Rome was not the only urban center in the empire. The Romans developed an extensive network of administrative centers and collection points for tribute, usually located at the intersections of trade routes. These administrative centers were populated by colonial governors, ex-soldiers, traders, and migrants from their hinterlands.

The capital city of Rome was tied to the provinces by tribute and resources to feed its population. State bakeries, for example, fed an estimated one-third to one-half of all of the families in the city. Thus, a drought in Egypt or other interruptions in food transport had severe repercussions in Rome. As the city grew in power and size, the fields encircling and sustaining it when it first emerged became ever more distant. Egypt provided the majority of the grain, and even Carthage was revived to serve as a granary.

With the fall of the Roman Empire the financial and transportation arrangements that had assured provision for the massive population of the city of Rome were upset. Therefore, shortly after the sacking of Rome in A.D. 476, its population fell precipitously. Concomitant with the decline of Rome and the empire, deurbanization took place throughout the West. It was to be more than a thousand years before the massive, complex coordination attained by the Romans would be equaled again.

The decline in urbanization

With the fall of Rome large urban settlements in the West virtually disappeared. Those which survived did so in reduced scale, sometimes only temporarily, and in widely scattered sites. The lack of a central governing authority and the defense previously assumed by Rome "is perhaps best reflected in the almost incredible proliferation of castles all over Europe" (de la Croix, 1972:32). Twenty thousand castles were built in Italy alone from the 6th to the 10th centuries.

Repeating the process of nucleation around granary and enclosure observed earlier in antiquity, the numerous castles at times became aggregating foci for populations; security and employment were their main attractions. As in the past, site selection was governed by ease of defense, irrespective of the difficulties of access. High hilltops had walls following the terrain; and strong walls were built around a central tower which served both as living quarters for some and as last refuge for all.

Ancient cities had been built on the trade routes that rivers and caravans created, on agglomerations of individual farms in fertile areas, and around administrative, religious, and military centers. These factors continued to shape settlements into the medieval period.

For some 400,000 years the species *Homo sapiens* had roamed the planet Earth, living a precarious existence, ravaged by the vicissitudes of a scarce and uncertain food supply and the depredations of other human beings. For at least 20,000 years modern human beings had suffered the same fate until cities emerged to revolutionize all life. Once that revolution was forged, the power of urban life was such that all who had experienced it or knew it even indirectly worked to make it manifest again.

In medieval times as in antiquity the countryside was the arena of violence, discord, poverty, and the short, brutal life. Outside the city, human life had no purpose other than survival, no security other than one's own arms, no goods or surplus beyond that produced by one's own labor or through exchange with distant neighbors. There was no contact or communication to widen one's horizons or to counter widespread ignorance. From the time cities first emerged to the present day, people have flocked to them whenever and wherever possible. The urban revival that began in the 9th century is only one manifestation of this continuing phenomenon.

The urban revival

In the founding, growth, and spread of urban settlements beginning in the West in the 9th and 10th centuries, some cities grew from centers ruled by bishops who located their cathedrals, or seats of power, where Roman armies and granaries had once been. Kings and nobles also fortified settlements, at times reconstructing the older Roman fortifications for their own uses. Antwerp, Hamburg, Prague, Warsaw, and Buda (later Budapest) were established in the 9th century A.D. In the 10th century such cities as Padua, Milan, Venice, and Genoa emerged, along with (somewhat later) cities in Scandinavia, northern Germany, the Baltic, and Russia.

Urban social organization was now known to the people, along with the means to protect it by walled fortifications. With the reopening of the trade routes made possible by enlargements of central authorities, the necessary economic base for urban settlement was available again. Old marketplaces began to grow and new ones to spring up. The growing power of the nobility increased the size of their residential compounds, and the settlements ruled over by church authorities also attracted increasing numbers of people.

It was the chartering of new municipalities by a sovereign, however, that gave the greatest impetus to urban development. In return for services rendered—troops or money for war, for example—or in promise of these, sovereigns could and did delegate certain "rights" to a settlement, the most important of which was the right to erect and maintain its own defense. Obviously a feudal sovereign did not grant such permission to a people initially or unreservedly, simply because the erection of such walls could be turned against the sovereign.

The right to hold a market and to pay a tax on goods sold was often granted first. The success and expansion of that venture might lead to permission of limited self-government. Civic improvements such as fire and police protection might follow. Then the increasing magnitude of the investment began to require protection beyond that available from the castle (Mumford, 1938; Sjoberg, 1960; Pirenne, 1925).

Enclosure also served as the sovereign's control over the population. Taxes were less easily escaped when access to markets could be controlled at the entry gates. Higher rents could be secured for land enclosed behind walls. A small deployment of troops could defend a walled city while the sovereign and the main body of the army were fighting elsewhere. Walls were thus to the advantage of the ruler as to the ruled, although they were sometimes turned against the ruler who had allowed their construction.

Cities were once again small; London had no more than 35,000 inhabitants as late as the 14th century (Holmes, 1952). Urban growth was kept closely in check by the locally available surplus as well as by war and disease. The need to care for the food surplus in times of attack led to the construction of stables, pigpens, and game coops within the city. Common pasture lands were provided within the walls. Later these shared lands developed into the commons of English cities, the plazas of Spanish settlements, and the municipal parks of the United States.

Sanitation usually was accomplished by open trenches running down the center of city streets. Community water supply came through common wells. "The *odeur de merde* was never completely absent from anyone's nostrils. People were used to it—the fastidious and very clean persons were rather few in the twelfth century, but they existed" (Holmes, 1952:39). Until the last hundred years or so sewerage was limited, and only the better houses had pits or privies. "Although streams of water were encouraged to flow down the middle of the streets, there was a shortage of drainage ditches for these to empty into. Fortunately many of the Paris streets sloped toward the river—filth found its way constantly into the muddy streets. Chamber pots and washbasins could be emptied too by pitching the contents from the window" (Holmes, 1952:101).

Overcrowding strained and often destroyed the always fragile balance between the city and its soil. Water supplies easily became contaminated, and poor sanitation carried and quickly spread disease. Urban populations were sharply reduced and sometimes decimated by smallpox, typhus, diptheria, typhoid, and the dreaded plague (McNeill, 1976).

City populations have rarely reproduced themselves. Birthrates have historically declined with urbanization. This means that if they are to grow, cities must receive migrants from the countryside. Since many migrants are needed simply to replace those lost to the city by death, an even greater migratory stream is necessary for population growth.

The fact that cities did grow throughout the Middle Ages testifies to their appeal and to their strength. The town's citizens built their own defenses, regulated and encouraged trade, raised taxes, and maintained order. Citizens took an oath acknowledging municipal authority. The social organization required to meet the city's needs also stimulated further growth. At times cities banded together to form leagues of mutual support. Occasionally their power was used to oppose the lord who had given them a charter. But no matter which of the many and complex ways they chose for managing their affairs, one thing was apparent: cities continued to create the material and nonmaterial wealth of the society.

AMERICAN COLONIAL CITY LIFE

With the discovery of the New World, colonial cities in the Americas were established. Not only were their settlement sites selected with great care according to colonial policy, but the basic layouts of the streets and the locations of the major buildings were planned in relation to current needs and in anticipation of the future.

Cities of the New World therefore represent a heightened consciousness of form. In deciding where and how a new city was to be built, the colonists relied on the traditions of the past. To illustrate, let us glance at American colonial urban life.

The city of Boston was founded as the hub of a New World empire called New England, which included all lands from Cape Cod to Newfoundland. The home of His Majesty's governor and his retinue, the court of law, the church, and the principal market were to be located in Boston (Shurtleft, 1871). Its site was selected with great care after preliminary experience elsewhere, with the defensibility of the site being as important as fresh water to drink. Defense and fresh water were both present on a peninsula with a narrow neck about a quarter of a mile wide. Since this neck was often covered with water at high tides and during storms, the site would be an island once it was walled where the peninsula joined the mainland.

Fort Dearborn, the earliest structure on the site which was to become Chicago, was also surrounded by water on three sides. In fact, the importance of water was a feature of a number of other American cities, as this quote indicates:

> In 1774 as Dr. Hamilton neared the Quaker City (Philadelphia) he had to ferry across the Schuylkill River; before he could reach New York he had to cross from Perth Amboy to Staten Island, to Long Island, and then back to Manhattan. Similarly, upon reaching Narragansett Bay, he took two boats to get to Newport and a third to leave Rhode Island (Bridenbaugh, 1938:36–37)

Early American colonial cities were coastal seaport cities and consequently a significant proportion of their populations was engaged in maritime and related pursuits.

> Statistics are scarce, but these "mariners"—local boatmen, watermen, fishermen, common sailors—always made up the largest segment of the urban working class, and in a very literal sense proved to be a floating population. . . . At little Newport, sooner or later, nearly every male above sixteen went to sea. . . . The fact that in 1742 Boston had over a thousand widows "in very low circumstances," because of losses from fishermen and commercial vessels, indicates that it probably had the largest seagoing population of any city. (Bridenbaugh, 1938:87)

Since the number of widows was large and the number of women whose husbands were out to sea even greater, many were led into the ranks of the gainfully employed.

> Merchants' wives, like Elizabeth Schuyler of New York, frequently retailed for their husbands, and during long lonely periods the spouses of sea captains kept shop with silks, yarns, shoes, pins, ribbons, threads, buttons, and yard goods. . . . Mary Singleton Copley ran a tobacconist's shop and eventually moved it from Long Wharf to the fashionable upper end of King Street in Boston. . . . Sarah Logan at Charles Town, Jane Blundell at New York, and Sarah Decoster, Susannah Newman, and Sarah Winser of Boston virtually monopolized the profitable trade with town and country in domestic and imported garden seeds. (Bridenbaugh, 1938:78)

As the city emerged in antiquity, we noted that the granary occupied its center. Later, as the church came to dominate the urban community, the cathedral, mosque, or other religious edifice supplanted the granary-fortress. In early American colonial cities the church, too, had its central place, but now along with court and market. But perhaps centermost in the hearts of Americans, if not exactly in the center of the city, was this often overlooked institution:

The tavern was the most flourishing of all urban institutions. The colorful signboards carrying such intriguing names as the Bunch of Grapes, Old Fortune of War, the Harp and Crown, and Ship-A-Ground were probably better known to the mobile colonials than the town halls and public buildings. Expanding its activities at all levels to meet the heavy demands of a growing population, the public house assumed new specialized functions. It served the cities chiefly as a place for male sociability, but it also provided hotel, restaurant, and political facilities. (Bridenbaugh, 1938:156–57)

City problems

Several other features of colonial city life deserve mention, lest we think that urban problems are the invention of our modern times. Traffic then was no less congested than now. A wide variety of animals filled the streets—those beasts going to and from markets and those used for transport—horses, oxen, sheep, goats, cows, pigs, geese, ducks, turkeys, hens. Vehicles included chaises, chariots, stagecoaches, tumbrils, carts, and huge wagons loaded with goods. Since there was no mass transit, the majority of the population was on foot and in competition with one another, with the porters and laborers, and with all the animals and vehicles for space to walk. Understandably, traffic safety was a serious problem. So was noise pollution.

In Philadelphia the steady procession of country wagons down High (or Market) Street to the wharves guaranteed a dissonance composed of wagoners' shouts and curses, cracking of whips, and clanking of heavy chains, in addition to the loud rumble of iron-tired wheels over cobblestone pavements. Passing traffic in King Street so interrupted the debates and proceedings of the Great and General Court of Massachusetts that in 1747 it forbade all vehicles to go on either side of the State House during its sessions. (Bridenbaugh, 1938:35)

Crime was another urban problem during the colonial era. In contrast to today's professional police forces, in colonial times it was the duty of each colonial male citizen to take his turn at enforcing the local ordinances. Bridenbaugh notes that, so onerous did this task become in Boston that only five males were sworn in as constables in 1743. Fifteen had been selected and not excused; the other ten preferred to pay their fines. He further states that criminal activity increased from the beginnings of urbanization in America, including counterfeiting, robbery, and violence. (Bridenbaugh, 1938:110)

In one respect at least, modern urban life is an improvement over colonial times—in today's relative absence of fires.

Probably Boston suffered more fires, in spite of its precautionary measures, than all the other cities put together; not a year passed without serious and extensive damage to property, and the newspapers reported many of minor nature. A fire in a warehouse in November 1743 caused a loss of between five and six thousand pounds. A midnight fire on Copp's Hill during bitter weather late in 1744 consumed three houses "occupied by a great many Families." On another occasion a spark from a South End smithy flew to an adjoining shop where it exploded an open keg of gunpowder "in a terrible manner." Boston lost its "spacious and Beautiful" State House along with valuable records, paintings, and books on December 9, 1747; . . . The worst fire in "upwards of Twenty Years" destroyed thirty North End buildings and much expensive merchandise near Bronsdon's Wharf in 1753. (Bridenbaugh, 1938:100–101)

Rural-urban relationships

Thus far we have said little about the wider complex within which each and every city exists. From the emergence of cities through the historical period about which we are now concerned, the city was dependent upon the country for food, for raw materials, and for people. Getting a supply of people has never been difficult—people have migrated to the city in large numbers for thousands of years. Getting supplies was a different matter—"not even a sheep gives up its wool willingly." Through conquest or other means of physical force, through tithes, tribute, or other general means of taxation, the city lived upon what it took from the rural areas.

> There is likely, therefore, to be a disparity of standards of living between the city and the rural area under this system. Whether the city or the rural area will have the higher standards will be a result of the policies of those who hold the taxing powers. Typically, it is the city which holds these powers and which, consequently, determines the tax rates, and, this being the case, the city usually has a higher standard of living than the rural area. Indeed, in most early periods, cities which taxed rural areas taxed these areas into poverty. The result was a very high standard of living in the city as compared with the rural area. (Gilmore, 1953:68–69)

The difference in the standard of living was therefore one source of conflict between rural and urban dwellers. Another source of conflict lay in the tax levied upon the farmer when he brought goods into town to sell. In addition to resenting any tax in the first place, the farmer had to pay the tax regardless of whether he made a profit. Bridenbaugh (1938) notes the continual trouble at Faneuil Hall in Boston over this issue. Ruralites were also quick to observe that they had no comparable way to tax the urbanites to benefit the rural areas.

The only time the countryfolk had an advantage was when essential provisions were scarce. Then they could pay the market tax and still make a handsome profit from the elevation in price brought about by war, drought, or other adverse conditions. Even as they enjoyed their infrequent and temporary advantage, however, the farmers had to bear the charges of hoarding and the insults which the urbanites hurled at them. The ancient and deep cleavage between city and country made its appearance in the New World less than a hundred years after the arrival of the first settlers. As we shall see in the next chapter, it was to become even deeper.

THE SYMBOLIC ECOLOGY OF THE CITY: SUMMARY

The origin and spread of the city to North American shores has now been traced from its beginnings to about A.D. 1800. The history of the city as the exclusive form of urban settlement extends from the incipient urbanization of the oldest known fortified settlement, Jericho of 8000 B.C.—nearly 10,000 years.

Walled settlements, what we called incipient cities, required the development of consensus. Whether achieved by a powerful ruler or by mutual agreement, spatial control was essential for social life.

As boundaries, walls surrounding the settlement set it off from other human populations. Further, the population was bounded according to spatial, not kinship, criteria. A person was either included within the boundary or excluded by it; he or she resided either inside or outside the settlement's walls.

In time the space enclosed by the walls was given a name, and as this new sociospatial form became known and spread throughout the ancient world, the form itself was given an identity, namely "a city." Pictographs showed it as a crossing of roads encircled by fortifications. The increased density of the incipient city increased interaction across the status divisions of kin groups and initiated the first co-residential relationships; sharing space had its integrative effect.

Walls were created for defense and virtually all settlement sites were selected on the basis of defensive considerations. Every meter that the walls were extended increased the magnitude of human effort required for construction. Therefore, the space enclosed was minimal at first, and the first walls increased population density at least by a factor of ten. Urban density increased and remained high through the next 10,000 years.

The environment enclosed by boundaries has configuration or form. In the walled city as it first emerged in Jericho, the spatial pattern was centralized. Whether the center was granary, fortress, market, citadel, temple, or some combination, all space was oriented to the single center. Since space may be centralized around more than one nucleus, for the sake of precision the first walled settlements should be described as both centralized and mononucleated.

The fortified center of a walled settlement is obviously the most secure location within the enclosure. Those people considered most valuable by their societies thus grouped at the center. As other interior walls went up, the population was spatially segregated by ethnicity and occupation in addition to class.

More significant is the rigid social segregation that typically led to the formation of "quarters" or "wards." In some cities (e.g., Fez, Morocco, and Aleppo, Syria) these were sealed off from each other by walls, whose gates were locked at night. The quarters reflect the sharp local social divisions. Thus ethnic groups live in special sections. And the occupational groupings, some being at the same time ethnic in character, typically reside apart from one another. Often a special street or sector of the city is occupied almost exclusively by members of a particular trade; cities in such divergent cultures as medieval Europe and modern Afghanistan contain streets with names like "street of the goldsmiths." (Sjoberg, 1960:117)

We can summarize the spatial pattern of the walled city as it first emerged as spatially bounded, limited in access, dense, centralized and mononucleated, and with occupancy organized by co-residence and with location determined by social position. The centralized and mononucleated pattern of the walled city made locations near the center most valuable. Outside the center, one location was about as preferable as any other. Land use outside the center was therefore heterogeneous: dwellings, shops, stables, and storage places were scattered throughout.

In the 10,000 years of its history, the walled or bounded city remained as only a more differentiated specimen of its initial form. Until superior defenses were invented, urban space was bounded, access was limited and controlled, and settlement size remained limited in most cases, its density fixed by the numbers that low-rise buildings could accommodate. The city was mononucleated and centralized, although its center varied from granary to fortress, palace, temple, plaza, and town hall. The city as the first urban settlement form may therefore be described as one which has:

> population—tens of thousands of people,
> limited to 5–10 percent of
> the total population
>
> organization—centralized and mononucleated units based
> on co-residence with controlled access,
> and areas or quarters for certain groups;
> densely compacted and bounded with
> heterogeneous land usage
>
> economy—preindustrial
>
> technology—primarily human or animal power and
> inefficient methods of food preservation and
> storage
>
> symbolism—"city air makes one free"—and better off.

STUDY QUESTIONS

1. How did the first cities change humankind?
2. What is "bounding" and what are its consequences?
3. What is the "urban revolution?"
4. What is a city?
5. What were the major problems of American colonial cities?
6. Summarize the symbolic ecology of the city.

SUGGESTED READINGS

Bridenbaugh, Carl. *Cities in the Wilderness: The First Century of Urban Life in America, 1625–1742* (New York: Ronald Press, 1938).

Childe, V. Gordon. "The Urban Revolution." *Town Planning Review*, vol. 21 (1950), pp. 3–17.

Sjoberg, Gideon. *The Preindustrial City* (New York: Free Press, 1960).

chapter 2

THE METROPOLIS

Historical Pictures Service, Inc., Chicago

METROPOLITANIZATION

A metropolis is not just a city grown large. Like the city which preceded it, the metropolis is a distinct pattern of urban settlement. The city and the metropolis differ not only in internal organization and size, but also in their relative self-sufficiency and specialization. In terms of population (P), the first settlements that we can call metropolitan contained hundreds of thousands and then millions of people. Their new organizations (O) distinctly departed from the city's part-time and frequently volunteer civic agencies, such as in law enforcement and fire fighting. Metropolitan economies (E) became more and more specialized, with urban land costs rising with the new skyscrapers. Industrial technology (T) came to the fore, as the mechanization of agriculture freed millions from the soil while creating jobs in vast factories located within and on the edge of metropolitan areas. In terms of symbolism, the older city or "polis" gave way to a "metro-polis."

The word "metro" may stem from the Greek word "mater," meaning mother, as in "alma mater." According to this derivation, a metropolis would be a "mother-city." A second and related symbolic meaning comes down to us through historical usage. In Western civilization, around A.D. 1535, there were metropolitan bishops who had responsibility for other bishops in their general geographical area. Metropolitan bishops came to be known as archbishops, but the community in which an archbishop lived and over which he presided came to be known as a metropolis. Eventually, the chief or principal city of a region or country came to be called a metropolis, whether or not it was the seat of a metropolitan bishop. Both by root and usage, then, the word "metropolis" suggests a dominant city. It is the first, the chief, the principal, the "metro" of all the "polises."

When can we say that the first metropolis has emerged? Not unexpectedly, the authorities differ in their answers according to the criteria they use. Beverly Duncan and Stanley Lieberson (1970), for example, date the emergence of the metropolis in Western Europe at between 1600 and 1700. Since these authors use economic organization—the dominance of markets—as their criterion, we can consider them organizationalists. Even considering just the organizational criterion, though, we would point out that political or religious dominance at times preceded the economic, and that other forms of organizational dominance have also occurred. In the same way, focusing primarily on any other single component would show the metropolis emerging at either an earlier or at a later date.

While each definition would contribute to our understanding of the emerging metropolis, we shall confine ourselves here to our perspective. Therefore, we shall say that the metropolis first existed when the five components were first joined in interaction in a way to produce it. The term "metropolis" may have been used as early as 1600, but our usage will begin with the settlement pattern emerging in America in the middle of the 19th century.

For the first third of the century in which the metropolitan form was dominant, many different solutions to the arising problems were attempted,[1] and so we differentiate the early maturing from the later phases of metropolitan development. And, as we shall see, changes were already underway toward the end of the century to produce yet a third pattern, namely, that which we will call the urban environment.

Because each form necessarily builds on its past, the process of metropolitan development will be seen to differ depending on when a settlement experienced its principal growth. Almost from the start, for example, Chicago took metropolitan form while Boston had to attempt to accommodate the metropolitan form to its "city" past.

American urban settlement patterns

The settlement of the United States began with the founding of coastal colonial centers through which immigrants later passed. Through the first century of American settlement, the majority of the immigrants located in rural areas. By 1743, Boston, then America's largest city, had a population of only 16,382 by actual census (Bridenbaugh, 1938:6). As the rural population increased, other urban settlements began to emerge and compete with the colonial cities. At times these new urban centers were located close to the colonial seaports—Salem across the bay from Boston, Brooklyn across the river from New York—and at times these new centers were established at points more distant—Portsmouth in New Hampshire; Providence in Rhode Island; New Haven, New London, and Hartford in Connecticut.

As modern historical research is now beginning to document (McCaffrey, 1976), Americans were a mobile people beginning with their migration to this country, moving in large numbers from port cities to other settlements further inland. In addition to population movements arising from the search for opportunities elsewhere, the War of Independence contributed also to a significant relocation of the population, even if only temporarily. In the year the war began, New York lost 80 percent of its population, dropping from 25,000 to 5,000; Boston went from 16,000 to 3,500; Philadelphia declined from 40,000 to 22,000; and Newport shrunk

---

[1] One interesting attempt to solve metropolitan traffic problems was Chicago's construction of "an elaborate freight subway system to move goods underground in and near the Loop, thus reducing truck and dray traffic on the surface. Originally, the subterranean network was created by a telephone company for its cables, but the excavations were large enough to accommodate two-foot-guage electric railway lines. . . . By 1914 there were 62 miles of tunnels under the major downtown streets, with 117 locomotives and 3,000 cars carrying goods, fuel, and workers throughout the business district." (Mayer and Wade, 1969:216–18)

from 11,000 to 5,300 (Bridenbaugh, 1938:216). After independence was achieved, urban growth outstripped rural rates.

From 1800 to the last census before the Civil War in 1860, the population of the United States grew by about a third every decade. For every person who settled in the rural areas, however, about twice as many settled in the cities; urban growth increased from a low of 33 percent between 1810 and 1820 to a high of 99 percent between 1840 and 1850.

Urban growth is to be differentiated from the *rate of urbanization*. The rate of urbanization is the change in the proportion of a population residing in urban areas. Thus between any given dates a city or metropolis may grow, but if the rural population grows faster, the rate of urbanization (the proportion of urban dwellers) actually will decline. Likewise if the proportion living in rural areas decreases, through famine for example, the rate of urbanization will increase even if the urban population does not grow (Davis, 1968). Whereas the rate of urbanization is a proportion, the term *urban growth* is used to describe the changes in urban population regardless of what occurs in rural areas. In these terms, the growth of urban settlements in America was large between 1810 and 1850, but the rate of urbanization only increased from 7.3 percent to 19.8 percent during that period.

These later figures are national averages, however, and do not reflect significant regional differences. By 1860 one of every three persons in the Northeast lived in an urban place, whereas only one in ten did so in the South. Until 1940 in the South, the caste system bound the entire rural and urban economy to agriculture. Cheap black labor discouraged labor-saving technological innovation, and change, including change through urbanization, was rejected, in part, because of fears that white dominance would be threatened. There was little in-migration but significant out-migration. Low per capita income, greater illiteracy than in other regions, and a relatively small middle class also discouraged southern urbanization. Finally, although cities were controlled politically by the rural areas elsewhere in the nation, southern cities depended most heavily on agriculture and so had to make additional concessions to ruralites (Reissman, 1954:80–81).

Urbanization was also unevenly spread within a single region. Before the metropolis emerged there were many cities, and they were in competition with each other—for markets, jobs, people, and prestige. Settlements on sites favored by deep and safe harbors enjoyed an advantage as did the long-established cities because their markets were organized and financing was available.

Of the 19 settlements in 1790, only 4 were not on the coast. By 1830, there were 29 settlements: 14 were on the coast and 15 were inland, but 6 of the inland were on major water routes (the Ohio, the Mississippi, and the Great Lakes). The 4,250 miles of canals built by 1860 tied this hinter-

FIGURE 2–1
Map of urban settlements: 1790 and 1830

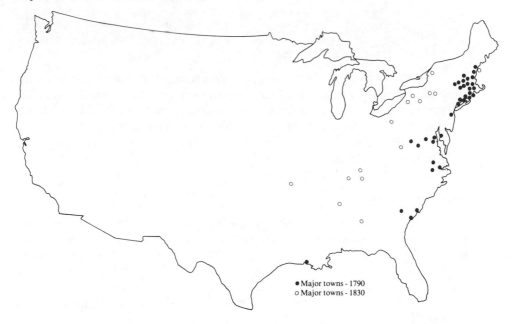

• Major towns - 1790
o Major towns - 1830

land together, establishing many local settlements, such as Terre Haute, Evansville, Syracuse, Utica, and Binghamton.

By 1870, the United States had two cities of 500,000 or more, five cities had more than one quarter million, and an additional seven had more than 100,000 population. There was then a total of 52 settlements with 25,000 or more population (Green, 1965). In virtually all settlement sites, however, space remained restricted. Living space contracted as old estate gardens were subdivided and built upon. Population density increased. The selectmen of Boston, for example, first filled in the Old Mill Pond and then expanded the entire peninsula from 783 acres to 1,829 acres by 1893 in an effort to create additional space. Two of Boston's three hills were leveled and the third significantly reduced to fill the Dorchester Flats (today the well-known South Boston). From 1791 to 1832 four bridges were built to increase access, adding to the number of people using Boston.

The central core of the settlement became too crowded for new factories to be established within the city. Textile mills with small towns, as in Newton Falls, Massachusetts, or Long Island City, New York, made their appearance—for there was then no commuting to or from the central area. A number of company towns were also established, complete with dormitories for the young female workers, as in Lowell, Massachusetts, or with homes for families, as in Pullman, Illinois, and in Gary, Indiana.

> Pullman City was designed to be good business, not philanthropy. The owner expected every part of the enterprise—the market, the hotel, the housing—to earn a modest profit on his investment. Moreover, the central consideration of the scheme was to make labor more efficient and more productive by providing an environment conducive to work and improvement. (Mayer and Wade, 1969:188)

The locations of these emerging new factories in America outside the older cities thus engendered the development of other, competing cities. As Pred puts it: "During the earliest phases of the 'industrial revolution,' the limited physical mobility of the working force and the modest scale of urban agglomerations were still the keystones of intra-urban industrial location" (1971:383).

Turnpikes and canals

The need for the transport of goods and people was felt both within and without American urban settlements. The financial success of the Philadelphia Turnpike, completed in 1794, helped stimulate the construction of the Knoxville Road, which linked with the Wilderness Road in 1795. The Old Walton Road then joined Knoxville to Nashville and gave rise to the Cumberland Turnpike linking Baltimore to the heart of Illinois in 1811.

The first run by steamboat from Louisville to New Orleans was made by the *Washington* in 1817 and for eight years that vessel hauled passengers on the lengthy trip for a one-way fare of $25 per person. The attractive future of water transport led to the digging of canals—to join the Hudson to the Delaware, the Ohio to the Mississippi and the Great Lakes, the Illinois to Lake Michigan, and the Hudson to the Great Lakes.

With the coming of the river steamer the one-way transport of floating goods downstream was ended. The relationship between rural and urban areas was changed because it became just as easy to ship goods in one direction as in the other.

> This new two way system rather early became capable of supplying farming and other raw material producing areas with the basic necessities of life, something which had seldom been possible under the old system. . . . Literally, up to this time, rural areas could export only their economic surplus, but, now, they could export their whole production if they could purchase their basic necessities from the outside. (Gilmore, 1953:60–61)

> Since most of the rural areas did develop during this period of cheap, two-way transportation, they developed from the start as commercial agricultural areas, rather than as self-sufficient farming areas. Furthermore, as commercial farming areas, each tended to develop an agricultural specialty, with the result that large specialized agricultural regions were developed which supplied each other with basic necessities to a degree never known before in any part of the world. In this system, the Southeast produced

cotton, the North Central States supplied corn and pork, the Midwest specialized in wheat, and the Southwest contributed beef, mutton and wool. The Northeast and Europe supplied the manufactured products. (Gilmore, 1969:65)

What had once been a number of loosely integrated cities and sparsely settled farming areas was now on the way toward functional integration and specialization. Thus the organizational form characteristic of metropolitanization had begun.

By 1850, turnpike and canal intersections had established and had swelled the populations of such cities as Cincinnati (115,000), St. Louis (28,000), Louisville (43,000), and New Orleans (116,000). As the new transport of goods and people improved, urbanization moved further inland, west to the Great Lakes, establishing such cities as Buffalo, Detroit, and Chicago. The Illinois and Michigan Canal then connected Chicago to the Mississippi. Traffic on it soared until it reached its "peak in 1882, and decline after that was precipitous" (Mayer and Wade, 1969:28).

In summary, American urbanization was dispersed for the first half of the 1800s. No one city or small number of cities dominated the others. As yet there were no definitive or mature metropolises.

Rail systems

Just as "canal fever" was at its pitch, railway companies were being formed to compete with the canal companies. Chartered in New York in 1826, the Mohawk and Hudson was the first. Its run from Albany to Schenectady paralleled a portion of the Erie Canal. Next to be chartered was the Baltimore and Ohio in 1828, which drove the Chesapeake and Ohio Canal out of business only one year after it had opened its waterways.

In 1835 the New England states had built 124 miles of railroads; by 1840 there were 512 miles. Just ten years later track mileage had soared to 2,507. Railroad construction in the East, however, was only a shadow of what it was to become on the broad expanse of the prairie. However often other sections of the country had used water routes, it was first the horse and then the Iron Horse that transported first goods and then people in the Midwest. And Chicago, of course, was the capital of the region.

> In 1850 only one railroad, the Galena and Chicago Union, entered the city. . . . By 1856 Chicago was the focus of ten trunk lines with nearly 3,000 miles of track; fifty-eight passenger and thirty-eight freight trains arrived and departed daily. (Mayer and Wade, 1969:35–38)

At the national level the integration by rail was also rapid. According to Gilmore, "By 1860, the United States had 30,635 miles of railroads, 52,914 by 1870, and 166,706 by 1890" (1953:57).

The significance of the railroad can be seen in many features of American metropolitan life, from the popular radio soap opera "Grand Central Station," to the lure of the steam whistle as it cried out on the prairie. After lying awake at night listening to that whistle, more than one American decided to attempt to follow it some day. The railroad was many things, but perhaps Mayer and Wade (1969:122), in commenting on the rebuilding of Chicago after the Great Fire, conclude with the true importance of rails:

> The railroads, too, moved to restore their facilities and renew regular service. Most of the freight terminals on the edge of town escaped damage, but nearly all the passenger depots were destroyed. The new stations expressed not only a faith in the revival of Chicago but also the central role of railroads in [its] life. . . . Companies lavished money and care in making them attractive gateways to the midland metropolis and symbols of its industrial power. Monumentally large and spacious, they were to the . . . [metropolis] what public buildings had been to Rome and the cathedral to the medieval town.

Although the first railroad companies were small—building lines between Boston and Worchester, or New York and Harlem, for example—they were quickly consolidated into regional and national empires. And as the rail system connected into first one city and then another, the dominance of those cities so connected was assured, if not extended. With competing canals out of business and with the time for transport now reduced by two thirds (from 20 days to 7 on the Erie route, for example), urban concentration in the United States accelerated. New York, where all roads began to run, went from a population of 123,700 in 1820 to 1,080,830 in 1860 to 3,437,202 in 1900.[2] In its expansion, the metropolis absorbed all towns within 15 or so miles of its old core and absorbed the growth of the settlements in its hinterland.

Transportation policy

Before continuing, it is relevant at this point to make brief note of the cost of these transport systems. Turnpikes, waterways, railroads, and other forms of transit or both people and goods were financed, as they are now, in part from public resources. By 1810, 180 turnpikes had been chartered in New England alone. For the nation as a whole, some 3½ million acres of public land were sold to pay for these wagon roads (Morris, 1953). State and municipal bonds were also sold to pay for the post roads and turnpikes.

When the construction of canals became possible the states and the

---

[2] The 1900 figure for New York includes the then recently (1898) annexed populations of Brooklyn, the Bronx, Queens, and Staten Island.

federal government subsidized canals with even greater enthusiasm. Between 1816–40, state governments had built 4,400 miles of canals, at a cost of $125 million—billions in today's monetary values (Mertins, 1972). To help the states pay for these necessary and valuable transportation routes, the federal government gave away nearly 7 million acres of land as grants for canal and river improvements alone (Morris, 1953).

Having invested more than 10 million acres of public lands and millions of dollars in bonds to construct turnpikes and canals, the same state and federal governments then subsidized even more heavily the massive railroad construction we have just reviewed. Even gross estimates of how much was spent are difficult to make, but one authority states that "up to 1837 [before the period of major rail construction] the states incurred debts totalling over $40 million in support of railroad development" (Mertins, 1972:7).

The land grant, the subsidy to railroad companies of public lands, was even more massive. If we just think of all the lands contained within the entire national park system (excluding Alaska)—the Great Smoky National Park, Yellowstone, Grand Canyon, Yosemite, Mount McKinley, Glacier, Everglades, Big Bend, Crater Lake, Shenandoah, Zion, Acadia, Bryce Canyon, Carlsbad Caverns, Virgin Islands, and the others—the total is about 14 million acres (*Columbia Encyclopedia,* 3d ed.), which is about the size of the land grants given to railroad companies to "encourage" them to build railroads which, if they were lucky, might make them a profit.

Excessive as such public doles to the railroaders may seen, the lack of any public control over route planning flies in the face of sanity. For even with this massive public support, what did the railroad companies take as their first mission? They first sought to drive all other forms of transport out of business.

In this mission the railroads were extremely successful. After some 11 years of work, the Chesapeake and Ohio Canal opened two years after the public had financed the construction of the Baltimore and Ohio R.R. whose route, of course, ran parallel to the canal. After one year of pointless operation the canal went into bankruptcy, and the public was left to pay its debts. The land that had been given to the canal company was, of course, unrecoverable. So having paid massively to build canals, the American taxpayer then contributed more resources to drive those canals into immediate bankruptcy.

This was far from being an isolated incident; indeed the American public continues to this day to subsidize the competition rather than the integration of transit systems. We are not discussing how massive public subsidy may be or should be. No doubt transportation is not only a necessity, but it is a valuable social and economic good, a sound investment for any country. Our point rather is that the public in the United States did not plan its transportation in accordance with sound policy. Canals could have carried goods to railroads, which would then take the cargo elsewhere. The potential for a fine national transport system was lost, just as it was lost again when the automobile and the truck replaced most of the rail system which we had supported so generously. In today's energy-and-resource-limited world, we ought not miss the opportunity again. Having thus argued our case for comprehensive transportation planning and policy, we can return to the impact the rails had on the concentration and dispersion of urbanization.

CONCENTRATION OF URBANIZATION

In the movement of goods by wagon on the old Boston Post Road, wagons typically stopped overnight at such places as New Haven, Hartford, and other small cities. Hotels, restaurants, and stables grew up in these locales to serve the early teamsters and the passengers of the stagecoaches. But since trains traveled day and night and needed to stop only for fuel and water, their crews did not need overnight services, and so one impetus to urban growth became concentrated at the origins and destinations of railroad runs.

At places where goods must be transferred from one vessel to another, from a ship to a train, for example, or from one train to another, labor is needed to load and unload those goods. Storage facilities are also necessary. And other institutions, such as banks and brokerage houses, are often needed, since at these points ownership frequently changes. Charles Horton Cooley termed these sites *breaks in transportation* (1930). Such breaks are one reason for urban growth. Compared with the distance between breaks for wagons and coaches, the distance between breaks for the railroads was much greater, and so urbanization in the United States became concentrated once again after the advent of railways. Therefore, during the period when railroad transportation was dominant, urbanization was concentrated. When urban development concentrated in only one settlement, that settlement became *primate,* or *primary* (Jefferson, 1939). And so in the competition between cities that hitherto had been approximately equal, intense battles were fought over which would get the railroad terminals, and over where the routes would be laid. Kansas City, Missouri, is a case in point.

Every settlement builds on its past, but it can also be strangled by it. Boston, New York, and the other colonial cities already serviced the needs generated by the "break in transportation" from seagoing vessels to land vehicles. These seaports had the advantages of already possessing a labor force for the new railroads, storage warehouses for their goods, and financial institutions to buy and sell these goods.

To bring the railroad terminal down to the dock, however, required tearing down houses and tearing up roads right through the heart of the city. Further, it meant laying track into the hinterland to buy and sell goods to ever more distant populations. To become dominant a city had to reach that hinterland first, before its inhabitants began to ship to another would-be metropolis and to buy its goods. In the "rail race," which was that era's version of the recurring space race within and between communities, some settlements "with more specialized commitments to an early technology faced partial eclipse or expensive adjustments. In short, technological changes either compounded or interrupted urban growth generated by initial advantages" (Borchert, 1961:47–70).

When urbanization is highly concentrated, as in the railroad era, *primate settlements* develop. Low levels of urbanization are further associated with the emergence of primate cities. *Dispersed urbanization,* by contrast, more evenly spreads development. As the process of urbanization matures to include 30 percent, 40 percent, or 50 or more percent of the population, urbanization tends to disperse. Rather than having one city or a few huge cities, or having a large number of very small cities with one or more primate ones, dispersed urbanization spreads urban settlements throughout the area, creating many competing cities. Thus, whereas low levels of urbanization are typically high in primacy, high levels of urbanization are characteristically low in primacy (Duncan, 1960).

In the history of the settlement of the United States, the few colonial centers began by dominating their hinterlands. The primacy of these seaports then declined as urbanization was dispersed. In the mid-1800s, primate settlements arose to dominate not only all communities in their proximities, but vast hinterlands as well. New York City is the classic example in the Northeast; Chicago perhaps best typifies the pattern in what was then considered the West.

New York had the advantage of history and the luck of location. The Hudson River provided New York with easy access to what was then called the Northwest, with the Great Lakes beyond. By water and then by rail, New York extended its hinterland far to the south and west, with each expansion multiplying its advantage. New York, once a small settlement on the tip of the island of Manhattan, became not just a metropolis, but the mother-metropolis.

Cut off by topography and by New York to the south and west, and by the formation of Canada to the north, Boston's growth slowed, barely keeping pace with national growth, until it became only a provincial metropolis. Its citizens responded by making it into a city that came to be widely regarded as one of the most beautiful of American settlements. Far to the south, Charleston was so far removed from industrialization and its rail system that it remained a city rather than becoming a metropolis, one of the few urban centers scattered throughout the South (Reissman, 1954:79).

Dominance

Were we to abstract the principles of metropolitan emergence from the American experience, we would observe from the early work of Harris and Ullman (1942, 1943) that there are three types of cities. Those which performed centralized services such as retail trade are *central place cities,* for they function to coordinate goods and services. *Transport cities* are, or course, those located at the earlier mentioned *breaks in transportation.* The third type of cities are those geared to *specialized functions,* such as resorts and recreation areas, religious shrines, or military headquarters.

Some cities may function in all three ways. And their combination at the same site may improve the advantages of each function. That is, retailing may be more easily accomplished in a city that also serves as a break-in-transportation because of the available transport. And the military may decide its best headquarters are in cities where alternative transportation and retail goods are available. When one settlement is able to function better in a variety of ways than another settlement, its chances of becoming dominant are naturally enhanced. In their studies of urban settlement patterns, urbanologists use the term *dominance* to describe what is called the "hierarchical ordering of urban communities."

The ways in which communities dominate each other are many and they change over time. In the days of the stagecoach, if you wished to go from Albany, New York, to Boston, Massachusetts, you could only get there by traveling several hundred miles south to New York City and then back north to Boston, a trip almost twice as far as a direct east–west route. In the days of the stagecoach, both Albany and Boston were dominated by New York.

With other forms of transportation—the canals, railroads, interstate highways, and air traffic routes (Taaffe, 1962)—dominance has continued although it may have favored different settlements. How is your own settlement dominated by others? Wherever you live, ask where you must go to travel to various destinations. Can you go to your own airport and get on a flight to Europe? . . . to South America? . . . to Canada? . . . to the South Pacific? Or must you first fly elsewhere in the United States before being able to leave it? The more a settlement dominates in transportation, the more likely a direct flight is available. And, the less dominant the settlement of origin, the larger the number of intermediate steps necessary to achieve one's goal.

Suppose, instead, you wish to place an ad in a newspaper. Does your community have its own newspaper or does it rely on one located elsewhere? When newspapers were our major source of communication, their circulations were a good measure of metropolitan dominance (Park, 1929).

Dominance may be found in transportation, communication, and in many other activities: banking, finance, governance, industrialization, medicine, law, education, wealth, and culture. As urbanologists have sifted through the statistics available on the various types of dominance, many have concluded that wholesale trade is the best measure today. For Vance and Smith (1954:14), "there is no question that the most important index to metropolitan status is the concentration of wholesale trade." Yet they question the utility of establishing definite boundaries for the dominance of a specific metropolis:

> It seems that efforts to mark off the areal limits of dominance by either trade or the closely associated newspaper circulation has meant too literal a tie to territory for the different contingencies on space involved in metropolitan influence. In certain specialized functions the whole United States may well be the hinterland of one city. On the level of consumer buying, the trade area marked off with pins on a map makes sense, but not for the complexities of economic structures." (Vance and Smith, 1954:126)

Through use of the mail, department stores and mail-order houses may serve national and even international populations, ones spread unevenly throughout a country. The same is true of television and radio stations, medical centers, governmental and financial institutions, and the other areas through which dominance is expressed. Therefore while we note that the dominance of one community over another is diverse and complex and not easily drawn on a map, metropolitan dominance is real. It is seen very clearly in our planet's *world cities,* which are at the apex of the order of dominance.

> These cities are the national centres not merely of government but also of trade. Characteristically they are great ports . . . great international airports. . . . Traditionally, the world cities are the leading banking and finance centres of the countries in which they stand.
>
> Each of the world cities has its great hospitals, its distinct medical quarter, its legal profession gathered around the national courts of justice. Students and teachers are drawn to the world cities; they commonly contain great universities, as well as a host of specialized institutions for teaching and research in the sciences, the technologies and the arts. The great national libraries and museums are here. Inevitably, the world cities have become the places where information is gathered and disseminated: the book publishers are found here; so are the publishers of newspapers and periodicals, and with them their journalists and regular contributors. In this century also the world cities have naturally become headquarters of the great national radio and television networks.
>
> Not only are the world cities great centres of population: their populations, as a rule, contain a significant proportion of the richest members of the community. . . . The traditional opera houses and theatres and concert halls and luxurious restaurants, . . . the variety theatre and revue, the cinema, the night club, and a whole gamut of eating and drinking places.
> . . . World cities go from strength to strength. (Hall, 1966:7–8)

One form of dominance leads to another, but dominance also leads to subdominance—the successful competition of those hinterland communities which accept the conditions imposed by the dominant city (Bogue, 1949). Thus, for example, while passengers must travel from Metropolis B to Metropolis A to go to Europe, for example, those from Metropolis C may find it necessary to first go to Metropolis B and then to A to take their European trip.

Dominance does vary from country to country, both in degree and relevant criteria to measure. It also varies regionally as well as within regions. And during the historical period with which we are now concerned, urbanization was highly concentrated within one region and in one settlement within that region. On the northeastern seaboard, population moved off the farm and away from the smaller cities into those which would quickly become metropolises. In the North Central, South, and West, however, urbanization within each region followed a much slower course. With this macropattern of urbanization in mind, let us examine the workings of the process within the emerging metropolis.

Annexation

In the initial phases of metropolitanization, many competing cities surrounded the early ports. In the 1830s, when the first railroads came into some of these communities, their initial effects were to link seaports to hinterlands. Although the construction of rail lines into these cities at times divided one section from another (the Back Bay from the South End in Boston, for example), the railroad had little other influence within the settlement at this time. With respect to suburban growth, the railroad's influence was also minimal, limited to allowing some wealthy families to live in country estates while commuting to the city.

The notion of rails, however, was extended in 1852 to create the horse-drawn streetcar in Boston. It was an instant success. The development of many competing lines followed, until by 1873 Boston was well-serviced to a distance of about two and one half miles out from the City Hall (Warner, 1962). In addition to transportation, city services now also included water and sewage mains, and citizens were prohibited from setting up or using their own systems. The demand for these services led many communities to seek incorporation into the central city. Typically these communities were encouraged to do so by their real estate profiteers.

For example, from 1868 to 1874 entire municipalities were annexed into Boston by the controlling state government, usually with the enthusiastic support of the citizens thus taken in. At the end of 1874, Boston included five formerly politically distinct communities—Roxbury, Dorchester, Charlestown, West Roxbury, and Brighton—a total landmass many times greater than the annexing city itself. And Boston is only one example: "in 1854, 28 cities, towns, and boroughs lost their local government and were incorporated into the city of Philadelphia" (Kotler, 1969). By 1890 the island of Manhattan was overcrowded and congested and the city was deeply in debt. The state legislature in Albany took advantage of the situation to establish Republican control over the traditionally Democratic city. By merging the five boroughs into a single government in 1898, Boss Platt achieved Republican control, despite the vigorous protests of the formerly independent municipality of Brooklyn (*New York Times,* July 8, 1886). "The fourteen incorporated villages of Manhattan, North New York, Port Morris, Wilton, East Morrisania, Old Morrisania, West Morrisania, Melrose, South Melrose, East Melrose, Woodstock, Claremont, Eltona, and Dove's Neck" (Kotler, 1969:3–4), plus the entire boroughs of Brooklyn, the Bronx, Queens, and Staten Island, with their hundreds of separate settlements, were all brought into a newly defined settlement called the New York Metropolitan Area.

Integration by transportation followed political integration. After 1873 the horse-drawn streetcar extended its lines out of the old Boston's boundaries, six miles out by 1890. In 1889 the first electric service became available, doubling the average speed of the streetcars while allowing them to carry three times as many passengers. Electric power was also cheaper than animal power, so the fare from one point to any other dropped to five cents. In the 1890s, with cars running every 10 to 15 minutes, less than an hour was required for the trip to work from the end of the line. And since the fare was within the means of many, the dormitory suburb came into popular existence.

Traction companies began to plan their routes and schedules to serve this growing commuting population, and soon streetcars, elevateds, subways, interurbans, and railroads integrated the former rim of the city into the central city itself. In Chicago, "by 1893 more than 500 miles of track crisscrossed the city, sustained by more than 200 million fares a year" (Mayer and Wade, 1969:140). In integrating this large landmass by a single interconnected rail system, the core area became the center, the chief, the principal city. A metropolis had emerged.[3] The formerly competing cities became dominated by one metropolis, and soon formerly heterogeneous communities became areas homogeneous in land usage. Urbanologists refer to these processes as centralization and segregation.

CENTRALIZATION AND SEGREGATION

Within the central city, railroad terminals were first built adjacent to the manufacturing plants and seaport warehouses. The availability of this terminal and its warehouses and facilities led other manufacturing concerns to locate in the same area, forcing out other types of land uses. The

---

[3] *Boston: The Hub of New England* provides a case study for the emergence of the metropolis in the videocassette prepared for use with this text. Order from publisher.

same centralizing and segregating processes went on at commercial locations. As one mass transit line terminated in the city's center, it gave rise to a connecting line. Quickly all lines saw the advantage of a central terminus. Commercial operations were attracted to this point of access because of the large numbers of people who congregated there. The largest of the commercial enterprises grew up at the center of the mass transit system and, in turn, generated the need for still more mass transit facilities—and then more stores to serve the additional population brought in.

> Between 1840 and 1870, an extensive warehouse district devoted to both manufacturing and commerce emerged as the dominant central urban land use, and, although the financial area was often well defined, it was very small. During the three decades that followed, the warehouse quarter continued to house wholesale trade and manufacturing industries, but financial and administrative districts were greatly enlarged and extensive new districts were developed to handle retail trade. (Ward, 1971:289)

Suburbanization

Families were thus forced out of the central city by the conversion of residential land uses to commercial uses. In addition, they were encouraged to go to the open spaces that mass transit now made accessible. In Boston, the only land lay to the west, and therefore the westward expansion of that city now began. This first major change in transport in the 10,000 year history of the city resulted in the first major change in residential patterns: the average person could now live in one community and work in another.

With rural residence and urban amenities thus joined, many understandably thought that the Golden Age had indeed dawned. Since the 18th century, many American cities had been surrounded by palatial homes of the wealthy.

> Nicholas Scull and George Heap issued a *Map of Philadelphia and Parts Adjacent* in 1750 showing about one hundred and fifty of the principal country places situated within a twelve-mile radious of the metropolis. (Bridenbaugh, 1938:145)

With the coming of rails the number of homes grew; members of the middle class and even members of the working class could afford suburban residence. The wealthy could go the farthest out, being able to pay the higher costs of travel, and they established their communities on the outskirts. Middle-class communities settled more closely in, followed by the working class. While large populations, unable to afford even the five-cent fare, remained in the central city itself, a significant portion of the population could and did leave the old city (Taylor, 1915).

In Boston, a typical middle-class Yankee community was Savin Hill.[4] On the bay, it had a magnificent beachfront and yacht anchorage a short walk from home, woods and fields for hunting, and ample space for family gardening. All the advantages of Boston were some 20 minutes away for the cost of a nickel. No wonder the urbanites fled the city in droves.

Many working-class families could also now afford to live outside the central city in more pleasant surroundings, and they too began to leave the central city. East Boston, for example, had earlier been connected to Boston proper only by boat. Now streetcar service by bridge transformed this summer resort area into a suburb for the increasing number of Italians coming into Boston. Like the Yankees of Savin Hill, they had their own beaches and recreational areas.

With the increased land made available to the city by the now well-developed mass transit system, facilities and institutions also moved outward, radially, along the streetcar lines, pulling the city's center behind them. In Boston, for example, the center of the city, originally located east of Beacon Hill, now shifted south down Washington Street and west into Back Bay.

Once an island whose spatial configuration had been shaped by its water transport from without and its pedestrians from within, the city of Boston had filled in its tidal flats and shallow bays to become the hub of a metropolitan area. Its initial growth had been limited to the distance that people could walk to work, to school, to stores, and to places of worship. Then in the first change in the primary transport used in American cities since their beginning some 250 years earlier, a system of mass transit developed to expand the growth potential of the city a hundredfold. Periphery was fused to central city; residential, commercial, manufacturing, and other land uses became segregated; and the entire urban settlement was centralized in the process.

Within each of the specialized areas of the city, however, from the central business district to the new dormitory suburbs, the nature of pedestrian traffic continued to shape their space. The transit system took its riders from one area to another, to home, to work, to stores, but once there they proceeded on foot. Thus the size of the areas, such as the central business district, or of the individual suburbs was still limited by walking distance.

The city as sociospatial form had given rise to its successor, the metropolis and its area. Whereas the city had once contained the entire urban population, homogeneous cells of commercial, residential, industrial, and institutional usage now dotted the urban landscape. Rail systems that radiated from the central business district outward, tied the original city,

---

[4] Photographs of this community are screened in the videocassette: *Boston: The Hub of New England.* Order from publisher.

now a commercial empire, to a vast area. Pedestrian islands tied together by mass transit—this was the newly emergent sociospatial pattern.

The hinterland

People went from one pedestrian island to another in the metropolis by rail car, below and above the street. And they traveled from one metropolis to another in the same way. These interurban routes had a significant impact on the people of the vast hinterland of the metropolis.

> For the first time, a farmer's wife was able to go into town, shop for an hour or two, and return to the farm by dinnertime. A resident of a country town could spend part of the day in the city and return home at his leisure.
>
> Even on the busiest railroad lines in the Midwest locals rarely ran more often than twice a day, but an interurban might schedule 16 cars a day. By 1909, the Illinois Traction was scheduling 106 trains a day in or out of Springfield, more than all the railroads combined, and in 1911, the interurbans regularly ran 140 trains a day in or out of Columbus. (Hilton and Due, 1960:91)

Since it must build upon the past, an individual settlement which had experienced its principle growth before this period of history developed into a relatively distinct central city or metropolis surrounded by communities which it dominated. When principal growth occurred during this historical period, though, the demarcation between metropolis and hinterland became blurred. Differences in temporal patterns of growth partly explain the differences in sociospatial organization of Boston and New York, for example. Even to this day, Boston remains more of a series of formerly independent but now loosely integrated communities, whereas New York evidences more a pattern of a single unbroken urban settlement.

One final detail needs mentioning before we examine other features of metropolitan population, organization, economy, technology, and symbolism. The initial railroad lines carried goods, not people, from one point to another. In fact, as Hilton and Due (1960) observe, passenger cars and trains were a long time in coming. Suburbanization during the emergence of the metropolis was therefore of people, not of economic activity. Business and industry could not move out on a massive scale until the invention of the truck made decentralization possible. Metropolitan suburbs were therefore truly *dormitory suburbs,* with virtually all shopping, employment, entertainment, and even worship centered "downtown."

The central business district

"Downtown" was, of course, the original city around which the metropolitan area was formed. As the central focus of all metropolitan activities except residence, and those requiring large space, its land was the most intensively used. Businesses such as department stores and the new movie theaters were dependent on access to people, and since such accessibility was highest within the center, competition for central locations drove up land values.

> Real estate on Manhattan Island was assessed at over five billion dollars in 1930; this was more than the value of the farm land in 23 states in 1925. The corner of State and Madison in the heart of Chicago's Loop was leased during the decade at a rate of $50,000 a front foot, a rate equivalent to $21,789,000 an acre. One small holding at 1 Wall Street in New York City sold for $100,000 a front foot, a rate of nearly $44,000,000 an acre.
>
> Inflation of downtown land values and the post-First World War prosperity of many sections of the economy stimulated the great era of skyscraper building in American cities. (Glaab and Brown, 1968)

The cost of the land as well as the crowds to which the businesses were attracted made "downtown" an undesirable location for nonbusiness uses, such as residence, recreation, or heavy industry, and therefore the center became the *central business district*.[5]

Within the central business district (CBD), businesses are distributed first of all by their degree of dependence on access to the general public. In the centralized metropolitan areas organized by mass transit, access was highest in the center, whether it was to labor, customers, goods, competitors, or associates. Since mass transit moved people but not goods, even the growing suburbanization of the population did not disturb the dominance of the central business district (Moses and Williamson, 1968). Thus "as late as 1910, 75 percent of the manufacturing employment in New York City was in Manhattan, 66.8 percent . . . in the small area south of Fourteenth Street" (Pred, 1971:383). The department stores, banks, professional offices, theaters, restaurants, libraries, and even grocery stores (then more specialized into meat markets, greengrocers, poultry and egg merchants) were found almost exclusively downtown.

Heavy industry and other economic units, such as nurseries, that required extensive space could not afford the cost of large tracts of land in the center, nor were they dependent on access to the public. They therefore located peripherally, tied to the core by rail lines. Public institutions, government centers, and nonprofit organizations located at various sites throughout the metropolis.

The central business district within itself was divided into relatively homogeneous areas according to the ability of a business to pay land

---

[5] Classical economic theory bases the foregoing sorting process on the differentiated ability of businesses and households to pay land costs, with the former able to outbid the latter. In addition to focusing attention on an inadequate set of variables, as shown for example by Alonzo (1971) when he is forced to equate a household's satisfaction with the profit of a business, such formulations obscure the economic consequences of social choice. Also, see Form (1954).

FIGURE 2–2
Concentric zone pattern of urban spatial organization

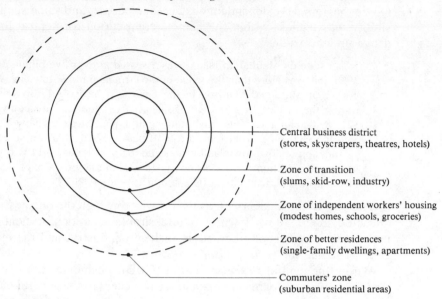

Central business district
(stores, skyscrapers, theatres, hotels)

Zone of transition
(slums, skid-row, industry)

Zone of independent workers' housing
(modest homes, schools, groceries)

Zone of better residences
(single-family dwellings, apartments)

Commuters' zone
(suburban residential areas)

costs. Shoe stores, for example, had similar abilities to pay costs because of their similar volumes, similar operating costs, and similar space requirements. By clustering together, they could also generate higher volumes than they could achieve individually. The CBD thus became subspecialized into concentrations of clothing stores, restaurants, theaters, financial institutions, and other specialized areas.

Within the boundaries of the CBD at any one moment in its history, the social status of the business establishments declined roughly with distance from the center. In addition, pawnshops, secondhand stores, and the less respectable places of entertainment, such as the "red-light district," were found on the trailing or older edge of downtown.

Cities are in constant motion and the CBD moves as well. For example, Caplow, Lovald, and Wallace (1958) plotted the movement of the Minneapolis CBD as it moved from St. Anthony Falls three blocks down Hennepin, turned left or northward down Washington Street for two blocks, was stopped by Post Office Park and forced to turn right, down Nicollet, where it had gone three blocks at the time of their 1958 study. Moving at a rate of about one block per decade, its leading and trailing edges significantly influenced the surrounding zone, as we shall see shortly.

The shape of the CBD is typically ovaloid, since pedestrians are willing to walk farther along the main stem than they are along its intersecting streets. Land values thus fall off most sharply on arteries perpendicular to the main artery, secondmost sharply toward the trailing edge, and least sharply toward the leading edge. Because the CBD is often growing in area faster than it is moving, leading edges may be created completely around the ovaloid perimeter. Those who own land just outside the CBD must therefore base their judgments on land value on predictions: will the CBD expand faster than it will move, and will it move in their direction? This ring which surrounds the CBD is called the *zone of transition* by Burgess (1925) in his *concentric zone theory*.

The zone of transition

The shape of this zone depends on the growth rate of the metropolis, the topography of the settlement, and the shape of the rail lines going to and from the CBD. Growth will occur along transit routes since access is higher on such transportation radii than between rail lines. This applies to all types of land usage—commercial, residential, and industrial. Topography initially influences where transit lines are located, and such surface features as lakes, rivers, hills, and valleys further influence development.

Taking such factors into account we can say that growth is axial, that is, along the axes of transportation. And since the metropolis is centralized around the CBD, we can add that metropolitan growth is concentric, therefore axially concentric. When and if the metropolis develops more than one center, that is, becomes polynucleated, the settlement's internal shape becomes a more complicated version of axial and concentric growth—provided the metropolis is developing within Western civilization and is capitalistic, industrially based, and centralized by rail routes.

Land in the zone of transition is far more valuable than the buildings on it because all structures would be razed for new commercial ones when taken over by the CBD. Building maintenance is therefore uneconomic, and so the structures are allowed to deteriorate. As a temporary expedient, at least at first, owners subdivide their buildings to rent them as residences. As this zone is composed of old hotels, office buildings, obsolete factories, warehouses, old commercial structures, and at times abandoned older middle- and upper-class homes, subdivision allows the per unit rental value to be low while the net rental value of the entire structure remains high.

Each floor of an old factory, for example, can be divided into hundreds of four-by-eight-foot cubicles, each being rented to a skid rower, for a mere 50 or 75 cents a night (Wallace, 1964). When the rent is multiplied by hundreds and compounded by thousands of nights of occupancy, the building can become quite profitable, even if not absorbed into the CBD. Other poor people can be housed the same way, and thus the zone of transition comes to include the lowest-status members of the city's population: the most recently arrived immigrants, the skid rowers, the prostitutes, the petty criminals. If the CBD fails to expand and move into the area, perhaps in part because its owners now require too high a price for their profitable though deteriorated buildings, the zone's status and ethnic enclaves remain standing as artifacts of the past.[6]

By the end of the 19th century, residential density in the zone of transition reached new and disturbing heights. In Chicago, for example:

> It was, according to one calculation in 1894, three times worse in the Polish district on the West Side than the most crowded portion of Tokyo or Calcutta. The extent of the crowding was hard to convey, but Dr. Frank Felter estimated in 1900 that if all of Chicago were as densely populated as its average slums (270 persons per acre) the city would have 32,000,000 people; if it were as densely populated as its worst slums (900 persons per acre) the whole of the Western Hemisphere could have been housed in Chicago. (Mayer and Wade, 1969:256)

Other zones and sectors

Beyond the zone of transition in the pattern shaped by mass transit, residences were distributed according to a given locality's accessibility, amenities (Hansen, 1959), topography, and history. Although closely related to distance, accessibility more importantly refers to the time it takes to reach a given destination. Since most persons had to work for a living, and since most work was located downtown, access in effect meant in this historical period (1850–1920) the time necessary to reach the CBD. In addition, most unskilled workers were hired by the day, and working hours were long. Residence adjacent the CBD was therefore highly desirable, even essential, for the poor since they could afford neither the time nor the cost of commuting.

The distribution by accessibility is far from absolute, however, since a location's amenities are also of importance.[7] For families with children, location may be chosen to secure better schools. Amenities for an orthodox Jewish couple might include walking proximity to the temple.

Topography also exercises an influence on the distribution of population. Wealthy districts may occupy areas along a beachfront, or hills with commanding views. How land has been used, its history, is the fourth variable that influences residential location. Sites whose past use is considered undesirable (slaughterhouses, cattle yards, red-light districts) are avoided, while historically prestigious areas attract (Firey, 1947).

Burgess's concentric zone theory proposes that the social status of the metropolitan population declined with distance from the center. Hoyt (1933), Hurd (1903), Harris and Ullman (1942), Alihan (1938), and others

---

[6] See the videocassette prepared for optimal use with this text: *Little Italy: An Ethnic Enclave.* Order from publisher.

[7] The following discussion has been freely adapted from Alonzo (1971), although he does not limit his application to the metropolis as historical form as is done here.

FIGURE 2–3
Sector theory of urban spatial organization

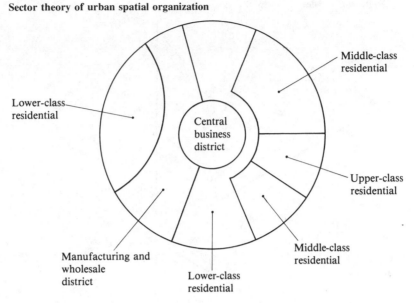

FIGURE 2–4
Multiple-nuclei pattern of urban spatial organization

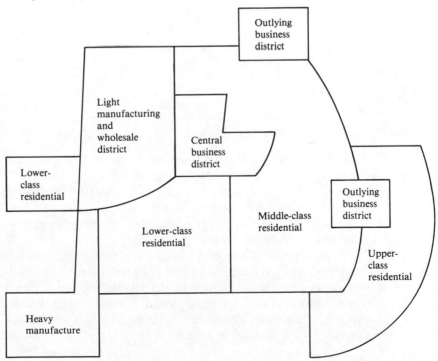

FIGURE 2–5
Radial or "star" growth of a city

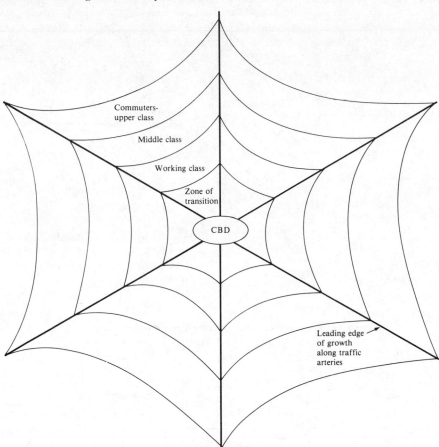

(Davie, 1937) have convincingly demonstrated the inaccuracies of that proposition. It was not even always true that the poorest lived closest to the center, as the history of Boston's fashionable Beacon Hill illustrates (Firey, 1945). Even with respect to the mass transit settlement he was writing about, Burgess's theory, while offering many important insights, must be highly qualified (Quinn, 1940).

The concentricity of the mass transit settlement has also been much debated, even though Burgess's initial sketch did show sectors, belts, and was given as an idealized form. In the city of Chicago, which he was observing, physical and temporal distance were closely parallel. If the investigator, however, completely ignores physical space and instead plots zones by the amount of time it takes to reach the CBD, access and topography both can then be taken into account. Changes in access as well as in nucleation would also be reflected.

If we add to these considerations the work of Homer Hoyt in tracing sectoral growth, and the Harris and Ullman contribution regarding polynucleation, then several other distributions become evident.

The intensity of land use decreases with distance from the center. Throughout the metropolis blacks and whites are highly segregated, rarely sharing as little as a single common block. The area highest in residential value forms a wedge from the center to the periphery. On either side of this most valuable wedge are belts of middle-class housing. Working- and poverty-class areas are also found in greater numbers on one side or within one sector than in another, although in general workers live closer to the center.

In the days when only wealthy city dwellers could afford transportation—that by horse and carriage—the principal roads and boulevards were promenades, routes on which the elites could and did maintain contact and communication. Upper-class residential growth was therefore axial, along the sides of these gracious routes. With the coming of the noisy trains, however, the wealthy avoided residence on principal thoroughfares and began to build their homes in communities with less traffic.

Once the organizational feature of segregation in land use became evident, newer developments self-consciously planned for such segregation. Again Chicago provides a clear example.

> Chicagoans introduced the organized industrial district idea to the United States. Under this scheme, the [industrial] district acted like the residential developer, assembling land, laying out streets, and installing utilities. It often also provided architectural engineering and financial services to the industrial clients; occasionally the district even furnished dining facilities and executive clubs. (Mayer and Wade, 1969:234)

METROPOLITAN PROBLEMS

The problems of the city not only continued into the metropolis, but they typically became much worse. Crime grew with population, and law enforcement became professional. Even though it was now highly integrated, traffic circulation continued to be a problem.

> The bitter competition for franchises so characteristic of the earlier period diminished; in 1907 the [Chicago] city council granted franchises to only five companies. Six years later, it put the entire system—nearly 1,000 miles of track—under the management of the Chicago Surface Lines, thus creating what Chicagoans claimed to be the largest unified street railway system in the world. Its volume of traffic reached 634 million fares in 1913; by 1929 that figure soared to nearly 890 million. (Mayer and Wade, 1969:208)

The problem of fire also continued, as dramatically illustrated by what Mrs. O'Leary's cow supposedly did to Chicago.

> The fire broke out just a few minutes past nine on Sunday evening, October 8, (1871). . . .
>
> The flames ate their way across the West Side, consuming a thousand shanties, houses, and planing mills. At Van Buren Street the fire vaulted the South Branch of the river. The gasworks at Adams Street went; then three blocks of pine rookeries called Conley's Patch; the "fireproof" mercantile buildings along LaSalle Street followed. The city now lay at the mercy of the fire's caprice. By one o'clock in the morning the Chamber of Commerce had fallen. Two hours later the Court House went down, its great bell pealing until the end. Soon the whole commercial center was wreathed in red and orange. The *Tribune* building, thought to be uniquely fire-resistant, was abandoned in the morning; two and a half million dollars' worth of stock and the marble magnificence of the Field, Leiter store lay in ruins. Having sacked the Near West Side and leveled the business district, the fire headed north across the main stream of the river. As if by instinct it hit first at the engine house of the waterworks, knocking out the water supply, and then proceeded to devour the frame buildings along the river. Almost nothing was overlooked. Wooden houses, commercial and industrial buildings, private mansions, and even markers in the cemetery were consumed before the lake confined the blaze. (Mayer and Wade, 1969:106)

With high metropolitan densities, better provision of safe water and waste disposal became essential. Again Chicago provides our example, although other metropolises may not have been as successful in solving the problem.

> Chicago's solution was bold—the construction of a canal across the drainage divide between Lake Michigan and the Mississippi Basin, the diversion of lake waters into the canal, thus reversing the flow of the Chicago River. . . . (Meyer and Wade, 1969:272–273)

In spite of its problems, the metropolis grew and grew and kept on growing. First the center and then other zones and sectors filled to the strangulation point, and then the metropolis itself began to decentralize.

> Boston contained a mounting proportion of the area's total population only until 1880; since that date it has shown a progressive decline. In other words, the outlying counties have exceeded the city in rates of growth since the 1880s. Much of this outlying growth, at least initially, must be attributed to the influence of the street railroad in the late 19th century. (Thernstrom and Sennett, 1969:248–49)

As the process of incorporation into the metropolis continued, expansion continued along transportation lines. Older residential centers were swallowed up, new areas appeared, and even larger landmasses were annexed. The resulting configuration looked like an irregular star whose framework was rail lines. Then a broad outer rail belt line was built, and sets of whole satellite communities grew up at the points of the star and on arcs between them.

The metropolis had indeed emerged. The pressure of population forced technological development, which in turn reorganized even larger populations into functionally interrelated units. Organization transformed environment, giving rise to a new symbolism—the towering skyscrapers of metropolitan skylines. Americans were on their way to becoming an urban, if not yet urbane, people.

THE SYMBOLIC ECOLOGY OF THE METROPOLIS AND ITS AREA: SUMMARY

The Bay of Massachusetts, the Hudson and Delaware river valleys, and the headwaters and mouth of the Mississippi were sites for numerous small settlements internally limited in size by the distance people were willing to walk. The bounded or walled settlement was limited in its possible expansion. Not until the invention of rail transit could a larger land area be urbanized. This first change in urban transport in the history of urban settlements created highly specialized commercial, industrial, institutional, recreational, and residential areas. Rail lines were first extended to what were at that time rival cities, making possible the spatial integration of much larger landmasses. The city that managed to become the core of the rail system could dominate and even annex its former rivals.

An area's series of bounded cities thus became spatially integrated into a single urban area dominated by a new metropolis. The metropolis and its area—the second sociospatial form in the history of urban settlement patterns—withdrew business and industry from its competitors because of its greater access to population and to transit facilities. It took its residential families and pushed them out into the lands of its former rivals, thereby transforming heterogeneous cities into homogeneous residential or industrial suburbs. To the specialization in land use—the separate areas for industry, commerce, recreation, education, culture, and the like—was added segregation by class, ethnicity, and occupation. The wealthy occupied one suburb and the middle class another, the Irish one locality and the Italians another, the craftsmen one area and the factory workers another. The metropolis and its area, in other words, became highly segregated by land use and population. The former heterogeneous and mixed land use pattern outside the center of the old city was no more.

The population continued to travel on foot within each area. They rode the trolley, the elevated, or the subway from home to work, but walked to and from the transit stops. The size of the work areas as well as the size of the residential areas was limited by the distance that people were willing to walk. These specialized and segregated areas were structured by pedestrian traffic, just as the entire earlier bounded city had been. The mass transit system had tied a series of these pedestrian islands together to form the metropolis and its area.

In summary, then, in terms of our ecological components, the metropolis and its area of the historical period 1820 to 1920 can be described as:

        population—hundreds of thousands of people,
                 10 to 50 percent of total population
    organization—centralized, first mononucleated,
                 then polynucleated,
                 dominated by CBD, segregated by land
                 use, social class, and ethnicity
       economy—industrial,
                 spatial occupancy determined by temporal
                 zones of accessibility,
                 differential definitions of amenities,
                 history, and ability to pay land and
                 transport costs
     technology—mass transit rail lines,
                 inanimate energy sources (coal, steam),
                 mechanization of agriculture,
                 sophisticated construction (skyscrapers)
     symbolism—prestige of dominance,
                 optimism engendered by material growth

STUDY QUESTIONS

1. Using the five components of the symbolic ecology approach, POETS, describe the metropolis.
2. What is the relationship between dispersed and concentrated urbanization, primacy, and dominance?
3. In what ways was the metropolis centralized and segregated?
4. Describe the concentric zone theory as formulated by Burgess.
5. Compare and contrast the problems of the city and the metropolis.

SUGGESTED READINGS

Burgess, E. W.   "The Growth of the City: An Introduction to a Research Project." Robert E. Park et al., eds., pp. 47–62. *The City* (Chicago: University of Chicago Press, 1925).

Mayer, Harold M.   "A Survey of Urban Geography." Pp. 81–113. *The Study of Urbanization* (New York: John Wiley & Sons, 1965).

Park, Robert E.; Burgess, Ernest W.; and McKenzie, Roderick D.   *The City* (Chicago: University of Chicago Press, 1967; originally published 1925).

Thernstom, Stephan, and Sennett, Richard, eds.   *Nineteenth-Century Cities: Essays in the New Urban History.* New Haven, Conn.: Yale University Press, 1969.

chapter 3

THE URBAN ENVIRONMENT

United Press International

URBANIZATION UNBOUND

Writing in 1915, the remarkable Patrick Geddes perceived a new form of urban settlement beginning to arise and named it a *conurbanation,* a growing together of many metropolises. Geddes saw and described what in 1964 Jean Gottman would call a *megalopolis*—"mega" meaning super, "polis" meaning city. Keeping in mind that Geddes was writing in 1915, let us read what he had to say:

> The present Greater New York, now linked up, on both sides, by colossal systems of communications above and below its dividing waters, is also rapidly increasing its links with Philadelphia. . . . For many years past it has paid to have tramway lines continuously along the roads all the way from New York to Boston, so that, taking these growths together, the expectation is not absurd that the not very distant future will see practically one vast city-line along the Atlantic Coast for five hundred miles. (Geddes, 1915:48–49).

Some 50 years later, Gottman (1964) described what he saw as an unbroken band of urban settlement stretching from Boston to Washington, including parts of ten states and the District of Columbia, 117 counties, and unnumbered cities. In the 1960s, Anselm Strauss observed that Americans were being told that soon they would be living in 15 nameless and shapeless communities—super-cities, strip cities, suburbia, exurbia, and inter-urbia (Strauss, 1961:246–54). We now turn to the emergence of this new pattern of urban settlement.

The self-contained and isolated city of the past had been succeeded by the much larger and more specialized metropolis. After about a century of metropolitan settlement form, urbanization burst out of its metropolitan confines and flowed out into the countryside. Small towns and cities, resort and recreation areas, dormitory suburbs, industrial parks, and even agricultural regions felt the impact of urbanization.

No longer was urbanization confined either by city walls or to the end of the mass transit line. No longer was the urban way of life confined to 5, 10, or even 50 percent of the population. With the third settlement form that we call "the urban environment," urbanization spread out to engulf entire national societies, among them the United States. In the 20th century, urbanization became unbound.

To understand how and why urbanization in this century spread nationally, and even internationally, we need to return to the metropolis when it was still dominant.

METROPOLITAN DOMINANCE

Intense competition and rivalry among metropolises marked the later phases of metropolitanization. St. Louis competed for dominance with Chicago, while Detroit struggled against St. Louis; Chicago, in turn, and virtually every other large center struggled with New York. By the turn of the century, the dominance of New York was so complete and so extensive that it had become our truly national metropolis. New York therefore became the symbol of urbanity itself—cultured, refined, and sophisticated on one hand; vile, vicious, and wicked on the other. In time the darker view would prevail, and the subdominant metropolises would band together to reduce New York's power. Remembering that all metropolises, in some way dominate the communities in their midst, and that dominance is relative and of many degrees, and that those dominated survive by fulfilling other functions in a subdominant position, let us examine in more detail this part of the history of the dominance of New York.

In our earlier discussion, we saw that dominance in one activity frequently gave a settlement an advantage that led to dominance in a second function. New York enjoyed the advantage of being a major port of immigration, and shipowners were eager to find cargo for the return voyage to Europe. With so many empty vessels to fill, shipping rates out of New York were low, and therefore many firms began shipping through New York. When more and more cargo became available for the return trip, other ships were attracted and changed their port of debarkation to New York, contributing further waves of growth in shipping activity. Since ownership frequently changes at breaks in transportation, New York also became an early leader in financial institutions, which were strengthened by the growth in shipping.

Governmental actions also contribute to dominance. If, for instance, the government designates one settlement rather than another as an official port of entry, that settlement obtains an advantage over its rivals. In areas low in urbanization, the location of the county seat frequently determined which of many small towns would become principal (Reissman, 1954). Because a metropolis is already fulfilling many functions, the addition of yet another by the government may not have as major an impact as this, but it will have an influence nevertheless. An example of the federal government's contribution to New York's dominance is seen in the National Banking Act of 1863, which made the Big Apple the only reserve capital for deposits of currency. Money started to flow from all parts of the nation into New York, giving those who controlled the New York banks tremendous assets to invest. The birth of a number of giant corporations, such as U.S. Steel, International Harvester, General Electric, and American Telephone & Telegraph, can be traced in part to the National Banking Act. The organization and the locus of such corporations heightened New York's dominance.

The ascendancy of New York banks affected assets and markets nationwide. Decisions made in New York raised or lowered prices in Boston, Pittsburgh, or St. Louis; non-New Yorkers were powerless when New York interests moved into stock market manipulation. New York brokers drove down the prices of stock in non-New York firms, so that they could later purchase them for a fraction of their value. They then added insult to injury by taking them over (McKelvey, 1968). Once corporate control had been seized, the firm's headquarters could be moved to New York and all its shipping routed through the port of New York.

In 1890, virtually all the land within the entire city of New York as it then existed (Manhattan Island only) was occupied. Through legislative action in Albany, the four surrounding boroughs were annexed to Manhattan, causing New York's population to leap to nearly 5 million by 1910. Nearly one of every five Americans lived in the New York metropolis. New York was the world's second largest city (London was first), and our one and only national metropolis.

At the turn of the century, each region of the United States had its dominant metropolis, while New York remained dominant over all. Chicago had become the metropolis for the upper Midwest and the Great Lakes, and was becoming the major financial, retail, and wholesale center of its region. At the mouth of the Mississippi, New Orleans dominated its lower valley and the lands for hundreds of miles to the east and west. At the confluence of the Missouri and Mississippi, St. Louis dominated the eastern areas along the Ohio as well as to its west. Going west from Kansas City, one had to travel to the coast and San Francisco, some 1,500 miles away, to find a city or metropolis. Nor were there cities in the western band from Canada to the United States–Mexico border.

The period of mature metropolitanism was a time of partisan politics, the spoils system, and political machines and bosses—in short, widespread corruption. Considering that the metropolis was so young, having emerged within the lifetimes of many former residents of the old cities, we should not find the inability of governments to keep up with the governed surprising. Although the annexation of large areas into the core city represented, in part, an effort to deal with the emerging problems, the effects of annexation all too often overburdened a government already overwhelmed. Political machines and their bosses stepped into the resultant vacuum, and Boss Tweed (New York), "Doc" Ames (Minneapolis), and James McManes (Philadelphia), among many others, became nationally known through the writings of muckrakers such as Lincoln Steffens (1931). Later studies (McCaffrey, 1976) have revealed that half of these bosses were Irish, Catholic, and Democrat, and some have suggested that they did serve their own well.

In the later metropolitan period, reform organizations arose to urge the assumption of local responsibility for municipal affairs, including ending machine control. Since cities were chartered agents of the various states, vital decisions concerning first the cities and then the metropolises were made at the respective state capitals. Annexation, for example, was decided at that time by the state, not by the people who were affected by it. Municipal taxes and expenditures were also frequently the responsibility of the state legislature, leading to municipal corruption through the channels of the state. The Citizens Municipal Reform Association had been organized in 1871 (McKelvey, 1963). Local political machines occasionally fought what were seen as abuses of state power.

Advocates of *municipal reform* also thought one solution lay in home rule for cities. The state of Missouri took the lead, granting home rule to St. Louis in 1876 (Barclay, 1962). A state municipal convention was held in 1877, and in 1885 the American Institute of Civics was organized. But although the officials and citizens of metropolises had begun to associate with one another on a national scale, none of the reform-minded organizations seemed to make much impact on metropolitan problems.

In 1894, the Municipal League was organized, to be succeeded by the National Municipal League, which had 180 affiliated societies by 1895 (McKelvey, 1963). Those who lived in the nation's metropolises were learning that their problems were common and that they could learn from one another. Problems needed to be studied and results published along with other information about urban settlements. To facilitate this, the Reform Club of New York established the journal *Municipal Affairs* in 1897.

The next series of events is one manifestation of the initial phases of the emergence of the urban environment. In a series of conferences involving delegations from across the nation, the National Municipal League worked out and adopted a model for what they called municipal reform.

This model rejected state or even national authority in favor of a home rule carried out under state administrative supervision. It called for the separation of power between the council and the mayor. A civil service system, a comptroller responsible to the council, a limitation on taxing and bonding powers, personal registration of all voters, and the secret ballot were some of the other provisions.

Other national organizations also signal the emergence of the urban environment. Through them common approaches to problems were developed: one settlement learned from the experience of another, metropolitan experience became national in scope, and increased contact and communication increased intermetropolitan migration.

In 1897, the League of American Municipalities endorsed standard accounting procedures in collaboration with the new National Association of Comptrollers. The National Board of Fire Insurance Underwriters urged other types of standardized practices, as did the (national) City Managers Association, which was organized in 1914.

Among the literally hundreds of other national organizations founded in the late 19th and early 20th centuries are: National Teachers Association (1857), which became the National Education Association (1906); the National Planning Association (1909); the National Association of University Professors (1913); and the National Association for the Advancement of Colored People (1910).

Dispersed urbanization

The period 1910–15 has been taken as the beginning of the end of the metropolis as the primary urban settlement form. This period also witnessed, of course, the beginning of the emergence of the urban environment. Symbolic of this shift was the change in the status of New York. In 1913 Wilson sided against what had come to be known as the New York "money trust" and established 12 central reserve districts, each with a central bank and one or two branch reserves. In that same year New York's dominance as an official port of entry was lessened by the establishment of 49 such centers throughout the United States. Others followed this decentralization of federal government activities. The Associated Press, for example, established eight regional press depots in 1914. Such changes were both the results of and the encouragement of the dispersion of urban settlements.

Blake McKelvey (1963) states that what he terms "metropolitan regionalism" culminated between 1910 and 1915. Although our concept and focus differ from his, we agree that what we call "the urban environment" began to emerge around 1915. McKelvey uses as bench marks that: between 1910 and 1915, railroads attained their maximum in mileage, the Federal Reserve system was reorganized, suburban growth began to mushroom, central city populations began to decrease, and factories began to disperse.

It was also after 1915 that urbanologists began to comment on the changes they were seeing in the metropolis. Since we have already heard from Patrick Geddes, let us turn to 1916 and Robert Park:

> Modern methods of urban transportation and communication—the electric railway, the automobile, the telephone, and the radio—have silently and rapidly changed in recent years the social and industrial organization of the modern [metropolis]. . . . These changes in the industrial organization and in the distribution of the population have been accompanied by corresponding changes in the habits, sentiments, and character of the urban population. (Park, 1925, 1967)

AUTOMOBILITY

In the search for the basis on which urbanization spreads, urbanologists have focused upon a wide variety of factors. For those who stress the importance of population (P), the lowering of the death rate and other improvements in public health are thought to be critical. Organizationists (O), have stressed the increasing power of the national government. Economists (E), observing the national integration of American business and industry, have argued that such economic integration provided the critical underpinning for the national urban environment. As even Robert Park observed, it was the technology (T) of modern transportation and communication which altered urban settlement form. Those urbanologists who have stressed the symbolic factor point to the emergence of national identities—Americans, English, French, Germans—a process in part stimulated by the First World War.

To return to the technological determinists, they argued that the main force for the creation of modern urban life was the automobile. Many volumes have been written analyzing the impact of the automobile on American life. No doubt the automobile has been and continues to be an important influence in shaping community life. Yet our continuing (and hopefully growing) ecological awareness leads us to insist that the other four components must also have had their influences. Obviously without people, without places to go, and without money to buy cars and build roads for them, the automobile would have been but another "newfangled" invention. And without the automobile's symbolism of power, freedom, and conception of self, Americans probably would have continued to ride the less expensive and more efficient rail car.

Happily, John C. Burnham (1961) has already given us a term that includes all our components. "Automobility" Burnham calls this combination, stating that this term "conveniently sums up the impact of the motor vehicle, the automobile industry, and the highway [industry] plus the emotional connotations of this impact for Americans." We then, now turn to *automobility,* using it to discuss our five components as they interact to spread urbanization.

The automobile first appeared on the American scene as an experimental vehicle in 1891.[1] Charles E. and J. Frank Duryea made the first sale of an American gasoline car in 1896 (Fink, 1975:15). Approximately 2,500 motor vehicles were produced in 1899, nearly all for the upper-class market. Not until the luxury market was saturated, shortly after 1905, did manufacturers turn their attention to the middle-class market. "The most successful was Henry Ford, who led the industry in developing the reliable, moderately priced, four-cylinder, conventional runabout with his 600 Model N (1906–07). Its successor, Ford's legendary Model T (1908–27), became the universal car that had been anticipated by many Americans since the turn of the century." (Fink, 1975:24–25)

For a number of reasons, Americans welcomed the new technological invention, making it an item of incredible mass consumption, appropriating millions of dollars for its routes, and reorganizing their settlements and ways of life to accommodate it. Due to the far-reaching impact of "automobility," the context within which the automobile was introduced bears examination.

---

[1] Invented by Henry Nadig and John W. Lambert, separately. Gottfried Scholmer and Frank Toepfer, W. T. Harris and William Hollingsworth followed in 1892, and Charles H. Black and the most famous of all, Charles E. and J. Frank Duryea, completed their first cars in 1893. For a detailed account of the origin and spread of the automobile, see: Fink, 1975.

We can begin with the frequently overlooked problems of the transport system which preceded it.

> In New York City alone at the turn of the century, horses deposited an estimated 2.5 million pounds of manure and 60,000 gallons of urine on the streets every day. Traffic was often clogged by the carcasses of overworked dray horses who dropped in their tracks during summer heat waves or were destroyed after stumbling on slippery pavements and breaking their legs. On the average, New York City removed about 15,000 dead horses from its streets each year. A 1908 estimate that tried to take all factors into account concluded that the cost of not banning the horse from New York City was approximately $100 million a year. (Fink, 1975:34)

Dysentery, diarrhea, and other serious problems, including loss of life and limb, were traced to the horse and its excreta.

The electrification of the trolley in 1889 and its rapid adoption throughout American cities did lessen reliance on the horse, but mass transit moved people, not goods. Metropolitan deliveries to home, factory, and store were still made by horse teams (Kirkland, 1948:15).

Mass transit was also expensive to construct and operate. Once built, its routes were furthermore inflexible—unresponsive to shifts in population distribution. Suburban development had to await the extension of transit lines, which became increasingly expensive as construction costs mounted in the 1890s. Articles published in *Scientific American, Harper's Weekly,* and *Motor World* also argued that traffic would be speeded up by use of the automobile, since autos, unlike streetcars, could bypass obstacles and one another.

The motorcar was considered cleaner, safer, more reliable, more economical, quieter, more flexible and maneuverable, more impervious to weather conditions and to fatigue; it depreciated less rapidly, did three times the work of a horse for about the same cost, and enhanced family life and individual mobility. It was also an ideal status symbol in American society.

There were other influences. The metropolitan press was enthusiastic in its praise of the automobile, and provided millions of dollars of free publicity by covering early automobile races and the introduction of new models to the market, and editorialized for improved roads and other facilities for the automobile. Federal, state, and municipal politicians initially supported the automobile by refusing to pass any special regulations governing the manufacture or use of the automobile, including limitations on its speed. Fink (1975:27) points out: "The 1905–1906 period marked the high point of restrictive speed laws. Before this few speed laws had been enacted; later, with the rapid diffusion of the motorcar, speed laws became progressively more lenient."

The early and rapid success of the automobile industry, which "leaped from 150th to 21st in value of product among American industries" (Fink, 1975:18) by 1910, gave it economic and political influence beyond any power the horse-drawn transit and mass transit interests might mount. By the 1920s automobile manufacturing ranked first among all industries.

Other businesses and industries quickly saw the advantage in promoting the automobile and did so in numerous ways. The automobile industry thus obtained the support of the oil industry, and also that of the rubber, glass, steel, advertising, real estate, finance, construction, engineering, trucking, motel, and used car interests, among others.

Finally, automobility was basically dependent upon the easy availability of inexpensive petroleum. In the early days of this century, in contrast to today, oil supplies were abundant, they were thought to be inexhaustable, and they were inexpensive. With fuel costs so low, the automobile could successfully compete with almost any other source of energy, including animal power.

That brief historical episode of abundant and cheap fuel is now over. Contemporary urban life is already witnessing the impact of resource scarcity, especially that of petroleum. Future urban settlement forms will no doubt be affected even further by rising gasoline prices. Thus, to the list of the factors promoting automobility must be added the cost of gasoline. Cost factors, combined with the many industries benefiting from use of the automobile, made the automobile dominant in a relatively short time.

The influence of powerful economic interests along with the public's embracing of automobiles help explain the massive effect the new technology had on the cities and metropolises of the United States. Whereas previous transit systems were integrated to some extent (for example, people at least had to walk through downtown after getting off the rail car), the automobile could compete even with foot traffic. Whether intracity or intercity, whether related to employment, recreation, family visiting, shopping, or worship, wherever their locations, one's destination could be reached by automobile. Getting there by auto did require roads, bridges, tunnels, service facilities, and parking lots, and paying for them necessitated the mobilization of political forces. But whereas the organizational forces promoting the automobile were centralized, the new technology was decentralizing.

Decentralization

Previous modes of transport served to centralize people and places. The automobile decentralized them. Rails brought hundreds of thousands of passengers to a central point where everyone worked, shopped, or carried out other activities, including embarking for another center, town, or city. But when automobiles converged on a central point the result was massive congestion.

Rail cars pulled into a station, their riders disembarked, and the train went elsewhere. By contrast, the automobile had to be stored at its destination until its riders returned. Whereas a single path was needed for hundreds of rail cars and their thousands of riders, auto vehicles required wider and wider paths. Land devoted to transport thus increased from approximately 15 percent to 40 or even 50 percent of the settlement's ground surface.

Recognizing that the impact of the automobile differed from one settlement to another, we can note that generally its effect was to push the boundaries of the metropolitan area farther and farther out, thus decentralizing the settlement and bringing into existence the urban environment. As a form of urban settlement, the urban environment includes the city and the metropolis and its area.

The decentralization engendered by the automobile was felt first at principal nodes, such as the central business district (CBD). Then it affected subcenters as well. As population density declined, the efficiency and profitability of mass transit also declined. As fewer riders used the transit system, its service deteriorated, leading still more people to purchase and use automobiles. Pressure for highway construction grew, and as each new highway that promised to relieve congestion quickly filled to capacity, another highway had to be opened—contributing further to the demise of the mass transit system.

Between 1880 and 1910, population densities in the central core and in the metropolis as a whole reached their maximums and began to decline. From 1880 to 1890 in Boston, for example, the core city began to lose out in population growth, a trend that continues to this day. Manhattan, or old New York, reached its maximum population in 1910 and has lost people ever since. Population moved from the core to the adjacent area, forcing people who lived there to move a little farther out. Residents of that area, in turn, moved into the area adjacent to them, leading to yet a third, fourth, and fifth relocation of the population. The density in virtually every zone and sector was reduced in the process, but since the landmass occupied by the metropolis swelled, the total number of persons in the metropolis increased. Therefore, although population size continued to increase, the greater distribution of the population in space lowered densities everywhere.

The decline of the CBD

Billions of dollars had been invested in downtown areas, money that investors tried in vain to save. As the annual output of passenger cars jumped from about 25,000 in 1905 to nearly 36 times that number a decade later, an average annual increase of about 350 percent (McKelvey, 1968:11), the mass transit system lost riders at a precipitous rate. Fares therefore had to be increased or operating subsidies provided. Boston abandoned the five-cent fare, and this increase led some transit riders to forsake the train for the automobile.

New York battled fiercely to retain that (5-cent) fare throughout its vast
system in order to assure the builders of the new towers that increasingly
covered central and lower Manhattan a sufficient flow of daytime inhabitants. Philadelphia extended its rapid-transit lines to serve its skyscraper
district. But Detroit, with 19 buildings of twenty or more stories and 100 of
ten or more, rejected a proposed subway in 1929; as the automobile capital,
it turned, with Los Angeles, to planning for the development of a
superhighway system and a widespread suburban pattern. (McKelvey,
1968:46)

The automobile was aided in its major influence on the erosion of the
metropolitan form by many other factors. In the 1890s electric power
became available and facilitated the suburbanization of industry.

The building of industrial towns and cities in the early part of the twen-
tieth century reflected a general pattern of decentralization clearly indicated
in statistics of manufacturing. A Census Bureau study of twelve of the
thirteen largest "industrial districts" showed that from 1899 to 1904 the
number of persons employed in industry in central cities increased by 14.9
percent while in the outlying zones the number increased by 32.8 percent.
From 1904 to 1909 the increase in central cities was 22.5 percent while in the
surrounding zones it was 48.8 percent. For the decade, the growth rate was
over two times as great for the suburbs—97.7 percent to 40.8 percent. This
trend toward industrial decentralization became even more pronounced with
the general acceleration of suburbanization after 1920. (Glaab and Brown,
1968:14)

The increase in the number of trucks manufactured, from 450 in 1905 to
74,000 in 1915, spurred the suburbanization of commerce. The first chain
store (the A&P) had been organized in 1864, but when the population
began to decentralize after 1900 many more were opened. The first F. W.
Woolworth Variety Store of 1879 gave rise to hundreds and thousands of
"dime stores," with one or more at each major traffic intersection. Chain
stores in tobacco, drugs, clothing, shoes, yard goods, and groceries followed (McKenzie, 1926).

By the late 1800s there was no space left in the CBD. Each square foot
was intensively used and extremely expensive. Land outside the CBD
was by contrast plentiful and cheap, leading many new businesses and
industries to establish facilities on the rim of the decentralizing metropolis. The central business district began a decline to which the automobile later contributed.

Freeways and parking lots

Efforts to accommodate the automobile were prodigious and ultimately
unsuccessful. The early parkways were progressively streamlined (first in
Detroit, of course) until the freeway with limited access, no grade cross-
ings, and service stations of its own came into being. Robert Moses built

one of the first of these in Manhattan's West Side in 1934 (Caro, 1974). It was called simply the West Side Highway by New Yorkers and the Henry Hudson Parkway by others.

The "cloverleaf" intersection, developed in 1930 in New Jersey, began to be widely used. J. C. Nichols built the country's first suburban shopping mall in Kansas City. The instant success of the Country Club Plaza and its parking lots led others to provide automobile parking in their new suburban shopping centers. When these new malls contributed to the further decline of the CBD, downtown merchants built parking ramps in an effort to save their enterprises.

Newer settlements, such as Detroit and Los Angeles, had the advantage. Because they did not have significant city or metropolitan pasts to reorganize, they could build with the auto in mind. St. Louis could propose a divided highway through the heart of the city; Boston's "heart" had to be torn out to accomplish the same ease of auto travel. Boston, in fact, provides a graphic illustration of problems caused by demands for freeways and parking lots.

By 1928, Boston was 300 years old.[2] In its past, a number of large projects had been carried out: draining the 50-acre Mill Pond, filling the 600-acre Back Bay, and commissioning a toll bridge to be built. Bostonian pride had been evident in the care exercised over these projects.

The talents of some of the nation's finest architects, such as Charles Bullfinch, had been employed in the periodic reorganization of the city. When the Mill Pond was filled in 1830, great care had been taken to integrate the previously isolated North End into the central city of Boston. Selectmen later reviewed plan after plan of solving the problems created by integrating 500 acres of landfill in the Back Bay, finally adapting the skillful and innovative proposal advanced by Frederick Law Olmstead (Whitehill, 1968).

Earlier, Olmstead had provided a series of parks along waterways, making recreational space convenient to nearly every area of Boston. This "emerald necklace" rivaled the park system of any city at that time, and helped make Boston perhaps the most beautiful city in the United States in the early 1900s. As the city expanded into the newly created areas, such as the Back Bay, though, its core was pulled west and south, leaving the original business district to deteriorate. With the coming of the automobile this deterioration accelerated. The old hub became an area of petty vice and crime, and as early as 1930, proposals were advanced for the clearance and rehabilitation of this area, then known as Scollay Square.

Boston during this historical period is especially interesting to the urbanologist. Always proud, overbearingly so to some outsiders, the city had seen significant change since its beginnings in 1628. Whether changes

---

[2] For further details, see the optional videocassette prepared for use with this text. Order from publisher: *Boston: The Hub of New England*.

occurred in government, spatial use, or expansion, the citizenry of Boston had sought to integrate the new in ways that protected and preserved the old. Perhaps more than the residents of any other city, Bostonians treasured their past and the beautiful city they had built. What absorbs us in observing Boston in the period between 1925 and 1955 is that she began to do what she had never done before—namely to neglect and to destroy her past.

Fine buildings were allowed to be razed to provide parking lots ("They paved paradise and put up a parking lot," J. Mitchell), expressways were thoughtlessly thrown across parks and rammed through communities, gasoline stations went up everywhere, and three centuries of thoughtful urban planning were rent asunder. In the central city, the North End, so carefully integrated in 1830, was once again isolated in the 1930s by elevated highways. These elevated roadways ignored the experience which cities, including Boston, had just had with elevated trains. The "El," or elevated, had been found to cause so much blight that it had been taken down in many cities, or at least not used in later rail construction. Now, just a few decades later, a new series of elevateds was built, repeating the same errors on an even more colossal scale.

Prior to the coming of the auto, the Charles River basin had provided Bostonians with recreational space on land and water. Then Storrow Drive was constructed, stealing that land from its citizens and cutting them off from easy access to the waterfront at the same time. The parks became filled with the roar of traffic and the stench of exhaust. Frederick Law Olmstead's magnificent Back Bay was cut off from its river frontage on the north. To the west his beautifully wrought fens and water gates into the river were paved over, bisected, used for supporting columns for elevateds, defaced, and significantly reduced in value. On the south the Massachusetts Turnpike roared its way along the old railroad tracks, separating Back Bay from South End as if they had never been joined with so much effort.

Outside the old city the havoc wrought by the auto was no less significant, no less depressing. The delightful community of Savin Hill was first cut off from its own beachfront by one highway. As a result, its fine beach became a mudhole. Then, Savin Hill was isolated from the rest of Dorchester on the other side by a second expressway. Rendered a much less desirable place to live, Savin Hill of course went into decline.

The first and most important influence on any settlement is its history. So powerful is the influence of the past that it has doomed thousands of large cities that proved unable to adjust to change. Walled cities at hilltops were abandoned; pony express and stagecoach station settlements lost their ability to compete; flourishing river port cities became little remembered names in history books. Settlements that have survived major changes often have paid a heavy price in terms of their previous investments.

Thus, despite the efforts of vigorous planners, such as Robert Moses, the population densities established during the city or the metropolitan phase typically overwhelmed the freeways built for the urban environment. As Caro documents in detail for New York, hundreds of thousands of people could be relocated and millions of dollars spent and yet the solution to automobile traffic congestion remained distant.

> By 1938, the parkway (Henry Hudson) was all hooked up and the double-decking of the bridge completed. . . . Traffic on the bridge had been 10,300,000 cars in 1937. By 1939, it rose to 12,700,000; by 1941, 14,300,000; it would finally top out at 26,000,000. In the face of such increases, double-decking a bridge hardly seemed to make any difference at all. Motorists pulling up to pay their tolls found themselves at the end of lines that seemed little, if any, shorter than the lines had been at the old Broadway Bridge, whose congestion New York had considered intolerable . . . the congestion on the old bridge had not been noticeably relieved. (Caro, 1974:563)

Settlements that grew up with the automobile were more fortunate in being able to allocate their space in harmony with the new technology from the beginning.

> Before the automobile a commuter could go, at best, six miles in sixty minutes, so that urban development was effectively restricted to a hundred square miles. The car and later the freeway increased the sixty-minute radius to 35 miles and thereby opened up two thousand square miles for settlement. In seventy years, the potential size of urban areas has multiplied forty-fold. (Fisher, 1976:207)

The dominating automobile

Given this vast increase in the landmass available for urbanization, communities could be built with houses spaced widely apart. Land throughout the settlement could be reserved for traffic ways and parking lots. Suburban facilities for offices, industries, and commercial activities could be built, with still more land available for parks and recreation. In such settlements the automobile did become dominant.

> Perhaps the best symbol of the new dominance of the automobile in the metropolis is the fact that the spot that the Burnham Plan had marked for the civic heart of Chicago is now the site of the most elaborate expressway interchange in the city. Just west of the Loop where Burnham had located a domed civic center, the Kennedy, Dan Ryan, and Eisenhower came together in a baffling maze of ramps, overpasses, underpasses, entrances, and exits. Just beyond this complex, however, and more in keeping with the spirit of the Plan of 1909, is the newly established University of Illinois Chicago Circle campus, probably the only campus in the world named for a traffic interchange. A frankly "urban campus," it is a series of varied buildings united by concrete walkways. (Mayer and Wade, 1968:442)

The dominance of the automobile was further entrenched by the Federal Highway Act of 1956, which called for the construction of 41,000 miles of highway at an estimated cost of $70 billion, about $350 per American adult or child for the federal contribution alone. Whether it was done intentionally or not, this act ended any competitive or possible complementary transport development by making the auto dominant and exclusive. For every dollar the state spent on this system the federal government was to spend nine dollars, and with the promise of such massive federal funds, state after state rushed to begin interstate highway construction.

The promise of federal funds became an attractive way of financing local circulation highways that could also carry interstate traffic. Relocating several hundred thousand people whose homes lay in upper Manhattan and the Bronx, Robert Moses secured interstate designation for the Cross-Bronx Highway and pushed its route through those communities. Boston established its Outer Belt, Chicago its Belt Loop, and many other settlements pushed the automobile to the fore.

The automobile and truck were not the only vehicles spreading urbanization. In the 1920s the newly invented airplanes were beginning to see domestic use, and the federal government announced plans for airmail service. In effect the government use of a transport for the mails is an indirect subsidy, and to this federal financial support of airlines the municipalities added the support of providing landing field construction and maintenance. Later such subsidies would grow at all levels to include weather reports, air traffic control, and safety and route regulation. When airmail service began in 1920, 21 cities had fields ready for use. By 1928 there were nearly 5,000 airfields.

The rail lines continued to lose passengers as more and more Americans bought automobiles and used airplanes. What had once been the only mass transit now steadily declined in passenger traffic to become less than 2 percent of the country's personal intercity travel (Mayer and Wade, 1968:432). Unable to compete with the auto for short trips or with the airline for long journeys, rail lines were abandoned, their rails sold for scrap, and the once famous train stations fell into disuse. Even Grand Central Station, whose keys had been thrown away upon its opening, found it had to close its doors at night in the early 1970s.

Sprawl

In the early phase of automobile traffic there were no fixed routes, and even with today's interstate and limited access routes, the automobile remains less tied to fixed routes than were rail systems. Previously inaccessible areas suddenly became urbanized by this revolutionary new form of transit. Just as mass transit had expanded the area that could be integrated into a common whole tens of times greater than that accessible to pedestrian traffic, the automobile expanded the city's areas far beyond that achieved by rails. With inexpensive land in generous supply removed from the congestion of the city, the suburbanization of the population intensified. The city was now accessible from previously distant and remote areas. So were other cities and remote places, such as lakes and beachfronts, accessible from the city.

First walls and then rails bounded the city. Outside the city walls or beyond the end of the line, the countryside began. The city was contained, bounded. High population density was both the consequence of and the support system for mass transit, since few wished to live far from mass transit. The nearly universal use of these transit facilities made them convenient, dependable, and inexpensive and profitable at the same time.

As a distributor of people in space, the land use configuration engendered by the automobile differed in nearly every respect from the mass transit pattern. There were no clear boundaries to the limits of automobile traffic. Although cities had always had scattered suburbs and metropolises had scattered real estate developments, those were limited in size and location until the automobile made remote areas accessible. With the automobile, people could live as far from work as they were willing to drive. The definite boundary of the city thus gave way to a ragged and unevenly developed rural and urban—*rurban* area. *Sprawl,* those "areas of essentially urban character located at the urban fringe but which are scattered or strung out, or surrounded by, or adjacent to undeveloped sites or agricultural uses" (Harvey, 1977), made its first appearance.

Harvey states that sprawl is "located at the urban fringe." But since sprawl may be found in more central locations, we include sprawl as one type of land use within the urban environment, differentiating three forms of sprawl: (1) low-density continuous development; (2) ribbon development, which extends axially and leaves the interstices undeveloped (the Strip City pattern); and (3) leapfrog development, or discontinuous patches of urban uses. In-filling may later transform the third type into the first or second type. Sprawl is a gluttonous use of land and stems from a combination of causes, including poor or nonexistent land use planning, which can sometimes be traced to lack of public regulation outside municipalities, independence of decision-making by land users, land speculation, and auto transit.

Suburbs

As noted in Chapter 1, suburbs—*sub* (beyond), *urb* (the city)—are nearly as old as the city. As noted in Chapter 2, suburban development

increased when rail systems made it possible to combine suburban residence with urban employment. Until 1920, however, the central areas of
the metropolises grew faster than the suburbs. After 1920, suburban
growth mushroomed and outstripped the growth of any other area.

The Great Depression and World War II temporarily slowed suburban
development in the United States, but it resumed on a massive scale in the
post-war years. Millions of returning veterans, former residents of central
cores, and even new immigrants settled in the suburbs. An extensive
literature swelled both in defense and in criticism of these suburbs. Instead of dealing with this phenomenon in our present examination of the
general outlines of the emerging urban environment, we have included a
separate chapter (10) on suburbs.

TRANSPORTATION POLICY

In conformity with the now familiar pattern of nonplanning for transportation in the United States, there was no requirement or even sugges-
tion that auto routes be integrated with any other type of transport. There
was no effort to "piggyback" cars or trucks by rail over long routes. The
$70 billion spent on highways in fact contributed to the further decline of
the national rail system. With generous federal outlays available for auto
traffic and none available for mass transit, it is a small wonder that local
and state governments gave priority to freeways. The funds made available for mass transit in the Housing Act of 1961 and in the Urban Mass
Transportation Act of 1964 were not based on the 90–10 formula used for
highways, and the sums involved were small (Winters, 1976). While such
funds may have been of little use to newer regions that had not previously
invested so heavily in transit systems, they were badly needed in the older
urban areas. By the 1960s, funds for mass transit were still not forthcom-
ing, but community opposition to intra-urban highway construction
began.

In 1958, Robert Moses proposed building in New York first a lower
Manhattan Expressway and then a four-lane trafficway through Washington Square Park. Because it was the only community park for some
220,000 people who lived in the area, the 19,000 daily users of this small
eight-acre park arose in wrath. They not only defeated the plan to destroy
the park, but were instrumental in eliminating the proposed Lower Manhattan Expressway as well. On the Upper West Side, a proposal to turn
the West Side Highway into an interstate route with eight lanes of traffic
through Riverside Park met a similar fate.

Community opposition was not limited to New York. In Boston in the
mid-1960s, when construction of Interstate 95 was proposed, the citizens
forced their elected officials to stop the destruction of their settlement by

the automobile. Aided by advocacy planners at M.I.T. and by other university faculties and students in the area, citizen groups built support over five years, then listened with satisfaction as the governor of Massachusetts suspended all highway construction within the metropolitan area, transferred funds from highway construction to mass transit, and began other programs for rebuilding the entire Boston metropolitan area (Fellman and Brandt, 1973).

The examples drawn from New York and Boston are only two among many. The construction of Interstate 95 down the eastern coast has been stalled in every metropolis in its path. Community opposition to intra-urban highway construction has also been expressed in Chicago and the Twin Cities, in San Francisco and San Diego, in Houston, Fort Worth, Dallas, Memphis, and New Orleans, among others (Manning, 1978).

The age of the automobile is certainly not over in Boston or elsewhere, but never again will city officials be permitted to rely exclusively on cars as transportation. The city's nondriving population, including the young, the old, the poor, and the infirm, must have a way to move around the city. An increasing number of people are also realizing that cities such as Boston simply cannot accommodate the automobile at their centers. Mass transit must be used in dense downtown areas; automobiles should be limited to getting people to and from transit lines to the centers. Much of the corrective for the traffic congestion caused by the automobile lies in integrating autos with other systems.

During the 30 or 35 years that the automobile dominated local transport in American cities, air travel became the primary means of traveling longer distances. In a development parallel to what was happening within the city, air traffic was pursued as the exclusive transport between cities. Just as railroad, streetcar, inter-urban, elevated, and underground transits were neglected within the city, so national rail and bus lines suffered while air traffic expanded disproportionately. And just as the automobile eroded the support for intra-urban rail transport, so air traffic reduced utilization of the inter-urban and transcontinental railroads. That rail system for which we had spent so much money and to which we had devoted such great land resources was abandoned. One rail route after another ceased operation, one railroad company after another went into bankruptcy, and the total rail mileage available in the United States continually declined.

Although system interaction and consequent change is unavoidable, neither the inevitability nor the desirability of change justifies our failure to anticipate and plan for it. As we have pointed out in some detail, American public investment in transportation has been massive. In terms of money spent, we should have the finest transportation system in the world. The fact that we fall so short of being any kind of model underscores the cost of *not* planning.

The Hoover Commission, the Brookings Institution, the Sawyer Report, the Weeks Report, the Nueller Report, the Doyle Report, the Fitch

Report, and others (Mertins, 1972) have all agreed on the need for a comprehensive transportation policy. Such a policy has yet to be adopted and made operational.

The creation of the Department of Transportation in 1966 was a step forward. President Johnson's special message to Congress on March 4, 1966, "stressed that the United States was the only major nation in the world which relied so heavily on privately owned and privately operated transportation. At the same time, however, the President noted that this reliance was made possible only by the extensive latitude that had been given to private enterprise by various levels of government, and by tremendous investment of public resources" (Mertins, 1972:79).

In the past, public monies built and maintained wagon roads, post roads, turnpikes, canals, and railroads; today public funds primarily support and maintain highways, truck lines, and air traffic. (The direct subsidy to Amtrak is small by comparison to the subsidies to the automobile through road construction and maintenance, traffic engineering, regulation, policing, health and medical costs, insurance, parking, air pollution, vehicle abandonment, and so forth.) Perhaps the time has come for the public to demand more for its money.

URBANIZATION RECONSIDERED

Urbanization is a revolutionary process. It is also ecological because its many components are interdependent. A change in any one of the components leads to changes in the others. If the economy differs in area A and in area B, for example, we will expect their urbanizations to differ. If during the time of the emerging metropolis area A already contains a city while area B has no urban settlements, we will expect area B to assume metropolitan form from the start and area A to manifest both city and metropolitan characteristics. Understanding such differences is critical to urbanologists, because it enables them to examine each settlement within its own context.

An embarrassing number of persons conclude that a particular settlement is not urban, not "a city," because it does not conform to previous or well-known patterns. Thus Bostonians made disparaging remarks about New York as it took metropolitan form in the mid and late 1800s. New Yorkers insisted that Chicago lacked some critical dimension of urbanism, even as it began to rival the Big Apple. More recently, the urban nature of Los Angeles has been questioned—"seventy-seven suburbs in search of a city," and "freeways filled with anomic, restless people hurrying from nowhere to nowhere." Stung by such remarks, defenders of Los Angeles have responded by claiming that urbanization as found in Southern California is "the ultimate city of our age."

At times urbanologists notice the same problem as they go from one country to another. In western Nigeria, for example, the observer learns that the Yoruba have traditionally been an urban people. Since the central area was already densely populated, European colonials, in introducing such institutions as department stores and banks, had to locate them on the outskirts (Fava, 1968). If the CBD was not in fact central in Ibadan, did that make Ibadan any more or less urban? Of course not. Urbanization is a process. It necessarily builds upon the past, and as times and places change so do the patterns produced by it. Thus, although we may speak of urban settlements as if they were the same, in fact we know them to be quite different. There is only one New York, only one Boston, just one historic Kansas City (now in Missouri), and only one Incredible Los Angeles.

Given these differences—which are reflected in such statistics as that most New Yorkers do not own a car and that nearly all Los Angelenos do—what set of terms and concepts can we use to describe urbanization in our own times? Suppose we were to list the characteristics of urban settlements and eliminate all those not held in common. We might find, for example, that, although not all urbanites own automobiles, the number of people living in urban settlements is always large. We might find that, although urbanites work in a wide variety of jobs, there are no farmers. Does urban therefore mean big? Nonagricultural? What do we mean by the word "urban"?

When we went back into the past to learn how, when, and where cities emerged, we raised the question, What is a city? We noted that different writers use the term differently and that, in part because of such differences in definition, they saw the city emerging at different times. Also using our own criterion, that of enclosing walls, we claimed that all five components were brought into interaction by bounding and that their interaction gave rise to incipient cities. In Chapter 2 we further noted that the term "metropolitan" is also used in a variety of ways. Although some urbanologists use the terms "city," "metropolitan," and "urban" interchangeably, we have not done so.

Throughout, the word "city" means to us that shape or configuration of population, organization, economy, technology, and symbolism (POETS) which emerged about 8000 B.C. and was supplanted about A.D. 1800. In our usage of the term, then, the city did not then die but rather was surpassed as the dominant settlement form. What emerged either from the old cities of the past or as entirely new urban settlements was that configuration we call a metropolis. And it, too, was eclipsed by a third combination of POETS as the central business district began to decline and the population within the metropolis began to move out. These and other massive changes which we have reviewed spread urbanization beyond the area of the metropolis. As more people and larger regions became integrated into a national urban society, urbanologists struggled to define this new settlement pattern.

Census Bureau definitions

To be able to report data accurately, the Census Bureau has offered its definitions of modern urban patterns. Prior to 1910, the Census Bureau simply used the corporate boundaries of a city for reporting data on urban population. Although lagging behind the actual changes that had taken place in American urban settlements, usage of the municipality reflected the historical importance of the legal boundaries of the city. By 1910, however, the Census Bureau recognized the massing of population around and outside the city. It therefore introduced the "metropolitan district" and defined one for every city over 200,000 in population. Basically this delineation served to distinguish urban from rural populations. Although used again in 1920 and 1930, dissatisfaction led to some changes in 1940. In that census, metropolitan districts were defined for each incorporated city having 50,000 or more inhabitants, and included adjacent and contiguous minor civil divisions or incorporated places having population densities of 150 or more persons per square mile.

The need for uniformity in reporting statistical data by government agencies led to devising the 1950 Standard Metropolitan Area. The SMA included one or more contiguous counties containing at least one city of 50,000 or more inhabitants. To determine what adjacent counties should be included in a particular SMA, the Bureau examined indices of their social and economic integrations with the metropolis, along with population densities (Berry, Goheen, and Goldstein, 1968). The metropolitan area concept adequately reflects the spatial manifestation of the metropolitan area, because it reflects a spatial continuity of populations at densities higher than those typical of rural areas.

In 1960, the word "statistical" was added to communicate better the purpose of the SMA of reporting data used by all federal agencies. The Standard Metropolitan Statistical Area (SMSA) took into account places of industrial and population concentrations and distinguished between metropolitan and nonmetropolitan areas.

Regarding Census Bureau definitions, Brian Berry points out that the 1910 definition of a metropolitan district was applied in 1920, 1930, and 1940. "In 1950 and 1960 the concept was but little changed, although the definition criteria had become more elephantine (remember, an elephant is a horse designed by a committee). . . . The concepts that were valid in 1900 have become so institutionalized that even the most urgent evidence that times have changed (and along with them the concepts that are valid) can elicit only marginal definitional shifts" (Berry, 1971:155).

Other definitions

In 1955 Howard L. Green compiled seven indicators of urban settlement boundaries, based on available statistics concerning transportation

FIGURE 3–1
Megalopolis or "Boswash"

loads and destinations, communications frequency, agricultural basins, recreation zones, manufacturing links, and banking controls. Using such indices, he then delineated urban areas; for example, he gave most of Connecticut to New York and eastern Massachusetts to Boston. Smailes (1947) and Friedman and Miller (1965) argue that recreational areas, such as ski slopes, should be included as urbanized areas since they are part of what they call the *urban field*. Friedman and Miller define an urban field as "a mosaic of different forms and micro-environments which co-exist within a common communications framework." Webber (1968) goes so far as to argue that communications is everything, that space means little if anything, and that today's population lives in nonterritorial communities of interest.

Daily urban systems have also been advanced to define the urbanized portion of an area. "Twentieth-century Metropoli have so burst their nineteenth-century boundaries that broad 'daily urban systems' now transcend all the traditional definitions: 'central cities,' 'urbanized areas,' and even the 'standard' limits of 'metropolitan statistical areas'" (Berry, 1971:153). Using this concept, the investigator includes all areas surrounding a central core from which a certain percentage of the population commutes to the core for work. Although commuting does offer insight into the pattern with which we are dealing, the lack of commuting to the core does not necessarily mean that a given community is not integrated into that core.

In 1942, Hope Tisdale stated that the increase in the rate of urbanization involves: (1) an increase in the number of points at which population concentrates, and/or (2) a growth in the size of these concentrations. From 1900 to 1970 the population did concentrate. But by 1975, the trend that had persisted from the beginning of the century had shifted. The *New York Times* reported the Census Bureau's latest findings: "Rural Population Gains Now Outstrip Urban Areas" (*New York Times*, May 17, 1975, p. 1, col. 3). Beginning in 1970 people began moving to small towns and rural areas "far away from any cities," as it was reported. Some otherwise usually accurate urbanologists even concluded that the American population was entering a phase of counter-urbanization.

> Counter-urbanization has replaced urbanization as the dominant force shaping the nation's settlement patterns. A similar tendency has been noted in other Western nations. . . . To mimic Tisdale: counter-urbanization is a process of population deconcentration: it implies a movement from a state of more concentration to a state of less concentration." (Berry and Gillard, 1977:1–2)

In what way does it make sense to classify now the some one million migrants to small towns and remote areas as "rural" residents? Few of these new migrants returned to any aspect of rural life other than residence in communities outside Census Bureau definitions of what is metropolitan. They took jobs in new decentralized manufacturing centers, worked in new sunbelt recreation areas, took up residence in new retirement communities, or perhaps registered in one of the newly developing community colleges and state universities. What is "rural" about that?

The urban environment defined

Our own ecological perspective seeks to avoid such confusion by refusing to rely on any one single component of urbanization. A population may move to a new environment, but when it takes an urban organization, economy, technology, and symbolism with it, it urbanizes that environment. From our perspective we would say that the sunbelt (Texas, Oklahoma, Arkansas, Tennessee, and the like) began to experience the process of urbanization in the 1970s, drawing population from older urban settlements. Such spread of urbanization beyond the confines of the metropolis is no different in kind from the urban developments outside the old walls of the city.

Urbanization in the 1970s carries within it a wide variety of sociospatial forms. Not only are the older city and metropolitan patterns now contained within it, but urbanization today also creates resort and retirement communities, large planned residential complexes, strip and ribbon developments, and exurbs.

Even the so-called rural areas have become integrated into the urban environment. Gottman noted this in including in *Megalopis* (1964) a chapter on "Metropolitan Agriculture" (written by Eugene Higbee). In the process of integration into the urban environment, the family farm has become large scale business termed "agri-business" by some. As agriculture has become a business, the "farmer" has been replaced by the manager of a multimillion-dollar enterprise. As the tractor parades of protesting farmers in the late 1970s illustrate, farm machinery today costs tens and even hundreds of thousand of dollars, and farmers and farm families are as much affected by government policy as anyone else.

Today urbanization has become relatively unbound, no longer contained in a specific territory called a city or metropolis. The process of urbanization now goes out on vast networks of electronic communication. It is not that space today has little or no meaning—rather, that space in the contemporary era is organized in different ways.

The name we have given to this new configuration of tens and hundreds of millions of people who are tied together by telecommunications, by air, auto and mass transit routes, is *the urban environment*. It is *a mosaic of interpersonal networks and social worlds which may or may not share common exclusive territory*.

Recognizing that the urban environment is the subject matter for the remainder of this book, we can now summarize its general features and then turn to a more detailed examination of it.

THE SYMBOLIC ECOLOGY OF THE URBAN ENVIRONMENT: SUMMARY

Throughout these three chapters of Part One we have traced the process of urbanization from the rise of incipient cities about 8000 B.C. to the spread of urbanism throughout national, continental, and even civilizational borders. Although we have used the settlement of the United States for our primary examples, the outlines of the process can be seen in many nations.

For better or worse, the urban environment is now with us. In the 1970s there were 49 million commuters. Some 18 million people live and work in what the Census Bureau designates the central city; 16 million live and work in the suburbs; 9 million commute from the suburbs to the central city; and 3 million people reverse commute from the central city to the suburbs (Taeuber, 1976). The extent and complexity of movement patterns within the urban environment reveals its areal specialization.

Whereas traditionally cities were located at breaks in transportation, today's urban environment contains hundreds of thousands of such breaks at widely scattered sites. All the technological developments of industrial times have reduced the constraints of geographic space, until today transport terminals can be located almost at will.

Coordination and control, a second major function formerly found exclusively in the city and then in the core of the metropolis, can be performed today at suburban, exurban, or other "noncentral" sites. And the third type of locational orientation of economic activities, that of specialized functions, can also be carried out wherever communications can be established.

The urban environment is thus characterized by high degrees of areal specialization. Within it the cities and the metropolises of the past are found, at times relatively intact. Ethnic and socioeconomic enclaves, millions of social worlds, vast areas filled by one or more institutions, suburbs of many sizes and types, satellite communities, exurbs, and inter-urbs are among the other sociospatial forms found within the urban environment.

As urbanization has spread across the land, creating and connecting the many units of the urban environment, space has been reorganized but not eliminated from consideration. As human beings we are space-using creatures and until we can mentally project ourselves in space, that is, develop the power of telekenesis, we will continue to be at least constrained by space. Therefore, it is incorrect to suggest that today we are spatially unbound, free from the frictions in overcoming space.

We do have the telephone and television and with them we do communicate across vast distances. Resources nevertheless must be constantly expended to traverse those distances. Without the necessary resources communication shrinks or ends, as gasoline shortages so vividly demonstrate. It is not that we have become nonterritorial or aspatial but that our territories, home ranges, orbits, and associations encompass larger and larger spheres of space—ones connected by transportation and communication.

Space within today's urban environment need not be contiguous. As the process of urbanization began to urbanize the entire country, it jumped over and went around some areas. Thus were we to attempt to map the boundaries of the urban environment for the United States today the map would include about 60 percent of the land surface and about 95 percent of the American population. Such isolated populations as those thinly scattered through the southern Appalachians and in Idaho and Montana are examples of the only areas excluded.

Our framework differs from that used by the Census Bureau, which continues exclusively to use place of residence to define an urbanite. According to Census Bureau definitions, the American population is about three quarters urban. Exclusive reliance upon the number of residents in a settlement ignores, of course, whether that settlement is a retirement community, a resort, or a county seat. It ignores the urbanization of agriculture, the spread of urbanism far beyond the confines of the metropolis, and the reorganization of space now prevalent within the urban environment. While size of community of one's residence is a valuable measure for some purposes, as we shall see later, it is an inadequate basis on which to delineate the urban environment.

Urbanization involves more than settlement in large population aggregates. It involves large populations organized in urban ways of life, which we soon examine in more detail. As urbanization spread from city to metropolis and thence began to encompass and make urban virtually the entire nation, the symbolism of urbanity spread with it. The urban environment can be summarized as:

population—tens and hundreds of millions,
      up to 95 percent of the total population,
      nationally integrated
organization—deconcentrated, decentralized,
      polynucleated,
      areal specialization
economy—post-industrial, agri-business, automation
technology—telecommunications,
      auto, air, and truck routes
symbolism—shopping malls, cultural centers,
      financial centers, sports complexes,
      cultural pluralism,
      many nationally shared experiences,
      events, and personages.

STUDY QUESTIONS

1. What is metropolitan dominance and subdominance and how are they measured?
2. What were the major forces leading to the dominance of the automobile as the major system of transportation in the United States?
3. How would you characterize American transportation policy?
4. Define: (a) sprawl; (b) municipal reform; (c) megalopolis; (d) agri-business; (e) SMA; (f) SMSA.
5. What is the urban environment?

SUGGESTED READINGS

Fink, James J. *The Car Culture* (Cambridge, Mass.: M.I.T. Press, 1975).

Gottman, Jean. *Megalopolis* (Cambridge, Mass.: M.I.T. Press, 1964).

McKelvey, Blake. *The Emergence of Metropolitan America, 1915–1966* (New Brunswick, N.J.: Rutgers University Press, 1968).

PART TWO

Urban populations and variations in urbanization

In Part One we examined three different urban settlement patterns, namely the city, the metropolis, and the urban environment. In that preceding analysis our focus was primarily upon organization, economy, technology, and symbolism, with the component of population being scarcely mentioned except for its size. This is not because population is unimportant but because it is so important that it needs a separate section.

In order to know how to secure adequate food supplies, sufficient water, housing, clothing, and many other essentials of human life, we need to know how many people there are, how old they are, and other related information. To plan for the future we need to know whether the number of people in a given area is expanding or contracting. Further, we need to know why a population is expanding or contracting in order to be prepared for changes in its size. For example, if the population is contracting because of an epidemic now sweeping the land, even though it has a high birthrate, we may expect this decrease to be temporary and the population to increase when the epidemic is brought under control.

More than 100 years of demographic research have documented systematic differences between rural and urban populations. Not all cities, metropolises, and urban environments are alike—far from it—but it is safe to say that each differs from its respective rural population.

Demography is held by some of its specialists to be an exact science. Whether or not it is an exact science we would not hazard to say, but we would readily acknowledge that the techniques of demography are exacting. Working with data banks, such as the U.S. Census, which contain hundreds of millions of cases must require refined techniques indeed.

This qualification is a preamble to saying: were we to attempt to introduce the urban student to demography we would need the remainder of this text. Since we have so many other topics to consider, however, we can only touch upon a few demographic characteristics, and these only in their most general forms. Just as we summarized the 10,000-year history of the city in a few pages by overlooking many exceptions and variations, so we shall again need to ignore many details if we are to glimpse a few general processes established by demography. The processes are examined in three subsections in Chapter 4, first the demography of the city, then of the metropolis, and then of the urban environment. The data, however, are extremely limited—to the West, especially to the United States in the last two centuries.

As ecologists we expect patterns, including demographic ones, to change in space and time. Thus, we expect that our statements about the population of "the city" probably do not apply to "Pre-Pottery Jerico A" of 7800 B.C. and do not necessarily apply to all cities everywhere since then.

Within our ecological perspective, understanding the interaction of components is critical. Whereas Chapter 4 attempts to do this with population, Chapter 5 considers other variations.

Many countries are divided into regions and rarely is urbanization spread evenly between them. How has urbanization varied regionally in the United States and what difference has it made? Such questions are raised in the first part of Chapter 5.

How has urbanization affected the location of markets? How are markets distributed within the urban environment today? Variations in the process of urbanization as they relate to markets comprise the second part of Chapter 5.

Urbanization is a worldwide phenomenon. It is accelerating in settlements throughout Asia, Africa, and South America. The third and final part of Chapter 5 explores urbanization internationally.

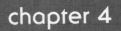

chapter 4

THE URBANIZATION OF
THE POPULATION

Photograph by Harold M. Lambert

When the city was the dominant sociospatial form of our ecological complex of POETS, its population differed from the rural population. When the metropolis arose its population also differed from the nonmetropolitan population. And if we examine these two sets of differences—those between city and noncity and those between metropolis and non-metropolis—we find that the pattern of differences changes. Although it is important to know the difference between the population included and that excluded by each historical settlement form, knowledge of how the pattern of differences changes over time will facilitate further comprehension of the impact of the urbanization process. Once we have grasped this more abstract patterning produced by temporal changes, we can then apply those broad generalizations regarding urbanization as it moves through space and time. First, let us briefly look at the nature of the urban population as found in the settlement called the city.

THE CITY'S POPULATION

Size and proportion

From the emergence of cities to their eclipse about 1800, there were few cities, and their populations were small. Of the total population, rarely more than 5 percent resided in cities by 1800. The city's population often consisted of a small power elite, a somewhat larger artisan-merchant class, and a large unskilled population little different from the rural peasantry.

Birth and death rates

Birth rates varied little between city and country. Because there were relatively few groups that had birth rates differing from the prevailing average, variations in overall rates within a country were slight during the age of the city.

During most of the history of the city, an understanding of the causes and spread of disease was minimal. Epidemics were common, and when a disease as virulent as the dreaded plague hit, it was not unusual for one of every three inhabitants of the city to be killed (Zinsser, 1935).

Over time and through painful and costly experience, city dwellers learned to regulate carefully the burial of human beings and animals, to safeguard water supplies and their catchments, to establish safe drainage routes for wastes, to pay bounties on rats, and to isolate those afflicted with disease. Hospitals were in part created to quarantine the ill, the afflicted, and the dying. Bridenbaugh (1955:54) observes that in our own American colonial cities, "by strenuous efforts to use every known theory and weapon against disease, the townsmen succeeded remarkably well for their times in combating all scourges except smallpox and yellow fever."

But despite the "strenuous efforts" of some cities, death rates were higher in the city than in the country. When an epidemic did strike, death rates rose precipitously, and then fell dramatically when the crisis abated. In addition to city death rates being higher than those in the country, then, they were also subject to dramatic fluctuations.

> It is a fact well worth attention that the death rate at Boston from 1743 to 1773 remained relatively constant in proportion to a constant population, except during the measles year, 1747, and the smallpox years, 1752 and 1764. Thus it cannot be said that this dread disease was a major factor in stabilizing the city's population. Child and childbed mortality, many losses at sea, the numerous accidental deaths of the time, war casualties, and such perennial ailments as dysentery, tuberculosis, and influenza seem to have been the principal reasons for death at Boston. (Bridenbaugh, 1955:328)

Population increase

If we take the number of births for a population and compare it with the number of deaths, we can tell whether that population is increasing by reproduction. Since this figure excludes any increase due to migration, demographers call it the reproductive increase—the excess of births over deaths, as distinguished from the net increase, population gain from all sources.

Since populations also differ by the number of males and females and by their age distributions, demographers term these simple measures we are using crude birth rates or crude death rates to distinguish them from more refined sex and age specific birth or death rates.

If the crude birth rates are approximately equal between city and country populations, and if city death rates are higher than those of the country, the reproductive increase of the rural population will be higher than that of the city. Since city death rates typically exceed city birth rates, there is a negative reproductive increase in the city; that is, cities lose population and must therefore depend on migration to replenish their populations and to grow.

Data from London illustrate this pattern. Between 1650 and 1750, "the crude death rate in London was substantially higher than the crude birth rate," (Team, 1973:13). To replace the population lost by death, an average of 5,000 persons had to migrate to London each year. To increase the population—and the population of London did increase by 2,750 persons each year throughout the century—another 2,750 migrants had to come to London each year of the hundred-year period.

Migration, however, is not confined to the flow from country to city. A number of persons also leave one city for another. The above figures are based only on net in-migration. We know that an even higher number of migrants had to come to London to replace those who had left.

Age and sex ratio

Who migrated to the city? Studies in historical demography indicate that it is the unmarried young adult, and, in Western civilization and among whites,[1] the males who left home to seek fortunes in the city. When this selective pattern of migration continued for a long period, the middle-aged, the old, and the children were left behind in rural areas, while city populations reflected a disproportionate number of persons in the age range 15–49. City populations also had a relatively greater number of unmarried persons and an excess of males over females.[2]

Interactional and residential densities

Population density in the city was high. Since the walls compacted the inhabitants into a relatively small space, every inch of the city was crowded. Because the city's center typically contained the principal church, the market, and the place for assembly, *interactional density* was highest in the center and declined out to the walls. The pattern of density population by residence was the reverse of the distribution by interaction. That is, since the wealthy lived in the center and the poor near the walls, *residential density* increased slightly from the city's center outward.

Summary

The city when defined by settlement pattern was small in size and contained a small percentage of the total population. City death rates typically exceeded birth rates, which were roughly equal to those found in the country. This meant that a large migratory stream was needed both to replace population lost by death and for the city to grow. Since cityward migrants were typically young, unmarried, and male, a greater proportion of these population segments was found in the city than in the country. Interactional density was highest in the center of the city and declined to the walls, whereas residential density increased slightly from the center outward.

THE METROPOLIS'S POPULATION

The demographic transition

When the metropolis began to evolve from the city around 1800, industrialization in the West also began. The twin processes of urbanization and

---

[1] Of American blacks, the female migrated in greater numbers in this historical period. See DuBois, 1899.

[2] As noted in Chapter 2, industrialization paralleled urbanization in the Western experience. While this is not true in many developing countries today, as Abu-Lughod (1964), Turner (1972), and others have demonstrated, the reader is reminded that we are speaking of a historical period in the West.

industrialization produced further changes in the urban population. In this *demographic transition,* death rates fell sharply while birth rates declined gradually, producing high levels of reproductive increase. At the close of the transition, birth rates had also declined with the consequence of lower rates of reproductive increase (Weber, 1899, 1963). Let us examine the population of the metropolis in more detail.[3]

Birth and death rates

The process of moving to the city initially changed one's residence; eventually urban life also changed one's values as well. Such changes were evident in the birth rates for different segments of the population. As urbanization proceeded, family size was first limited by the newly emerging middle class. Families of higher and then lower status followed suit. "During 1885–1920 there was a sharp widening of fertility differentials by occupation. There has been a sharp trend in the other direction since 1940" (Kiser, 1970:45).

Birth rates were also lower in urban areas because a larger proportion divorced or never married. For those who did marry, the average age of entry into first marrige was higher than for nonurbanites. In the metropolis, therefore, birth rates are generally high initially, gradually declining through the stage of mature metropolitanism.

To complete this picture of the pattern followed by metropolitan birth rates, the effect of the high proportion of males must be noted. Since the sex ratio greatly favored males at the beginning of the period, it had a significant negative influence on the crude birthrate. It declined in importance toward the end of the period, though, as the sex ratio became nearly even. Incidentally, one reason demographers use more refined rates is to restrict the influence of such changes as those of the sex ratio and thus to be able to get a more accurate portrayal of the situation.

Within the metropolis in its early phases, compaction of the population, often adjacent to factories and without any sanitation, raised metropolitan death rates even higher than were those of the city. Modern sanitation, public water service, decreases in residential densities brought about by the newly invented mass transit rail systems, and other factors, such as a rise in real wages, combined to lower death rates dramatically in the metropolis in the last half of the 19th century (McKelvey, 1963). Rural mortality rates also declined, but more gradually, during this period.

Death rates also varied widely within metropolitan populations. Osofsky observed that: "Of all the peoples in New York City, foreign-born as well as native, Negroes had, proportionally, the highest mortality

---

[3] For part of the following summary we are indebted to the research of Janet Abu-Lughod (1964), herein revised and adapted to our sociospatial models.

rates. In 1890, for example, 37.5 Negroes in every thousand died contrasted with 28.5 deaths in the white population" (1966:88).

The direction of the trend in all segments, however, was the same. Mortality was high, at times climbed higher with beginning metropolitanization, and then steadily declined throughout this historical period. Negroes had higher death rates than whites at the beginning and at the end of the period. Negro mortality, however, had been virtually cut in half. DuBois observed: "The average annual death rate among Negroes in the 1820–30 period was 47.6. At the end of the century, the rate has dropped to 28.02" (1899, 1967:149).

Population increase

With high birth and high death rates at the start of the metropolitan form, followed by rapid reductions in the death rate and a gradual decrease in births, the rate of reproductive increase went from less than replacement at the beginning to stable population size and then to some natural increase.

> Because the population is known to have halved its rate of productive increase, and also to have enjoyed lower death rates, during the sixty years between 1830 and 1890, the inference that birth rates were reduced drastically during this period is inescapable. If, during this period, the crude birth rate dropped from about 50 per thousand residents to about 28 per thousand, and the death rate dropped from about 25 to 15 per thousand, the annual rate of reproductive increase dropped from about 25 per thousand to about 13 per thousand. Although the rates given above for the beginning of the period are only guesses, they are probably accurate enough to illustrate the magnitude of the change." (Bogue, 1959:15)

Immigration during this period in the United States was massive, growing from an average of about 170,000 every year at midcentury to nearly one half million every year in the decade after the turn of the century (Cole, 1958). Improvements in agricultural techniques also displaced many from rural areas. To the "push" from abroad and from small towns and rural areas was added the "pull" of industrial employment. Men, women, and children found jobs in the early factories, and the availability of such employment swelled metropolitan populations (Stouffer, 1940, 1960).

Abu-Lughod notes that as "incipient" industrialization reached its "take-off point," urban growth attained a momentum of its own. The metropolis was now able to offer sufficient employment opportunities to draw even more migrants. The number and percentage of persons engaged in urban types of occupations increased, and as these workers became socially mobile and culturally assimilated into metropolitan society, fertility declined. The remaining rural population, being unaffected by such changes, maintained its high fertility rate. Sharp metropolitan-rural demographic differences emerged.[4]

As the era of the metropolis closed, the proportion of the population classified as urban had increased to about half the total population—nearly tenfold over the city. Although the difference in rural-urban death rates had declined significantly, there was more of a difference in birth rates because fertility had decreased in the metropolis. Migration from rural areas continued and increased. As earlier migrants had aged, married, and had children, and as their children married at the younger ages permitted by prosperity, rural-urban differences in age and the sex ratio had diminished. Further, as mortality rates favored females, the larger metropolises had begun to show an excess of females over males.

Age and sex ratio

Typical migrants from rural to metropolitan areas were young adults, but whether they were male or female depended on prevailing gender role employment opportunities. In the United States the overall pattern showed an excess of males in the initial phases of urbanization, followed by a gradual reduction in the sex ratio. As mature metropolianism emerged, the sex ratio went below 100 with an excess of females.

> While the national sex ratio increased with continued immigration [from 103.6 in 1840 to 104.7 in 1860], however, that of Milwaukee declined, so that by 1860 the city definitely reflected an urban rather than a frontier sex pattern, with females outnumbering males [133.5 in 1840 to 98 in 1860]. (Conzen, 1976:48)

Seattle, as McKenzie noted in 1925, was typical of a newly urbanizing area, having 113 males for every 100 females. He further observed that the sex ratio declined from the center outward, going "from 300 to 500 males to every 100 females" in the downtown district to the reverse "in the outlying districts of the city."

Alvin Boskoff (1962:94) explains the process in this way:

> In the first phase, industrial needs attract high proportions of male migrants, though mill towns constitute a clear exception. The second phase involves commercial and clerical functions as supplements to, or competitors of, the industrial focus. Females are consequently attracted in this phase. A third phase accompanies a more balanced economic base and increased opportunities for family life in the city and in an expanding suburban fringe. At this point, sex ratios tend to move from the 80–90 range to the upper 90's—the continuing "excess" of females reflecting differential mortality rather than differential migration.

---

[4] Such demographic differences contributed to the intense rural-urban conflict found, for example, in the United States as noted in Chapter 2. Also see Strauss, 1961.

Variations in the sex ratio, once thought to be associated only with changes in the rate of urbanization, also depend on prevailing race and gender role opportunities. For example, the sex ratio among whites was observed to be high in the initial phases of urbanization and to decline and then reverse in later stages. Among American blacks the situation was reversed. "In 1890 there were 810 Negro men for every thousand Negro women in New York City; in 1900, 809 for each thousand; in 1910, 850" (Osofsky, 1966:4). Further, more than twice as many Negro women were employed (59 percent) as either foreign-born (27.2 percent) or native-born (24.6 percent) white women (Osofsky, 1966:5).

In Philadelphia, an excess of females in the Negro urban populations was reported by DuBois.

> The cause of this excess is easy to explain. From the beginning the industrial opportunities of Negro women in cities have been far greater than those of men, through their large employment in domestic service. At the same time the restriction of employments open to Negroes, which perhaps reached a climax in 1830–1840, and which still plays a great part, has served to limit the number of men. The proportion, therefore, of men to women is a rough index of the industrial opportunities of the Negro. (DuBois, 1899, 1967:54–55)

Residential population densities

Residential density in the city as settlement form increased slightly from the center. In the initial residential density distribution created by the mass transit of the metropolitan area, density increased at the center, extended farther out, and fell off more steeply.

As land use segregation transformed the core of the city into the central business district (CBD), emptying the area of residents, the density distrubition over time became wavelike, as Blumenfeld (1954) accurately calls it. He estimates that in the history of Philadelphia this wave pushed outward at a speed of one mile per decade. The amplitude of the wave decreases with distance from center; in other words, the crest of the wave is steeper in the inner zones. Observing that this "tidal wave of expansion" had approximately a 50-year period per undulation, Blumenfeld concludes by noting that the wave could be reflected, as it was by city walls we would interject; diffracted, moving around obstacles; or refracted, pushed up or down. The outward expansion of the urban area is thus achieved by the emptying, the displacement, of the core (Boyce, 1971).

Measurements of population density distributions by Muth (1969); Newling (1971), and others (Team, 1977) demonstrate a negative exponential distribution. Leaving the mathematical formulas to specialized texts, we can briefly explain the *negative exponential density distribution* (n.e.d.d.) as follows. The average residential density of population declines with distance from the center of the city in a systematic way, and the decline is exponential. This means that every increase in distance from the center results in a lowering of the residential density by a fixed proportion. This proportional decline is greatest near the center and gradually becomes less as distance increases—that is, it is a negative exponent.

For example, if the residential density in a city is 100,000 persons per square mile at one mile from the center, and 50,000 persons per square mile at two miles, it can be expected to be 25,000 at three miles, 12,500 at four miles, 6,250 at five miles, and so forth. It declines—that is, it is a negative distribution—and it is exponential.

The data given by Clark (1966), Muth (1969), and Newling (1971) indicate that the rate at which densities decline becomes less over time. We add to that our own observation that the absolute level of density also becomes less. For example, Paris in 1817 had both a higher density at its center and a greater rate of decline from the center than were found for 1931 (Team, 1971). It is evident within our framework that metropolitanization was at work. As the city gave way to the metropolitan area, the new system of mass transport made possible the urbanization of a much larger landmass and reduced population densities in older areas. As Blumenfeld indicated, an outward displacement of the population took place, thinning out first the core and then successive adjacent areas.

Our addition to the research on the negative exponential density distribution, which reflects the effects of transit available, gains further support when settlements are examined according to their principal growth periods. The borough of Manhattan in New York City was solidified by 1910, and New York's densities remain high. Los Angeles, which may come closest to being the antithesis of the settlement pattern of New York, experienced its principal growth in the age of the mass use of the automobile, and its density is low in comparison with New York at any period (60,000 per square mile compared to 140 for New York in 1950). The fact that population densities of both settlements have decreased over time does not change the basic difference. The period of principal growth is important because it establishes the base on which later urbanization builds.

The negative exponential density distribution, then, summarizes the finding that urban residential densities decline exponentially from the center out. The rate of decline decreases with time, and absolute levels are established during principal growth periods.

Interactional densities

The research done on the n.e.d.d. has been exclusively based on residential populations. It does not take into account where people go or meet each other but only where they sleep. It is a useful measure but has limitations. Wall Street, for example, would have a population density of nearly zero, using a residential base. Central business districts, shopping centers, depots, and terminals would also have zero population densities[5] according to residence.

A second measure of population density is based on the number of persons using an area—entering it, for example. We term this measure the *interactional density* of a population.[6] Interactional densities are highest in the center of most metropolises, where, as we have noted, residential densities are low. This inverse relationship between residential and interactional densities is only true at the center. Just outside the center both types of densities are high and both decline with movement out. Suburbia, at the city's edge, is low in both residential and interactional population densities.

As a measure of interactional density, the number of persons passing a specific point who could choose to stop is highest when the point is in the center of the CBD. Furthermore, the number of persons passing is higher on a major street than on a side street. It is higher at intersections than in the middle of a block. For businesses oriented to the general public, those who pass are potential customers. The higher the number passing, the greater the potential business. Therefore, the higher the interactional density, the higher the commercial value of the land. (See Chapter 5.)

Land values

Interactional population density is highest in the center and so are land values. Interactional population density is lowest at the edges of a settlement, and so land values drop there. Major thoroughfares have higher land values and higher interactional densities than do side streets. Dead-end streets are low on both. Note that we said we would only count the people passing who could stop. Hundreds of thousands of persons may pass our point on a rail route, but they become potential customers only when the train stops. Land values are therefore high at train stations and low between stations.

There is another reason that land values are highest in the center and decline regularly outward. Surface area increases with the square of the radial distance from the center point. The land at the center is therefore doubly valuable; it has the greatest accessibility and is in the smallest supply. In American settlements during this period (1820–1920) building height so closely followed land values that the student can easily visualize the graph of land values by observing how the skyscrapers were concen-

---

[5] Or nearly zero, because some few persons may live in these places. Grand Central Station, for example, was reported to have a small but unexpected and largely unknown resident population. Even subways may have "residents." See Love, 1957.

[6] In the literature, these populations are sometimes called the daytime population; see Foley, 1952. Entertainment areas, those with nightclubs and bars, however, may have high "daytime" populations at night, or nonresidential "nightime" populations, and for these reasons the distinction between interactional and residential densities seems less confusing.

trated at the center, then how the height of the buildings declined outward. Even the higher land value ridge lines along axial transport routes,
the subnodal peaks in value at major intersections, and the valleys midway between rail lines can be visualized in this manner.

Urbanologists have studied such distributions of land values and their
effects in considerable detail (Hurd, 1903; Hoyt, 1933; Firey, 1945;
Alonzo, 1971). True to the interdisciplinary nature of much urban research, no single set of economic, geographic, or social variables is sufficient to embrace all of the factors involved. What follows then is an
integration of the contributions of several disciplines, organized in terms
of the ecological processes already introduced. The reader is reminded
that we are concerned now exclusively with the metropolitan area historical period when space was organized by mass transit.

With access determined by sharply defined boundaries and movement
by rail, the network of the metropolitan area as a whole was highly centralized. Nuclei were located at the intersections of rail transport routes.
Settlements of small and moderate size, such as Knoxville or Minneapolis
in 1900, had only one center; larger ones such as New York displayed
several nuclei. Areal specialization and polynucleation increased with settlement size throughout this period.

Residential density has been observed to decline from the center, and
the core has been seen to yield to business, which drives out residences.
Over time, business areas become more and more deserted after business
hours—Wall Street on Sundays, for example. Before mass transit made it
possible to extend the distance between place of work and place of residence, residential and interactional densities were closely related. Non-
residents did come in during business hours to such places as Haymarket
Square in Boston, but many people also lived in and around these same
districts. When it became possible for a person to live miles away from his
or her place of employment, residential and interactional densities began
to follow separate distributions. We have seen that residential population
density follows a negative exponent, which is summarized in the negative
exponential density distribution. Interactional density distributions have
yet to be determined precisely.

Summary

In the initial phase of metropolitanization, both birth and death rates
were high. Dramatic reductions in death rates followed while birth rates
declined more slowly. The result was an increase in the population,
which, when combined with heavy in-migration from nonmetropolitan
areas and from abroad, swelled urban populations to about 50 percent of
the total, or ten times the proportion represented by the city. The young
and unmarried constituted the bulk of the migration. Males outnumbered
females among whites; the reverse held true for blacks.

Residential density distributions in the metropolis followed a negative exponential pattern, the central core being lowest in density. Interactional densities were highest in the center of the metropolis, and high along major thoroughfares and at intersections, but low between them. Land values paralleled the interactional densities.

THE URBAN ENVIRONMENT

In reaching out to encompass great masses of land and population, the urban environment urbanizes both space and people. This is seen in the reduction of rural-urban differences (Ogburn and Duncan, 1964).

Cities and metropolises today are part-societies in which all activities are related to a larger whole—the national urban environment in which 95 percent of Americans now live. What Park (1939) said about the city can be applied to the urban environment: "The city is, in fact, a constellation of natural areas, each with its own characteristic milieu, and each performing its specific function in the urban economy as a whole." For example, Keyfitz (1964) reports a reconvergence to a uniform family size. Twenty-five years ago the Canadian province with the highest birth rate had double the rate of the province with the lowest rate. Today the difference is only 20 percent.

Birth and death rates

Fertility began to decline during the period of the metropolis and continued to decline until 1940, aside from a sharp but temporary change during World War I. Beginning in 1940, the 125-year pattern of decline was reversed, going from low to moderate. Bogue (1959) points out that the prevailing rates after 1940 were similar to those between 1890 and 1930. In part because of this rise in urban fertility, but also due to continuing declines in rural rates, rural-urban rates became similar.

The sequence of population segments through which changes in birth rates proceed is of considerable interest to the urbanologist, since it reflects the pattern through which urbanism spreads. Abu-Lughod (1964:486) points out that fertility "declines first within the newly emerging professional and managerial class," followed by the older aristocracy, the urban lower-middle class, the semirural or migrant city dweller, and, finally, the rural dweller. "*Note that the sequence begins with urban subgroups and terminates with rural groups.* Therefore, urban-rural fertility differentials will appear to develop along a U-shaped curve, minor at the point when the fertility transition begins, maximal toward the middle, and negligible at the terminal phases of the transition." As the process of urbanization flows out into the countryside, transforming it into the sociospatial form of the urban environment, then rural-urban differences diminish.

The city and then the metropolis had long been known for high death rates. As modern methods for the treatment and prevention of disease were discovered and applied, and as the water and sewage systems we now take for granted came into use, death rates began a precipitous decline. Given our typical absence of epidemics and the urban location of modern medical facilities, it is not surprising that urban death rates are now often lower than those for rural areas. As Woodrow, Hastings, and Tu (1978) document: "for males the age-specific mortality rates are markedly higher in the rural area than in the urban area in the first four years of life, and slightly higher for ages 5 to 45. After age 45 age-specific mortality rates for males in the urban area exceed those observed in the rural area." A similar pattern is found among females.

Within today's urban environment, differences in fertility and mortality are typically due to such factors as the degree of urbanization of an area and the social and economic characteristics of the population, rather than to their place of residence.

Population increase

The metropolis grew in part by absorbing all growth around it. The urban environment increases by urbanizing previously unurbanized areas. People do not have to move to the urban environment to be touched by it; it reaches out and embraces them. Discounting this urbanization of rural areas, "real" urban population growth is moderate and largely a function of planned fertility.

Urban growth from immigration peaked in 1907 and fell precipitously with the outbreak of World War I, after which immigration laws, the worldwide depression, and World War II kept it below 100,000 for most years. So after World War II urban growth stemmed from internal migration and a rise in urban birth rates.

> The effect of urbanization upon fertility is not necessarily limited to urban places. Urbanization can be viewed as a shift of population from rural to urban centers, increasing the proportion of the total population having relatively low fertility; it can also be viewed as a diffusion of values typical of urban centers to smaller urban places and rural areas, thus lowering village and farm birth rates and narrowing the rural-urban differential in fertility. (Dinkel, 1954:78)

Net urban reproduction rates in the 1930s "were about 76 percent, an indication that urban population would decline by 24 percent without the counterbalancing effect of migration. Since the mid-forties, however, American urban regions have become self-sufficient in population growth" (Boskoff, 1962:94).

Migration today is within, rather than to, the urban environment. The *velocity of migration* is the proportion of the migrants in a stream to the "home" population, multiplied by the proportion of the population in the specific destination area to the population of all potential areas of destination. Such calculations indicate that the velocity of migration "is lowest for urban to rural migration, rural to urban, and suburban to rural types. The highest velocity seems to be found among rural to rural and suburban streams. In short, urbanites are more 'stable' than our folklore suggests, while the greatest proportionate movement is really among the suburbanites and ruralites" (Boskoff, 1962:91–92).

Age and sex ratios

In lowering birth and death rates and increasing life expectancy, urbanization raises the average age of the population. Again Woodrow, Hastings, and Tu (1978:7) nicely document this relationship.

> Our current analysis of rural-urban differences in mortality shows that the average life expectancies at birth are higher for females than males regardless of residence. Further, urban females are expected to have greater longevity than rural females. Similarly urban males, on the average, should survive to an older age than rural males.

The net effect of these differentials is to raise the average age of populations as they become progressively urbanized and to shift the sex ratio to favor females.

Interactional and residential densities

In the urban environment, the displacement of residential population, when its density was at its peak in the center, flattened the density distribution and extended it farthest out. Winsborough (1963:567) found that the population density of Chicago declined throughout the period 1860–1950. The greatest reductions took place in the 1880s, reflecting effects of rail transit, and the 1920s, when use of the automobile became widespread.

> In 1950 about 15 percent of the United States population lived at genuinely urban densities of more than 10,000 persons per square mile, but by 1970 this had dropped to only 10 percent of the nation's population. Below the 10,000 level, major clustering into centers cannot occur, although densities of 1,000 or more people per square mile are considered urban since they signify that the land is built up and no longer available for agriculture or open space. (Fava, 1975:14)

With the emergence of the urban environment, residential density was lowered in the older areas and raised nearly everywhere else, including at and beyond the old metropolitan perimeter.

The rise of the urban environment split the density distribution into residential and interactional densities, each today assuming a separate pattern. As interaction has been progressively freed from the requirement of physical proximity, "people may interact with one another at rates far exceeding those that could be tolerated in older urban forms. No adequate measure of this dynamic density of interactions has yet been developed, much less accepted, although several writers have recently advocated some measurement based upon 'bits of information'" (Abu-Lughod, 1968).

The importance of interactional densities as contrasted with purely residential densities is underscored by Gottman's (1964) research. He reported that two thirds of a million people entered the midtown and lower portions of Manhattan every day in 1956 and that there were 123 planes in the air at one time (10:30 A.M., July 14). Whereas Washington, D.C., then had nearly 2 million residents within its metropolitan area, almost as many (1.8 million) entered its hub on an average weekday.

Even more of a contrast is seen in the example of London (Menzler, 1952). The residential population of the City of London, the ancient core city, is less than 10,000 residents, but approximately half a million people work there.

> A study made of London's daytime population in 1949 indicated that the central commercial area had a resident population of 170,000. During the day this was swelled to 878,000, an increase of over 700,000. Sharp shows that from 3:00 to 5:59 A.M. the population of the central business district of Flint, Michigan, was 458. From 6:00 to 8:59 A.M., 6,313 were in the central business district. From 12 noon till 2:59 P.M., 18,637 people were in the district. (Cole, 1958:134)

Interaction in the central core is much more intense than residence alone would imply.

Summary

In the urban environment, birth rates fell to their lowest levels ever and then increased to a moderate point, leveling at a point slightly lower than rural fertility. Death rates declined, descending beneath the historically lower rural rates. Today, urban mortality is lower than that found in rural areas. Population increase has been from low and stable with respect to reproduction and low with respect to immigration. Migration today is largely within the urban environment, with suburban to suburban shifts predominating.

As urbanization matured, the population aged and the sex ratio favored females, a result of lower female mortality and higher female longevity.

Residential population densities began to decline in the most populous centers in 1910, a decompaction that continues today. In fact, since 1970 nonmetropolitan areas have grown faster than metropolitan areas, a reversal of the previous 50-year pattern in the United States. Residential densities have progressively been reduced in the older core areas, and increased outside the cores, reflecting a flattening and outward extension of the distribution.

Interactional density no longer follows residential density distributions but instead follows its own shape. Central core areas remain high in interactional density, but there are many high interaction nodes as the urban environment polynucleates.

APPLICATION TO SETTLEMENT SIZE

Just as we may say that a country with 50 percent of its population living in urban settlements is "more urban" than a country with 25 percent in urban areas, so we may apply the generalizations we reached about urbanization according to the size of settlement. That is, we may assume that a settlement with a million inhabitants is "more urban" than a settlement with only half a million. While we may not assume that the former is "twice as urban" as the latter, research does indicate that larger settlements are nevertheless "more" urban than smaller ones.

Fertility, for example, may be predicted to decline with increases in the size of settlement. Mortality is likewise inversely related to settlement size. The average age of populations of larger settlements is older than smaller ones, and the larger ones also have more females.

Understanding this series of relationships underscores that urbanization is a process. As a process it revolutionizes space and people, but by degrees. The ruralite does not arrive in Manhattan and overnight become urban or urbane. The process takes time and change comes slowly.

STUDY QUESTIONS

1. For the city as historical settlement forms, what were its birth and death rates, its population increase or decrease, and its age and sex ratio?
2. Repeat the above for the metropolis.
3. Repeat the above for the urban environment.
4. What is the difference between residential and interactional densities, and how are they distributed in the city, the metropolis, and the urban environment?
5. How can changes in birth and death rates be applied to the rate of urbanization?

SUGGESTED READINGS

Bourne, Larry S., ed. *Internal Structure of the City* (New York: Oxford University, 1971).

Burgess, Ernest W., and Bogue, Donald J., eds. *Contributions to Urban Sociology* (Chicago: University of Chicago Press, 1964).

DuBois, William E. B. *The Philadelphia Negro* (Philadelphia, University of Pennsylvania Press, 1899; republished by Schoken, 1967).

VARIATIONS IN URBANIZATION

Photograph by Harold M. Lambert

The process of urbanization varies, as we have seen, from one historical period to another. Depending on when an area experienced its principal growth, its settlement form will change. History is but one part of the process of urbanization, and as other components of the process change, variations in urbanization will become evident. Once again to illustrate the basic conditions involved, three of these variations are reviewed.

First we study variations in urbanization by regions of the United States, with primary focus on the South. Second, the urbanization of markets is reviewed. Finally, as the nations of Africa, Asia, South America, the Middle East, and others are now experiencing intensive urbanization, we ask: what are some of the variations in urbanization internationally?

URBANIZATION REGIONALLY

At the time the city walls began to come down (about 1800) and urbanization travelled out along rail lines into what then became the area of the metropolis, only 6.1 percent of the United States was classified as urban. The greater part of the urban population, however, was located in only one region—the Northeast—9.3 percent of which was classified as urban. Next came the South, which was 3 percent urban. The North Central region and the West had no urban settlements.

At midcentury 15.3 percent of the United States was classified as urban. The Northeast had increased its share of the urban population to 26.5 percent of its total. The North Central region had surpassed the South, 9.2 percent to the latter's 8.3 percent urban. The West registered 6.4 percent of its population as urban.

After another half century, by 1900, almost two thirds of the population of the Northeast was urban (61.1 percent), but the South trailed far behind (only 18.0 percent urban). The North Central and the West was about 40 percent (Bogue, 1959), near the national figure.

At the turn of the century there were few urban settlements in the South. By 1920, however, about half the population of the United States was urban. Three of every four persons were urban in the Northeast; about one in four was urban in the South. By that year, New York's population exceeded 6 million, while the largest city of the South, Atlanta, had but a quarter of a million. Some southern states, such as Mississippi and Alabama, were almost exclusively rural, and large portions of most southern states were also rural.

Why did urbanization in the South lag so far behind that of other regions? What difference did the later urbanization make? In order to answer questions about this region's urbanization, we now need to define the South.

The definitions of regions

A region stems, in some ways, from physical geography. For millions of years there has been an east coast, a west coast, and a gulf coast on the North American continent. There has "always" been a great river draining land between the eastern and western mountain ridges. As one of the "Deans of the South" puts it:

> All the changes—past, present, and future— . . . have taken place and will take place against the background of the physical geography of the South. Geography separated this area by large water bodies from Europe and South America. Geography attached it to the southeastern part of the North American continent, but geography failed to separate it by any effective natural barrier from areas to the north and west of it. In the opinion of many southerners this was a mistake on the part of the Creator. Geography does not favor secession. (Thompson, in McKinney and Thompson, 1965:452)

Geography did not favor Southern secession, nor does it provide the meaning of the orientation implicit in the terms north, south, east, and west. By itself, physical geography is without meaning. A place is north of what? Canada may be "the north" to inhabitants of the United States, but the United States may be "the north" to Mexicans. South Americans see Mexicans as living "north." Regional designations contain the prevailing symbolic orientations of peoples, and as the people change so does their regional designations. Although the rivers and mountains may not have moved, the symbol systems giving them meaning change.

Consider some changes in regional designations. Where is "the Northwest" in the United States? The famous Northwest Territory for which Jefferson issued his ordinance in 1787 lay east of the Mississippi, extending to the Ohio River, and north to the Great Lakes. It included the present states of Ohio, Indiana, Illinois, Michigan, Wisconsin, and part of Minnesota, most of which are now called "North Central." "The South" at one time was considered to include Delaware, Maryland, and West Virginia. Thompson (1965) suggests that "the area we now call 'the South' was originally not south at all." It was north—that is, north of the Caribbean, the area with which "the South" traded.

Partridge (1959) informs us that in Old English, "sunth" is "the land that, to the Old World of the Northern Hemisphere, lies in the sun." During the same period Southworth (then "wark") was the southern fortifications. And since the Saxons were then fighting one another rather than the Anglos or the Puerto Ricans, "suffolk" meant "the southern" folk, the South Saxons, who lived in Sussex.

Notwithstanding the "abiding earth" and the relative lack of change in physical habitat, regions are everywhere defined by people, and their designations indicate their relationships to each other. The relationships between people change and they change unevenly. The world is indeed shrinking, but it does not shrink evenly. The outbreak of war distances two peoples just as peace brings them closer together. The loss of air service by a small town likewise makes it more remote than when it had such service.

In analyzing regions, urbanologists begin with the relational designations and then seek to establish their boundaries in one of two ways. First suppose that they delineate a wheat-growing region, an urbanized region, or perhaps the area where those "Saxons" live. They take a characteristic, such as wheat or Saxony, and include all those areas containing that characteristic. Often urbanologists use a percentage, saying that if a county or perhaps a state contains 50 percent or more of its population in urban settlements, or if some percentage of its farms grow wheat, then the entire area will be considered urban or wheat-growing. Statistics are reported only by areal units—by counties and states, for example—and either all of that area or none of it must be included in a specific statistic. This type of definition uses *uniformity* as its criterion.

A region may also be defined by its *node,* its center. If we were to travel the highway between New York City and New Haven, Connecticut, we would observe a band of relatively unbroken urban settlement the entire distance. Where can New York City or New Haven be said to end? We may use commuting to work as the criterion, as the previously reviewed daily urban system concept does, saying in effect that if people commute to New York, or if a certain percentage of them do, then the areas from which they commute should be included with the Big Apple. New York would be treated as one node and New Haven as another, with the boundaries of each established according to its relationship to its fringe.

Regions, then, refer to relational designations of peoples (Reed, 1972) and can be defined either in terms of the uniformity of some characteristic or by nodal orientation. Both are useful and both change. Let us now turn to the example of the South.

The South defined

The "central theme" of the South, according to historian U. B. Phillips, is "white supremacy." If we use that as our criterion, will we then include all areas exhibiting that criterion—including South Boston—in what we call the South? Should we include all states south of the Mason-Dixon line, including West Virginia? If we include only the former slave states, what do we do with Oklahoma, which did not become a state until after slavery was abolished? If we define the South as the 11 states of the Confederacy, we exclude Maryland, Kentucky, Missouri, and, some would insist, Tennessee, which, during the Civil War, followed its tradition of being the "volunteer state."

Thompson (1975) has defined the "essential" South by the plantation.

The plantation, he argues, gave meaning and organization to the deep, rich soils of the coastal plains, the river valleys, and the delta. It produced cash crops from a labor-intensive industry and developed the lowlands of the South into a center for national and even world cotton production. Because thousands of men, women, and children were needed by the plantations, high birth rates were encouraged. High death rates also prevailed, of course, especially among infants and children. Even so, there was an excess of population which moved west to open new territory for agricultural exploitation. After the Civil War, former slaves became sharecroppers, and the plantation continued and prospered.

Were we to define the South as that region where the plantation flourished, though, what do we do with those southern areas that lacked them? On the thin soil of the rugged uplands of the Appalachians and in the red hills of the Piedmont, as well as on the pine barrens of the sandy plains that stretch down to the Gulf, a different form of economic and agricultural production emerged. These large areas of the South contained the self-sufficient subsistence farmers and appropriators of natural resources. There the plantation and the widespread use of slaves was not found. This division between uplands and lowlands continues to be cited today as part of the intraregional differences within the South.

How does the U.S. Census Bureau define the South? Its definition has changed over time. Today, even though Missouri's southern heritage (it was a slave state) persists, the Census Bureau places it in the "West North Central" region. Arkansas, Louisiana, Texas, and Oklahoma make up what the Census Bureau calls the "West South Central" states. The division between upper and lower South is bypassed by the Census Bureau in favor of an east and south division. Kentucky is put with Tennessee and Alabama and Mississippi to make up what the bureau calls the "East South Central" states. Delaware, Maryland, the District of Columbia, and West Virginia are grouped with Virginia, North and South Carolina, and Georgia, and, perhaps because there is no other place to put it, Florida, to complete the "South Atlantic" region.

Even the most recently arrived alien, a Yankee in the South, knows that southern Florida is Yankee country. And West Virginia? How can miners be considered "southerners"? And as far as the distinctions between West South, South Central, and the like, Thompson (1965:545) explains:

> To southerners themselves it is "South for sure," and no funny business such as "Southeast" or "Southwest" will do; it must be the South, the sunny South, the magnolia South, or nothing.

Once again the familiar problem of definition appears—different criteria produce different areal designations. Certainly some definitions are better than others, but the more essential point to understand is the way in which something is being defined. Understanding how words are being used may save pointless argument, and may also help in understanding why a given definition is employed.

We will combine all the census definitions that mention South, and differentiate between an 11-state core and a 5-state and district fringe. The core includes: Virginia, North Carolina, South Carolina, Georgia, Florida, Kentucky, Tennessee, Alabama, Mississippi, Arkansas, and Louisiana. The fringe includes: Delaware, Maryland, West Virginia, Texas, Oklahoma, and the District of Columbia.

FIGURE 5-1
Regions of the United States

Source: U.S. Bureau of the Census, *United States Census of Population*, 1970.

Obstacles to urbanization: Slavery

The urbanization of the South lagged far behind the rest of the nation for many reasons. The plantation system, which continued to dominate in the South until the 1920s, kept people too poor to even move. In his introduction to Johnson's *Shadow of the Plantation*, Robert Park (1934:xi) observed:

> One can hardly escape the impression in viewing the facts of this survey that it is the inheritance of a tradition, embodied in the present plantation system, which more than anything else inhibits the progress, not merely of the black tenant but the white landlord, and that with the persistence of that tradition the small and independent farmer cannot make headway.

Under these conditions the Negro rural school, instead of creating a settled class of Negro peasant proprietors, seems, particularly since the World War, to have conspired with other tendencies to hasten the movement from the rural South to the northern cities.

Among the "other tendencies" to which Park refers was the "inhospitality" of southern cities to blacks. "In 1820, 37 percent of all town dwellers were blacks; by 1860 that portion had dropped below 17 percent. Urban slaves fell from 22 percent to 10" (Wade, 1968:335). The problem with slavery in the cities was the nature of the urban settlement itself. Given the separation of place of residence from place of employment, the basic problem was the supervision of blacks when not at work. As Wade (1968:336) observes:

> The problem was not what happened in the factory or shop but what happened in the back street, the church, the grocery store, the rented room, and the out-of-the-way house. It was not contact with machines or an industrial process which broke the discipline, it was contact with people of all kinds in numerous ways which generated the corrosive acids.
> "The city, with its intelligence and enterprise, is a dangerous place for the slave," wrote a shrewd analyst. "He acquires knowledge of human rights, by working with others who receive wages when he receives none; who can come and go at their pleasure, when he from the cradle to the grave must obey a master's imperious will. . . . It is found expedient, almost necessary, to remove the slave from these influences, and send him back to the intellectual stagnation and gloom of the plantation."

Southern cities sent their blacks back into rural ignorance as their first measure of control, particularly young male blacks who were at times so transported by the infamous chain gangs. A second general movement was to separate blacks and whites from all walks of life in all of life's ordinary encounters. As this movement was elaborated it came to embody "most of the features later identified as segregation" (Wade, 1968:342). The basic principle, as Wade puts it, was this: "Increasingly public policy tried to separate the races whenever the surveillance of the master was likely to be missing." Wade gives us an important insight into the power of symbolism when he describes how the separation was brought about: "To do this, the distinction between slave and free Negro [before emancipation] was erased; race became more important than legal status; and a pattern of segregation emerged inside the broader framework of the 'peculiar institution'" [of slavery] (Wade, 1968:344).

Poverty   Earlier in our account of the emergence of the urban environment the impression may have been that whenever and wherever cities and metropolises emerged the millions who migrated to them had simply decided to move. That has probably never been the case. Just as the Greeks and Romans controlled residence, so did feudalism in medieval times. Even in the 19th century, serfdom, slavery, and abject poverty tied people to the soil. Would the Irish have left their native land in droves without the potato famine? The Italians without their wars of nationalism? Migratory streams always flow, or just trickle, depending in part upon the push from behind.

The rural areas of the South, which included three quarters of its population, did have high rates of reproductive increase. Plantation life may well have been intellectually stagnant and filled with gloom, but an even worse fate awaited blacks in southern cities. An annual average of only about 30,000 blacks left the South at the turn of the century. The vast majority remained where they were. And when they did leave, their urban destinations were north not south.

Migration north   The total (black and white) migratory stream out of the South was about 90,000 per year at the turn of the century. The first three decades of the 20th century witnessed increases in southern out-migration, of which blacks were an increasing proportion. Population had built up in the rural areas, the boll weevil and a drop in the price of cotton drastically reduced labor needs, and the Northeast was perhaps never more prosperous. Total out-migrants went from 90,000 per year to 120,000 between 1910 and 1920, and then to 170,000 from 1920 to 1930. The black portion of the stream went from one third to one half and then to nearly 60 percent, or some 97,000 per year.

The out-migration of whites peaked in the decade of the 1920s, but the black migration did not peak until after World War II. After dropping significantly during the Great Depression to 65,000 a year, the population migrating from the South swelled to a record 213,500 per year from 1940 to 1950. Three fourths of these migrants were black.

By 1933, all states had adopted uniform birth and death registration. These reports allow urbanologists to calculate highly refined age and sex-specific death rates. As a result we have learned that changes in public health are first reflected in changes in infant and child mortality. The urbanization of the South provides a case in point, with reductions in the infant and child death rates appearing in the 1940s and 1950s and continuing through the present. Death rates for the total population are slower to decline, but are on the decrease as urban health practices and facilities spread outward with the urban environment.

We now have far more complete and accurate data on migration than in the past. Nationwide, the most mobile people are the 18- to 22-year-olds. Whites are more mobile than blacks. And changes in the equality of the sexes are seen in the equal mobility of males and females. (There is some variation by sex in migration within some age categories, but overall the rates balance out.) These national patterns hold for the South, although the migrants into the South are somewhat younger than the migrants into other regions (Ford, 1962).

Currently available data also make possible some generalizations with respect to education. There is a positive association between education and migration. That is, persons with college or postgraduate education are more likely to migrate than persons with lower levels of educational attainment. During the many decades in which the South lost population, it lost greater proportions of its more educated residents. This was even more true of better educated blacks, who were more likely to leave than better educated whites.

As the number of in-migrants began to match the number of out-migrants, the South was the beneficiary in augmenting its better educated segment. As the balance shifted to become a net in-migration, the South benefited even more (McKinney and Thompson, 1965).

It is crucial to keep these general relationships in mind if we are to understand the very complex process of urbanization. We should observe that what was just noted about the South can be reversed and applied to New York. Not only has New York lost population since 1910, but it has lost persons of the younger ages, the unmarried, the whites, and the better educated.

Populations in American cities are therefore becoming "darker" in skin color, in part because blacks are left behind by the greater mobility of whites. As blacks become urbanized, they, too, will be influenced by the revolution that urbanization brings about. As their birth and death rates decrease, as their health, education, and working skills improve, their social and residential mobility will also increase. As they become more mobile they, too, will leave the central areas in large numbers for the suburbs. (That is, unless the energy shortage or other conditions change current patterns—as well they might.) Urbanization must always be understood in its context.

Mid-20th century urbanization

The watershed year for the South, both in terms of its relations with other regions, and within the region itself, was 1950. Before that year, southern cities had "depended upon outside migrants much less than northern and western cities have depended upon recruits from outside their regions. The South has both peopled its own cities and sent large contingents of migrants to the urban areas of other regions" (Hitt, 1954:59–60). From 1940 to 1950 "extraordinarily large increases in the urban population . . . occurred in the South" (Bogue, 1959:67). This trend continues to the present. As Reissman (1954:92) observes:

> The unity of the region—politically, socially, economically, and ecologically—is a thing of the past. The new urbanizing forces that have been acting on the South since 1940 have fragmented the region irreparably. What we can now observe is a transition period during which a new coalition of metropolitan sections in the region will emerge: that is, conurbation that will transcend existing state and local boundaries and that will seriously rearrange the urban ecology of the South.

White southern outmigration had peaked in the 1920s. In the 1950s, white migration in and out was nearly equal, reversing to favor in-migration in the 1960s and 1970s. Black out-migration peaked in the 1940s and was reduced in the 1950s and 1960s. A sizable in-migration of blacks began in the late 1960s and continued to grow in the 1970s. The states constituting the fringe areas of the South all recorded a net in-migration of blacks in the 1950s, a decade earlier than the black in-migration to the deeper South. The District of Columbia, the most urbanized section, also lost whites, reflecting a pattern observed nationally in American urban settlements.

The basic process behind all these trends is that of urbanization. Just as New York, our first city to be intensively urbanized, began to lose population in 1910, so the South, the last to be urbanized, is now experiencing population growth through migration (Vance and Demerath, 1954). Although it is popular to point to the attraction of the sun, it shines no more today than it did tens or even hundreds of years ago.

As urbanization proceeds fertility declines, as we now know. In the South the birth rate among whites is close to the national average, while for blacks it is higher but declining. The more urbanized blacks of the North have lower birth rates than their more rural southern counterparts.

URBANIZATION AND MARKETS

The city in history arose around the granary, which later became fort, religious and political center, and market. The influence of the market on the city has been so significant that some investigators have seen in the market the basis of urban life. For our purposes it is sufficient to note that markets have played a vital role in the expansion and prosperity of the urban settlement. Variations in urbanization stem from the importance of markets, their location, and the publics they serve.

Market location

The basis on which urban markets are organized has been the subject of considerable research, especially with respect to the central business district. Harris and Ullman (1942) identify three principles of city location that can be applied to markets. First, some cities are located at "central places," locations where the performance of centralized services, such as retail trade or political administration, is most easily accomplished. Second, there are "transport cities," places where goods must be transferred from one type of transport to another, from oceangoing to land vessels, for example, or from camels to river barges. Third, there are "specialized function cities," places chosen as military or religious center, or perhaps developed as recreation centers.

Within the urban settlement, economic activities are also located with respect to these three principles (Berry, 1971a). That is, some economic activities seek central places, others follow the transport networks, and other economic activities are located by design or survive in those locations conducive to specialized functions. Note that none of these theorists are stating that all economic activity is so rational and well founded on empirical data that location always follows these principles. At times, economic activities are located at unfavorable sites but they usually do not survive. Therefore, central place theorists argue that markets are either initially located at or survive in central, transport, or special function sites. The generalization is based only on the survivors.

In the historical growth of American cities, the initial settlement had a center which combined on the same site all location principles. The single nucleus of New York in the 1600s was central place, "break in transportation," and contained specialized functions as well. As new transport networks integrated large populations into the core, land within the entire city, including its central areas, became specialized, with different location principles operating in one area more than another. That is, while settlements of several thousand population typically have but one center which contains all retail, wholesale, and related exchanges, the central area becomes internally differentiated when larger populations are served. Increases in urbanization lead to increases in market specialization—we may conclude.

The hierarchy of business centers   Five zones or areas of commercial activity are typically recognized in the urban literature, and these five zones are ordered into a hierarchy. This *hierarchy of business centers* includes: (1) the *central business district;* (2) *regional shopping centers* with department stores, music, hobby, toy, photo, and other shops; (3) *community business centers* with variety and clothing stores, bakeries, florists, post offices, and banks; (4) *neighborhood business centers* with small supermarkets and grocery stores, drugstores, laundries and cleaners, barber and beauty shops, and small restaurants; and finally, (5) *isolated convenience stores* on street corners serving populations within two to three blocks.

The threshold of a central place   Each unit within this hierarchy has a range, which is the area necessary to sustain that particular commercial activity. When a range sufficient for the support of an activity is reached, central place theorists refer to this as the *threshold*, the condition of entry of a business. Threshold is operationalized as the minimum sales volume required to support that establishment. Each unit within the hierarchy thus has a different threshold.

The corner convenience store supplying toiletries, tobacco, newspapers, and daily-need groceries can be sustained by the people living in the adjacent two or three blocks, while a music store may require an area which includes 10,000 people. If the people are both wealthy and music lovers (of the kind of music sold in this store) then the area needed, the threshold of entry may be smaller than if the people are both poor and tin-eared. As the central place theorists express it, as the amount of purchasing power available per unit decreases, the range increases, and commercial activity centers are therefore more widely spaced apart. The reverse is true as well. A hierarchy of central places also exists because centers of lower order tend to "nest" within the hinterlands of the next higher order. Between regional shopping centers, in other words, several community business centers will be found, and areas between these will in turn contain several neighborhood business centers.

A *central place* may therefore now be defined as a cluster of service functions located at the point most accessible to the maximum "profit area" that can be commanded. The specific point will, of course, vary with the activity under consideration; for example, whether it is a music or department store.

> The hierarchy results because (a) on the supply side, different commercial functions have different conditions of entry (thresholds), and thus demand minimum trade areas of different sizes for their support, and (b) on the demand side, consumers spend differing proportions of their income on different goods and services, and purchase them with differing degrees of frequency. Low threshold, high frequency functions are found in lower-level nucleations ("convenience good centers") whereas high threshold, low frequency functions are found in higher-level nucleations serving larger trade areas ("shopping goods centers"). (Berry, 1971a:363)

Other commercial activity areas   Before returning to this herarchy and its consequences let us note three other commercial activity zones. After the hierarchy of business centers there is a zone of *highway oriented commercial ribbons,* what planners often call strip development. Highway oriented ribbons "serve demands originating on the highways and increase with traffic volume" (Berry, 1971a:364). When routes are relocated or when an interstate bypasses an older route, these commercial activities decline and disappear. Their location, in other words, is with respect to the highway traffic. They are thus on the highway itself if the route is of unlimited access, and if, as with interstates, the route is of limited access, they are located near the exit ramps, with billboards telling the motorists to "Take Exit 29, turn left for. . . ."

As we previously noted, some businesses find it advantageous to locate near each other for a variety of reasons; sharing customers, communicating most easily, or relying on a common supplier. Commercial activities located on a *highway oriented ribbon,* however, display no such *economies of agglomeration,* as it is called. Instead they are scattered almost at random, without planning or functional relation. From the customer's point of view, stops at them are single purpose; for instance, to get a hamburger or a taco, to stop at the cleaners or the liquor store.

Second are the *urban arterial commercial developments.* Visits to them are also single purpose, and again there is no functional relation between units. They are oriented to the locality, and they need space, so much space that they cannot afford to locate in the CBD. They include auto repair shops, furniture and appliance stores, office equipment suppliers, funeral parlors, and lumberyards.

Finally, there are the *specialized functional areas,* where there are close linkages between activities, as found in the comparative shopping that takes place on "automobile row" or the system of referrals that takes place among certain medical specialists or between medical laboratories and professional offices. The location of these specialized functional areas is usually planned, according to Berry (1971a), but once begun, the agglomerating process leads to further specialization.

The pattern of land values generally parallels these zones of commercial activities, with the highest peak in the center of the central business district, then along ridges of land values as they decline out from the center but remain high along ribbon developments, with cones at street corners and other intersections. If the value of the land in the CBD is taken as the base, land values along commercial ribbon developments will be about one tenth the CBD base. Land values will be less than one hundredth the CBD base for local street corner nucleations. Planned shopping centers, however, do not usually conform to this pattern of land values.

Central place theory assessed

Central place theory, while commendable in its specificity of concepts and valuable in understanding commercial location, needs to be supplemented by additional components. Here, as elsewhere, ecology operates. Central place theory assumes a uniform transport surface—that is, that access is solely a function of distance. It fails to consider the impact of transport access, which lays down its own topography over that which naturally exists. Further, the theory assumes that each individual has equal access to whatever system of transport is in operation. While certainly not invalidating the theory, addition of the operation of actual access improves the power of the theory to explain commercial location both within and between zones of activity.

The central business districts of all urban settlements today, whether or not specialized into separate financial, retail, and administrative centers, are organized on the basis of pedestrian traffic. Both highway oriented commercial ribbons and urban arterial commercial developments, by contrast, are organized on the automobile. Outside the CBD some regional shopping centers are organized in terms of pedestrian traffic, while others are oriented to the automobile. Community business centers are also mixed in their traffic modes, while neighborhood and convenience centers in dense settlements depend on the traditional foot for people to get to them. Taking for illustrative purposes the CBD oriented to the pedestrian

FIGURE 5–2
Central place diagram

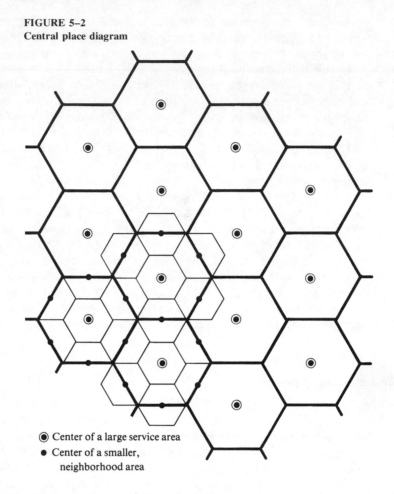

⊚ Center of a large service area
● Center of a smaller,
    neighborhood area

and the highway ribbon oriented to the automobile, let us examine how different transport networks further organize commercial activity.

Pedestrians and the CBD   Pedestrian traffic determines the shape and size of the CBD. The shape is oval, with one dominant axis, since foot traffic will not move far off one central route. Neither will pedestrians easily patronize shops separated by open spaces—by parks, for instance. Oval shape with limited activity only a few doors down side streets and no interruptions in flow are the essential features of pedestrian markets, as seen in the CBD. Wall Street, Thirty-fourth and Forty-second streets in New York, the Combat Zone in Boston, Brattle Street in Cambridge, Ponce de Leon in San Juan, Market Street in San Francisco, and Peach Street in Atlanta are among the many instances of this pattern.

The size of the market area is determined simply by the distance that pedestrians are willing to walk, between one quarter and one half mile. The availability of several mass transit stops within the market area may expand the size of the market somewhat, but without moving sidewalks or some other form of transit to assist the pedestrian, the size of a market nucleus remains limited.

Areal specialization within markets also evolves from the nature of pedestrian traffic. Shoe stores, clothing stores, camera and hi-fi equipment, movie theaters, and other types of economic activities establish themselves near each other due to the advantages of agglomeration. Each benefits from the customers others bring into the market, its sales volume exceeding that which it could command in an exclusive location. As an area becomes known for its concentration of an activity, other persons are attracted to the area, which leads other similar businesses to locate there. In a great metropolis like New York, such specialization has created literally hundreds of specialized clusters, many of them further specialized by price categories.

Autos and strip markets   The shape, size, and specialization of markets serving pedestrians stands in sharp contrast to those whose patrons arrive by the automobile. Markets organized by private automobile traffic are linear, with virtually no commercial development on secondary, intersecting streets. Residences, schools, hospitals, golf courses, parks, vacant land, and a wide variety of other noncommercial uses characteristically lie behind the strip development of markets oriented to the automobile.

The size or, more precisely, the length of these linear markets, is limited primariiy by the local and/or highway population, by the number of businesses that can be supported. The market on Route One in Boston is nearly 10 miles long, Kingston Pike in Knoxville, Tennessee, about half that, while Sunset Strip in Los Angeles extends for over 15 miles. Intersecting arteries, such as the Outer Belt in Boston, may delay development on the other side, but over time such interruptions of traffic have relatively little influence.

Markets oriented to the automobile are not specialized. Nightclubs, fast-food dispensers, furniture stores, funeral parlors, veterinarians, gas stations, cleaners, and pubs do business side by side. Stops at them are single purpose, and after accomplishing it the customer drives elsewhere, so no functional association between businesses evolves.

Linear, lengthy, and unspecialized, such a market may cause its users difficulty in locating any business on it. Once in the general area, known perhaps by a curve in the road or a hill, the motorist slows down to search the numerous competing signs for the desired destination. Not infrequently turns are missed or made prematurely, sometimes leading the customer to park in the lot of one business while shopping in another. Likewise, when residents are asked for directions to a specific establishment, instructions are vague, limited to orientation to one side of the street, nearness of the more predominant signs, and/or ''a little while after'' a certain traffic light. Linear strips lack *imageability* (Lynch, 1960:1976).

Regional shopping centers may depend on the automobile to bring their customers to their acres of parking lots, but may be organized by pedestrian traffic within them. Yet the spatial organization of activities for pedestrians and automobiles are basically oppositional. Cities that have attempted to save their downtowns by making them accessible by the automobile often have found they have destroyed the CBD in the process. And where planners have favored pedestrians over vehicles, traditional markets have often flourished (Wood, 1968). A number of cities have therefore restricted or even eliminated automobile traffic from their pedestrian centers, thus revitalizing central cores. Many American cities, however, having experienced their principal growth in the age of the automobile, have no such central pedestrian areas to revitalize. In these instances the question becomes what to do with central city land.

Life cycles of markets

Birch (1970) has examined the life cycle of the metropolitan area and suggests the likely future of the central areas in newer urban settlements. Grouping SMSA's according to the decade in which each area qualified as an SMSA in the U.S. census, his data ". . . suggests a sequence whereby younger cities chew up low-density land at a good clip with manufacturing floor space, parking lots, and road networks. . . . As the city ages and becomes more densely populated, central city land becomes more expensive, and manufacturing declines in significance, as does retail and wholesale trade. Services, in contrast, appear to thrive on concentration. . . ." In this sequence the CBD tends to become an elite service center, one which caters to other businesses rather than to individual consumers.

The foregoing projection for the future of the CBD parallels Vernon's (1962) summary of the activities sustained by the central core. He indicates that those activities (1) that require face-to-face communication, (2) that need to minimize the risk of uncertainty, and (3) that profit from external economies of scale thrive in the CBD. The central area is therefore becoming the favored location for coordinating institutions, as in finance, insurance, real estate, law, and government. Such specialization is seen in the proportion of office workers per population. Thus whereas jobs in manufacturing and retail and wholesale trade have increased in the suburbs, elite service center employment has increased in the city center. Such employment is highly specialized, serves a wide region, and is dependent on contact with related concerns.

The pattern today

The urban environment today displays wide variation in market ecological configuration. The once dominant central business district is becoming a specialized center for such coordinating institutions as government, finance, and insurance. Regional shopping centers now serve retail distribution for durable goods, with community and neighborhood clusters providing daily need items and services. Isolated convenience stores continue to decline with each improvement in transportation. The older pattern of mononucleated centralization has been replaced by multinucleation and relatively low levels of centralization, with many unfocused strip developments scattered throughout the modern urban environment.

URBANIZATION INTERNATIONALLY

After beginning in the East, urbanization spread to the West, where it intensified tenfold with industrialization. Today many Western nations are almost totally urban, with 90 or 95 percent of their populations living in settlements defined as urban. If the definition of urban is not based on place of residence but upon integration with the urban society, then the urban proportion rises to 98 or 99 percent of such countries as England, Sweden, Germany, the United States, and Japan.

The Western and industrialized (the two terms are closely associated but not identical) nations, however, include only one third the world's population. About 2 billion people live in nations which are now beginning to industrialize. They are called developing nations. They are also experiencing urban growth. The question urbanologists ask concerns what pattern this new urbanization in developing countries will take. The answer is important, because being able to predict some of the consequences of urbanization aids, among many other things, in planning and providing urban goods and services (see, for example, Turner, 1969, 1973).

Urbanization and urban growth

Urbanization is the proportion of the total population which is urban, and when we look at the rate at which developing nations are increasing their proportion urban we find the rate is moderate to low and even negative in some cases. The rate of urbanization is low, however, only because the entire population, rural and urban, is increasing at a rapid rate. How rapid? In countries such as India, the population is predicted to double within 30 years. The urban population is therefore expected to double, but since the rural population also will double, the rate of urbanization is low.

Urban and rural growth is rapid, but, as the population expands, the urban growth increases at an accelerating rate. Why? First, as populations expand, the size of a settlement grows, to be reclassified as urban. (The United Nations *Yearbook* defines urban as a settlement of 20,000 or more.)

Second, throughout the developing nations the birthrate is high, much higher than the death rate. This is, of course, the reason why the population everywhere is expanding so rapidly. But this factor also favors urban growth because the death rate in cities of developing nations is lower than the death rate in rural areas. This is in contrast to the Western experience with urbanization.

Third, hundreds of thousands and millions of people migrate from rural to urban areas. In this there is no change, since people have done that for centuries. The difference between the Western history and urbanization experienced in developing countries, according to some experts, is that there is insufficient employment in the urban areas for so many migrants. They call this overurbanization.

Overurbanization

The urban populations of developing nations grow rapidly but their economies industrialize at a much slower rate. The result is widespread and often increasing unemployment and underemployment. The condition is termed *overurbanization* and is thought by some to depress economic development. When overurbanization and the growth of primate cities occur simultaneously, economic development may be concentrated entirely in one area. Urban areas outside the primate city and rural area may experience economic recession, leading more of their inhabitants to migrate to the primate city, further straining the already inadequate rate of development there.

The two components of population and economy at times combine, then, to create new patterns of organization. The young unmarried males who are most often the current migrants, as they have been in the past, may be unable to have their families join them. Instead they may return home and then go back to the city next year. Over time a seasonal migration pattern may develop in which many migrants are in the city but not of it. Such migrants may retain their hinterland, tribal, territorial, and/or clan identity, bringing ancient countryside conflicts into the urban arena. Such an organizational pattern has a different impact on symbolism—the values of the migrants—than we had noted before.

Upon going home other migrants find that however bad conditions are in the city, they are far worse where they came from. And, whereas there is some basis for hopes of a better future in the city, the future of the small town and rural area is grim. Having come to the same conclusion themselves, some urbanologists have criticized the very concept of overurbanization as being out of touch with reality as the migrants see it.

With urban populations growing by 50 or even 60 percent every decade, it becomes impossible to provide even elementary urban services. There is no housing available so the people build their own. Huge areas grow up without street planning, water, electricity, sanitation, fire and police protection, schools, churches, medical facilities, or recreation or health services. Unemployed or underemployed, with even the little they have threatened by the thousands of newcomers who arrive every day, these masses often develop political unrest.

As POETS combine in yet new patterns in developing nations, urbanologists seek to better understand urbanization. Increased understanding helps the wide variety of urban officials to plan more effectively. With resources already strained by population increase, the resources available should be used optimally.

SUMMARY

Three sets of variations in urbanization have been examined. Urbanization, we learned, varies by region of the United States (and elsewhere), by market activity and location, and by nation of the world. We know that the basic components of urbanization are POETS, but we do not know the pattern they will display.

STUDY QUESTIONS

1. What is a region and how is it defined?
2. What differences do regional variations in urbanization make?
3. What is the hierarchy of business centers?
4. How do pedestrian-oriented and automobile-oriented markets differ?
5. What is overurbanization?

SUGGESTED READINGS

Berry, Brian J. L.   "General Features of Urban Commercial Structure." Larry S. Bourne, ed., pp. 361–67. *Internal Structure of the City* (New York: Oxford, 1971).

Fava, Sylvia, ed.   *Urbanism in World Perspective* (New York: Thomas Y. Crowell, 1968).

Reed, John S.   *The Enduring South.*

PART THREE

Urban communities

Our study of urbanization began far back in history; in telling that story we used as our unit of analysis the entire urban settlement, the city, the metropolis, and finally the urban environment. The impact of the process of urbanization on the human population was the first subject of Part Two. Second, we examined regional, market, and international variations in urbanization. Thus, once again our analysis dealt with large-scale developments.

The historical review of patterns of urban settlement and urban population characteristics is essential for understanding the urban environment. The urban environment contains the past, and its contemporary development is in large part structured by that past. If urbanization began in one settlement hundreds of years ago, its pattern of POETS will differ significantly from a second area that has urbanized in the last 20 or 30 years. The relevance of era of principal growth, which is the way we express the historical dimension, will continue to be evident as we turn to an examination of the internal characteristics of the urban environment.

First let us observe that today's urban environment contains hundreds of millions of people. Indirectly they relate to each other through the sharing of goods, services, and space. This is evident in how many people were involved in growing, processing, distributing, and marketing the food we eat every day. How many were involved in recruiting, training, organizing, and broadcasting the sports events we watch on TV? As you read the newspaper, or fill your car's tank with gasoline, ask yourself how many pooled their efforts so you could engage in these routine activities? And if you estimate the number of people with whom you share the sidewalks and the streets, who ride in the same bus or car, eat in the same restaurant, sit together at the movies—in a single day the average urbanite may come up with a number in the thousands. Clearly, lives in the urban environment are lived with many others.

In personal terms, our lives are lived with persons whom we know—family, friends, neighbors, acquaintances. But these persons constitute a minute fraction of the throngs of people with whom we are indirectly involved and who are unknown to us. As we walk down the city street we see, as Saul Bellow (1956:124–25) put it: " . . . the great, great crowd, the inexhaustible current of millions of every race and kind pouring out, pressing round, of every age, of every genius, possessors of every human secret, antique and future, in every face the refinement of one particular motive or essence—*I labor, I spend, I strive, I design, I love, I cling, I uphold, I give way, I envy, I long, I scorn, I die, I hide, I want.*" We do not know their names, their ethnicity, national origin, race, religion or anything else—and usually we do not care. Those who bake our bread or prepare our paycheck are important to us only because they are useful. "People live together on the whole, not because they are alike, but because they are useful to one another" (Park, 1952:80).

Millions of strangers provide us with a vast pool from which to take our friends and associates. No matter what interest or form of association we prefer, others in that vast urban environment share them or perhaps will share them for a price. Whether we wish to skydive, go spelunking, or customize automobiles, we can draw upon hundreds of thousands and millions of other persons to find associates for these and virtually any other ventures.

In the isolated rural village, and to an even greater extent back on the self-sufficient farm, life must be lived within much more restricted confines. What one eats is limited to what that person and a handful of others are able to grow. The topics of conversation, the types of entertainment and recreation, the available worship services, and all other activities are limited to what can be sustained by a few hundred or perhaps a few thousand others.

The vast, even overwhelming, variety of ways of life possible in the urban settlement is certainly a major reason for its widespread appeal. Whenever and wherever urban centers have appeared throughout the last 10,000 years, people have flocked to them when they could. And once the urban way of life has been experienced, few have ever voluntarily forsaken it.

Wanting to pursue our own lives, and having countless others with whom to form our associations, however, is not sufficient in itself. We must somehow locate these potential mates, friends, and associates somewhere in the vast urban population who can meet our needs and gratify our desires. The problem becomes: how can we meet those with whom we would like to share? Share what? Since any human activity requires space, we can answer: those with whom we would like to share space.

Sorting through people for those with whom we would like to share space is only one side of the coin, however. Just as there are people with whom we would like to share space—our bed, dwelling, neighborhood, or church—so there are others with whom we do *not* wish to share space. We may wish to go to bed with one type of person, but definitely not with other types. We may wish to neighbor with those who speak our language and not some other. And we may wish to dwell with friends and not enemies.

To include some is to exclude others, as the first wall around the first urban settlement did. To establish a boundary is to specify who may and who may not enter. The boundary makes it possible for those included within it to engage in common activities, and, at the same time, to exclude others from participation in the activities of the "in" group.

The very first group-established boundaries were those of kinship. The city, the first human association formed by the sharing of space, gave rise to hundreds of territorially organized social groups. Today's urban environment contains countless associations based on the sharing of space.

The bounding of space by social groups into communities is the subject matter of Part Three. To learn how different types of communities include some and exclude others, we shall examine the nature of urban communities. We shall continue in subsequent parts to analyze smaller and smaller units, until we examine the individual urbanite.

chapter 6

SYMBOLIC BOUNDING

United Press International

133

SOCIAL DIFFERENTIATION

Whether we live in a hugh metropolis of millions of people or in a smaller settlement of hundreds of thousands, or perhaps even among merely tens of thousands of others, if we list all our family, our friends, acquaintances, and other associates, our list will include only a small fraction of the people in our settlement. And yet each of us can choose our associates from thousands and millions of others. On what basis do we exclude more than 99 percent of all those other potential associates? We live our urban lives with less than 1 percent of those with whom we share the urban environment. How do we select that 1 percent? To answer, we can ask another question: in what ways do we think we are different from others and in what ways do we think we are like them?

As we think about the characteristics of the people who live in our settlement, we discover hundreds of ways in which we think people resemble us or are different from us. We differ in our height and weight, but there are many others who are similar to you or to me in height and weight. The color of our eyes, hair, and skin also varies widely, and there are many who have the same color eyes, hair, or perhaps the same complexion as you or I may have. Differences and similarities also exist in clothing and adornment styles.

When we turn from physical appearance to speech, we hear many different vocabularies, different accents, and different languages, just as we recognize many whose speech is similar to yours or mine. Behavior gives us another long list of ways in which we differ from or perhaps are the same as others. Among the population of any segment of the urban environment, people differ in the foods they consume or avoid, the substances they smoke or avoid, the entertainments they seek or shun, the organizations they join or oppose, the beliefs they practice or perhaps pretend to practice.

Any sizeable population differs in literally hundreds of ways, and the characteristics that a specific individual shares with one group may not be shared when he or she encounters another group. In this long list of similarities and differences, however, some characteristics will be more important to us than others. As individuals, we may not care that another person's height differs from our own, but we may care whether he or she speaks our language. We may be relatively unconcerned about a person's clothing or hair style, yet be deeply concerned about whether that person shares our own sexual preference. Although we as individuals may not be concerned about the color of another person's skin, our families or our neighbors may consider skin color to be more important than any other characteristic of a potential neighbor.

The basis upon which we see some people as being like us and others as being different is called *social differentiation*. Although it varies from one individual, family, neighborhood, and community to another, and although it changes over time, at any one point in space and time there will be broad agreement about the basis for social differentiation.

To say that someone is like us and another is different is to include one within our group while excluding another. Those with whom we see some commonality become "us"; those who differ are called "them." Social differentiation is a process of inclusion and exclusion, dividing a population into an in-group and an out-group.

In-groups and out-groups exist at many different levels between the individual and society—the family, the neighborhood, the community—and there are similarities at all size levels in the process of inclusion-exclusion; we limit our initial consideration to an analysis of relatively large-scale social differentiation, namely that found among communities.

Ethnicity

Although in-groups may be based on many different characteristics, it is convenient to begin with those based on ethnicity. What is your own ethnicity? Many of you would answer: "American." Suttles (1968:10) relates that when he gave "American" as an answer to that question, his interviewer replied:

> "Geraldo, you're just an American." She did not mean it as a compliment and afterwards I remember being depressed. In the Addams area, being without ethnicity [i.e., American] means there is no one to whom you can appeal or claim as your own.

For this woman, and for many others, "American" is not thought to be an ethnic term. Where were your parents born? . . . Your grandparents? . . . Your great-grandparents? If you respond to these questions "the United States," your questioner might finally ask: "But where did your family originally come from?" Note that this question assumes your family did in fact originate somewhere. But any "origin" selected is arbitrary. Why say your family came from Scotland when the Scots were formed from many peoples who came from elsewhere?

To use the Scots as merely one example for all others, their ancestry in part stems from Ireland, England, Sardinia, France, Spain, Portugal, Scandinavia, and Germany. In addition, peoples who spoke Celtic and Gaelic also genetically contributed to those people who we call Scot. Scotland itself came into being about a thousand years ago from four peoples—Pict, Scot, Briton, and Angle—who lived in what was formerly known as Pictland.

The ancestors of all of us extend back through ages of countless migrations and mixtures from lands whose names have changed even as the continents have shifted. Recognition of the arbitrary nature by which we answer questions of social differentiation, such as ethnicity, underscores the symbolic processes involved. Although our forebears extend back through thousands of years, we nevertheless claim one or another ethnicity, on the basis of a commonality which we *assume* with others.

Arthur Haley began his *Roots* with the departure of his ancestor from Africa. Why did he begin there? Were he to trace his roots among earlier generations, what different peoples would he find? The point is that our assumption of peoplehood is arbitrary. It is equally arbitrary to select some point in time from which "we" "originated."

Tracing one's own family tree has lately become a popular activity. When I began my own work in 1954 on "our" segment of the Wallace clan, I found that just three or four generations of "my family" numbered more than several hundred people. Even if one restricts oneself to blood relatives, the number of ancestors increases geometrically: 2 parents, 4 grandparents, 32, 64, 128, and then to 256 progenitors in just eight generations. Given vast migrations, voluntary and forced, and countless changes in the boundaries of social groups, to say that I am Scot, German, Croatian, or Druid is again quite arbitrary. Out of many possibilities, one selects those given importance by the symbolism of one's time and place.

Throughout the centuries there have been countless peoples. Eventually, regardless how great the differences between them, people sooner or later become integrated into a single unit. As Shibutani and Kian (1965:571) observe, "the only exceptions are those few cases in which one group has been completely exterminated." Policies such as separate quarters or ghettos, apartheid, and other devices to maintain separation have been attempted many times. "When seen in historical perspective, however, they are but transitory phases in a seemingly inexorable process" (Shibutani and Kian, 1965:571).

Peoplehood

Social differentiation, the process of inclusion and exclusion, leads to the formation of in-groups and out-groups. We call such groupings *people*, saying that those involved share *peoplehood*. Again let us keep in mind that ethnicity is but one basis for peoplehood. But of what does ethnicity truly consist? Max Weber (1958a) defines an ethnic group as a human collectivity based on an assumption of common origin. The "common origin" may, as Gordon (1964) notes, be based on race, religion, national origin, or some combination of them.

To be a member of an ethnic group does not necessarily mean that one is a member of a minority, or the working class, or that one is an immigrant. The basic point is that, for some persons, their conception of themselves binds them into a social world: the members of an ethnic category see themselves as a people; they share peoplehood.

A *people*, then, are those who so call themselves, whatever the basis for their assumed commonality. Shibutani and Kwan (1965:588) add the important point that those who define themselves as a people must be so regarded by others. Thus a person may not be a Jew unless he or she is so regarded by other Jews and gentiles (Dashefsky and Shapiro, 1974:8), but may be regarded as a Jew irrespective of his or her own individual conception. The assumption of real or imaginary peoplehood may be made voluntarily by those who identify with one another, or one group may impose its definition on those who may not have been previously associated. To cite an example of the latter case, Rogler (1972:4) notes that the Puerto Rican becomes a member of a distinct cultural group, an Hispanic, in part upon confronting residential segregation outside of Puerto Rico.

An ethnic group, then, is one whose members share a sense of peoplehood, whether they voluntarily embrace "their people" or whether they are identified with "them" against their wishes.

Inclusion-exclusion

The assumption of commonality includes some and excludes others. The process of inclusion-exclusion may be by custom or it may be incorporated into law. In Nazi Germany (Hughes, 1971:516–24), formal statutes specified the criteria by which people were to be classified by "race," or peoplehood as we call it. Ethnicity is one way of differentiating populations into various in-groups and out-groups: white and nonwhite, Jew or gentile, occidental or oriental, and other sets of terms that distinguish between "us" and "them," between "my people" and "your people."

Back on the farm (where most of us have never been), everyone personally knew one's own people. As everyone was acquainted with everyone else, at least through another, the stranger in town was automatically "one of them." When we meet someone in today's urban environment, frequently we do not know if he or she is "one of us" or "one of them." For some classifications, physical appearance may give us an indication, but by itself such clues are unreliable bases on which to initiate interaction. The first time that a white answers us in German, Spanish or perhaps Arabic, or that a black responds to us in French or perhaps with a British accent, quickly teaches us this lesson.

Even after commonality in language is established, we will still have little idea of whether the person is "one of us." Furthermore, who "we" are and who "they" are depends on where one is. Traveling through Europe, "we" may become just "American" without further distinction such as southern and northern Americans, Catholic or Protestant Americans. As one enters Africa and Asia, and as the number of Americans traveling decreases, as it does especially from October to April, the "we" with which Americans identify and are identified expands to be simply a "Westerner." When my family traveled in sub-Sahara Africa, the resident people really did not distinguish between Europeans and Americans; we were all just Westerners. Who we think "we" are depends on where we are, just as who "they" are also changes in space and time. Applied to the urban environment in the United States, one may simply be an "easterner" in Mississippi. In New Jersey there are no "easterners" but there are, of course, "southerners." One is regional, in other words, only outside one's region.

Within the region one is from this state or that state; within the state one is expected to indicate from what community in the state. And finally, within one community, the person is expected to identify where he or she lives within the community: Beacon Hill, the Upper East Side, Orange County, the Haight.

Why do we frequently begin our interaction with: "Where are you from?" "Where do you live?" The spatial location of a person helps us to identify him or her as a member of a particular social group. To respond that we are from Spencer, Iowa, and now live on Fifth Avenue (New York, of course), supplies social information, since physical space is symbolic. When we later discuss the individual urbanite we will note how everyone has a mental map of a settlement in which areas are characterized by their status. Herein it is sufficient to note that to give an address or location is to identify one's membership in particular social groups.

The identification between location in physical and social space comes about because people often wish to live near those with whom they assume some commonality. We should remember that commonality can also be imposed by external factors. Thus if one is poor, he or she is not expected to live anywhere else but with others who are poor. The wealthy could easily afford housing in "poor" areas, but social pressures within their own group, in addition to their rejection by the poor, prevent them from such deviant location. Although the example of the rich and poor may seem farfetched, the same process can be seen in the lives of the middle-class persons who purchase housing in poor, innercity areas. At times they are resented by the local people, and their friends may be reluctant to visit them in their new neighborhoods.

An area of the settlement, in summary, becomes *symbolic*. To mention the North End (Boston), Watts (Los Angeles), Chinatown (San Francisco), Park Avenue (New York), Levittown (New Jersey), or one of the hundreds and hundreds of other areas is to symbolize a social group. So powerful are the symbolic meanings of an area that if one does not fit the public stereotype, he or she must do a lot of explaining or move. Middle-class in-migrants to an area, for example, may add after stating where they live: "We're renovating an old house" (*New York Times,* July 7, 1978). Persons living in a mobile home may volunteer the additional information: "We're both in school and won't buy a house until we find out where we're moving."

The symbolic nature of physical space is also seen in the way in which boundaries will expand and change as the symbolic meaning of an area changes.

It was only in the late 1940s that the old Bedford and Stuyvesant Heights neighborhoods came to be called the Bedford-Stuyvesant section, designating the Negro ghetto. . . . As Negroes moved into new areas of central Brooklyn, the name Bedford-Stuyvesant followed them across Atlantic Avenue into Crown Heights and extended the ghetto almost to Eastern Parkway. However, it was not until the riots of 1964 that the central Brooklyn ghetto attained its full public identity. Only then did the newspapers omit the designation ''section'' or ''area'' and from then on simply call the ghetto Bedford-Stuyvesant. (Etzkowitz and Schaflander, 1969:4–5)

The same process can be observed in the changing boundaries of all areas of the city. The area included within the South End, Greenwich Village, Society Hill, the Highlands, or Watts changes as the society's symbolism changes.

In summary, our argument has been that social differentiation divides a population into peoples, each of whom includes some while excluding others. We then noted that often those of a people desire to live near one another, but that others may also force a people into common residence. Whether brought about voluntarily or involuntarily, the identification of a people with a specific space has been so pervasive that some urbanologists have mistaken the ecological consequence for the cause. That is, these urbanologists have assumed that because a people lived in a certain area, that area was somehow different from others. The importance of understanding the relation between social differentiation and spatial organization is critical to understanding any aspect of the urban environment. As symbolic ecologists we know that the difference lies in the area's symbolism.

Utilizing the ecological perspective in our study of the urban environment may be likened to watching a movie. We can either observe the way in which the pattern changes over time, or we may observe a given settlement at one moment in time, as in a single frame of a movie. Knowing that it is more difficult to ''see the forest'' when one is in the middle of it, and since our ''forest'' is the urban environment in which all of us live, we feel it is perhaps more effective for our education to begin with the changes over time that have produced a specific sociospatial order. Let us then for the moment ignore whatever now exists and begin with people moving into an area.

MIGRATION

Just as the first city grew by people moving into it, so urban settlements since then have involved the movement of population. People may move individually or collectively, and they may move voluntarily or involuntarily. Whatever the combination of these two dimensions, the pattern will differ. Since we cannot discuss all combinations, and since the Western pattern has largely been voluntary and individualistic, let us examine just that one type of migration.

According to the MacDonalds (1964), there are two types of individual and voluntary migration: that which is impersonally organized, by an employment recruiter or perhaps a company that tells a person where to move; and that which proceeds by chain migration, wherein the migration of one member of the family leads to the migration of others from that family, their friends, or their acquaintances. *Chain migration* can be defined as that movement in which prospective migrants learn of opportunities, are provided with transportation, and have initial accommodation and employment arranged by means of primary social relationships with previous migrants. *Impersonally organized migration* is movement based on impersonal recruitment and assistance. The arrangements for selection, transportation, reception, instruction, and placement are made by agents not personally known by the migrant.

In addition to the contrast of impersonal and chain migration, there is also the distinction of place and stage migration. In *place migration,* a specific destination is sought, while in *stage migration,* successive moves are made until a final destination is reached. These various types of migration have consequences that we shall serve later.

All four types of initial migrants, whom we can call *beachheaders* even when they were recruited by strangers, serve as sources of information about their new location to those left behind.

> The most important publicity for Wisconsin and Milwaukee, however, was found in the unsolicited testimonials which filled the letters to those left behind in the old country. "I thank God for giving me the idea to emigrate," one Milwaukeean wrote. "One must work hard with all one's strength and zeal, but one has hopes that his labors will be rewarded. I believe that if William were here, he and his family would fare better than in Germany." Such a measured judgment from a relative would be carefully considered back home and could be expected to bear more weight than a guidebook or other publicity to one conscientiously weighing immigration. (Conzen, 1976:37–38)

Clustering

In many instances in the United States the beachheaders were housed together by the employment agent. He could control his new recruits more easily if they were living close to one another and could make sure they got to work at the correct place and were sufficiently comfortable to continue working. And aside from the advantages to the sponsor of the migrant, clustering had a number of advantages for the migrant.

> The Negro who ventures away from the mass of his people and their organized life, finds himself alone, shunned and taunted, stared at and made uncomfortable; he can make few new friends, for his neighbors however well-disposed would shrink to add a Negro to their list of acquaintances. . . . Consequently emigration from the ward has gone in groups. (DuBois, 1899; 1967:297)

In addition to needs of physical safety, security, and friendship, Timms (1971:100) points out that:

> Since association demands contact, and contact may be seen as a function of spatial propinquity [living near one another], it follows that the manipulation of residential location may be regarded as a strategy for optimizing the probability of desired association. Individuals who wish to interact with each other are likely to wish to live in close proximity.

Clustering is further reinforced by the fact that since migrants often have similar incomes, the areas in which they can afford housing are likely to be similar. Another important economic factor is the cost of transportation. Some housing may be less expensive on the outskirts of the settlement, but migrants will not be able to live in remote sites if they cannot afford the cost of commuting. Apart from rent and transit costs, such noneconomic factors as the kind and quality of schools, the availability of familiar foods and worship services, and the presence of friends may make certain locales preferable to a particular group of migrants.

> "West Fifty-third Street, the pastor of Bethel African Methodist church remembered," was the principal place of resort for *our* group. On this street could be found, in 1900, or shortly thereafter, many of the major institutions of Negro New York: Negro political clubs, Mount Olivet Baptist Church, St. Mark's Methodist Episcopal Church, St. Benedict the Moor Roman Catholic Church, offices of the major Negro fraternal societies, two Negro hotels, varieties of small businesses and the Negro YMCA. (Kusmer, 1976:15)

These processes occurred, not only among blacks but among Germans, Poles, English, Irish, Norwegians, and others, as we document in later examples. Clustering is neither confined to one people nor to one country.

> In Great Britain approximately two-thirds of the colored population live in ethnic islands. . . . In Kampala, Uganda, there is no zoning by ethnic groups, but most natives live in the "African area." . . . In Batavia during the colonial days of the Dutch East Indies, the administrators and traders lived in spacious villas in the most desirable areas; the Indonesian middle class and some Chinese lived in brick houses in more crowded areas; and throughout the city, wherever they were tolerated, there were kampongs for the lower-class Indonesians. (Shibutani and Kwan, 1965:163)

The advantages of *spatial clustering* were even more evident when the second wave of migrants landed in the United States. The beachheaders temporarily doubled up in their housing, making the adjustment of the second wave of migrants easier than it had been for their hosts. The beachheaders were often able to get jobs where they worked for the newcomers. Jobs were secured so often in this way that at the turn of the century in the United States, certain crafts and trades came to be dominated by certain ethnic groups. "Irish immigrants first helped to build, and later found employment in, the warehouses and terminal facilities of the business district, whereas German immigrants found employment in the sewing machine and port supply trades'' (Ward, 1971:295). Many Italians became construction workers (Wallace, Harrison, and Nacarano, 1974).

Spatial clustering also created employment for "one's own" in the developing enclave.

> . . . being Jewish within the Jewish community provides one with an economic position within a subeconomy. The Jewish professional or the Jewish merchant has his own clientele, the members of the Jewish community. This is based on friendship and family relationships, a sense of supporting "one of our own" among the Jewish clientele, and, not the least significant, particularly in terms of professional services, a trust in the competence of the Jewish practitioner.

When housing had to be located for newly arrived immigrants, it was sought in the immediate area where the beachheaders had first established themselves. This was in part because they knew their area of the settlement better than any other, but it was also because of the mutual advantage of having one's people nearby.

Invasion

Invasion is the name given by ecologists to movement of a different people (or land use) into an area. Invasion is not by any means confined to black, Hispanic, or immigrant invasion as the white invasion of black areas of Philadelphia's Seventh Ward indicates (Baltzell, 1899; 1967:xxxiii).

Reaction to invasion depends in large part on the current occupants of the area. Some residents of an area being invaded will resist the arrival of even one of "them," but a significant majority will often not object until the number of newcomers reaches some critical point. The size of that critical point varies according to the social distance that two peoples wish to maintain from each other. Italians may not object to the invasion of their area by 50 or 100 Puerto Ricans, but they may object to the arrival of one black family. Norwegians may accept hundreds of Swedes, but resist the invasion of their area by a single Italian.

Invasion also refers to the entry of an establishment with a different land use from that prevailing in the area. Retail businesses, for example, may move into a predominantly residential area, or an institution such as a university or hospital may invade an area devoted to business. Although the processes involved in either the invasion of one people by another or one land usage by another are similar, we confine our current discussion to the former at this point.

Upon initial invasion a people may rally to defend their area. If successful, the area retains its previous character, becoming what Suttles (1972) terms a *defended neighborhood*. Recognizing this as one outcome, let us turn to another possibility. Attempted defense may be unsuccessful, or no defense may be attempted. The host people may accept those entering the area, or they may abandon their area to invade in their turn another area.

The process can be demonstrated by the findings of some research on blacks and whites. Frequently, as Farley, Schuman, Bianchi, Colosanto, and Hatchett (1977) point out, researchers have asked whites the question: "Would you sell your home to a black?" This question obscures the critical point of whether the hypothetical buyer is to be first black in the neighborhood, or the second, third, or even last. Although some may derive satisfaction from the findings of research asking this question— about 75 percent of the whites would accept a "black on the block"— neither blacks nor whites need an urbanologist to tell them that the first black is likely to be followed by a second, a third, and so on. Continuing to use the careful research by Farley and his associates, let us observe the process in detail.

Farley and his associates began by limiting the hypothetical neighborhood to 15 units and asking whites if they would remain in a neighborhood if one black family moved in. As corobrated by other research (Taeuber and Taeuber, 1964, 1965), three quarters said they would remain, about one fifth said they would be uncomfortable, and the remaining (7 percent) said they would move.

The number of whites who said they would move jumped to one fourth when the number of blacks increased to two families, and then to 40 percent when three of the 15 houses became filled by blacks in the hypothetical example. Let us now switch our attention to who would be moving in.

While more than nine of ten whites said they would stay in their neighborhood if one black family moved into it, one in four whites said they would not move into a mixed neighborhood. Most blacks would not be willing to be the first black in a white neighborhood, but 25 percent would be willing to be the second black family. When the third black family was added to the hypothetical 15-unit neighborhood, the number of whites who would be willing to move into such a neighborhood decreased to less than half. The number of willing blacks increased to about half. When the neighborhood reached 40 percent black, few whites said they would be willing to move in, whereas almost all blacks said they would be willing to do so. Thus, the probability that an in-migrant will be black increases with the number of blacks already resident in the area, while the probability of an in-migrant being white decreases rapidly to zero.

As the number of blacks in the neighborhood increased, so did the number of whites who said they would move. Because an increasing number of whites would move out, then, the probability that they would be replaced by blacks increased quickly to 1.00 (certainly in a probability model).

Throughout our examination of the urban environment we have studied and continue to study various settlements, populations, communities, and peoples as examples. Let us keep in mind that these processes can be applied to many other settlements, populations, and peoples. Today some people flee from Chicanos, Hispanics, West Indians, (white) hillbillies, Jews, Catholics, and Poles. In earlier eras it was the Methodists, Baptists, or perhaps the Mormons, and earlier still it was the Quakers, or perhaps the sheepherders or the sodbusters who were to be feared. Our examples are just that, and we use a variety of them to demonstrate their universality.

The tipping point

Returning to our example of blacks and whites, we see that unless an area is successfully defended against invasion, or unless the number of in-migrants is limited, the entire area may quickly change in composition from one people to another. The point at which it changes is called the *tipping point*.

Whether or not a tipping point exists depends on the relationship between the two peoples.[1] Kitians (people from St. Kitts) may accept any number of people from St. Croix as in-migrants, and the Irish may accept any number of Scots. Both the existence of a tipping point and the number of inmigrants needed before the earlier residents flee depends upon who is invading whom.

When there is a tipping point between two peoples, the initial clustering turns into predominance of the people moving in.

> Fifty years ago Watts was an orchard of orange trees tended by a handful of "Anglo," Negro, and Mexican-American farmers. As people moved outward from the city center, small suburban houses in the 1930 Spanish style sprouted among the farms, and Mexican-Americans came to dominate the region. But with the unprecedented influx of Negroes in the late 1930s, the whites and most of the Mexican-Americans departed, and Watts became the "port of entry" for hundreds of thousands of Negroes who gradually moved north toward the civic center and south toward the ocean. As the census maps of 1950 and 1960 show, Watts became solidly black. (McCord et al., 1969)

SUCCESSION

The operation of the tipping point is what turns a cluster into an area predominantly or exclusively occupied by one people. When this point is reached, ecologists say one group has succeeded another—that invasion has led to *succession* (Park, 1936; Cressey, 1938; Ford, 1950). The entry of

---

[1] For some of the many studies of "tipping" and the criticisms of the concept, see: Caditz 1976; Freeman and Sunshine 1970; Ginsberg 1975; Goering 1978; Kantrowitz 1973; Taeuber 1965; Wolf 1963.

one, ten, or a hundred members of a people new to that area leads to their exclusion by the current occupants, or to the abandonment of the area to those newcomers. (In many cases, the newcomers may be accepted, but then succession does not take place.)

When does the ecologist say that succession has been reached? Again it depends on the peoples involved. When the Italians invaded the portion of New York between Canal and Houston streets, west of the Bowery, the area was known as Irish. Although both peoples were Roman Catholic, the Irish excluded the Italians from the churches they considered their own—for example, St. Patrick's. The Italians responded by organizing their own parishes, recruiting Italian priests to staff them. Later, as many of the Irish left the area, the Italians took over St. Patrick's. Long before the last Irish family departed, the Italians had succeeded the Irish, and the area became known as Little Italy. In part, then, succession is the point at which a people come to predominate; in part, it involves the direction in which change is moving.

Cultural intensification

We pointed out that when the walls first went up around the settlement that was to be called a city, the commonality of the people enclosed was increased. We call this process *cultural intensification*. Being boundaries, walls intensified the interaction of those within. The "walls" that now surround the "people" we have been observing are, in most instances, purely social, but they are boundaries nevertheless. And these social boundaries also intensify the interaction of those included. "As soon as admission into defined space is allowed, various norms, such as certain legal rights and duties, are expected to operate" (Hiller, 1941:197).

Living with one another in a specific section of a larger settlement, people can communicate easily and effectively. Through communication they can develop common understandings, which are the essence of a culture or subculture. "If new communication channels are established, those who had been strangers are able to share their experiences and in time become more alike culturally" (Shibutani and Kwan, 1965:573).

Currently sharing space, the ethnics can organize and sustain their own churches, schools, and community activities. Regarding the Italians, Firey (1945:146) notes:

> . . . proximity, or at least common residence in the North End, greatly facilitates participation in the *paesani* functions which are so important to the first generation Italian. Moreover, it is in the North End that the *festas*, anniversaries, and other old world occasions are held, and such is their frequency that residence in the district is almost indispensable to regular participation. The social relationships comprised by these groupings, as well as the benefit orders, secret societies, and religious organizations, are thus strongly localistic in character.

With co-residence, ethnics can mutually celebrate St. Patrick's Day, the Passover, or Martin Luther King, Jr.'s birthday. They can continue the feasts and the rituals and can observe baptisms, christenings, bar mitzvahs, weddings, funerals, or any other occasion they wish to share. Each has others with whom he or she can speak the same language or use a common vocabulary, dialect, or accent. And they can do all these things without fear of being condemned, punished, or even ridiculed by "them," those other "people" who do not understand.

> . . . the survival among the Poles of their native language is encouraged in a variety of ways by community agencies. Thus, Polish is an optional subject for students in the Hamtramck high school. . . .
>
> Above all, the Polish language is preserved through the church services, through the Polish newspapers in Hamtramck and Detroit, and through numerous community gatherings and societies where Polish is spoken. (Wood, 1955:38–39)

As a fully developed social world emerges, the common activities, institutions, and interests strengthen the development of common values, beliefs and sentiments. Common association in turn creates or enhances an awareness, in many, of their status as "a people."

> The notion of a "special bond" between people whose only common characteristic is their being Jewish appears again and again in casual conversation among Jews. As upper-middle-class members of American society, many Jews are international travelers on business and/or pleasure trips. Hardly one of these trips passes without the travelers telling about this Jewish couple (fellow travelers) or Jewish merchant (native) whom they met in Paris or in San Juan. Jews will say that they seem "just naturally" to gravitate to other Jews at a party or at any sort of meeting. Regarding more long-term, intimate relationships, the vast majority of Jews indicate that most if not all of their closest friends are also Jewish. (Dashefsky and Shapiro, 1974)

Within their own communities and through the strength of unity, they can even ridicule, laugh at, and condemn those "whiteys," "goys," "gringos," and the other epithets for one's respective out-group.

> Our folkways also included a warning song, *"Shikker iz a goy vayl er iz a goy."* (As long as a man is a non-Jew, he's a drunk.) It was a song from Russia and Poland used against the *pogromchiks,* and it had a mocking racial air. You laughed, felt superior—being nonalcoholic—and you went on to other rational matters.
>
> *Goy,* then, was as much a word denoting a possible Christian drinker who might drink too much as it was a word merely denoting a Christian. (Roskolenko, 1971:168)

The strength of social pressures within the spatially concentrated people may be seen in the heightened political activity of those on the inside.

. . . members of ethnic minorities, whether based on race, religion, or nationality, may become active in social and political affairs because of social pressures exerted upon them within their ethnic community. Members of such an ethnic community are often more aware of their common bonds and hence are more socially cohesive. . . . "As a consequence, their ethnic communities serve as a salient reference group for them." (Warren, 1975:74; in part quoting Olsen)

The consequences of contact with those outside may be especially evident in mate selection.

I had thought that she would like Barbara . . . [but] my mother hated Barbara, hated her helplessly, depthlessly, felt for Barbara a revulsion so deep that she could scarcely bear to look at her. . . . "Now, you know," she said to me darkly, once, "that is not what I raised you for. That was no part of my calculations, young man, and you might as well know it front as back."

"What are you talking about, Mama?" I knew what she was talking about. She could almost never bring herself to mention Barbara by name, but the tone was unmistakable.

"I mean, I am not going to have no fair-haired, blue-eyed baby crawling around here and calling me Grandmama. *That's* what I mean. You know damn well what I mean." (Baldwin, 1968:261)

The feeling of being among one's "own" may become so strong that few will voluntarily leave the area, and those who do leave may be seen by others as having abandoned or even having repudiated one's own people. Firey (1945:146) notes with respect to the Italians of Boston's North End:

Residence in the North End seems therefore to be a spatial corollary to integration with Italian values. Likewise emigration from the district signifies assimmilation into American values, and is so construed by the people themselves. Thus, while the area is not the conscious object of sentimental attachment, as are Beacon Hill and the Common, it has nonetheless become a symbol for Italian ethnic solidarity. By virtue of this symbolic quality the area has a certain retentive power over those residents who most fully share the values which prevail there.

Those who do leave the area or otherwise fail to conform to the values of the in-group are also ridiculed and condemned. Calling them such epithets as "Oreos," "Shiskas," or perhaps "Apple-Indians" applies pressure for their conformity.

Given the attractions of conformity, the condemnation meted out by the in-group for deviance, and perhaps the lack of welcome elsewhere, it should come as no surprise that the formation of a social world attracts others to it. In a study of Chicago's Jews, Jaret (1977) reported "a high degree of Jewish residential clustering on blocks, both in the city and the suburbs." Further, in the 14-year period of mobility which he studied, Jaret found that most Jews moved to blocks which contained either more or an equal proportion of co-religionists than did their former neighborhoods: "45 percent of the households in the sample [n = 6000] moved from less to more Jewish blocks . . . and 23 percent moved to blocks that had about the same percentage." This pattern was more pronounced in city-to-city moves than in city-to-suburb moves. And "Orthodox and Conservative Jews moved . . . more often to blocks that were of higher percentage Jewish than did the Reform and nonaffiliated Jews."

Having examined the process of social differentiation and having seen how it may manifest itself in space, we can summarize it as follows.

An assumption of commonality by self and/or others, when it leads to spatial clustering, sets in motion cultural intensification, which leads to the formation of a social world, whose members share common activities and institutions, common interests, values, beliefs, and sentiments, an awareness of their status as "a people," a feeling of interdependence with others in the same peoplehood, and a sense of unity that forms the basis for a potential to act in union. (Adapted from Williams, 1964:356.)

Spatial organization

Now that we have seen how social differentiation may give rise to the spatial concentration of a people, let us look at what, if any, commonality people share who occupy contiguous (adjoining) space. People may identify with one another and then move into common space, but does that mean common space will usually be occupied by people who identify with one another?

When urbanization spread into the countryside in the settlement form we have identified as that of the *urban environment*, the outward displacement of the population reduced the populations of the core. Included within the decline were many of the older ethnic communities—Little Norway, Germany, Poland, and Italy. As the members of such ethnic groups moved out into the suburbs, these former members of the same people became relatively dispersed. While five, ten, or even more families from the "old neighborhood" often clustered near each other in their new suburban locations, the clusters did not lead again to the development of an exclusive area for these peoples.

Observing the declining populations of Little Italy, Little Poland, and the Jewish ghettos, among others, many investigators have concluded that all ethnic groups in the United States are melting into one common population. With reference to the Jews, for example, Wirth (1928) states that with each generation of Jews in America, "not only does the Ghetto tend to disappear, but the race tends to disappear with it." For Wirth the ghetto is a geographical-physical unit and an ethnic group; it is a place and a state of mind, an area and an institution.

Given this fusion of place and people, Wirth and others like him think that were people no longer identified with a specific space, they would eventually lose their sense of peoplehood. That is, if it is true that bounding intensifies interaction, strengthens community, and itensifies common culture, as even we have argued, then should not spatial dispersal decrease interaction, weaken community, and decrease commonalities in culture? Is it not true that social processes operate in both directions?

So many investigators have equated the spatial form of ethnic concentration with the ethnic community that many have answered the preceding question in the affirmative. Little Italy is disappearing, and therefore so are the Italians; they are assimilating, leaving their Italian community and identity. As these observers have noted the decline of German, Swedish, Norwegian, Polish, Slavic, and other communities, they have seen them all as declining in importance for their members. Extending this process, they have concluded that such assimilation is the "natural" way of all peoples.

In our own assessment these urbanologists are mistaken in several ways. The way in which space is shaped depends fundamentally on symbolism, on the specific operation of the social processes at a specific time and in a particular place. There is no one-to-one relationship between people and space. Antiblack racism with regard to blacks was present in both the North and the South, yet black/white space was organized differently in both regions. The same symbolic processes may configure different arrangements of space.

Jesuits who move from their father houses to become dispersed throughout the world are rarely "lost" to the community of Jesuits. Members of fanatical sects likewise survive without exclusive territory (Coser, 1974). Ethnic peoples, such as gypsies, have continued to function in spite of changes in their residential concentration-dispersion. Therefore, to conclude that certain communities are disappearing because of changes in their previous spatial manifestations is to ignore their symbolic basis. As the settlement pattern in the United States was changing from metropolitan to urban environmental form, some ethnic communities changed their settlement patterns as well. Whether their changed spatial configuration represents a "loss" or a "gain" in community is an empirical question, not one to be decided on the assumption that any change means loss.

As an empirical matter we know first that there is no single pattern into which all peoples may be placed. The experience of migrants depends upon the pattern of POETS at the time of their migration. Knowing this most basic point, we expect and find that the experience of Germans, Scots, and Swedes has been different from that of blacks, Chicanos, and Jews. At this time blacks and Chicanos have little opportunity of living outside the areas in which they are now the exclusive occupants. If they were to become residentially dispersed, would the black and the

Mexican-American cultures and communities continue to exist? The answer to that question, it should be clear by now, is that it depends upon the symbolic—not the spatial—processes.

People may communicate across distances, just as they may *not* communicate with those nearby. Although the Jews are no longer required to live in designated areas, Etzioni (1959) points out that they are not distributed at random in space. On the one hand the majority do not wish to live in an exclusively Jewish area, because that would give them "a feeling of segregation." Yet, Etzioni continues, nor do they want to be without Jewish associates and institutions. Therefore, Jews cluster together in several suburbs. Interaction is maintained through common activities and networks, by telephone and perhaps newsletter (Lavender, 1977). Such communication and participation creates and sustains Jewish culture. As Etzioni (1959:258) concludes: "a group can maintain its cultural and social integration and identity, without having . . . [a territorial] basis." We agree and add that communal forms are not fixed in space. Communities can survive, have survived, and will survive in a variety of spatial forms. And apparently identical spatial forms need not have identical symbolic components. A concentration camp or a military encampment may fulfill all the spatial criteria of a community without being one.

We therefore conclude that people living next door to one another may or may not share any significant commonality. If they are strangers to one another, that does not mean they lack friends elsewhere. And, the members of communities in the urban environment need not live next door to one another to maintain interaction.

Territory

Note that we have thus far avoided using the terms "territory" or "turf" for the space with which a people may become identified. To call a certain area a "territory" implies that it is possessed, occupied, and defended by a people. As our examples have indicated, whether a people defends its space depends on the relationship of the resident group to those entering. Further, the extent to which a people identifies with a locale depends upon the organization of the people. *Territoriality,* in other words, is a response to space (Suttles, 1968), not a condition that can be assumed to be universal. To illustrate this let us look at one example of a previous pattern of territorial organization.

The following findings come from a study of the distribution of denominations in Philadelphia carried out by Johnston (1968:248):

> . . . the Presbyterians are most likely to be found sharing residential space with Episcopalians and are found sharing that space with Methodists only when the other two denominations are present in significant numbers. . . . Baptists, however, share residential neighborhoods alone with Methodists or are in an enclave of their own.

Territorial organization, as this example and others indicate, was formerly on the basis of religion and ethnicity—both, of course, linked to class. And prior to 1890 there were only clusters of blacks in American urban settlements in the North and South. The emergence of exclusively black areas did not develop until the early 1900s.

> As early as 1860, most of Cleveland's black population resided on the East Side, and the center of the Negro community was the old haymarket district on Central Avenue. Prior to the 1880s, however, there was no noticeable trend toward the ghettoization of the black population. Before then, in fact, no ward in the city was more than 5 percent black; and although blacks were concentrated essentially in three wards (the First, Fourth, and Sixth), they were thoroughly integrated in each. No segregated neighborhoods as such existed. Nor were blacks housed primarily in multiple-unit dwellings; in 1880 almost 70 percent of the city's Negroes lived in single-household units.
>   . . . it seems doubtful that anything even remotely resembling a real black ghetto existed in American cities, north or south, prior to the 1890s. (Kusmer, 1976:12)
>   (For a possible exception, see Johnson, 1968:346.)

Rather than speaking of territoriality, symbolic ecology first examines social differentiation. The way in which social differentiation leads to a particular organization of space depends on the symbolic framework of society. The so-called "territorality" of any people depends upon the way in which they symbolically differentiate themselves. Their defense of a space, their territorial behavior, is only one of their many responses to space. In this, social organization and social psychology go hand-in-hand.

SUMMARY

Social differentiation, the process of inclusion and exclusion, leads to the formation of in-groups and out-groups. We call such grouping *peoples,* saying that those involved share *peoplehood.*

Ethnicity is one basis for peoplehood; other bases include race, religion, national origin, sexual preference, and life style. A people, then, are those who so call themselves, and/or are so regarded by others. Peoplehood is based on the assumption of commonality.

A people may desire to live near one another and/or others may force a people into common residence. Whether migration is individualistic or collective, voluntary or involuntary, clustering frequently occurs. The similar incomes of the migrants, their similar abilities to afford the cost of transportation, and the availability of familiar foods, worship services, and friends reinforces the tendency of migrants to cluster.

When a new people enter an area, ecologists call this *invasion.* The reaction of the current occupants to those invading depends upon the relationship between the two peoples. The occupants of the area may rally to defend it, they may accept the newcomers, or they may abandon the area in turn to invade another area.

The point at which invasion accelerates into succession, changing the composition of an area from one peoplt to another is called the *tipping point*. Whether a tipping point exists depends on the relationship between the two peoples.

When there is a tipping point, the initial invasion gives way to *succession,* the predominance of the invading group in the area. Areal predominance facilitates the creation of a social world based on peoplehood. Space turns into territory.

Although the creation of territory supports and enhances community, a people can maintain its cultural and social integration and identify without territory. Commonality may instead be maintained through common activities and communication networks, through common associates, institutions, and organizations. Territory is a response to space which flows from community.

STUDY QUESTIONS

1. What is social differentiation and what are its consequences for the organization of space?
2. Describe the process of invasion and succession.
3. Ethnicity is but one type of peoplehood. What are some other types?
4. How is the social world which may be created by social differentiation like the first cities that emerged?
5. To the symbolic ecologist, what is territory or turf and under what conditions is it present?

SUGGESTED READINGS

Shibutani, Tamotsu, and Kwan, Kian, M.   *Ethnic Stratification: A Comparative Approach* (New York: Macmillan, 1965).

Suttles, Gerald.   *The Social Order of the Slum* (Chicago: University of Chicago Press, 1968).

Williams, Robin M., Jr.   *Strangers Next Door: Ethnic Relations in American Communities* (New York: Prentice-Hall, 1964).

chapter 7

GHETTOS

The Photography of H. Armstrong Roberts

In the last chapter we examined how a population differentiates itself into peoples. Our next task is to observe how the social differentiation we are studying leads to spatial differentiation—that is, to the concentration of one people in one area and another people in another area.

SPATIAL CONCENTRATION

Urbanologists distinguish three types of spatial concentration of peoples: a specific area may be said (1) to have a concentration of, (2) to be predominantly occupied by, or (3) to be exclusively occupied by persons with some common characteristic.

The first measure, that of concentration, refers to the relationship between the total number of a people in the entire settlement and how many of them live in a specific locale. In a metropolis of 8 million, for example, although there may be only 100,000 Jamaicans, they may be concentrated in one specific section. Thus we may say that three quarters, or 75,000, of all Jamaicans are concentrated in a specific area. This statement would remain true even if there were 200,000 Antiguans also living in this same area. To be concentrated in an area does not necessarily mean to be the majority in that area.

In the second measure, to say that an area is predominantly Chicano or Hispanic is to measure concentration by the proportion of one people relative to others in that area, disregarding how many may live elsewhere. Thus a specific area may be two thirds Chicano, one sixth Hispanic, and one sixth black. Other areas may also be predominantly Chicano. To predominate does not necessarily mean to be the majority. The West End of Boston that Gans studied (1962) was known as an Italian area, but Italians were only 42 percent of the population. The area also included Jews, Poles, Irish, Albanians, Ukrainians, Greeks, gypsies, homeless men, middle-class professionals and students, homosexuals, artists, and bohemians.

A third measure of spatial concentration is the exclusive occupation of an area by a people. Rarely does exclusive occupation mean 100 percent. By "exclusive," urbanologists mean greater concentrations than predominance, i.e., areas where there are "few" others.

These three degrees of spatial concentration delineate three types of areas. When a people is concentrated in an area, we will call this a *cluster*. When a people predominate in an area, we will call this an *enclave*. And when an area is exclusively occupied by a people, we will call this a *ghetto*.

Index of segregation

The *index of segregation* (or dissimilarity) (Duncan and Duncan, 1955) refers to a measure of the concentration of a people. To understand the basis on which this index is computed, let us assume that a given settle-ment as a whole is 20 percent black and 80 percent white. If there were no segregation, each block or other small area such as a census tract would contain the same proportions, that is, 80/20. If all areas did contain the same proportion as found in the total settlement, the index of segregation would be zero. If, at the other extreme, each block were occupied exclu-sively by blacks or whites; that is, there were no integrated areas at all, the value of the index would be 100. The index of segregation can there-fore be defined as the percentage of whites or blacks (or any other groups) that would have to change their residence to produce total integration. At zero, no one would need to move. At 100, half of each group would need to move.

Students should be aware of the influence that the size of the unit of analysis has on the value of the index of segregation. If the investigator uses larger spatial units, such as census tracts or wards, the values tend to be smaller—that is, to reflect less segregation. By contrast, there is a tendency for the value to rise the smaller the unit of analysis; for example, when block or precinct data are used.

Exclusive occupation

While people who assume some commonality with one another may wish to live in proximity, rarely does every member of a people wish to live exclusively with his or her people. Human beings are simply too different from one another for such uniformity. Earlier we mentioned that one in four whites would accept at least one black as a neighbor. In the sample (n = 400) of Farley (1977) and his associates, 62 percent of the blacks rated as "most attractive" a neighborhood which is one half black and one half white, and another 20 percent stated that such equal compo-sition was their second choice. Thus the majority of blacks do prefer inte-grated neighborhoods, as a number of other studies have also documented (Pettigrew, 1973; Duncan, Shuman, and Duncan, 1973).

As another example, Jews also prefer integrated residential areas. While the majority wish to live in neighborhoods with co-religionists nearby, the majority also wish to live in an area not exclusively Jewish (Etzioni, 1959; Jaret, 1977). Given then the assumption that all members of a people may not wish to live together, as well as the empirical re-search which indicates the desire of the majority for integrated neigh-borhoods, how do areas exclusively occupied by one people arise?

Exclusive areas arise, in part, simply because some peoples have no choice: others tell them where they must live. Regardless of their ability to afford the cost of housing elsewhere, in spite of their ability to pay for the additional cost of transportation, and in spite of their possible preference for other locations—near schools, churches, and other institutions of their choice—the fact of the matter is that others will not accept them outside certain areas. A ghetto—an exclusive area, in other words—is in part formed because people have no choice. To a large extent, residence in a ghetto is involuntary (Clark, 1965; Warren, 1974).

The involuntary residence in a ghetto does not by any means indicate that none who live there desire to do so.

> I was born into a self-contained Yiddish ghetto. Though we were the majority, the ghetto also housed Poles, Russians, Irish, and Italians. All of us had our special places, dictated to us by our faces, our speech, our jobs, our music, dances, and looks—and, of course, our religion and country of origin. Each one lived in a ghetto within a ghetto. Did we mind it? We wanted to be among our own people, our own language, our own religion, and to be ourselves down to our last Jewish roots. (Roskolenko, 1971:168)

Our usage of the word "ghetto" as an area of exclusive occupation of a people is in keeping with its historical derivation as a quarter to which the Jews were restricted. The word itself was initially the name of a small Venetian islet called "getto" to which the Jews were expelled in 1516 (Sachar, 1964). Subsequent Jewish quarters came to be called ghettos. Today the term is used to refer to the exclusive residential concentrations of a variety of peoples.

Predominate occupation

Ghettos are distinguished from enclaves where a people simply predominate. The predominance of a people in an area is usually voluntary. "Norwegians have not been segregated from native whites, nor is there any evidence that they have been discriminated against in any way as far as choosing a home is concerned. The clustering within the area is therefore voluntary" (Jonassen, 1954:39).

The distinction in theory between enclave (voluntary) and ghetto (involuntary) co-residence having been made, it needs to be pointed out that the distinction is often difficult to make in practice. If a particular area of an American city contains mostly Jews, is that area a ghetto or an enclave? Is the Black Belt of Chicago or the Watts area of Los Angeles a ghetto or an enclave? How about Chinatown? Little Italy? El Barrio? As these examples suggest, any given community may be formed and maintained by both voluntary and involuntary forces. The difference between ghetto and enclave, in other words, is one of degree rather than of kind. Examining an urban community as a ghetto should not blind us to the fact that many of its residents may prefer to live there.

Whether enclave or ghetto, areas where a people are concentrated represent the spatial manifestation of social differentiation. These areas constitute a social world for their inhabitants. Let us examine some of the many social worlds which are thus created. Because ghettos are the most distinct, and since blacks are often the current occupants of America's ghettos, we will use blacks as our example. In doing so, we should keep in mind the words of the chairperson of one of Chicago's Mayor's Committees of the 1940s: "No people can live decently unless they can live freely. The ghetto is a feature of medieval Europe that has no place in America" (Drake and Cayton, 1962:12).

Concentration

The initial movement of a people into an area rarely provokes immediate segregation. Prior to the latter part of the 19th century, blacks were only loosely clustered in certain areas. A large number of blacks lived outside any residential clusters of other blacks, sharing common activities and institutions with other peoples.

> In 1832, less than five years after its organization, the First Baptist Church accepted its first black member. . . . [Other] blacks entered the congregation, and by 1836 there were at least eleven blacks among the one hundred or so members. (Katzman, 1975:51)

As the metropolis emerged in the second half of the 1800s, the population became increasingly segregated.

> Detroit, like most American cities, was a conglomeration of ethnic and racial neighborhoods. In the 1860s, 1870s, and 1880s, Corktown, Dutchtown, Kentucky, Polacktown, and Piety Hill were common community names in Detroit. By the turn of the century less explicitly descriptive epithets would be used, but Detroiters still could identify the east side with the Irish, the St. Antoine district with Negroes, Gratiot with Germans, Hastings with Polish and Russian Jews, Hamtramck with Poles, and Paradise Valley with Italians. (Katzman, 1975:55)

As the metropolis expanded, many people began to move to the growing suburbs. Those who moved out were those who could afford to do so, generally the older immigrant groups. And as they moved out they dispersed. As outward expansion continued, more recent immigrant groups became involved in the process.

THE GHETTO HYPOTHESIS

The pattern of movement of urban populations seemed clear by the 1920s. Immigrants initially settled in areas adjacent to the central business district. In this ring around the CBD that Burgess had called the zone of transition, the ethnic enclaves and ghettos were established. As the immigrants and their later generations increased their economic resources, they moved outward from the CBD—first into Zone III, then into Zone IV, and when they were very successful into Zone V.

As the descendants of the old immigrants moved out, many urbanologists thought that they were leaving behind their ethnicity. Migrants to the outer zones were thought to be assimilating into an "American" way of life. And as migrants left the old ethnic community, its internal cohesion was weakened, and assimilation increased there also.

In spatial as well as cultural terms, then, the urban analysts of the 1920s thought they saw the coming of a great American melting pot whereby formerly diverse peoples would become one. This point of view became known as the *ghetto hypothesis*.

Could an ethnic community survive without a territory of its own? The ghetto hypothesis argued that it could not. Could a community be created and sustained through the concentration of a population in an area? Those who accepted the ghetto hypothesis answered that sharing space did promote community. Both answers, however, were qualified by later research.

In the first place, later analysts observed that a population may be concentrated in an area primarily on the basis of economic class, not peoplehood. Consider the experience of American blacks as an example. At the same time that many immigrant populations were scattering outwards, blacks were becoming ever more concentrated. Whereas the index of segregation for many peoples decreased after 1910, the index for Negroes increased (Kusmer, 1976:164–65). Why were they an exception to the general pattern of residential dispersion which was followed by many, although not all peoples?

Economic discrimination

The reason for the increasing concentration of blacks at the turn of the last century lay in the economic discrimination to which they were subject. When the metropolis as settlement pattern radically altered the face of urban America, the economy was also undergoing massive change. Industrialization on one hand led to the development of massive plants with their thousands of workers. On the other hand, both traditional craftsmen and small farmers were displaced by the "massification" of American economic activity. When blacks attempted to enter these newly emerging employment centers, though, they found their entrance blocked.

> In Cleveland, of seventeen hundred men enrolled in apprenticeship programs in 1910, only seven were Negroes. Second, no economic necessity compelled employers to hire blacks until the outbreak of hostilities in 1914 sharply reduced the stream of European immigrants that had previously provided American manufacturers with an abundant supply of cheap labor. . . . Finally, many trade unions affiliated with the American Federation of Labor refused to accept black members. . . . In 1870 fully 31.7 percent of all black males in Cleveland had been employed in skilled trades; by 1910 this figure had dropped sharply to 11.1 percent. (Kusmer, 1976:67, 70)

Ethclass

Economic discrimination, when based on ethnicity, limits an entire people to one economic class. Ethnicity thus combines with class to produce what Gordon (1964) has termed an *ethclass*. Under ethclass conditions, community may not arise or be sustained even though a people are spatially concentrated.

Among the consequences of ethclass is homogeneity—especially in terms of needs and the resources to fulfill (or fail to fulfill) them. The more homogeneous a population, the less self-sufficient and sustaining it will be. It will lack its own leaders, be unable to direct and control its own fate.

A contemporary example of ethclass is found in some housing projects. To get into the project, a household must have a minimum income— enough to pay some rent. But if and when a household earns over the maximum income allowed by project rules, the people comprising the household must leave. Those between the minimum and maximum income form a homogeneous class. If they are also of the same ethnicity, an ethclass exists.

The ghetto hypothesis had postulated that spatial concentration of a people would foster community. But the research on ethclass has indicated that spatial concentration based on ethclass may well undermine community. Spatial concentration by itself is no guarantee of community.

Ethstyle

Not all immigrant groups moved to the suburbs, even when outward migration was economically and socially possible. Within some ethnic communities, the more "successful" individuals did not move away and thus possibly weaken the group—rather they remained where they were. Under these alternative conditions, as Conzen (1976:64) notes, the community becomes more heterogeneous and "presumably more self-sufficient and sustaining. . . ." Since the community retains its members, it produces its own leaders, its own varied organizations, its own techniques for internal and external communication, and even, to some extent, its own economy. Under these alternative ghetto formation processes, what we shall term an *ethstyle* (parallel to Gordon, 1964) emerges— distinctive life based on style rather than class.

According to Conzen's examination, the German community's exclusive area of Milwaukee is illustrative of what we term an ethstyle. It should be understood first that those included within "Deutschland" were not there entirely voluntarily.

> The Germans avoided the Irish, almost everyone avoided the Germans, and the Yankees and the British sought out one another. . . . While native and Irish householders were scattered somewhat more evenly throughout the

city ten years later (1860), the Germans clung even more tenaciously to their own neighborhoods. (Conzen, 1976:127)

Little Germany, as we noted earlier of all ghettos, was maintained by both voluntary and involuntary forces.

Whether pushed or pulled into the community, the initial migrants and several generations after them were of the same general class. (The voluntary migrants out of most communities are drawn from a limited segment of that parent society. See Chapter 2.) Over time some Germans were successful in business, trade, or other economic activities, and thus could afford housing elsewhere. As members now of the white collar or even upper class, these German-Americans also would have been accepted. For a complex of reasons that Conzen notes in detail, however, many Germans remained in the area they exclusively occupied.

The increasing heterogeneity of the ghetto based on ethstyle is what differentiates it from an ethclass. The community based on ethstyle becomes better able to develop and sustain its own leaders. The needs of its people are varied, and so are the resources the community can mobilize to fulfill its needs. Over time, the consequences of ethstyle are such as to produce a miniature society, a social world so complete for its inhabitants that they need have little, if any, contact with the outside world. Reciprocally, outsiders have little access to those on the inside of this type of ghetto: the boundary of an ethstyle people has highly restricted access.

Community control

To the degree to which a ghetto restricts access, it intensifies interaction, which in turn promotes communal solidarity and cultural homogeneity. Thus, after generations of ghetto experience, blacks who had been involuntarily taken from different African tribes, communities, nations, countries, and regions, now come to share a common culture derived from all heritages and from their American experience.

> Soul is a reflection of oppression and hardship, of faithlessness from other people, of lack of control and of the battle of the sexes. There is impiety and bittersweetness, and soul is almost literally an involvement with personal feelings, a turning inward rather than toward the community. (Warren, 1975:88)

Hannerz (1969:177) provides us with another description of black ghetto culture.

> Among the components of this ghetto-specific complex are for instance female household dominance; a ghetto-specific male role of somewhat varying expression including, among other emphases, toughness, sexual activity, and a fair amount of liquor consumption; a relatively conflict-ridden relationship between the sexes; rather intensive participation in informal social life outside the domestic domain; flexible household composition; fear of

trouble in the environment; a certain amount of suspiciousness toward other persons' motives; relative closeness to religion; particular food habits; a great interest in the music of the group; and a relatively hostile view of much of white America and its representatives.

Capitalizing on an idea frequently found in literature, Merton (1957) applies what he calls the *self-fulfilling prophecy* to individual behavior. He notes the tendency for people to conform to the predictions they make about themselves: they think they will succeed or fail, and thus they do. Extending this notion we may say that involuntary imposition of people-hood, on the assumption of commonality, may produce common charac-teristics even where none existed before, a kind of *socially fulfilling prophecy.*

> An ethnic culture does not have to be foreign, and all those who are one hundred percent American are not American in the same way. There is a black culture largely evolved in America as a response to black American conditions, just as black has become a term for an ethnic group only in America. As Singer describes it, there has been an ethnogenesis on Amer-ican ground. (Hannerz, 1969:104)

As Drake and Clayton (1962) put it, there is even an advantage to such homogeneity.

> Race consciousness breeds a demand for "racial solidarity," and as Ne-groes contemplate their existence as a minority in a white world which spurns them, they see their ultimate hope in presenting some sort of unified front against that world.

Such creation of commonality may be seen among many peoples; again, blacks have been used simply as one example among many.

Living in a social world filled with one's own people has many advan-tages. In locating and securing housing, finding employment, assuring help in emergencies, and in protecting life and property, the ghetto com-munity can be of great assistance. The assistance, however, has a price.

On one hand, the members of ghetto escape the personal control which nonghetto dwellers might wish to impose. Within a ghetto one may speak a language different than that spoken on the outside, one may worship a different god, eat different food, and behave in other ways that deviate from what may be expected outside the ghetto.

On the other hand, the members of a ghetto increase their control over each other by their very abandonment of those outside. The smaller na-ture of the social world of the ghetto permits greater surveillance. As in a small town, ghetto dwellers know a great deal about each other. They are "actual or potential participants in close personal relationships with one another" (Hannerz, 1969:12). Deviants from the values of the ghetto are therefore few. Should surveillance, gossip, and perhaps warnings fail to correct the errant one, the group has within its sole power the ultimate weapon to control the individual—expulsion.

Without the boundary that sets off the ghetto in the first place, expulsion would mean far less. Since the boundary makes possible the creation of the social world of the ghetto, however, to be expelled means to lose no less than one's world. As if having one's world at stake were not enough, there is no guarantee that others will accept the banished. On the contrary, membership in one people may mean automatic rejection from other peoples. For these reasons the community in a ghetto has significant control over the individuals who live there.

Ghetto and community

Let us now apply the principles of group control to ghetto communities based on ethclass and on ethstyle. Within the ethclass one must conform to both an ethnicity and to a specific class. Within an ethstyle the degrees of freedom are greater, because conformity to ethnicity alone is demanded. Extending this principle, we may add that, since exclusive occupation of an area restricts access between groups but intensifies it within, pressures toward conformity are greater in a ghetto than in an enclave. Mere concentration, a cluster, exercises the least control of all.

The ghetto hypothesis therefore must be qualified in yet another way: the survival of ethnic communities is more likely when they are based on ethstyle rather than on ethclass. Although the ethclass community demands greater conformity, it is also less complete and autonomous than an ethstyle community. When we add this second qualification to the previous one, that spatial concentration in itself is no guarantee of community, the ground is prepared for the third and final revision of the ghetto hypothesis.

Is it possible for a community to be created and/or sustained although its population is dispersed and scattered throughout a settlement? Whereas the ghetto hypothesis argued that communities broke up if dispersed, later investigators found that this was not necessarily the case. Through common places to meet and to talk to each other, through common activities and events, a people may create and sustain community. Today in the United States many ethnic groups are scattered, yet ethnicity continues to be important for many Americans. This is one indication that spatial concentration is not necessary for a community to exist. Many immigrant groups did move from the innercity to the suburbs, but they often took their ethnicity with them.

Ethnicity today is maintained as it was in the past—through social interaction. Such interaction may take place among people who are not neighbors, just as neighbors do not necessarily communicate with each other. Thus whereas spatial concentration is no guarantee of community, symbolic identification with others does create community, even without spatial concentration.

THE SYMBOLISM OF THE GHETTO

For some, ghettos are places where "they"—other people—should live. By isolating "them," some people think that the quality of their own lives is raised. Contact with others degrades, and therefore walling them inside a designated place prevents degrading contact.

As Louis Wirth (1928) observed, the ghetto can also be perpetuated by walling one's own inside a designated place. Others are not considered to be among the "chosen," and those chosen deign not to have contact with the unchosen but rather to be safely fortified.

Whether reserved for chosen peoples or for degraded others, the symbolism of the ghetto legitimates one standard of housing in the ghetto and another outside, one standard of housing code enforcement inside and another outside, one price for goods and services inside and another outside, and other double standards in mortgage financing, insurance, and such professional services in health, education, welfare, and police.

It is the symbolism of the ghetto that leads people to interpret unconsciously the same behavior in different ways. Asked why he had not taken up jogging, a ghetto resident reported that anyone running through the ghetto was likely to get arrested. Sure enough, as Hannerz (1969) reports, this same respondent was later arrested while running to the hospital to see his stricken mother.

The symbolism of the ghetto is also partly based on the assumption that peoplehood cannot survive if one people has contact with another. As we have already noted, contact can lead to communication, and communication does help to foster the intermingling of peoples. It may take a few centuries or even longer for a people's boundaries to change, but they do. The final question therefore becomes: is spatial segregation necessary to control contact between two or more peoples?

North-South variations

The symbolic (not spatial) nature of community and the different spatial forms that symbolism may take are evident in American regional differences. In Chapter 5 we examined the southern experience of late urbanization. In part because massive urbanization did not arrive in the South until the 1940s, northern and southern black/white relationships evolved in different ways. In the South, as blacks and whites came in contact with each other on many occasions, a system of "racial etiquette" became established: the Jim Crow "back of the bus," Jim Crow drinking fountains, Jim Crow entrances, or Jim Crow Bibles for witnesses in court. This racial etiquette served to keep the peoples socially distant from one another.

When the social distance between peoples is great, there is less need for spatial segregation. Slaves, for example, can live in the master's house, perform domestic tasks, and help raise his children, including nursing them. In American southern cities and towns, blacks could live just behind the houses of the white families for whom they worked.

By contrast, as social distance decreases, contact between peoples becomes regulated through space rather than by enforced standards of "proper" behavior. Ethnicity then becomes a set of boundaries governing spatial inclusion and exclusion.

Thus in northern cities the blacks became residentially isolated from whites. The Jim Crow practices were not necessary since social contacts between blacks and whites were infrequent. As blacks and whites, in other words, did not use the same establishments, separate drinking fountains, for example, were not regarded as necessary. In the North, spatial segregation accomplished what social distance achieved in the South.

> The urban ghetto . . . performs many of the same functions, both social and spatial, as the plantation. Both the plantation and the ghetto are adaptations in space and time to the racism of the society in which they exist. (Davis and Donaldson, 1975:4)

These regional differences could be observed in white/Chicano relations in the Southwest, to Hispanic/black relations in the North, as well as in other groups within and without the United States. Once again we see that segregation is a symbolic, not purely a spatial, process. Did blacks in the South live lives any less segregated than blacks in the North? Not in terms of symbolic ecology, which conceives of segregation as a symbolic process whereby a people is set apart from another, not necessarily spatially.

NONETHNIC GHETTOS

There are other bases of ghettos in addition to those of ethnicity, religion, national origin, and race. Skid row, where the author lived in order to study (1965, 1968), is based on an assumed commonality. In the perception of the respectable members of the larger society, skid rowers are all "bums." The fact that some of them have worked all their lives and then have retired to skid row because they preferred living on their meager pensions or from irregular sources rather than in state institutions makes no difference; they are all "bums."

Skid rowers have common activities, such as attending mission services, asking for handouts, and socializing in their taverns and bars. They also help each other to find a flop for the night, instruct each other in how to manipulate the police, and tell each other where jobs can be found. They also share common values in believing that they are exploited, treated unfairly, and stereotyped (Blumberg, Shipley, and Shandler, 1973). Without power of any kind they are unable to act on the sense of unity that they have, but that does not stop them from distinguishing between "us" and "them," nor from condemning what they see as their own turncoats—the mission-stiffs. Skid row, in summary, contains the same features that constitute an exclusive area as does one based on ethnicity.

Clark (1973) has used the term in describing what she sees as "geriatric ghettos": in this case, economic discrimination makes the elderly less able to move outward with the rest of the population. Trapped behind in decaying areas, they experience involuntary residence. La Gory (1977) argues that such age segregation is positively related to racial segregation.

John Lofland (1968) has described the concentrations of youth around large universities as "the youth ghetto." In his discussion he draws on parallels to the ethnic ghettos of the past and relates this to the increasing territorial segregation of the aged.

SUMMARY

Urbanologists distinguish three types of spatial concentrations of peoples: a specific area may be said (1) to have a concentration of (a cluster), (2) to be predominately occupied by (an enclave), or (3) to be exclusively occupied by persons with some common characteristic (a ghetto). The index of segregation measures the relative segregation-integration of peoples, where a value of zero reflects complete integration and 100 equals total segregation.

The majority of people prefer integrated residential areas. Therefore the exclusive occupancy of an area by one people indicates, in part, that residence in a ghetto is involuntary to a large extent (although some do prefer to live there).

The ghetto hypothesis held that immigrants settled in the zone of transition when they first arrived and that, as economic resources permitted, they moved outwards from the center, leaving their ethnicity behind, and assimilating into a common "American" way of life in the suburbs. Later revisions to the ghetto hypothesis traced differences in ethnic communities to ethclass as compared to ethstyle. This comparison indicated that spatial concentration by itself was no guarantee that the residents would form a community.

Community control of its member individuals does increase as the boundary surrounding the community restricts the access of outsiders to it. Restricted access is accomplished through social interaction, which may or may not involve spatial proximates. Thus although spatial concentration is no guarantee of community, symbolic identification and interaction with others does create community, even when its members are spatially dispersed.

Whether withdrawal of a people takes place because others consider themselves to be superior to that people, or whether that people consider certain others to be inferior, the fundamental fear is that of contact with "them." In thus distinguishing between "us" and "them" a double standard is erected—reflected in housing, prices, services, and basic values—and legitimated throughout the society of which the ghetto is but a part.

Therefore, although the ghetto is an area—a place with a population (black, Jewish, German), an organization (bounded, with restricted access and exclusive occupancy), an economy (single or multiclass), a technology (walls, newspapers)—most fundamentally it is a symbol, a place where someone else may belong. Since others may someday decide that that someone else is us, the only safe and sure course is to abolish the ghetto for all—beginning with the racism on which it is usually based.

STUDY QUESTIONS

1. Differentiate between a ghetto, and enclave, and a cluster, and give an example of each.
2. What is the difference between an ethstyle and an ethclass?
3. What is the symbolism of the ghetto?
4. What is the relationship between social distance and spatial segregation?
5. What is spatial determinism?

SUGGESTED READINGS

Cozen, Kathleen Neils. *Immigrant Milwaukee* (Cambridge, Mass.: Harvard University Press, 1976).

Hannerz, Ulf. *Soulside: Inquiries into Ghetto Culture and Community* (New York: Columbia University Press, 1969).

Wirth, Louis. *The Ghetto* (Chicago: University of Chicago Press, 1928).

chapter 8

ENCLAVES, CLUSTERS, AND VOLUNTARY ASSOCIATIONS

United Press International

SOCIAL AND RESIDENTIAL DIFFERENTIATION

Social differentiation is a universal human phenomenon and without it society would simply cease to exist. Categorizing people goes along with differentiation: we differentiate between people on the basis of their assumed membership in groups in order to survive in a *World of Strangers,* as Lynn Lofland (1973) puts it. The process of social differentiation only becomes destructive when such definitions are imposed and without valid knowledge, and when the label hides the individual.

Social differentiation leads to *residential differentiation,* and this phenomenon also is universal. Separate areas for different peoples are found in urban settlements ancient and modern, in folk, preindustrial, industrial, and postindustrial societies, in planned and in sprawling settlements, in socialist and capitalist urban areas, in military, religious, and commercial centers (Timms, 1971).

The universality of residential differentiation suggests that it is important to the urbanite. Living near "one's own," the vast population of the entire settlement is reduced to a small community of those with whom one can comfortably live. As Timms (1971:5) notes: "The effect of residential differentiation is to divide the urban fabric into a series of more or less distinct subcommunities." One of the effects of this differentiation is to make the city more manageable for its residents. (We see this more clearly when we examine the individual urbanite in Part Five.)

Residential differentiation leads to ghettos, enclaves, and clusters; our concern now is with enclaves. Enclaves are formed by people who desire to live near "their own kind," whomever their own kind may include. Unlike the ghetto in which the area is exclusively occupied by one people, in the enclave one people only predominate. We must remember that for a people to predominate they need not be the majority; rather, there just must be more of them than of any other single group.

Voluntary co-residence

Although they may live elsewhere, many peoplehoods prefer to live near one another, thus creating an enclave. Is it possible for a people to prefer to live together but also for them to be rejected by others? Of course. Human behavior often springs from more than one source of motivation. For some, whether or not they are rejected by others is quite irrelevant to their needs.

They need to speak the same language: German, Yiddish, street talk, or jive; they need to eat "decent" food: soul, southern, Puerto Rican, or Chinese; they need to have the savage beast within them soothed by "real" music: the blues, acid rock, Muzak, or maybe baroque. Only one's own people know how to entertain "properly," discuss politics, analyze problems, worship, drink, dance, and behave.

To satisfy these basic human needs, then, one must seek out one's own regardless of whether rejected by "others." Further, if one's own did not or could not satisfy one's need, why live among them?

But if rejected by others, does one have a choice of residence? Herein lies the distinction between ghetto and enclave. The ghetto dweller has little or no choice but to live among whomever others consider to be his or her own. "Wherever I go the police arrest me, not for anything I have done but for what I am, a bum. So I live here on skid row where they leave me alone." "I'd like to get out of this dump but no one in the other neighborhoods will rent to me."

Such illustrative comments by ghetto dwellers indicate that residence in a ghetto is largely involuntary. Involuntary residence does not mean that many would not live there even if they had a choice. Why, then, do they want a choice? The reasons include both abstract principles such as freedom and practical desires, such as choosing one's own neighbors. It is our conviction that everyone ought to have a choice, and furthermore a choice among as many alternatives as possible. The ghetto is a spatial concentration of people which can only be formed under conditions of no choice. When people are given a choice, ghettos disappear and are replaced by enclaves. What is lost with the disappearance of ghettos? Nothing positive, in our assessment.

Enclaves are quite different. The fact that enclaves include other people, as well as the fact that the members of such peoplehoods live in other areas, testifies to the voluntary nature of enclaves. To destroy them would be to lose much of the pluralism of contemporary society. Without the many types of enclaves we now have, the urban environment would become far more homogeneous, far more uniform from one part to another. Few would find any satisfaction in such a "1984 world."

LITTLE ITALY: AN ENCLAVE

Enclaves are symbolically organized by attraction, while ghettos owe their organization more to rejection. Voluntary and involuntary forces are at work in both; nevertheless their different mixture makes a real difference. In an effort to understand ghetto life we used blacks as our primary example, indicating that there is nothing inherent in any people that links them always to any specific sociospatial form. This holds true for enclaves as well. Different peoples may be found in enclaves, and the same "people" may be in enclaves in one era but not in another. Recognizing these variations, we will use Italian-Americans as our example of enclave residents, just as we used blacks as our example of ghetto residents. It is convenient to use them because we have data from four studies of Italian-American communities extending over 35 years.

In 1947 Walter Firey published his study of the symbolic ecology of Boston, including the North End, which was (and is) a traditional Italian community. In 1962 Herb Gans published his findings on the Italian-American community of the West End of Boston. In 1968 Gerald Suttles published his research, which was based on field work in the Addams area of Chicago, an area with many Italian-American residents. Finally, with Joan Nacarano as field director and Jerry Harrison as an associate in 1974, the author published a study of "Little Italy" in New York City. These four studies, as well as others (Cordasco and Bucchioni, 1974; Lopreato, 1970), provide us with detailed knowledge about Italian-American enclaves.[1]

Migration and clustering

Clustering, rather than enclave or ghetto development, is the only alternative possible when the numbers of a people are small. As noted in the previous chapter, blacks were initially clustered at many points in New York City prior to their increase in numbers and the development of Harlem. The Italians, too, followed that pattern. Before 1860, only about 20,000 Italians had entered the United States. While the majority landed at New York, nine out of ten of them moved to other cities as well as to rural areas. With negligible numbers even in the largest city—1,463 in New York—only weak clusters were evident (Park and Miller, 1921).

In Chapter 2 we discussed the "push" and "pull" factors in migration. Both are evident in the changes in the Italian pattern of migration. As background factors, civil war and strife marked Italy both before and after its unification in 1870. The social and economic upheaval initially characteristic of the northern provinces, especially Liguria, swept nationwide and perhaps even intensified in the south, especially in Sicily. The "pull" factor was the need for labor in the booming industrialization then underway in the United States. The yearly average number of Italians entering the United States first quintupled to 5,576 in the 1870s, then swelled to first 30 and then 65 times the 1860 figure in the 1880s and 1890s. This migratory stream became a torrent when more than 185,000 Italians entered annually after 1900, nearly 2.5 million entering from 1900 to 1910 (DiPalma, 1905).

Given these large numbers, although tens and even hundreds of thousands left their port of entry for interior settlements and rural areas, hundreds of thousands still remained where they had entered. They, in turn, clustered at hundreds of different locations within their settlement, in New York in our example.

The consequences of chain migration are evident in the homogeneity of the origin of each cluster's inhabitants. Within each growing spatial concentration, most persons were not only Italian but they were from the

---

[1] Students would also profit from screening the videocassette especially prepared for this section. Order from publisher: *Little Italy: An Ethnic Enclave.*

same region, province, and often even the same hometown. Park and Miller (1921), Riis (1898), and the MacDonalds (1964), who all offer evidence on this point, note as examples the concentration of Sicilians from the town of Cinisi in midtown Manhattan, those from Avigliano (Basilicata) in East Harlem, and the Calabrians on Mulberry Street. Recognizing that the development of many clusters, among Italians and non-Italians alike, followed the same process, let us focus in detail on the cluster that was located on Mulberry Street.

Mulberry Street Bend

The original Dutch town of New York was laid out on a gridiron plan, and in spite of protests, including one by Frederic Law Olmstead, the grid was successively extended until the entire island of Manhattan was uniformly gridiron pattern. Streets that depart from the decreed uniformity are so unusual that New Yorkers seem to take notice of them. Thus, while bends in streets are common in many places and not paid the slightest attention, a very slight turn on a street on New York's Lower East Side has for long been known simply as Mulberry Street Bend (Bengough, 1895).

The Bend and the streets around it have been hosts to many different immigrant groups. Canal Street, which lies about one and one half blocks to the north of Mulberry's bend, was, of course, originally a canal. The canal carried refuse and raw sewage from the old Collect Pond, an open sewer noxious to a degree difficult to imagine today. The area was also near the employment centers downtown, and in other ways conformed to Burgess's description of a typical zone of transition. For these several reasons, anyone with a choice lived elsewhere, and those without resources, usually the latest immigrant group, were the only ones with no choice but to live here.

As an interesting aside, this area of New York City, known as the Lower East Side, became so identified as a receiving basin for immigrants that it continues to function in that capacity today—currently housing large numbers of Puerto Ricans.[2]

Bounding the enclave

The Germans had moved into Mulberry Bend sometime after 1800. They were invaded by the Irish and so moved north to create what be-

---

[2] Lest my friends and former neighbors on the Lower East Side (at 12th and C in the early 60s) think I am saying that only the most recently arrived or impoverished live on the Lower East Side, let me hasten to say "nay, not at all." In addition to students of many sorts, professors, artists, models, theater-types, junkies, speed freaks, and assorted loonies far beyond our powers of description, there are also traditional religious (Hasidic Jewish), bohemian (Greenwich Village), and deviant communities (Bowery) found there, among others—as devoted New York buffs (who are usually nonnatives) will tell you.

came known as Kleindeutschland (Little Germany) in the same general area as the Little Italy we studied. The Irish were invaded by Italians, Chinese, and Polish Jews in the latter part of the 1800s. The Irish moved north and invaded Kleindeutschland, eventually succeeding the Germans and turning the area into an Irish ward.

The influence of physical development on the organization of space (what might be described as human-created topography) is evident on both Canal and Bowery streets. In 1834 a rail line was laid along the Bowery, and in 1870 the rail line was elevated. Homeless men were among those who lived under the El, and thus the Bowery became a boundary for groups moving north, dividing them in general into eastern and western streams.[3] Second, the construction of the Manhattan Bridge in 1909 made the widening of Canal Street necessary. Once this formerly narrow street became a major thoroughfare, the Italians living south of it felt cut off and so moved north of Canal Street. Movement northward was also forced by the demolition of many tenements near the Bend and by the creation of Columbus Park.

As the Italians moved north of Canal Street they invaded the Irish, who in turn moved farther north to become invaders of other people's spaces. Rarely are these invasion-succession transitions made without conflict, and the present instance was no exception. Although the Italians could not literally transplant their peasant villages to America's largest urban center, they carried over patterns that existed in their agricultural villages, attempting to transform space according to the Southern Italian traditions. Closely grouped living conditions characterized the rural life of the southern Italian, but in New York they were confronted with a new environment of different spaces, densities, disorders, and distances (Handlin, 1973). Given their near-indigent economic conditions, as well as their symbolic identification with their community, the Italians stayed within their immediate area.

Ethnic division of labor

Paradoxically, while it was overwhelmingly the males who established the beachhead in search of employment, the women and children who arrived later frequently found more employment opportunities than did their men. The southern Italian male immigrant was one of the least prepared by previous background to cope with the environment in which he debarked in New York. Predominantly peasant farmers, Italian immigrants of the time were without economic resources to move inland or to purchase farmland, livestock, and machinery. Per capita cash-on-hand on arrival, as documented by Di Palma (1905), was so limited as to require

[3] The Bowery served to divide only after the skid row was fully developed and after the Italian bocce courts had been established several blocks east of Little Italy, on the other side of the Bowery.

immigrants to seek the cheapest housing available that was also close to their jobs.

Given this paucity of resources, men had to accept employment that others refused to take and/or allow their women and children to take jobs as operatives, especially in the garment district. Summarizing the literature they reviewed, the MacDonalds (1964) point out the threat this employment posed for the traditional male-dominated southern Italian family structure. Such stresses were, in part, minimized by careful selection of the type of employment taken up by women and control of the work place itself. Southern Italian women "avoided work as domestic servants, which was regarded as a threat to their chastity" (MacDonald and MacDonald, 1964:91). They chose instead industries where they were not forced to work with men, and then relied on their relative ethnic concentration at work to chaperone one another. This system was beneficial to employers who used parental authority "as a form of sub-management whereby young girls were put to work under their mothers or aunts" (MacDonald and MacDonald, 1964:92).

Although chain migration was the pattern followed by many southern Italians coming to the United States, the data for the period from 1880 to 1920 are inadequate to show just what proportion of the migrants followed this pattern. Shipping companies, employment agencies, the Mafia, and others lured unsuspecting persons into migration only to abandon them after they had been exploited; (even the "benevolent" *padroni* received a 10 percent commission for financial backing of immigrants' ocean passage in steerage). Also, no doubt some kin also failed to honor kinship obligations and left the newly arrived to fend for themselves. Given the almost catastrophic social and economic conditions of southern Italy from the 1860s through the turn of the century, no doubt still others who had no kin in this country fled their homeland. The magnitude of chain migration, however, is evident to some extent from the developing ethnic division of labor that emerged during this same period.

In the 1850s, forms of employment particularly "Italian" had been organ-grinding, pasta-making, confectionery and artificial flowers, child musicians, and fruit stands. Only 5 percent of the Italian population had been employed in manual labor. Economic and social upheaval after 1860 forced thousands of persons ill-equipped for urban living to migrate, and left them no choice but to seek employment in already densely crowded districts (largely in central locations), where newcomers were totally lacking in political power and ability to compete for jobs.

Some employment became available through the provision of ethnic goods, foods, and services, which as we noted were also found in the ghetto. Italian pushcart peddlers and vendors of other goods were commonplace in the Little Italies, in Greenwich Village, and in Harlem. The greengrocers often expanded their trade areas beyond the confines of their enclaves, selling to other segments of the urban population.

Hand in hand with concentration in particular kinds of employment came residential concentration. As noted, immigrants tended to live within walking distance of their jobs, partly due to long hours, low wages, and daily-hiring practices by employers who were located principally within the central business district. Residential segregation throughout New York City took place by ethnic affiliation. While not every person in an enclave was a member of that ethnic group at any given moment in its history, the largest number of its inhabitants were of that group and gave the area its identity. As Handlin points out in *The Newcomers* (1959), "For most New Yorkers, ethnic affiliation remained significant to the third generation and beyond. Even in the 1920s, the great-grandchildren of the German or Irish immigrants of the 1830s or 1840s and the great-great-grandchildren of the Yankees of 1800 still had meaningful ties to the groups of their ancestors. Those ties established the character of the group's identification."

Internal residential differentiation

Southern Italian enclaves were organized by values important to these immigrants: beginning with region, province, and hometown. We have already noted that, within the Little Italy which we studied, not only were the majority from the same region (southern) and province (Calabria), but that, within the enclave, entire streets or perhaps contiguous tenements were filled by persons from the same hometown. Although only traces of this pattern could be seen in the 1970s, Park and Miller (1921) reported this pattern as widespread in the early part of this century.

In the beginning, the Italians occupied the least desirable blocks of the old East Side. They lived at first in rear tenements behind the Irish, then moved out to better quarters as their position improved and as their predecessors left. The district was also transformed in the 1890s by the new-style tenements (first built by philanthropists and located near Elizabeth Street and Mott Street), which were built to hold a far larger population than ever before (Handlin, 1959:34).

In his 1926 publication, Zorbaugh observed how natural and human-created boundaries frequently divide a settlement into separate areas. In examining the development of Little Italy we also have noted the influence of the Bowery and of Canal Street. Recognizing that wide thoroughfares are obstacles to neighboring, Houston Street, another wide and heavily traveled thoroughfare, became the northern border of this ethnic enclave.

Canal Street on the south, the Bowery on the east, and Houston Street on the north constituted stable and long-lasting boundaries of the emerging Little Italy. On west, however, the boundary line fluctuated between Broadway and Lafayette Street, which is lined by factories and warehouses that extend westward to the contemporary artists' community of Soho. Little Italy, then, became bounded by physical barriers to outside contact as organized by its members' values.

Ecological order within the enclave

Italian use of space was strongest in Little Italy from 1900 to 1940. It was during this period that the area was vital and unmistakably southern Italian in character. Having defined space as their own, and having given selected boundary streets significance, southern Italian immigrants proceeded to shape their community according to their unique cultural values.

Southern Italians historically have used Little Italies to reinforce religious and family solidarity. By restricting intrusion and maintaining internal solidarity, the group created its own enclave. It is important to note here that Italians neither wanted nor chose to be part of the larger foreign society. Because the Italians actively sought to remain within their designated boundaries, various social institutions developed that both fulfilled the needs of the residents and enforced conformity to traditional values. Given the external isolation and the internal organization of life within the confines of the enclaves, Little Italy became a microcosm within a larger urban environment.

To understand and appreciate the quality of life in Little Italy, we must understand that religion and the family were extremely powerful social institutions for the southern Italian. For the peasant immigrant,

> . . . the very process of adjusting immigrant ideas to the conditions of the United States made religion paramount as a way of life. It was unthinkable not to be a member; it demanded a considerable feat of the imagination to conceive of what it would mean to be excluded, to draw down the censure of the entire community, to be barred from every social occasion. (Handlin, 1959:117, 119)

Family and church determined the quality and even the existence of other social institutions.

In the southern Italian peasant community, family life was considered the norm to the extent that individual ambition was not enthusiastically favored. The emphasis was conservative, as in religion, and on family honor. Family solidarity was the basic code and was manifested by uniformity of behavior and strict adherence to family traditions.

The extended family has traditionally been a core institution of the Italian culture, even in America. Two and three generations of a family have lived for many years, if not in the same apartment, then in the same apartment house. The solidarity of the extended family was so strong that moving to a new residence was often contingent on one's parents moving, too. The Italian family structure stressed intergenerational continuity, which helped to create and maintain a characteristically Italian neighborhood such as Little Italy.

The father held the authoritarian position within the Italian family. The male made most decisions, especially those involving the family. His position was accepted by the women and children. Wives were in a subordinate position; their lives revolved around the home and the Catholic church.

Outside the home, men and women were rarely seen together in Little Italy. While the women went to shops or stayed at home, groups of men were frequently found in front of the many social clubs or societies in Little Italy. Inside the clubs the men spent hours sitting around tables, deeply involved in card games. These male societies had a great social and religious importance to their members and further served to keep the southern Italian within his community. They provided insulation from the outside. The members of each club came from the same village or town in southern Italy. These clubs illustrate the stratification of Little Italy by subsections based on native Italian geography.

In terms of spatial considerations, "intense family interaction is congruent with low separations of people from other people" (Michelson, 1970), a principle demonstrated in the interaction of the southern Italians. Through intense contact and interaction, the conservative bent was supported by a near-universal surveillance which, in turn, supplied needed behavior control. In the streets, in hallways, staircases, apartment doors, in the spaces connecting apartment buildings, and inside the home, privacy was minimal.

Symbolic boundaries that reflected Italian-American values were evident everywhere in Little Italy. For example, there was rigid segregation by sex. As Gans (1962:48) noted in his study of Boston West Enders:

> . . . much of their segregation of leisure takes place within the home: the women sit together in one room, the men in another. Even when everyone gathers around the kitchen table, the men group together at one end, the women at the other, and few words are exchanged between them. Men are distinctly uncomfortable in the company of women, and vice versa, but the men find it harder to interact with the women than the women with the men.

The importance of religion was demonstrated by the many Catholic churches within Little Italy. The churches in the Italian enclaves were organized with respect to the patron saint of a city or a peasant village in southern Italy or Sicily. However, the largest church in Little Italy is Old St. Patrick's Cathedral at Mott and Prince streets. Built during the War of 1812, it was, as we have previously noted and as its name suggests, an Irish parish. The invasion and succession of the Italians, combined with the departure of the Irish, forced the church to orient itself to its new parishioners. This church did not reorient itself until the Italians, denied participation, formed their own parish with Italian priests. Only much later in the invasion process was St. Patrick's taken over by the Italians, who then reoriented it. One such orientation was educational services.

St. Patrick's Grammar School illustrates the interaction between the needs of the Italians, the needs of the church, and the laws of the state. Italian parents sent their children to this school rather than to public schools outside the community—slowing the assimilation process by partially insulating children against the influence of other groups. St. Patrick's today also provides the community with a senior citizen's club and with an active youth center. These facilities demonstrate the desire of Little Italy's residents to pass time within the confines of their community, not outside its borders.

Even today, outsiders who walk along Mott or Mulberry streets might find it difficult to believe that they are in the same city that harbors Lincoln Center, Radio City Music Hall, and Saks Fifth Avenue. The grandeur of New York City has not been permitted to permeate into this community. Life within Little Italy seems uncomplicated and untouched by the greater problems that usually plague urban dwellers. The general impression is that Little Italy is a small village where everyone knows one another.

People seem to be in constant motion, walking up and down the narrow streets, shopping and talking to shopowners and pushcart dealers. Groups of boys cluster outside the many cafes. Mothers with carriages meet on the streets. Men gather in front of the numerous social clubs. More than in other communities, local streets seem to serve a great social function for Little Italy's residents.

The sidewalk becomes an extension of the home, and many family activities occur on the streets. People remain close by their buildings, as if guarding their territory. On nice days, Little Italy's residents bring out their kitchen chairs and remain outside talking to friends or relatives, playing cards, or conducting business for hours. Coffee is made and brought to the streets to drink. Young children remain close to their parents, playing on the streets under their watchful eyes. Adolescents gather and "hang around" together—sitting on cars, playing stickball, or just talking. Once again, street life is segregated on age-sex lines—that is, age peers of the same sex share the same locations. "Nearest their house stoops are the women and the old people followed by infants, young girls, young boys, and adult males in that order" (Suttles, 1968:74).

Residents appear to be expressing a desire to remain within their community and to keep contact with outsiders to a minimum. The residents find their enjoyment within the neighborhood, and particularly on the streets, partly because there are few public parks. But even more important, the residents do not want to leave Little Italy, and thus generally make do with what is there. Their isolation is voluntary.

Youngsters also use available space for amusement. Parking lots, street corners, and doorways provide them with places to play. When they do leave the neighborhood seeking other diversions they usually go as a group. This enables them to reinforce their group identity in other locations. They are also able to protect each other if need be.

While the street provides a significant social function for Little Italy's residents, it also has become the place for the Italian *fiesta*, not only for the immigrants but for people from the surrounding area. The street festivals demonstrate the spatial expression of religious traditions. The social clubs sponsor these feasts in honor of various local patron saints. People from outside the community who wish to share in the richness of the Italian heritage jam the streets for blocks, eating, playing games at the many concessions, or just walking up and down. The celebration of religious events has continued in part because it gives immigrants an opportunity to renew or strengthen their identification with old customs.

Enclave decline

During the 1940s and 1950s a slow movement of residents out of Little Italy occurred for a variety of reasons. The pattern of immigration changed. Fewer and fewer Italians entered the United States, and those who did enter frequently settled where their relatives had now moved, in suburbia. As the population that was left behind in the traditional enclave aged, natural increase diminished. Family size also shrank, as within the American population as a whole. These conditions were intensified in the 1950s and 1960s and thus Little Italy began to lose its vitality and Italian character. The decline of Little Italy is still in process at the present time.

Italians in Little Italy are no longer of sufficient numbers to compete successfully for space in a high-density area of the city. Previous boundaries have been permeated by other ethnic minorities, by derelicts, and by commercial enterprises that have taken over space. Although the Chinese have lived in Chinatown south of Canal Street for many generations, their swelling numbers require additional space. The Chinese are therefore crossing into Little Italy from the south in numbers constituting a major invasion. They are willing to crowd large families into tenements that recently housed lesser numbers of Italians. The present pattern of Chinese immigration, by the way, resembles that of the Italians at the turn of the century.

While the skid row population of the Bowery is not as large as it was in the past, many derelicts still live there. Whereas previously skid rowers were not able to penetrate into Little Italy, the conversion of former tenements into flophouses, combined with the overall decrease in Italian neighborhood control, means that an increasing number of derelicts and alcoholics roam the streets of Little Italy. Although they have not taken over the physical space, they have disrupted community life in Little

Italy. This indicates that Italians can no longer defend their territory against unwanted intruders.

In addition to the intrusion by the Chinese and the skid rowers, another ethnic group has begun to move into Little Italy. Hispanic peoples are starting to create their own territories in the blocks just to the west of the Bowery and south of Houston Street. Spanish grocery stores, Spanish restaurants, even an Hispanic men's social club now exist in this area. Spanish masses at Old St. Patrick's began nearly a decade ago and now are very well attended. Masses in Italian are less and less frequent and attendance at them is poor. As a further example of invasion and succession, now even the bocce courts are attracting Latins.

The Italian population continues to decline as the old people die and are not replaced by younger people. If the current pattern continues, Little Italy will no longer exist. The space once defined as "Italian" will probably be redefined by the Chinese population pushing its way north of Canal Street. When and if this occurs, the stage of succession in the ecological cycle will once again have taken place.

The future of Little Italy is partly in the hands of its present residents. If Little Italy is to survive, these people must remain in their ethnic enclave, maintain its Italian character, and increase their numbers. To a great extent, the few remaining residents understand this. They know that their community's continuance depends on their ability to make the area attractive once again to Italians.

An affirmative response has been the creation of the Little Italy Restoration Association. This organization is trying to encourage the City Planning Commission to designate Little Italy a historical district. It is hoped that in this way the identity and character of the Italian community can be preserved.

In spite of their efforts to preserve their nearly century-old community, the obstacles the residents of Little Italy face are enormous. To change not only the number of southern Italians entering New York but to change the present pattern of where they settle, from suburbia back into the central city, seems beyond the abilities of the present population. It therefore seems likely that within the next decade the various invasions that we have reviewed will have moved into all but a small central core of Little Italy. Although the core itself may survive for a time as a tourist attraction, even the tourist commercial establishments may disappear without its supporting community.

The Germans withdrew and were pushed out of the Lower East Side by the East European Jews, who in turn shifted north and east as the Irish moved in. Then came the Italians, who were being pushed from behind by the Chinese, and who in turn pushed out the Irish. Now it is the Chinese and the Hispanics who are doing the invading, and it is the Italians who are doing the retreating. The ecological process of invasion and succession goes on.

CLUSTERS

Population, organization, economy, technology, and symbolism may combine in yet a third way to produce what we have called a cluster. Although both ghettos and enclaves begin as clusters, this does not mean that clusters necessarily develop into either enclaves or ghettos. Further, as the examples of the Jews and of the Italians in suburbia suggest, clustering may follow earlier enclave or ghetto existence.

An example of contemporary clustering is that found in the Haight of San Francisco. First the beatniks were clustered there in the 1950s (Kerouac, 1958), the "hippies" were then concentrated in the area in the 1960s (Yablonsky, 1968), and now the "street people" live there. According to Baumohl and Miller (1974), the street people are the uneducated, the unskilled, the disoriented (often from drug usage), the lame, and the addicted. Downwardly mobile, mostly white and under 30, four of five are male. In Baumohl and Miller's assessment, the street people cluster in the Haight as it is "a community in which no questions are asked and in which they can lose themselves."

While many examples of clusters could be given, perhaps two others will provide the necessary context for our analysis. Pilcher studied the longshoremen of Portland in detail, concluding that they represented a dispersed community. In our terms they are clustered, not residentially, but through their hiring halls. Since this example underscores the communication basis of our symbolic perspective of communal life, some attention to their ecological pattern is in order.

> The union is the basic institution since it regulates the hiring and the work and transmits a sense of identity to all of its members. . . .
>
> The longshoremen are not hired by company representatives nor do they consistently accept employment from certain stevedore companies, rather they are dispatched from a union operated hiring hall on a rotating basis. . . .
>
> The hiring system also has the effect of bringing all the longshoremen together in the hiring hall in an entirely random manner. Each longshoreman will at some time be in the hiring hall with every other longshoreman in the port and will undoubtedly have occasion to engage in sociable conversation, play cards, or have coffee or beer with every other longshoreman. . . .
>
> After the hiring, many of the men who have not secured employment for the day hang around the hall on the chance that they will be hired for a late job after the regular hiring period, thus creating another opportunity for social contact with other longshoremen.
>
> This effect is again heightened by the necessity to take part in the operation of the union. All union members are required to attend monthly meetings, and to vote in all elections. (Pilcher, 1972:114–15)

As this example indicates, social interaction may be intensive and collective, shaping a community, even though its members do not live next door to one another. Thus whether people live in the same locale is not of primary interest. The fundamental question is not who are one's next-door neighbors, but with whom one has symbolic interaction. While in earlier eras interaction may have been possible primarily with spatial proximates, the people next door, that is no longer true in today's urban environment.

Clusters of "gay people" represent but a variation of the same symbolic processes. Gays are drawn from a wide variety of religious, racial, national origin, and income groups. They assume commonality because of their sexual preference, in spite of the many other ways in which they differ.

Using what he considered to be the "most current and accurate" of the gay directories, Martin Levine (1977) plotted the locations of institutions (bars, bookstores, steam baths, churches, restaurants, cruising districts, and movie theaters) which serve the male homosexual in Boston, New York, Chicago, San Francisco, and Los Angeles. Summarizing the number of such places in each of the concentrated areas in which he observed them to be located, he used the percentage of an area's total to the total in each city as one of his two measures of areal concentration. The second measure was the "ratio of the total sum of the land mass of each area compared to the total land mass of the city." Just as gay institutions were found by Levine to be concentrated in specialized areas, so were the areas found to be but small portions of the total area of the cities: for example, Boston has 83 percent of gay locations in less than 2 percent of the total city landmass.

With respect to the culture of the area, Levine notes that gay language is used, gay fashion is "ubiquitous," and gestures of affection between men are openly exchanged.

> For example, two men are frequently seen walking with their arms around each other's waist or holding hands. These open displays of homosexuality rarely envoke sanctions. . . . In other places, this behavior quickly elicits harsh sanctions. (Levine, 1977:13)

Regarding their isolation, again Levine, among others (Humphreys, 1970) observes:

> Gays, whether their condition is known or hidden, are always aware that heterosexuals regard them as socially unacceptable. As a reaction to this, many homosexuals have withdrawn from meaningful social relations with members of conventional society and have restricted their social life and primary relations to other homosexuals. (Levine, 1977:15)

While there are substantial numbers of gays living in such areas as Beacon Hill, Greenwich Village, New Town (Chicago), and West Hollywood, and while they even may predominate in such areas as Castro Village and the Boy's Town area of West Hollywood, at least an equal number of homosexuals live in widely scattered parts of American cities. The undeniable phenomenon of the gay social world indicates that communities may be created on nonterritorial bases.

To summarize, clusters may be spatially located or they may be dispersed. In either case their basis is symbolic interaction. Those members of a cluster who do live near one another may move elsewhere and yet continue to participate in the cluster through symbolic interaction. Living near one another, however, usually does make symbolic interaction easier and therefore strengthens the group provided symbolic identification continues.

VOLUNTARY ASSOCIATIONS

A final variation on the symbolic processes creating communal environmental forms concerns the role of voluntary associations. While such associations flourish in ghetto and enclave alike, as we have already observed, they can exist outside either. Taking on some of the functions of ghetto and enclave, voluntary associations may provide for the recent migrant a link between the traditional and the urban way of life. While numerous examples could be drawn from our own American experience, including the recently arrived Puerto Ricans (Rogler, 1972), conditions are such in West African urbanization as to make an example drawn from there more effective.

As Kenneth Little (1968:312, 322) points out in his study of the role of voluntary associations, West African urban workers frequently spend only part of the year in the urban settlement: "They may own property, make repeated visits, spend part of the year there, but . . . their social life remains in some other part of the country." Given such conditions of temporary residence, voluntary associations take on added importance.

> One of the ways in which associations aid the migrant's adaptation in these respects is by providing him with information about what is going on in the town. . . . An association keeps him in touch not only with its own people at home but with the town's institutions. It serves as a go-between if, for example, he needs an interpreter, and it introduces him to useful contacts, such as employers of labour. . . . The association also reduces the migrant's isolation by acting as a "civilizing" agency on his behalf. It inculcates new standards of dress, social behaviour and personal hygiene; . . .
>
> What the migrant learns is also very helpful to him in practical terms. There are, for example, the association's rules, including fines for late attendance at meetings, which teach useful habits of punctuality. Thrift is encouraged by the demand for regular payment of dues, and its practice is taught by mutual benefit schemes as well as by savings clubs themselves. . . . They teach him, in fact, how to keep an account of cash and the safest way in which to conduct his own business dealings. More specifically, associations concerned with a particular trade accept initiates for training. . . .
>
> Finally, associations which have a tribally mixed membership enable the migrant to meet on friendly terms people of different origin. (Little, in Fava, 1968:314–15)

Voluntary associations are an important part of urban life—or that of urban political life. Harwood observes:

> The Irish arrived with family traditions, parish-church organizations, and associations devoted to the cause of national liberation. They had ward heelers and elective officials who had come up from within their ranks and who saw to it that able-bodied male constituents were kept employed. Indeed, the political power that the Irish mustered in the large eastern cities has no parallel within the Negro communities. This enabled the Irish to stabilize their economic situation and even overcome discrimination against Irish workers. The ability to grant franchises, tax concessions, and public-works contracts gave the Irish politician a control over the Irish urban fate that no other immigrant bloc ever achieved to the same extent through the political offices of the city. Spokesmen for "reverse discrimination" or even "black power" could, if they wished, point for justification to an old American political tradition which, if not exactly hallowed, was a recognized fact of life in many cities for a long time. Since the Irish and other ethnic blocs used political power to achieve a kind of reverse discrimination in their favor, it seems perverse to deny to Negroes these avenues for self-fulfillment and mobility. (Harwood, 1969:23)

The importance of voluntary associations as the nuclei of communities has been well put by Greer and Orleans (1968), who call them "parapolitical."

> Parapolitical organizations may be identified as voluntary associations based on the routine of everyday life, which represent an area of autonomous social value, and which can represent that value in political terms if necessary.

It remains to point out that ghettos, enclaves, clusters, and voluntary associations differ in the control they can exercise over the lives of their participants. The more restricted the entry, the more difficult the exit. The reward for such association, however, lies in the protection, the security, and the advantages which a group may also provide its members.

SUMMARY

Symbolic ecology is the term we have proposed to facilitate understanding of our urban settlements. The term "symbolic" is critical because it directs our attention to social processes. Early in American history, religion was the primary basis of social differentiation, linked of course to class. Religion as the basis for social differentiation gave way to ethnicity. Because the basis of social differentiation changed, so did the spatial manifestations of social differentiation. Baptist, Presbyterian, and Episcopalian social worlds faded as such configurations as Little Italies, Chinatowns, Germantowns, and Irish wards came to the fore.

Pluralism in today's urban environment is increasingly expressed by life style. While German, Swedish, and Norwegian social worlds have declined and even passed from the scene, organization on socioeconomic and dependency status, marital status, sexual preference, and political ideology have become more important. The process of social differentiation continues; its bases and the way in which space is organized has changed.

STUDY QUESTIONS

1. What is the basis of residential differentiation, and in what kinds of settlements does it occur?
2. What are the advantages and the disadvantages of living in an enclave? a cluster? of belonging to a voluntary association?
3. What is the ethnic division of labor?
4. Within an enclave, how do a people organize themselves spatially? Give some examples.
5. Within the perspective of symbolic ecology, what kind of spatial concentration do voluntary associations represent?

SUGGESTED READINGS

Gans, Herbert J. *The Urban Villagers* (Glencoe, Ill.: Free Press, 1962).

Pilcher, W. W. *The Portland Longshoremen: A Dispersed Urban Community* (New York: Holt, Rinehart and Winston, 1972).

Suttles, Gerald. *The Social Order of the Slum* (Chicago: University of Chicago Press, 1968).

PART FOUR

Urban aggregations

PHYSICAL BOUNDING

In Part Three we examined ghettos, enclaves, clusters, and voluntary associations as examples of communal bounding. When we examined a variety of peoples settling themselves in space in relation to one another, we ignored their specific locations. We did so because we wished to emphasize the primacy of the symbolic processes bringing about the variations in locations. Ghettos, for example, may be formed in central or suburban parts of the urban settlement, depending upon the combination of POETS dominant at any one historical time and in any one specific place. Indeed, the exclusive spatial concentration from which the word "ghetto" took its name was an islet. Enclaves and clusters likewise have been located in many different areas within urban settlements during the 10,000 years since urban settlements began.

To stress the symbolic nature of bounding is not, however, to deny the importance of physical location. Whether people are located in central, suburban, or exurban areas does make a difference. If they reside in outlying areas but work "downtown," they must spend time and money traveling back and forth. If they live near the center and lack transportation but the jobs are available only in the suburbs, they will have high rates of unemployment. There are other consequences to be expected if people live in one suburb and their friends live in other suburban areas, if they live in one area but must shop in another, and if they live distant from their families.

When urbanologists recognize the importance of the symbolic processes, they also know that location has consequences for the urbanite; accordingly, they find that sections of the urban settlements are usefully categorized according to their location.[1] Thus we speak of central or innercity areas, of suburban and exurban places, and of other distinctions based on location. Location, of course, symbolizes relationships between areas.

When we examined symbolic bounding in Part Three, Urban Communities, we were discussing the processes which create communities. We pointed out that while a community often is concentrated spatially, a community may also exist although spatially dispersed.

In the chapters of Part Four, we pursue the same topic of the relationship of people to space, but with primary focus on space. In Part Three a basic question was: how do people who assume commonality with one another locate in space? Now we ask: what commonality do people have who share space?

Community can exist without territory, we concluded in the last chapter. Anticipating the subsequent chapters we can say that sharing space does not necessarily create community. For this reason, we title this section: Urban Aggregations.

Continuing to examine large scale units, let us now turn to examine first innercity areas and then other organizations of physical space.

---

[1] Classical ecology has been criticized for what was considered to be excessive reliance on physical characteristics. But a pioneering ecological work by McKenzie (1926) defined an ecological unit as a relation between units, thus interpreting physical relationships symbolically.

chapter 9

THE INNERCITY

The Photography of H. Armstrong Roberts

Thus far we have used the word "city" only in reference to the centralized urban settlement that emerged first in history and was succeeded by the metropolis. Our specialized usage differs from the practice of the majority of urbanologists, who use the term city interchangeably with urban. In keeping with their general usage, they refer to the "inner-city," the central core of a metropolitan area. This central core is surrounded by suburbs, which are often divided into older and newer suburban growth rings.

What is called the innercity is frequently compared to the suburban ring since, together, they constitute almost all (except for the rurban, exurban, and/or fringe areas) of the metropolitan area. The populations characteristic of the innercore (innercity) and outer (suburban) areas have been studied in detail by many investigators.

DEFINITIONS: URBAN

As first the city, then the metropolis, and finally the urban environment dominated as settlement patterns, the Census Bureau has changed its definition of urban in an attempt to keep pace with these changes. When the city dominated, urban simply meant any community having the legal status of an urban community. When the metropolis at times swallowed up previously independent communities but was unable to annex those that had already achieved legal incorporation, the Census Bureau used size or population density, or both, as the definition of urban. With the advent of the urban environment, none of the three previously used criteria—size, population density, or legal status—was sufficient, so in 1950 the Census Bureau adopted some new definitions, ones which have been used since then.

Urban places

Urban places now are defined by the U.S. Census Bureau as places with 2,500 or more inhabitants, whether or not such settlements are incorporated and regardless of their population density. Had this change not been made, many of the tens of thousands who had moved outside the legal limits of the metropolis to unincorporated places would have been classified as rural according to the pre-1950 definition.

Urbanized areas

Urbanized areas are defined as places having a core (central city or cities) population of at least 50,000 plus the surrounding urbanized territories. All population with an urbanized area is classified as urban, regardless of its size or legal status. Therefore, people who are actually suburbanites commuting to the core to work are included as urban, not as part of the rural population, regardless of the size of the community in which they live. Likewise, incorporated places located within the metropolitan area, regardless of the size of their populations, are included in the one urbanized area rather than classified separately. This, too, made sense, because the populations of such incorporated communities really are part of the urbanized area rather than separate communities.

When applied to a specific settlement, the actual area included within an urbanized area will change over time, reflecting the growth or perhaps the contraction of the settlement. On one hand, the urbanized area is an accurate measure of the influence of the metropolis; but, on the other hand, comparison from one era to another may be difficult precisely because the boundaries have changed. In part for this reason, some investigators prefer to use the third new definition the Census Bureau introduced in 1950, the *Standard Metropolitan Statistical Area* (the SMSA).

Standard Metropolitan Statistical Area

The concept of a metropolitan area was not new; nor was the addition of the word "standard." But why call the Standard Metropolitan Area, the SMA, a "statistical area?" The word "statistical" was purposely included to stress the function of this concept in providing uniformity in reporting statistics. Use of the same areal definition by the Departments of Health, Education, and Welfare, and by Labor, Commerce, Interior, and others would help coordinate many operations and strengthen the information necessary for planning. Use of the word statistical also differentiated the SMSA from the earlier used Standard Metropolitan Area (SMA).

Like the urbanized area definition, the SMSA has its starting point at a core population of 50,000. Whereas the urbanized area concept uses whatever cities or parts of cities that are relevant, the SMSA uses the entire county which contains a city or cities of at least 50,000. In deciding the extent of territory surrounding the central county or counties, the SMSA continues either to include or to exclude entire counties. Generally, the Census Bureau examines the social and economic relations of the entire population of an outlying county with the central county, as revealed, for example, in the pursuit of agricultural or nonagricultural work. If more than 25 percent of the outlying county's labor force pursues agricultural work, the entire county is classified as part of the agricultural hinterland, not as part of the SMSA. Since the entire county must either be included or excluded in the SMSA definition, whereas parts of counties may be included or excluded when the urbanized area definition is used, some population classified as urban in the SMSA will be considered to be rural if the urbanized area definition is used. This does not mean that one definition is necessarily better than the other, rather it underscores the price paid for the greater uniformity and temporal comparability of the

SMSA. We could also add that "reality" has a way of confounding our best definitions of it. Actual people do seem to have a way of failing to fit precisely the categories we create for them.

Suburban

Our discussion of Census Bureau definitions has special relevance for the definition of suburban. When the legal entity known as New York City was redefined to include not just the single borough of Manhattan but also four other boroughs, the problem of definition was no different in kind than the problem created when the city walls were expanded. The new definition artificially expanded the core's population and reduced the number of people considered to be living on the fringe. And when people began living in New Jersey, Pennsylvania, Connecticut and parts of other states and yet worked, shopped, visited, and in other ways were socially and economically integrated with New York, the problem of how that "city" should be defined continued. The SMSA and the urbanized area are two solutions to this old problem, the SMSA using counties and the urbanized area using smaller units. Urbanologists outside the Census Bureau have proposed other definitions of which we need to be aware.

Index of centralization

Suburbs were defined by one major investigator, Leo F. Schnore (1963), as the urbanized area outside the central city (which had a population of 50,000 or more by definition). He then constructed an *index of centralization*. The index was designed to reflect the degree to which the suburban population differed from the central city population. It was so constructed to make a score of 100 represent equality between city and suburb, with values greater than 100 representing relative concentrations in the city, and values below 100 representing suburban overrepresentation of people of given characteristics. Specifically, Schnore wanted to find out if suburbanites were of higher or lower socioeconomic status than central city residents. As his measure of socioeconomic status he used the educational attainment of males 25 years of age or over.

ECOLOGICAL VARIATIONS

The importance of the ecological perspective is forcefully established by Schnore's work. While it is true that among the entire population of the 200 urbanized areas in 1960 the city residents had lower socioeconomic status than those residing in the suburbs, any generalization based on the aggregation of all 200 would be misleading, he pointed out. Disaggregating the 200 urbanized areas existing in 1960, that is, examining the 200 for systematic differences within them, he found that settlement size and age (together closely related to what we have called "era of principal growth") made a significant difference. Whereas larger and older urbanized areas had concentrations of lower-status persons in central cities, smaller and newer urbanized areas reversed this pattern. Continuing to use educational attainment as his indicator of status, he stated that: "the proportion of persons completing at least a high school education is consistently higher in the suburbs of the older cities, while newer cities tend to show the opposite pattern."

Not only must size and age be taken into account in discussing city-suburban differences, but region also makes a difference. Working with John Palen, Leo F. Schnore (1965) then considered the impact of racial composition upon city-suburban differences. Excluding all nonwhites from analysis, they first reported that among whites the findings previously reported remained stable. Among nonwhites, however, city-suburban differentials varied by region. In the North, nonwhites followed the same pattern as that found for whites, namely higher-status suburban than central-city populations among the larger and older urbanized areas. In the South, however, the suburban nonwhite population as of the 1960s had higher status in the smaller and newer urbanized areas but not in the larger and older ones. Palen and Schnore state: "the most probable reason why Southern non-whites fail to show the usual city-suburban status differences is that in the South, as opposed to the North, the poorer and less advantaged non-white residents traditionally lived on the periphery of the city." In a third publication, Schnore (1967) extended his findings to SMSAs, finding results similar to those given by his analysis of urbanized areas. Pinkerton (1969), Gist and Fava (1974), and others (Colins and Smith, 1970) have also examined, extended, and commented upon Schnore's contribution.

In the first phase of the process of urbanization—that of the "city"—the upper-status groups lived in the center while those of lower status occupied the outer edge. Social status thus declined from center to periphery. In the second phase—that of the "metropolis"—the wealthy began to move out into the suburbs while the poor tended to migrate into the center. The middle classes settled between the rich and the poor. This configuration is essentially that described by Burgess in his concentric zone theory: social status increased from center to periphery.

Within the third and contemporary phase, the urban environment is seen to include both the previous patterns, as well as the contemporary configuration. To understand the contemporary pattern for any specific settlement, whether defined by the urbanized area or the SMSA, the era of principal growth is of critical concern. Thus we need to know not only when a settlement was established but also when it reached the 50,000 core population needed to classify it as an urbanized area or as an SMSA. Ideally we also should know when was its dominant growth period: when it experienced its most sizable growth. For instance, it may have reached

50,000 in 1860, but not have grown significantly until the years immediately after World War II, when it grew by several hundreds of thousands. Given the critical importance of era of principal growth, it is misleading to talk as if there were but one pattern of relations between cities and their suburbs.

Regional differences

Because the process of urbanization never spreads evenly over any land, region must also be taken into account. As Chapter 5 indicates, regions, too, have different eras of principal growth. Therefore, the settlements within one region will tend to display commonalities with one another and systematic differences from settlements in other regions. The urbanized areas of the Northeast are larger and older than those elsewhere in the United States. Having experienced their principal growth during the metropolitan settlement form, they tend to display common characteristics. By contrast, because major urbanization was not experienced by significant portions of the West Coast until after World War II, West Coast urban settlements differ from northeastern ones, while displaying certain commonalities among themselves.

When characteristics of the population, such as race, are differentially distributed regionally, as blacks are in the North and the South, the population (P) and its organization (O) must also be taken into account. When the economy (E) changes from industrial to postindustrial, when the technology (T) changes from foot and hoof to rails, or perhaps from autos to bicycles, the fourth component of the ecological complex must be considered if we are to understand city-suburban differences.

Given the foregoing variations in POET, we note that neither all of our innercities nor all of our suburbs contain homogeneous types, although symbolism (S) may ignore this evidence. As the data reviewed make abundantly clear, and as Gist and Fava put it, "there is no single kind of central city or one kind of suburban ring." A summary of the six basic patterns established by Schnore using the 1960 census, and reconfirmed for the 1970s, makes these variations obvious. Recall that in this work Schnore is comparing city-suburban differences. Have suburbanites completed more years of education than innercity residents? he asks. Disaggregating the data for all 200 SMSAs, he establishes six patterns, three of them included here. We have named the patterns, which Schnore simply lists by alphabetical letters.

Schnore's typology

The *old city pattern:*

> This type (exemplified by Tucson, Arizona) is perhaps the most interesting of all since it represents the reversal of the "expected" pattern. Persons

with no formal schooling or with very little education are underrepresented in the city itself. Those who have completed high school and those who have attended college are slightly overrepresented in the city. This means that the suburbs of Tucson and those of 13 other areas like it showed a systematic selection of persons at the bottom rather than at the top of the educational ladder (i.e., status) in 1960, which is the exact reversal of the common image of suburbia.

The *mixed city and metro pattern:*

Los Angeles is the largest example. Persons at both extremes are overrepresented in the city. While the earlier encounter with this pattern suggested that this pattern might be a deviant case, [the data] show that it is actually the modal type for 1960, for 70 out of the 200 urbanized areas showed this pattern.

The *metro pattern:*

The expected pattern is perfectly illustrated by New York City. The pattern consists of continuously declining values, which leads to two indications: (1) that the city in 1960 was characterized by an overconcentration of persons with minimal education, and (2) that the suburbs of New York were populated by a larger than expected proportion of persons with higher educational standing.

Although it is beyond our purposes to examine all the types established by Schnore, further description of one pattern will facilitate our understanding of the urban environment. Placing his types within our framework leads us to examine the type of innercity that experienced its principal growth in the era of the metropolis (approximately during the 19th century)—the metro pattern in Schnore's work.

INNERCITIES OF THE METRO PATTERN

Settlements experiencing their principal growth before 1900 are obviously older than those developing in later periods, which also means that their buildings, transportation systems, sewage and water mains, and the balance of what is often called the physical infrastructure are also older. Just because the physical plant is old does not at all mean that it is obsolete. Many houses throughout the United States are hundreds of years old, yet are in fine condition. Transportation systems established at the turn of the century may also be in excellent condition. Office buildings and factories that were built long ago may in fact last longer than many being built today. The current renovation and conversion of many old buildings in American cities testify to their continuing value. Age, in and of itself, is not the problem in physical plants.

The basic problems in the physical plant of a settlement are need for maintenance and changes in function. Changes in function, of course, are related to the lack of maintenance; but such changes are not the only cause of obsolescence, as some would have us believe. It is probably fair to say that Americans often have been shortsighted, oriented to the present, and without adequate concern for past and future investment. Rather than considering a building or a transportation system as representing an investment by previous generations, perhaps we have been too quick to tear down what their resources, their labor, and their taxes have provided for us. Earlier we mentioned the massive investment which our forebears made in canals and railroads. To that we may add the entire inventory of the built urban environment as we have received it.

Perhaps as Americans we have also been insufficiently aware of the costs of maintaining that which we possess. In 1956 we authorized the expenditure of some $70 billion for an interstate highway system without considering how much it would cost us to maintain that national motorway. Today it remains common practice to purchase an automobile or a house without awareness of the future costs of maintaining that physical property.

It must be said that the obsolescence of much of the physical plant of our American urban settlements does stem from lack of maintenance. Provision of adequate subway cars, replacement of track, rebuilding of roadbeds, repair of buildings, update of sewage and water mains and equipment, and a plethora of other maintenance expenditures have simply not been made. The result is the deteriorated condition of much of the physical plant of the older SMSAs.

In the innercore of some of the older and larger SMSAs, streets have been repaved so many times that their curbstones have disappeared. Without barriers to water as well as to traffic, sidewalks have become tilted to the streets and destroyed by the unanticipated weights of vehicles. Staircases from sidewalks to buildings have fallen away, in turn, and the combined effect has accelerated the deterioration of the buildings. Underneath sidewalks and streets, the water and the sewage mains, simply worn out from decades of use, seep their contents underground, being repaired only when giving evidence of a major rupture.

For about 40 years new subway cars were not purchased for the New York system, and roadbeds and rails were not properly maintained. The once even elegant subway stations, insufficiently cleaned or otherwise maintained, became as shabby as the 1920 cars on the track. Because these systems were built for the some half million riders then, but with eight times the number of riders now, such intensive usage should have increased, not decreased, maintenance. In office buildings, stores, warehouses, port facilities, bridges, tunnels, and elsewhere throughout the built environment, the evidence of the decay of neglect is evident.

However much we would like to recover our forebears' bequest to us, the fact is that much of the innercore of the older and larger SMAs is simply beyond redemption. Government policies, such as urban renewal and some tax policies, have also contributed to the destruction. For many reasons we failed to maintain what was ours, and now the strands of the solution are even more numerous and closely intertwined.

Changes in function have also had a major impact. Although many would agree that we have indeed squandered much of our legacy, it is both unrealistic and foolish to attempt to stop change. When people moved off their farms into the city, they, too, abandoned previous investments in houses, barns, and cleared land. They would not have contributed to us, though, had they failed to grasp the opportunities of urban life. When later generations left the innercity for the suburbs, they, too, left houses and other physical facilities in which they and others had invested. In these and many other examples, it is obvious that some change is both inevitable and beneficial, though perhaps costly in economic and human terms. The basic point is that not all change is progress, nor are all things "modern" necessarily better. Our task, as was our forebears,' is one of directing and guiding change to build upon the past rather than to attempt to destroy the past.

The innercity has changed in function over the last 50 years, with accelerated change taking place in the last 25 years. In those settlements that experienced their principal growth before these changes began, the impact has been extensive. Again to use New York as our example, population density in the innercore reached its peak in 1910 and has declined ever since. The composition of the population has also changed.

By the mid-1800s, the then new railroad system had made it possible for the wealthy to move to distant suburban locations, such as Harlem about ten miles away. Although many retained town houses and even mansions near the core, an increasing number took up full-time and year-round residence outside the old city limits. The middle class left next, commuting to work by means of the new streetcars.

The upper and middle classes were replaced nearest the core by the impoverished, the most recently arrived immigrant group. The better-off segments of the working class moved in turn into areas previously occupied by both middle and upper classes, usually subdividing old middle- and upper-class homes to accommodate multifamily usage. Developments in the late 1940s, 50s, and 60s intensified these patterns until the innercity of New York today contains a concentration of persons with minimal education and the suburbs contain more of the better educated.

Employment

When people began to move out, retail enterprises followed them. First what are known as *convenience stores* established suburban locations, selling such daily needs as bread, milk, and tobacco.[1] Later *neighborhood*

---

[1] For a valuable bibliography of research on these markets, see Brian J. L. Berry and Allen Pred, *Central Place Studies: A Bibliography of Theory and Applications* (Philadelphia: Regional Science Research Institute, 1961).

business centers developed, with small grocery stores, drugstores, cleaners, barber and beauty shops, and small restaurants. As clothing stores, bakeries, florists, post offices, and banks clustered together, *community business centers* developed. Finally, *regional shopping centers,* with department stores, music, hobby, toy, photo and other shops began to develop in the suburbs (Berry and Gillard, 1977).

These four types of markets contributed to the decline of the fifth and final type of market, the *central business district* (CBD). Retail trade first began to decline in the CBD. As the number of shoppers decreased— in spite of increases in the population of the total settlement—movies, restaurants, cocktail lounges, and other facilities dependent upon shoppers relocated to suburban sites. In turn, the innercore lost a significant number of jobs in retail and related employment.

Manufacturing also began to decline in the core of these older and larger SMSAs, in spite of increases in total settlement employment in manufacturing. Wholesale trade grew but slowly, not in proportion to its increase throughout these older and larger settlements. As employment opportunities decreased "downtown" and expanded in the suburbs, additional population moved out of the central city. Those who could move were generally white and middle class. Although some white working-class persons also relocated to the suburbs, generally in these older SMSAs the blacks and the working class were left behind. Black, Hispanic, and/or working-class populations also continued to migrate into the core areas, the result being nonwhite and poor central city populations, with white middle-class suburbs surrounding them.

Jobs were lost first in retail, then in manufacturing, and finally (but only proportionally) in wholesale trade in the core of older SMSAs. In the fourth and final type of employment, that of selected services, however, the same core areas have experienced an increase. Although the proportionate increase in selected services was higher in younger SMSAs, regardless of their size, the gains registered in these services by the older and larger SMSA core areas were sizable. What are these selected services? They are those that require extensive personal communication, as among corporate lawyers and executives, stockbrokers and large investment firms, or among bank executives and accounting firms. In addition to the foregoing firms, which have been called "elite service centers," other specialized services that do not rely on public contact are also found in these older core areas. These data seem to indicate that the older core areas are successfully changing their functions and so may yet survive. Why then their continuing difficulties?

In our own assessment, aside from the negative view which many Americans have about large (and older) cities, the most fundamental problems of older core areas are two: unemployment and fiscal problems. Let us now analyze just these two problems, recognizing, of course, that there are other problems.

Unemployment

Unemployment results from the loss of jobs in the core areas, added to the lack of transportation to the suburban sites where the new jobs are to be found. As we observed, retail and manufacturing jobs have decreased "downtown" since about 1910. Also, employment in the wholesale trade area has also declined relative to its growth throughout these older SMSAs. The only sphere registering net gains has been in selected services, an area for which the vast majority of metro pattern innercity residents are unqualified. Thus, for most of this type of innercity residents, employment opportunities have decreased throughout their own and their parents' lifetimes. Why do the poor not move to the suburbs where the jobs are available? As we shall observe when we examine the suburbs, the poor are unwelcomed and effectively blocked from moving to suburban locations. Finally, mass transit from central city to suburban employment sites is typically unavailable. Even the suburbanites who commute by transit to the city find it necessary to drive first to the train station.

Having mentioned the suburbanite, the jobs he or she seeks are the ones expanding downtown: professional, managerial, and clerical. The suburban dweller thus has suburban employment opportunities in retail trade, manufacturing, and wholesale trade in his or her own suburb or in an adjacent one—and selected service jobs downtown. The innercity resident is most qualified for the jobs he or she cannot reach, and is least qualified for those positions available nearby. High rates of unemployment are the inevitable result.

Fiscal problems

The fiscal problem is held by many to be a shrinking tax base. Strictly speaking, this is not true, for all older SMSAs have experienced steady if modest increases in real estate valuations through the 1970s. Rather, the fiscal problems of the innercities of the metro pattern stem from their pattern of ecology, especially their past as it has shaped their present and future.

The way in which the components of the ecological complex have interacted to create fiscal problems for metro pattern innercities is seen in Bridgeport, Connecticut, which Kurt Schlichting (1975) has studied. Bridgeport will be used as our example since it fits exactly the type of older and larger SMSA we have been discussing.

Using Schnore's index of centralization, by which 100 represents an equal (proportional) distribution between central cities and suburbs, Schlichting's figures for Bridgeport are as follows. For those without any formal education, 165 in the innercity, 47 in the suburbs; for 1–7 years of elementary school completed, 148 in the central city, 58 in the suburbs;

and at the other end of the educational ladder, those with a college educa-tion or more, 54 in the center, 121 in the suburbs.

Half of the families living in the innercity have annual incomes of less than $10,000, while the average income for suburban families ranges from 20 to 65 percent higher. In terms of families with the lowest annual in-comes, "of the 5174 families . . . classified as below the poverty line, 3423 of them or 66.1 percent live in the innercity" (Schlichting, 1975:133). On the centralization index, the score for the central city's concentration of families with poverty incomes is 164; for each of the seven suburbs the range varies from 31 to 73. With regard to occupation, Bridgeport once again fits the metro pattern in having the highest percentage of blue-collar workers in the innercity and the highest percentage of white collar work-ers in the suburbs.

The innercity and the suburbs, in spite of their differences, are parts of the same metropolitan area. About three of every ten employed suburba-nites comes into the innercity area to work. In part as the hub of the transportation system, and in part to serve the commuting population, the innercore devotes about one fifth of its land to transportation uses. A disproportionate number of public and private institutions, such as schools, hospitals, and churches, are also located in the center, together occupying 12.1 percent of its total land surface. Although many of these institutions serve the entire SMSA, the innercity population dispropor-tionately pays for their support because they are tax exempt. When Schlichting added all nontaxable property, including the public housing which is virtually exclusively located in the innercity, 45 percent of the land was so included. When he computed an index of taxable property for innercity and suburbs, he established a score of 61 for the innercity, and from 109 to 149 for the suburbs.

Although it is indeed one metropolitan area, the legal limits of the city of Bridgeport encompass only the innercity area. The suburbs, too, are separate areas, ones typically excluding the working, welfare, and pov-erty classes, public institutions such as schools and hospitals, and the bulk of the transportation facilities. The city of Bridgeport is the innercity. The seven suburbs have separate names. As we continue with the example of the SMSA of Bridgeport, let us now use their separate names, calling Bridgeport the "city" or innercity.

Bridgeport (the innercity) does contain the population most in need. It contains not only more school age children than do the suburbs but also more poverty level families, more persons needing aid to dependent chil-dren, more health and welfare case, and the like. Forced in addition to assume a disproportionate share of tax-exempt properties, such as churches, hospitals, and housing projects, Bridgeport's tax rate is under-standably higher than any suburb. The property tax rate is the amount of tax a property owner must pay according to assessed value. As the rate is based on units of a thousand dollars of assessed value, it is called the mill rate. In Bridgeport the mill rate was 76.4; in the suburb of Fairfield the mill rate was 46.2

The student should understand that municipalities differ in their assessment procedures. Some assessors may be directed to assess all property periodically at its estimated market value, and other districts may change assessments only when property changes hands. One municipality may assess at 50 percent of market value, while a second may levy taxes according to a higher or lower percentage of assessed value. Municipal governments may therefore raise property taxes by (1) increasing the mill rate, (2) increasing the assessed value, and (3) increasing the assessment ratio. With one exception in the Bridgeport SMSA, all assessment ratios stood at 70 percent. Assessed value increased about 20 percent in the city during the 1960s, while all suburbs experienced increases in property values in excess of 100 percent. Given this situation, the city had only one alternative in order to meet increased costs and this lay in raising the mill rate, which it did by 87.9 percent. Each of the suburbs raised its mill rates only about half as much.

Finally, Schlichting examined the pattern of expenditures in the central city, as compared to the suburbs. Again computing an index of centralization, he learned that the score for welfare expenditures for the core was an incredible 234, while for suburbs welfare expenditures varied from 13 to 2. In terms of public safety, Bridgeport again led the list, with an index of 139, compared to scores of 100, 85, 82, 49, 42, 33, and 5 for each of the seven suburbs. In terms of expenditures for education, the scores were reversed. Now Bridgeport had an index of 73, while all suburbs except one had scores of 100 or above, with one having a score of 191.

In summary, Bridgeport has the highest proportion of tax-exempt properties (e.g., hospitals), the highest percent of its land devoted to nontax producing uses (e.g., highways), and the highest expenditures for police and fire protection. In large part this situation prevails because Bridgeport is the hub of the metropolitan area, servicing the hundreds of thousands of other persons, including suburbanites, who enter the hub to work, to shop, to obtain health and medical care, to attend concerts, to eat at restaurants, or perhaps to have a drink "downtown." Although Bridgeport undeniably provides many services for all residents in the entire SMSA, the population of Bridgeport alone pays for them. How much do the citizens of Bridgeport pay?

Innercity subsidies to suburbs

To estimate the cost of services provided by the hub to the entire "wheel," Schlichting computed the cost differential if such facilities were evenly distributed between city and suburb. For example, let us suppose that Bridgeport had the same percentage of tax-exempt property as the suburbs—10.1 percent, instead of 24.9 percent. If Bridgeport's excess

14.8 percent of tax-exempt property were producing tax revenues, the city would have received an additional $9,160,120 in taxes. By the same logic he reasoned: what if streets and highways were evenly distributed? They, too, take land off the tax rolls and lower the tax revenues. Assuming Bridgeport had the same proportion of land used for transportation as the average in all of its surrounding suburbs, and assuming that the excess produced the same revenue as the average parcel in Bridgeport, an additional $6,254,685 in tax revenues would have been generated. The entire 1971 budget for the city of Bridgeport was just over $56 million. Thus, the "subsidy" of innercity to suburb, more than $15 million, is quite high.

In some related research, Amos Hawley (1951) hypothesized that the larger the proportion of the total population of a metropolitan area resident outside the central city, the higher the expenditure of the city for the services it provides as the center.[2] Hawley argued, as did Schlichting, that "some of the activity and hence some of the need for city services arises from the population residing outside the city boundaries." In an article published in 1967, Kie tested Hawley's proposition and found it to be supported. In related research, Curran (1963) and Brazer (1962), also in general, supported the contention that central cities pay a disproportionate part of their share of metropolitan area wide services.

The evidence, however, is not all on one side. A study by Hirsch and associates (1971) flatly concluded that whatever central cities may lose through support of commuter services is generally offset by increased revenues generated through such sources as sales taxes. John Kasarda (1972) went so far as to argue that increased suburban growth either has no effect on central cities or it benefits them.

How should the student of urban studies attempt to understand such apparently contradictory data? Throughout we have argued for a perspective that takes context into account. Components are interdependent, and if urban phenomena are analyzed out of their own context, we fail to understand the true situation. Examining the data for context, we find that Hirsch and his associates and Kasarda and others fail to disaggregate their data, to specify the types of innercities and the different types of innercity-suburban relationships they are talking about. This point is evident if we take as a hypothetical example just two contrasting types of innercities and their suburbs. Let us suppose, for example, that in the first type the innercity is filled with lower-income populations while the suburbs contain those with higher incomes, as was true in Bridgeport. Let us suppose then that the second type is the reverse; that is, the upper-income population lives in the innercity, the lower-income population in the suburbs, as found in what we called the old city pattern. Were we to aggregate

---

[2] This hypothesis is in keeping with McKenzie's (1926) early proposition that the center, being the locus of coordination and control, would grow disproportionately to the growth of the region. Kasarda (1972) tested McKenzie's hypothesis and found it to be supported by the data.

these two types, to put them together in our analysis, the differences between them would be cancelled out.

Such inaccuracy is the reason we say that it is necessary to disaggregate the data by ecological type. When we do so, we are able to understand more thoroughly the types of innercities and their corresponding relationships with the types of suburbs that surround them. We can then understand the additional finding of Warren (1966), who argues that the effects of suburbanization on the central city have been exaggerated. His data are based on Los Angeles, whose ecological configuration is different from that of Bridgeport. Within the type represented by Bridgeport, the innercity may in fact be exploited by the suburbs surrounding it, whereas in other combinations of POETS, such exploitation may not occur.

SUMMARY

A review of the definitions of the innercity indicated that the innercity is typically defined as that which is not suburb or CBD. Innercity is a residual term, one delimiting that physical area which lies between the old CBD and the suburbs.

As a physical area, the innercity population constitutes an aggregation, not a community. As Schnore's work indicated, there are several different types of innercity populations, and there are several different innercity/suburban patterns. In some metropolitan areas of the United States, as elsewhere, the wealthy and the middle class live close to the center and the working and poverty classes reside on the outer fringe. In other metropolitan areas, rich and poor live in the innercity and the other classes are found in the suburbs.

The symbolism of the innercity as a vast slum with crime and disorder widespread must be dispelled as a myth. The preconception that the innercity population is homogeneous, that it is a single, united urban community, must also be abandoned. Urban settlements, including their innercities, can only be meaningfully analyzed within their own ecological context.

In some metropolises that experienced their principal growth in the 19th century, the working and dependent classes do predominate in the innercity. Our analysis of one metropolis of this type, Bridgepoint, Connecticut, indicated its primary problems. The innercity and its population had been left behind in the center as the employment sites of the jobs for which they were qualified moved to suburban locations. Without the education and the skills needed for jobs whose number is increasing within the CBD, and lacking the necessary transportation to get to suburban retail and manufacturing centers, high unemployment rates among innercity residents are among the consequences.

A second major problem of the metro pattern SMSA is the innercity's inability to tax the users of its resources. Thus while hundreds of thousands of suburbanites regularly travel to these types of innercities to work, shop, attend theater, or perhaps to go to the hospital, the burden of the cost of these services is borne by the innercity residents alone. In this way, then, some innercities subsidize their suburbs.

STUDY QUESTIONS

1. Define the following terms as used by the U.S. Bureau of the Census:
   a. Urban place
   b. Urbanized area
   c. Standard Metropolitan Statistical Area
   d. Innercity
   e. Suburban
2. How do some 20th-century innercities subsidize the suburbs that surround them?
3. What are some of the ecological variations in types of SMSAs that were established by Schnore?

SUGGESTED READINGS

Pinkerton, James R. "City-Suburban Status Differences." *Urban Affairs Quarterly,* vol. 3 (September 1967) pp. 95–108.

Schnore, Leo. "The Socio-Economic Status of Cities and Suburbs." *American Sociological Review,* vol 28:1 (February 1963) pp. 76–85.

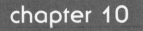

URBAN GROWTH: SUBURBS AND THE URBAN FRONTIER

Photograph by Harold M. Lambert

203

SUBURBS DEFINED

The word "suburb" literally means near to the city (from the Latin *suburbium* and later the French, *suburbe*). Although suburbs are historically associated with aristocratic life, the lower classes in French and Spanish settlements, among others, were often obliged to live in suburban locations (de Hostos, 1948). Historically as well as in the contemporary urban environment, suburbs have been and are filled with many different types of populations. Furthermore, there are manufacturing, mining, transportation, retailing, single industry, and resort suburbs.

Suburbs are old and so are criticisms of them. In his unexcelled *Decline and Fall of the Roman Empire,* Gibbon describes the criticisms leveled against the Roman suburbanites who were said to be apolitical, without culture or taste, and given to excess. In 1936, Cassady in the *Atlantic Monthly* lamented suburbs in the United States for their lack of "real culture" and for the "distasteful" similarity of their homes.

Suburbs are old, but they mushroomed, first with the coming of rail transport and then with the widespread use of the automobile. As millions of people moved out to the new fringe of the urban settlement, many social scientists saw significant changes taking place in these people. Those who moved to suburbia were said to become anti-intellectual and culturally deprived. Suburbia was seen to represent a dreary blight of monotonous uniformity, in houses as well as people. For many commentators in the 1950s, relocation to the periphery also meant a change from liberalism to conservatism in politics, from individualism to familism in life style, and from involvement in to escape from the problems then facing us.

Surburbia also had its defenders. There were those who thought that a revolutionary "New day" had finally arrived. With new and larger housing, neighbors like themselves and grass everywhere, Americans and their families could at last return to no less than Nature. With all this and a sense of community in these new tracts, too, what else could one want!

Positive or negative, such views are called the *suburban myth* by urbanologists with 20-20 hindsight. Like the myth of the unitary and homogeneous innercity, the suburban myth was also predicated upon preconception. As research evidence accumulated, suburbs were found to be of many different types, composed of many different populations, to vary by era of principal growth, and to differ in many other ways as well.

When the metropolis expanded and evolved into the urban environment, its fringes were then the suburbs. Those who moved to the outer parts of the same single urban settlement did so for a complex of reasons *not* including abandoning the urban way of life.

They lived in what was then countryside and worked, shopped, ate, worshipped, and carried on other nonresidential activities downtown. As the suburban ring grew, as it did sizably after World War II, the "new" suburbs became "old."

Urbanologists recognize this by referring to the old suburbs, the old suburban ring, as that which developed prior to 1945. The new suburbs are those that developed after 1945. The era of principal growth makes a difference for suburbs as well as for entire urban settlements. We see this in the phases through which an area develops into a suburb.

PHASES OF SUBURBANIZATION

The reasons for suburban migration have changed from one historical period to another. Without going back in history to understand the forces at work, we can grasp some essential points by examining first the suburbs most distant from the center and then by discussing those closer to the innercity. Examining space by proximity to center within the same time frame is but another way to help us understand changes through time, since the suburbs most distant today are likely to be "closer" to the center in the future. Space and time are reciprocally related.

Exurban

In a popular treatment of the initial phase of suburbanization, the outermost settlements were called *exurban*. According to Spectorsky (1955), the exurbanite establishes residence in the following order: "summer renter, year-round renter, summer-cottage owner, year-round owner, acreage owner (as opposed to lot owner), and finally property owner." We should note that the process often begins with temporary seasonal residence. Since such residents are often the first wave of urbanites who will be moving into the area, exurban is also called "pioneer," "incipient," or "pre-suburban."

Who are the exurbanites? Again, according to Spectorsky (1955:167):

> Exurbia is filled with intelligent, witty, amusing, clever people, people who are fun to be with and provocative to talk to. Indeed, they have to be, for in many ways it is their profession: wit, comedy, brains, intelligence, and animal cunning are the commodities they have to sell—to the advertisers, the producers, the publishers, the broadcasters. . . . So it is reasonable to conceive of Exurbia as the brains and sense of humor of America. We must look elsewhere to find America's heart, America's hands and muscles, or America's conscience.

Advertisers, writers, commercial artists, and others like them live in exurbia because their working hours are flexible and because they frequently do much of their work at home. They are the people, in other words, who can afford the time and cost of a lengthy trip to their place of employment. They are also the people who can afford the relatively scarce housing available in these outlying sections.

Due to the intensifying construction of large tracts of middle-class housing, as well as improvements in transportation to and from these exurban areas, the status of later migrants decreases as their numbers increase. As the incoming population becomes a mass movement, the area becomes suburban in character. Urbanologists divide the suburbanization process into (1) developing, (2) mature, and (3) absorption phases.

Developing

When tract housing construction begins in an intensive way, the *developing phase of suburbanization* is under way. The area at this point is characterized by mixed land uses, often with suburban tracts scattered among the farms that they are invading. Developing suburbanization has been described as "leapfrog" because it jumps over farms, bypasses lower-intensity uses, and is uneven. Growth is rapid.

Mature

As suburbanization reaches its *mature phase,* the former rural land uses disappear; they have been pushed out by the more intensive urban land use patterns. Whereas in the developing phase the newcomers complained about the lack of services—schools, law enforcement, sanitary collection—in the mature phase many of these services are available. The rapid and large-scale growth characteristic of the developing phase also falls off to slower rates of growth.

When parcels of land that were passed over in the leapfrog stage begin to be developed, urbanologists say that *infill* has begun. This, too, is a characteristic that differentiates developing from mature suburbanization. Finally, population densities in the mature phase reach their highest point.

Absorption

As population increases so does the demand for shops, stores, and other commercial enterprises. Whereas most of the land until now has been used for residential purposes, the need for commercial facilities at this point typically leads to redevelopment. Pressure to rezone some residential land for commercial uses intensifies. As the phase of suburbanization called *absorption* emerges, it is not unusual to witness some suburban houses being torn down to make way for stores, even though such housing may be but 10 or 15 years old. Such displacement of residential populations, combined with the now intensifying commercial development, may lead population density to decrease. As redevelopment occurs, the area is absorbed into the core urban community. Whether this absorption involves annexation or some other form of political integration, depends upon highly varied state and local conditions.

In summary, the process of suburbanization begins with the development of exurbs—settlements of pioneer urbanites who establish second homes, weekend or perhaps vacation residences in rural and/or resort areas. This population is composed of upper-income and professional persons who can afford the costs of such distant construction and transportation. The phase of developing suburbanization begins with the large-scale construction of tract housing, whose residents and their school-aged children swell the demand for services. Land which was skipped over in the leapfrog pattern of the developing phase begins to be developed in the infill that is characteristic of mature suburbanization. Population density increases although overall rates of growth slow down. The final phase, that of redevelopment and absorption, begins with the intensification of commercial development and the displacement of some residents.

GROWTH BY DISTANCE

The above phases of suburbanization examined a single area as it changed over time. It is also useful to examine different areas at the same point in time. Thus if we begin at the outermost perimeter of an urban settlement and then examine areas closer and closer to the center, we will find the temporal phases we have just discussed at various distances from the center. This means that areas of an urban settlement differ in part according to their distance from the center.

Although metropolitan areas differ in the way in which their populations are distributed—with the wealthy in the center of some and on the periphery of others—virtually all large urban areas have some discernable distribution. Keeping such differences in mind, let us examine one configuration. It is also the distribution most often found in American SMSAs (Schnore, 1963), especially in the older urbanized areas.

Axially

Urban growth takes place along axes of transportation, such as auto routes. Growth along such axes is called "axial" or "sectoral." Examination of the 223 SMSAs of American cities indicates that such characteristics as the education, occupation, and income of the population differ systematically by sectors. In New York City, for example, the wealthy may be distributed primarily along portions of York and Fifth Avenue, while the poor are found in the sector known as the Lower East Side. In Kansas City the wealthy sector may be along Brookside, while Prospect Avenue is the axis of the working class. Thus we may say that the socio-economic rank of the population varies axially (Berry and Kasarda, 1977).

Higher-status sectors generally follow desired amenities—the higher ground with views, beachfront areas with access to the water, or areas of historical importance. Lower-status sectors follow lower-lying lands, often on industrial-transportation arteries.

Concentrically

In perhaps the most widely reprinted article of all the urban literature, Ernest Burgess (1925) outlined his concentric growth theory. While not necessarily subscribing to his theory, we may use the technique of dividing an entire urban settlement into concentric rings and then examine who lives in each ring. The radius of these rings may be one, two, three, or more miles from a point taken to be the center of the settlement or the size of each ring may be smaller or larger. Regardless of ring size, urban populations have been found to vary systematically by each ring from center outward. Such distribution by ring is termed "concentric."

The age of people and property varies most systematically by concentric ring. The age of the housing and the average age of the population decreases from center to periphery (Berry and Gillard, 1977). Because age is closely related to population density, the number of multiple housing units, the proportion of renters, and the proportion of women in the labor force, these also decline from center to periphery. That is, the larger families with younger adults in which the wife does not work live in the outer concentric rings, while the rings nearer the center have smaller, older families with fewer children and more wives working (Berry and Kasarda, 1977).

Urbanism has been defined in many ways, but female participation in the labor force is one widely used index since it is expected to increase as the population becomes more urban (Shevky, 1955). Fertility rates are also used as a measure of urbanism because they have been found to decline from rural to urban areas, and from small to large urban settlements. Either or both measures are called the *Urbanism-Familism Scale* (Bell, 1953). Using this scale we can say that urbanism-familism decreases concentrically.

Axial-concentric

The distribution of the population differs by social rank according to axial sectors of the settlement. Urbanism-familism, by contrast, differs concentrically. Thus in any one specific concentric ring, the age of the population will be similar, as will be the population density, the number of multiple housing units, the proportion of home owners, the proportion of children, and the proportion of women in the labor force. This generalization holds even though the social rank of the population differs from one part of the same concentric ring to the other according to axial differences.

If we turn to examine any one specific axial sector, we will find that along each axis the population will systematically vary by concentric ring, and that one sector will differ from another by social rank.

The population is also distributed according to local patterns of segregation. Throughout the United States, for example, blacks and whites are so thoroughly segregated that axial and concentric variations must be examined separately for each population. When this is done, principal growth among black areas is seen to be primarily if not exclusively axial (Palen and Schnore, 1965; Muth, 1969). That is, even black suburbanization has largely taken place by the axial expansion of black areas. Spatially compressed into only one sector, the black population differs concentrically by both social rank and by urbanism-familism (Davis and Donaldson, 1975).

Although the configuration just reviewed is but one type, in all urban settlements some pattern predominates. Nationwide and worldwide, populations of different incomes, occupations, and educations have rarely lived together, nor have those families with children lived with those without them. In other characteristics, such as age and home ownership, the people of the many areas constituting the urban settlement are remarkably similar to their neighbors. Given the high degree of homogeneity of an area's population, and the persistence of such homogeneity in spite of many changes in the entire settlement, the question arises: how is such homogeneity created and maintained?

CONTROLLED GROWTH THROUGH EXCLUSION

In our discussion of suburbanization, we have observed that often it was the wealthy who first moved out of the innercity into the distant exurban perimeter. The middle class followed, leaving primarily the working and dependent classes behind. The income, and the occupational and educational status of the population thus rose from the center to the periphery, at least in the metro pattern. Once located in exurban and suburban areas, the resident populations acted to keep lower-status persons out of their communities.

The techniques for exclusion are many. Among the most powerful are the economic. By zoning an area for lots with a minimum of one half acre, one acre, two acres, or more, the residents make sure that only those who can afford to pay the costs of large parcels of land will buy land on which to build. If land costs $150,000 an acre, for example, zoning regulations that specify minimum lot sizes effectively exclude lower-economic classes.

In addition to minimum lot sizes, it is also common for subdivision regulations to specify a minimum house size, expressed by the number of square feet in finished rooms, excluding basements, porches, or balconies. If it costs $40 a square foot to build a new house, and the smallest house one can build is one with 2,000 square feet, then one must have sufficient resources to build a $80,000 home, as well as the funds necessary to buy the land. The minimum may be 3,000 square feet, or 4,000, or just 1,000 square feet. The cost of new construction may also vary. Regardless, the principle remains the same: regulations concerning minimum-sized lots and minimum-sized houses effectively exclude those unable to purchase that minimum.

Some subdivisions also own and operate communal swimming pools, tennis courts, clubhouses, and the like, and assessments for these facilities contribute to the additional economic class homogeneity of the residents of a subdivision.

Economic restrictions are not always sufficient. However much housing may cost, even when it is in the hundreds of thousands of dollars or more, there may still be some persons who can afford even very expensive homes, but whom the residents do not want to have as neighbors. To exclude such "undesirables," many subdivision residents were earlier required to sign restrictive convenants before they could purchase their homes. These restrictive convenants consisted of legally drafted formal documents wherein the parties agreed not to sell their homes to persons of specified races, religions, color, or perhaps of certain national origins, whatever the price offered.

When these restrictive covenants were declared not legally enforceable in 1948 in the *Shelley* v. *Kramer* decision, some people thought that this would produce higher rates of integration. If black-white residential patterns are used as a measure of one type of integration, the hopes of one side and the fears of the other side of the restrictive covenant issue were both unfounded. As the Taeubers (1965) and many others have documented, blacks and whites remain to a high degree segregated from each other. This is because restrictive covenants were but one of the many forces at work segregating peoples.

Regardless of the legal status of restrictive covenants, many people are unwilling to sell their homes to persons to whom they think their neighbors will object. The black, Puerto Rican, or other minority person who makes an offer on a house for sale in a white area may be told that an offer has already been made, or perhaps that one offer has been accepted. They may be quoted higher prices than others would be told, and in other ways discouraged from buying in that neighborhood. Among blacks, Farley (1977) points out: "They perceive differences in how welcome they would be in the different suburbs and realize that moving into any of them entails greater difficulty . . . than moving into the northwest corner of the central city" where many blacks already live.

Federal law prohibits such discrimination and there are agencies to which people may appeal. Remedies take time, however, and many prefer to avoid such hassles. They know, furthermore, that discriminatory practices are but surface evidences of deeper problems which they (and often their children) would face. Symbolic forces thus join with the economic to continue the observed patterns of residential segregation.

Although nearly one half million blacks moved to the suburbs during the 1960s, the areas to which they moved were usually sectoral extensions of central city ghettos. "The vast majority of blacks who currently reside in the suburban ring reside in close proximity to other blacks" (Rose, 1972:18).

Through economic and symbolic processes, the techniques of exclusion operate both to create and to maintain the homogeneity of an area's population. When change does occur, the entire area is likely to change, with one group moving out when another does manage to move in. The first in-migrants to an area may therefore signal the beginning of a complete turnover in the population of an area. Experts therefore intensively study even slight changes for evidence of what may be coming. Let us examine one such recent change.

BLACK SUBURBS AND WHITE CITIES?

Beginning in the late 1960s and continuing through the present, a number of urbanologists noted increasing rates of black suburbanization and an increasing number of whites moving to central cities. Katheryn Nelson, in a lecture as part of the 1978 William E. Cole Lecture Series, examined recent trends to determine the magnitude of these shifts in black-white patterns. She reports that indeed: "Black migration patterns have markedly shifted since 1970 to be directed away from central cities toward suburbs."

Blacks moving to suburbs include both those formerly resident in the central city as well as those in-migrating. Both migratory streams are a reversal of pre-1970 patterns and are of sufficient magnitude "that by 1975 black migration was on net directed away from the central city in each SMSA studied." When Nelson disaggregated the migrants by family income, she found that, as with whites, black suburbanization was largely among the upper-income households.

While blacks are moving to the suburbs in greater numbers, whites are moving in greater numbers to nonmetropolitan and to central city locations. The magnitude of the cityward migration, however, varies highly from one SMSA to another and represents a consistent turnaround only in one metropolitan area, that of Los Angeles. In the L.A. SMSA, "by 1974 whites were on net moving from the suburbs to the central city, . . . while rates of central city inmigration and selection definitely increased, and the white share of central city inmigrants also grew." Who are these white in-migrants?

While the higher income groups have been and continue to be those who move to the suburbs, among blacks as well as whites, age is the more significant factor in the white in-migration to central cities. In Chapter 2 we noted that generally it is the young who migrate, and in the white in-migration to central cities this generalization remains true. Persons aged 20–34 constitute the bulk of the migratory stream, and their rates have increased slightly since 1970. Analysis of this pattern is difficult since there are many persons in these age groups, 20–34, in the suburbs, the children of the baby boom of the 1950s. Yet even taking this into account, the central city seems once again to be a magnet for young adults. Marriage postponement, divorce, separation, single parent families, lowered fertility, and increased participation of women in the labor force among the 20–34-year-olds all appear to strengthen the return migration to the central city. Should these trends continue, there may be a significant revival of central cities in the future.

Migratory streams compared

Although there is a sizable return migration to the central cities, when compared to all migratory streams, it is the least important. The most important migratory stream remains that from "frost belt" to "sun belt," generally from Northeast to South and West. This migration is from metropolitan to nonmetropolitan areas. The number moving to the suburbs from the innercities is second most important in magnitude. And third, the metropolitan areas continue to grow on their perimeters, transforming former rural areas into exurban ones. Therefore, on the whole, the American population continues to decentralize, and the entire country continues to urbanize.

In the midst of this decentralization, which has been going on at least since 1920, there is a small countertrend of movement toward the innercity. The significance of this trend lies in its reversal of the pattern of the previous half century, not in its current size. In addition, since it includes a significant number of young persons, this may be an initial wave of the future.

THE URBAN FRONTIER

We began with the innercity and now have described intensifying urbanization as rural areas were made into exurbs, suburbs, and then swallowed completely into the urban core. As the last section on black suburbanization and white in-migration makes clear, change is not limited to the edges of the urban settlement. Or, as some would put it, the "edge" of the urban settlement has shifted to the center. The "frontier," some argue, now lies in the old urban heartland. Let us then conclude this section by looking in detail at one population of persons living on what they call the *urban frontier*. Once again we use them as examples of persons who can be found in virtually every older urban settlement.

Just as rural areas evolve into exurban and then into suburban areas, innercity areas also change. In a pattern characteristic of many central cities, the wealthy left the city for suburban and exurban sites, and their homes were taken over by middle- and upper-middle-class persons who subdivided them. Thus a large house which formerly provided residence for only one family came to house two, three, or even more families. Then, as the middle class departed, that same dwelling was often further subdivided to house four, five, or more households. Originally middle-class dwellings were also converted from single-family to multifamily dwellings.

In the 1960s the typical pattern of conversion to more intensive usage began to change in some old neighborhoods. Young, middle-class persons began to move in and to renovate these old structures. Some buildings, which formerly housed four or five families, were changed to house one or two. Some formerly elegant old hotels, which had been converted to rooming houses, were redesigned to house a smaller number of households. Throughout, the direction of the change was toward less-intensive usage, and therefore it is generally called *deconversion*. As the structures were deteriorating, if not deteriorated, a significant amount of renovation also typically has taken place.

Donald S. Bradley (1977) studied such an area called Virginia-Highlands in the city of Atlanta. This area had been developed, beginning in 1910, as a white, middle-class area. Fifty years later its population was aged, with a third over 55, most were renters, they were working- and dependent-class, and they were white. There were a number of vacant and abandoned buildings in Virginia-Highlands, and "rooming houses, pornography shops, liquor stores, and fast food restaurants thrived along its two main commercial streets."

In 1970 a young, middle-class population began to move into the area. Bradley reported that the 118 new homeowners he studied in Virginia-Highlands had a median age of 27, were college graduates, had incomes of about $17,000, were married, generally without children (only a third of all households had children under 18), were white, were native American, and were southern, Protestant, and urban born.

Eighty-seven percent of Bradley's "restorers" indicated that before moving to Virginia-Highlands they had lived elsewhere in the central city. Thus the majority of persons in his study did not move in from the suburbs, at least on this last move. Perhaps they had some suburban experience, however, for Bradley reports that they rejected being "suburbanites." They also took great pride in living on what they called the urban frontier. They desired to be near the central business district where many of them worked, they said they preferred old houses to new ones, and they liked the relatively low cost of their housing.

The innercity neighborhoods of many American and European settlements are experiencing such revival. Predictions regarding their abandonment may indeed have been premature. Yet the countermigration cityward should not be overestimated. Although it does represent the young and therefore may be the beginning of a larger future in-migration, it is by far the smallest stream today. Its direction represents a reversal of the pattern of the last half century, but then so does the movement from metropolitan to nonmetropolitan areas. Therefore, the only conclusion we can reach at this point is that we need to continue to examine such trends in the future. And perhaps as urbanologists we should also note the tendency of the urban environment to defy even our most precise predictions about it.

SUMMARY

Suburbs are those areas of growth on the fringe of the urban settlement. In the past as in the present, different kinds of people have lived in different types of suburbs. The conception of a homogeneous suburbia, however glamorous or dreary, is known as the *suburban myth*. Old suburbs are those built before 1945; new suburbs are those built afterward.

Suburbanization begins with the development of exurbs—settlements of usually upper-income pioneer urbanites who establish second homes or vacation residences in rural or resort areas. The phase of developing suburbanization begins with the large-scale construction of tract housing, whose residents and their school-age children swell the demand for services. Infill characterizes mature suburbanization, while the intensification of commercial development marks the beginning of the absorption of the suburb into the urban settlement. The phases of suburbanization also can be seen by distance from the center, with exurbs located on the fringe and absorbed suburbs closer in.

Urban growth in American SMSAs has taken place along axes of transportation, such as auto or rail routes. Such growth is called axial or sectoral. The education, occupation, and income of the population differs by sectors.

Growth is also concentric, in terms of rings around the center. The average age of the population, its density, the number of multiple housing units, the proportion of renters, and the proportion of women in the labor force declines with distance from the center.

The growth of black areas is primarily if not exclusively axial. Socioeconomic and racial homogeneity is created and maintained through zoning, minimum lot sizes, minimum home sizes, restrictive covenants, discrimination in advertising and sales, and social rejection. Even though law does prohibit discrimination in housing, homogeneous residential areas persist.

Growth through migration today is primarily from the frost belt to the sun belt; that is, from Northeast to South and West. This migration is from metropolitan to nonmetropolitan areas. The number moving to the suburbs from the innercities, including an increasing number of blacks, is second most important in magnitude.

Third, metropolitan areas continue to decentralize, as they started to do after 1910. Reversing this long-standing trend of the past, today there is a small number of migrants into the innercity. Although it is the smallest of the migratory streams, this cityward movement is significant because it reverses an old pattern and it includes young adults. These middle-class, childless, college educated, white Americans are renovating and deconverting many old homes in the urban frontier areas of many American settlements.

STUDY QUESTIONS

1. Describe the process of suburbanization through its three phases.
2. How do urban populations typically differ axially and concentrically?
3. What are the techniques of exclusion?
4. Compare and contrast the various migratory streams within the urban environment.
5. What is the urban frontier?

SUGGESTED READINGS

Berry, Brian J. L., and Kasarda, John. *Contemporary Urban Ecology* (New York: Macmillan, 1977).

Clark, S. D. *The Suburban Society* (Toronto: University of Toronto Press, 1966).

chapter 11

PLANNED ORGANIZATIONS OF PHYSICAL SPACE

U.S. Department of Housing and Urban Development

217

CONTINUING EXPERIMENTATION

Not long after the evolution of the settlement we know as the city, various attempts were made to improve upon that form. Each time a new settlement was founded, new ideas regarding the "best" urban form were put into practice, with gains as well as losses in the quality of subsequent urban life. These experiments continue through the present and will undoubtedly continue into the future. It is to them that our attention now turns.

A *new city* is an entirely new settlement established as a whole and intended to be relatively autonomous. There are many historical examples of the founding, laying out, and initial construction of a new city; for example, our own capital, Washington, D.C. The establishment of cities such as Brasilia testifies to the continuance of this practice.

On a smaller scale than an entire city, *new towns* have also been established. They represent the desire to establish a new settlement, but they go further; they also represent the desire to eliminate the mistakes made earlier, whatever they may be. In the industrial era, the problems were inadequate housing, poor sanitation, the proximity of dwellings to factories, and the dearth of housing codes. New towns, such as Pullman, Illinois, and Lowell, Massachusetts, were created to solve those problems, while providing their residents with the advantages of modern, industrial planning.

On a still smaller scale, what are called *new communities* have also been established. As with the new towns, new communities are established to solve old problems and to create new solutions. These intentions are evident in the statement of goals of the U.S. 1970 Urban Growth and New Community Development Act, and its 1968 predecessor, Title IV of the Housing and Urban Development Act.

> (1) increasing for all persons, particularly members of minority groups, the available locations for living and working; (2) helping to create neighborhoods designed for easier access between the places where people live and the places where they work and find recreation; and (3) providing adequate public, community and commercial facilities (including facilities needed for education, health and social services, recreation and transportation). (Kaiser, 1976:xvii)

In addition to new towns and new communities, there continue to be still other experiments based on reorganizations of physical space to solve the ills of modern urban life. Communes or intentional communities are among such experiments. They, too, have a rich historical legacy, and they also continue into the contemporary era.

> Communitarians are not only concerned with building alternate models for social and economic relations but also with shaping the values which inform our political culture and provide legitimacy for the political order. They are

addressing an external problem of man in society: the search for purpose and for mutual support which is the crux of community. (Bouvard, 1975:21)

These four types of communal organization are also parts of the urban environment. Let us now examine some instances of each type.

NEW CITIES: BRASILIA

"Building Brasilia, Brazil's new national capital in the interior, was perhaps the largest single coordinated city-building effort in modern times" (Epstein, 1973:a). Ed Bacon, an architect, describes Brasilia as "The Great Effort." "Besides Chandigarh, India," he continues, "the one other measure of the maturity of the architectural profession today is provided by the great new capital of its country." (1967:283). "Brasilia stands in contemporary architecture as the most significant example of a city designed as a whole . . . Costa [the designer] made it clear that Brasilia was never intended to be a model for a typical city. It was meant to be a unique capitol for a great nation." And, " . . . the gift of Brasilia is not primarily the form of its structures or the formal symmetry of its composition, but rather the reformulation of the vision of the city as a totality" (Bacon, 1967:221, 227).

The creation of this entirely new city, then, was undertaken in large part for symbolic purposes, to build a symbol and base for future greatness. The city was also founded in the desire "to move the capital to a made-to-order, modern, perhaps even utopian capital" (Epstein, 1973:28). Proponents of the scheme also argued that the new location in the interior would speed up that region's economic development and help orient governmental policy toward national development. The creation of a new capital was seen as a way of escaping from the many problems of the old capital, Rio de Janeiro, not the least of which was its cumbersome and inefficient bureaucracy. In Epstein's (1973:24) words, "the move in space was seen as a relatively painless means of effecting a revolution in mentality and methods."

Ten criteria were specified and given weights in deciding where to locate the new capital, including a favorable climate, a water supply sufficient for a population of one half million, and access to ground and air transport. An international jury was empaneled, competitors submitted their designs, and Lucio Costa's plan was judged to be the winner. All of the foregoing was done according to the plan of the president of Brazil at that time, Juscelino Kubitscheck de Oliveira.

Kubitscheck then pressed forward with especial vigor to complete the building of the city before his five-year term in office expired. If the entire city could not be finished (a likely possibility in the less than four years remaining after site selection and plan adoption), at least enough construction had to be completed to force any subsequent government to carry on with the project. The haste with which the project was therefore implemented contributed to at least some of the problems which developed.

Initial migration

The site and the plan were entirely new, but the old laws of migration reigned as construction commenced. By now even the least attentive of students should be able to predict that the young, the males, and the poor (but not poverty-stricken) would constitute the bulk of the migrants to the new capital. They were followed almost immediately by the prostitutes and the gamblers, the saloonkeepers and liquor providers, and the others who service a predominately young, male population. For this army of workers and their "support personnel," Costa's grand plan had made no provision. The workers responded in the only reasonable way, they built their own homes.

Every city has its temporary structures and cities that are growing rapidly have more of them. Although the development of shantytowns could easily have been predicted even by beginning students of urban studies, their development in Brasilia seems to have taken the authorities by surprise. Official policy was inconsistent, changing from ignoring the presence of shanties, to tearing them down, and to attempting to control at least their location. Their residents responded with whatever opposition they could muster, as well as with the more usual tactic of rebuilding elsewhere following the destruction of their dwellings.

Favelas

> Lucio Costa's plan divided Brasilia into two principal parts, the Monumental Axis and the Residential Axis, the latter in turn being divided into what have come to be called the South and North Wings. . . . The government buildings largely correspond to the Monumental Axis, the superblocks to the Residential Axis, the city center to their intersection. Axes, intersection, and the local feeder roads constitute the vehicular circulatory system. (Epstein, 1973:54)

To this grand plan the workers who built the city added their settlements, called *favelas*. The planners, having failed to incorporate working class districts into the plan for the new capital, in spite of earlier assurances to the contrary, produced this consequence:

> . . . the lower class was virtually eliminated from many aspects of life of the planned center of Brasilia. . . . The people who built Brasilia are permitted to look at the city and to serve there in menial tasks, but rarely do they live there. (Epstein, 1973:94)

Socioeconomic integration

The early plan also called for "the co-existence of various social classes in neighborhood units." Instead, as built, residential sectors are homogeneous in the social rank of their inhabitants and different sectors are well separated from each other. "While calling for an equality not existing elsewhere in Brazilian society, the planner produced, it turns out, a blueprint for a city of inequality and class separation" (Epstein, 1973:94).

So also has Brasilia failed in its attempted orderly compartmentalization of urban services. Whereas the plan projected a series of semiautonomous superblocks and neighborhoods, each with its own educational, commercial, recreational, and related facilities, this, too, has failed to materialize.[1] Epstein concludes: " . . . one implication of this study is that the construction of Brasilia has fallen short of many of its declared goals."

Urban impact

In spite of all the problems of Brasilia, especially for the workers and for their families who have now joined them or have been created in the new capital, that revolution we call urban has now touched their lives. And what we must remember about the urban revolution is that, however terrible urban life may be, it has typically been an improvement over that which preceded it, in Brazil as well as elsewhere. As Epstein (1973:179) puts it:

> It would be simply quixotic to suppose that any large number of urbanites (even squatters) would consent to return to the economic exploitation, isolation, and lack of social services that characterize rural Brazil under present conditions.

NEW TOWNS: COLUMBIA, MARYLAND

New towns differ from new cities in consciously being a part of some larger settlement. One of America's early new towns was that of Pullman, Illinois, which was built in the 1890s by the Pullman Railway Car Company. Other examples include Gary, Indiana, built in the first decade of the 1900s; Lowell, Massachusetts, built in the 1920s; and Radburn, New Jersey, built in the 1930s. During the New Deal, the Resettlement Administration built three "greenbelt towns" in an effort to relocate unemployed urban males and their families. In all such cases, the new towns were established with the purpose of eliminating old urban problems by new planning. An example of one such attempt follows.

---

[1] Except for primary and elementary schools, which are based on neighborhoods.

The master plan

As our example of a new town we have chosen Columbia, Maryland. It was developed in the mid-1960s on 18,000 acres located midway between the beltways surrounding Washington, D.C., and Baltimore, Maryland. The basic unit of Columbia's master plan was the neighborhood, each having from 2,000 to 5,000 residents. The neighborhood was organized around a center that included:

> an elementary school, park and playground, swimming pool, community center building, and, in some cases, a convenience store. Two to four neighborhoods [were] then combined to form a village of from 10,000 to 15,000 people. Village centers provided supermarkets and other convenience shopping facilities, community meeting facilities, land for middle and high schools and major community recreational facilities. Nine villages surrounded a town center complex that included a regional mall, office buildings, a hotel-motel, restaurants, theatres and a 40-acre town center park and music pavilion. More than 20 percent of Columbia's development acreage [was] set aside for open space, with another 20 percent reserved for business and industry.
>
> By 1972 Columbia's residents had access to a wide variety of community facilities and services. These included an assortment of recreational facilities . . . a professional dinner theatre, an outdoor concert pavilion, several restaurants and lounges and hundreds of acres of parks and open spaces. Shopping facilities included the Columbia Mall, a regional center with two department stores, and three village centers with supermarkets, banks, drug stores, gas stations and assorted specialty shops. The Howard County Public Library operated a branch in Columbia, and four college-level institutions were present in the community. . . . Over 65 firms had located in the Columbia industrial parks. Total employment in the community was more than 15,000.
>
> Columbia's growth and development had also been marked by a number of institutional innovations. Recreational facilities, early childhood educational programs and a community transit system were operated by the Columbia Park and Recreation Association, a unique automatic membership homes association that was incorporated in 1965. . . . Catholics, Jews and Protestants shared common religious facilities in The Interfaith Center, located in Wilde Lake Village. The Columbia Medical Plan, a prepaid group practice health care program provided by the Columbia Hospital and Clinics Foundation in affiliation with The Johns Hopkins Medical Institutions, was formed to meet community health care needs. Innovation in the schools, including operation of a model high school in Wilde Lake Village, had drawn national attention. (Kaiser, 1976:147–49)

Problems

Persistent problems in new towns, including Columbia, include (1) the failure to include income, racial, and ethnic minorities; (2) the failure to integrate households with significantly different incomes, and (3) the failure to compartmentalize urban services into ordered residential units. These criticisms are the same as those made of Brasilia and other new cities. To them we can add a fourth, for new towns: the failure to provide sufficient employment for their residents, many of whom end up commuting long distances elsewhere to work.

NEW COMMUNITIES

The term "new community" is used in the U.S. Urban Growth and New Community Development Act of 1970. The term differs from that of new towns in referring to settlements that are both smaller and less autonomous in conception. In a number of ways, however, new communities are similar to new towns. That is, both attempt to integrate income groups, to lessen distances between work places and residences, and to order facilities and services by locale. In addition, the 1970 act sought to achieve some racial integration.

New communities can be divided into those assisted by governmental programs and those which are purely private enterprise projects. Eight volumes entitled the *New Communities Research Series* (see Kaiser, 1976) report studies of 17 federally assisted projects and 19 paired conventional projects,[2] all under the direction of the Center for Urban and Regional Studies of the University of North Carolina at Chapel Hill.

The seventeen new communities aided by the federal government had received $361 million in governmental commitments, as well as private investments in the billions of dollars before the program was sharply curtailed in 1974. According to the population projections for all these projects combined, they would house almost a million persons.

Communities compared

Kaiser (1976) analyzed a random sample of 5,307 households in federally assisted and nonassisted types of communities, separately analyzing those with and those without subsidized housing. He found that the reasons for selecting an assisted new community differed little from those for selecting a conventional community. Both types of movers based their choice on such considerations as climate, nearness to the natural envi-

---

[2] The Federally assisted communities about which these extensive data are available, are: Columbia, Md.; Elk Grove Village, Ill.; Forest Park, Ohio; Foster City, Cal.; Irvine, Cal.; Jonathan, Minn.; Laguna Niguel, Cal.; Lake Havasu City, Ariz.; North Palm Beach, Fla.; Park Forest, Ill.; Park Forest South, Ill.; Reston, Va.; Sharpstown, Tex.; Valencia, Cal.; Westlake Village, Cal.

The conventionally sponsored new communities which were studied, are: Norbeck-Wheaton, Md.; Schaumburg, Ill.; Sharonville, Ohio; West San Mateo, Cal.; Fountain Valley, Cal.; Chanhassen, Minn.; Dana Point, Cal.; Kingman, Ariz.; Tequesta, Fla.; Lansing, Ill.; Richton Park, Ill.; West Springfield, Va.; Southwest Houston, Tex.; Bouquet Canyon, Cal.; Agoura/Malibu Junction, Cal.

ronment, and convenience to work. Of 19 characteristics on which they all rated their respective communities, only two—overall planning and recreational facilities—were mentioned significantly more often by federally assisted new community residents. "Households moving to new communities were like those moving to the nearby, more conventional suburban communities in their profiles of family life cycle stage and socioeconomic class" (Kaiser, 1976:45). Movers to new communities were found also to have higher incomes than the general population of metropolitan movers. This was particularly true with respect to blacks.

> Black households moving to new communities were likely to be families with children and good incomes, who were buying a house and planning to stay. They were much more like their white new community neighbors than like movers to the black suburban communities, and they were not very representative at all of the general profile of black metropolitan movers. (Kaiser, 1976:83)

Jonathan described

For the example of a federally supported new community we have chosen Jonathan, Minnesota.

> Jonathan . . . is located in rural Carver County, 25 miles southwest of downtown Minneapolis within the Twin Cities Metropolitan Area. Jonathan is located a short distance north of and has been annexed by the farm-center town of Chaska which had over 5,000 residents when the study began in 1972. . . .
> As originally planned, the community was to be developed on about 3,000 acres in two upper- and middle-income residential villages. In 1966, the scope of the project was expanded to encompass 4,800 acres with a target population of 41,300 persons after a 20-year development period. Finally, the project was further expanded when Jonathan finalized its application for a federal loan guarantee under Title IV. The project area was expanded to 6,000 acres (and subsequently to over 8,000 acres), projected population was increased to approximately 50,000, industrial acreage was expanded from 500 to 1,989 acres, and a commitment was made to provide over 6,500 housing units for low- and moderate-income families.
> The design concept for Jonathan is shaped by the existing road system and a 1,700-acre open space grid (21 percent of the site) following the natural ravines and drainage courses through the property. Within the matrix of existing highways and proposed open space, five villages, each to house approximately 7,000 residents in a variety of housing types, were proposed. Village centers were to provide basic facilities for daily living, including shopping, post offices, municipal services and elementary schools. A town center was to serve as a regional multifunctional center with major retail, medical, office and entertainment facilities.
> In 1972, when Jonathan was selected for the study, the population of the community stood at 1,500 persons housed in 420 dwelling units, 148 of which were constructed under the FHA Section 235 and 236 subsidized housing

programs. The initial phase of the first village center was in operation and provided some convenience shopping facilities. A man-made lake had been constructed adjacent to the village center, with an accompanying recreational pavilion. Walking paths connected homes to the village center, the lake, and a neighborhood park with a baseball diamond and tennis court. Although schools had yet to be constructed in Jonathan, the industrial park was growing, with 45 firms providing 1080 jobs by the end of 1973.

Reflecting the character of the Twin Cities area, Jonathan's population was predominantly (97 percent) white. However, because of the high proportion of subsidized housing, the median income of the Jonathan households, $11,800, was the lowest of any of the communities studied. Almost two-thirds of the household heads had attended college and three fourths were employed in white collar jobs. (Kaiser, 1976:159–60)

When the author visited Jonathan four years after Kaiser's study, it had grown very little, to about 2,500. A few additional firms had located in the project, to increase the number of available jobs to about 1,200. Some 97 percent of the population was white and the low average income reported by Kaiser continued.

Problems

From the foregoing description of Jonathan, as well as the analyses available in the *New Communities Research Series,* it is clear that the problems of new communities are essentially the same as those of both new towns and new cities. In spite of their attempts, even when federally assisted, such communities have failed to include low-income and significant portions of different racial groups. They have become, at least at the current stage of their development, as segregated and homogeneous by income and race as old communities. The populations they have attracted have been the higher-income households, among blacks as well as whites. They have largely failed to provide employment for their residents, who must therefore commute long distances to work since these new communities are typically in outlying sections. And finally, they have for the most part been unable to order urban facilities and services to areas and neighborhoods within them.

OTHER EXPERIMENTS

The urban environment also continues to include a number of people who think that they (and possibly their associates) have the answer to the assorted ills which plague us. Without public or even very much private financial backing, primarily with only their own lives, they create their own new communal structures. Such persons are ignored in much of the conventional urban literature, in part because their numbers are small, in part because they frequently locate in remote areas, and in part because knowledge of them is scanty and unsystematic.

Yet their residents are urban born and urban bred. Their recruits learn of the existence and location of communes through urban sources of communication. Through modern means of communication and travel they relate to one another in the exchange of information, goods and services, and in the exchange of members. And in other ways as well, communes, intentional communities, ashrams,[3] and other such experiments with communal life are distinctly urban.

At least one reason that communes are largely ignored in the urban literature stems from the difficulty the urbanologist experiences in securing information about them. Those who experiment in "alternative social structures" have learned that there is little to be gained from publicity and often much to lose. Publicity brings tourists, curiosity-seekers, pulp-magazine and book writers, a breed of "commune-followers," and (worse yet?), some sociologists. Through loyalty and love, to protect the individual commune even from its most ardent admirers, those "in the know" are at least discreet in passing on information about the location of a communal group. Such reticence, of course, produces scores of rumors about this group "in Tennessee," and that one "on the Lower East Side," and then that new one "just outside Boston." Since actually knowing about a real-live commune also appears to make one seem "with it" in certain circles, the number of phantom communes far outstrips the number ever in existence. Some people also frequently talk about forming a community—you know, "a commune"—and such talk gets repeated as accomplished fact. Finally, communes break up and their members disappear literally overnight, so no one is ever really sure about the reliability of information about any commune save his or her own, and he and she may have frequent doubts about even that one.

Data biases

Time-consuming field research is therefore the only way data can be collected, but the same reticence that prevents knowledge of their existence also causes the would-be investigator problems.

> If members of the broader society have reservations about the community movement, this caution is returned by the new communitarians. They welcome visitors as possible recruits to a new way of life, but they have taken considerable pains to protect themselves from the mass media and the intruding desire to sensationalize their life in common. Visitors must write

---

[3] Although more specialized publications often distinguish between communes, intentional communities, secular and religious communities, and other experiments in community living, for our introductory purposes all such experiments and alternative social structures are analyzed together. We will use the common terms for them interchangeably. For other studies, see: Abrams and McCulloch, 1976; Erasmus, 1977; Houriet, 1971; Kanter, 1972; Kephart, 1976; Melville, 1972; Roberts, 1971; and Zablocki, 1972.

ahead and state their purpose before receiving permission to visit an intentional community. Communitarians generally devote the majority of their
time to community affairs and have few hours to answer questions and
shepherd visitors about. Also, given the small size of the communities, the
possibility that visitors might outnumber the membership is a very real one.
Besides the sensation seekers, communitarians avoid social scientists. The
ground for this reticence is the desire to prevent definitive descriptions of
their attempts while they are still in the stage of experimentation. Also, they
fear what they call the "exploitation" of their daily life. (Bouvard, 1975:4–5)

In spite of Bouvard's problems in gaining access, she nevertheless
continued her research, spending a year living in different communities,
informally questioning their members, and learning about them through
participant observation. What communities did she study? "Because
there are literally thousands of these small communities, I decided to
focus on some of the most important types of groups rather than examine
all of them." How Bouvard knew what types existed without some, at
least preliminary, research is not known. Without such information the
communal groups selected by Bouvard must be acknowledged to be
biased. Whether or not they are representative of the others or not we
cannot say, nor does Bouvard. While she does provide us with valuable
data, the information must be analyzed with caution.

A second data set is available to us, but it, too, is biased and of unknown relationship to the thousands of what we call communes that exist
today. From 1965 to 1970, Wallace collected data on some 15 communes,
indirectly observed the activities of 8, and participated in the origin and
development of 1. All of these are, or were, located in northeastern section of the United States and the portion of Canada bordering it.

Both data sets are biased. Also, the nature of the communal groups
these two studies describe are different. Some argue that the communities
themselves have undergone a transition, and that it was primarily the
nondrug-oriented groups which survived. Thus, whereas communes and
drugs may have been closely linked in the 1960s, today the literature
suggests that most experimental communities eschew the use of all drugs,
including alcohol and tobacco. On the other hand, the difference in the
data sets may stem simply from differences in biased samples. Caution in
interpretation must therefore be exercised.

Commune commonalities

There are several immediate generalizations that can be made about the
communes of the 1960s, which are included in the Wallace sample. First,
three fourths of them were connected with the psychedelic drug culture.
Most of their participants used such drugs regularly or whenever available. One fourth of the total number dealt in drugs as well.

Dealing in drugs was one way to help support communal finances. Seven of the 24 communes were financially self-supporting, albeit in three cases on a subsistence scale. The majority depended on sources of support unconnected to the commune. Regardless of income source, finances were a continuing problem for most experimenters in "alternative social structures."

About half of these communities had one or more children, who were typically under five years of age. Almost all of the communes Wallace examined were related to various universities in some way; that is, some communards were on university faculties or, more typically, they were students, at least sometimes.

The age range for participants was between 18 and 45, with modal ages being from 20 to 35. Aside from one group, which persisted for some time as exclusively male, no commune had a greater imbalance of two to one in the sex ratio, most were roughly evenly divided, and any excess was usually but not always male. Finally, all of the communes had one person, and usually no more than one, who was considered by most to be the principal leader or organizer.

The communes—or "communities," as she calls them—which were studied by Bouvard in the 1970s are reported to be quite different in several respects. First there appear to be many, many more such experimental groups today than there were in the 1960s. Bouvard hazards the estimate of 500 communities for the state of Vermont alone, and over 100,000 communities in the United States. An article in the *New York Times* in 1974 estimated the number of persons involved in intentional communities in the Northeast alone at in excess of 400,000.

There is a second important difference: according to Bouvard, many people have a negative image of "intentional communities as communes where free sex and drugs are the main focus of daily life." Bouvard states that "among the purposes of [her] study are the desires to dispel [such] widespread misconceptions. . . ." Certainly among the Koinonia Partners of Georgia; the Hutterite community of North Dakota; the Bruderhof of New York, Pennsylvania, and Connecticut; the New Testament Missionary Fellowship and the Children of God communities, all included in Bouvard's study, there does indeed appear to be little "free sex" or use of drugs. Also in support of Bouvard's view is the argument that groups heavily into drugs presumably had the lowest survival rates. Indeed, Wallace's data suggest about 18 months as an average length of existence for such communes. Finally, even among peoples committed to experimentation, the period of community founding is likely to be relatively more experimental than later in the life of the community. Several explanations thus point in the same direction, namely that the other experiments we are discussing have changed somewhat in character from the 1960s to the 1970s, even as the larger society itself has changed.

Problems

More importantly, however, the communes have not changed at all in one critical respect: they have not changed in the composition of their resident population. Repeating each other almost word for word, both Wallace and Bouvard point out that the overwhelming majority of communitarians are "white, middle-class adults in their early 20s and 30s." Thus, as was observed for the other new organizations of physical space, the communes have also failed to achieve the integration of different racial and socioeconomic groups.

Second, these experiments in community creation have failed to provide employment for all or even most of its members. For the majority, income is secured through jobs taken elsewhere, often at distant locations. Small in size and eschewing the need for many services, though, the new communes are successful in matching facilities to an immediate locale.

SUMMARY

In large-scale planned organizations of physical space in entirely new cities, as well as in new towns, new communities, and other experiments in community creation, all have failed to attract minority-income or racial groups. All, too, have failed to integrate different economic classes; but instead are relatively homogeneous by income, education, and occupation, by stage in family and life cycle, by race, religion, and national origin. Having earlier noted the widespread pervasiveness of residential differentiation in unplanned communities, we can now add that experimental efforts also evidence this.

The previous two sections—the first on symbolic bounding (Part Three) and the second on physical bounding (Part Four)—thus merge at this juncture.

Symbolic bounding, we argued in Part Three, consists of the formation of groups tied together by communication. Physical bounding consists of being enclosed in the same space with others—in the innercity, the suburbs, or perhaps in a new town.

"Peoples" are symbolic, we argued, composed of those who assume commonality with each other. Aggregations are physical, we continued, and there is nothing necessarily symbolic about them. Thus we examined physical urban space—the innercity, suburbs, new towns, and communities to determine, among other things, their symbolic natures. What have we learned? Although the investigator cannot assume that physical space (where I am) and symbolic space (who is included in my "people") are identical, the overlap between them is sufficiently high as to justify as a routine matter empirical investigation of the connection.

STUDY QUESTIONS ———————————————————————————

1. How did the initial migrants to Brasilia differ from migrants to other cities? How did they differ from migrants in earlier historical periods?
2. What impact did the urban revolution have on the residents of the *favelas*?
3. What were the four basic goals of new towns and new communities?
4. How does residential differentiation differ in planner organizations of urban space?

SUGGESTED READINGS ———————————————————————————

Kaiser, Edward J. *Residential Mobility in New Communities* (Cambridge, Mass.: Ballinger Publishing, 1976).

Kephart, William M. *Extraordinary Groups: The Sociology of Unconventional Life Styles* (New York: St. Martin's Press, 1976).

PART FIVE

The urbanite in public, in private, and in person

The "net" we cast upon the waters of urban environment grows to its smallest size in the three chapters of this part. Beginning in Part One we examined entire urban settlements: the city, the metropolis, and the urban environment. In Part Two we observed how population changes with urbanization. Symbolic groupings of peoples were then analyzed in Part Three, and physical aggregations became the focus of our investigation in Part Four. As the size of our unit of examination narrows to finally apprehend the individual urbanite, each of the foregoing sections provides the context for our concluding study.

Neighborhood, housing, and urban life all vary according to the settlements in which they are located. To live in a neighborhood that was part of a settlement closed in by walls was significantly different from today's neighborhoods of the vast urban environment that is bounded by electronic communication and modern transportation. To live in a two- or three-story house, without water, toilet, or ovens, as was true in the settlement form we have called a city, created different patterns of interaction than found in the fully serviced modern house or apartment.

Urban populations differ in family size, mortality, and life expectancy, in sex ratios and other demographic variables, and this, too, makes a difference in neighborhood, dwelling, and individual life. The additional contextual variable of region was also stressed in Part Two; urban life we now know, varies by whether one is southerner or easterner, by whether one lives on West Coast or perhaps in the Southwest.

Who one considers to be one's people determines who one's neighbors are most likely to be—as Part Three pointed out. And whether one lives in innercity or in suburb with one's people influences the nature of neighborhood life and the housing one occupies.

Given these many contextual variables, our approach here as elsewhere will be to examine the research for the principles of urban life it reveals. Knowing the variations in the context of urban life, empirical studies can be examined according to the context in which they were done. Thus, with our ecological framework guiding our inquiry, perhaps we can avoid overgeneralization even as we reconcile some apparent contradictions in the findings of urban studies. We hope that in the process of apprehending the urbanite in public, in private, and in person, we will learn some additional principles.

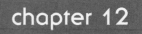

chapter 12

THE URBANITE IN PUBLIC

Photos courtesy of
Samuel E. Wallace

233

PUBLIC DEFINED

The word "public" means many things: national, not concealed, shared by all, the people of a country or locality. However, the sense in which we use the term refers to those places where a person can be observed by strangers, usually many of them. Driving to work, watching a movie in a theater, and shopping in a department store are a few of the many places we frequent where strangers can and do observe us.

Urbanites are in public for much of their lives. From childhood through at least 16 years of age, urban youths attend schools that are public. (Even the small number who attend private schools are "in public," as we are using the term.) Throughout adulthood, again most urbanites spend large portions of their lives at places of employment that are public in nature. In terms of daily life as well, the urbanite, whether walking, riding, eating, drinking, dancing, worshipping, or engaging in many other activities, often is in the presence of others whom he or she does not know.

It is impossible for us to examine the nature of all public places; there are simply too many of them. And we cannot even examine a sample of public places. Here once again we must resort to the use of illustrative examples.

PUBLIC PARKS

The example of public places that we have chosen is public parks. Parks are lands that have been set aside to be held in common and used by the public. Within public parks, we can (and usually do) observe others who are strangers, just as they observe us. Parks are public places. Also, going to a park is voluntary, whereas going to work, among other public places, may not be voluntary in the same sense. Let us then observe the urbanite as he and she voluntarily go to public parks.[1]

TYPES OF PARKS

The classic seven-volume study entitled the *Regional Survey of New York,* which was conducted in the 1920s (and remains highly recommended), devoted considerable attention to the provision of parks (see: "Public Recreation," vol. 5). Integrating the park materials of the *Regional Survey* with our data, which were collected about a half century later, we can distinguish three types of parks, which we will study. There are many other kinds of parks, which space makes it impossible to discuss here, including county, state, regional, and national parks.

---

[1] The data on parks was collected in a series of studies conducted at New York University and at Queens College of the City University of New York. The study of Washington Square Park was directed by Professor Patricia Sexton and the author (1974), and the other studies by the author. All studies, however, were carried out by students, who are acknowledged herein, when possible, and in the acknowledgements.

The first type of park to be studied is *local parks*. New York park planners have said that there should be one local park within one fourth mile of every resident, but the goal may differ in other settlement patterns (city or urban environmental.)

To a considerable extent, the use of a park depends on the size of the population. Population size, of course, is only one of the factors that influence use of parks. The age, family status, mobility, and socioeconomic status of the population also change park use. Nevertheless, total population is related to park size as a gross measure, both as ideal and actuality. The *Regional Survey* suggested that there should be one acre of local parks for every thousand residents.

Whereas the *Regional Survey* suggested the optimum size of a local park to be five acres, contemporary planners stress the value of even very small parks, called vest-pocket parks, and what about less formally designated areas which are used as parks?

Scattered throughout every settlement are places to congregate, sit, gossip, read, doze, and do other things human. The place may be the steps of the courthouse, the street-corner hangout, the site where teenagers gather with their cars, or perhaps the benches in the middle of the block where senior citizens visit. Although not called parks, or even necessarily having names, such areas serve as parks. Their existence indicates that people shape space—and not always in the forms their officials provide for them. Knowing this about people, as urbanologists we should be wary of relying exclusively on official forms.

For example, officially the residents of the borough of Manhattan in New York have only 2.17 acres of all types of parks per thousand population. Conventional new suburban communities have an average of 21.6 acres (Kaiser, 1976), about ten times the New York figure. Federally assisted new communities have 40.6 acres of parks per thousand residents, 19 times the Manhattan figure. Citing such statistics, some have reasoned that the only solution is to tear down enough of New York to give New Yorkers their proportionate share of park space.

The approach advocated herein starts—but does not stop—with what we may term the official (or officials') view of reality. After interviewing officials, reading their reports and studying their statistics, we left their offices to study firsthand the places officially designated as parks. Then we left the official parks to look for other spaces that were used as parks.

Unofficial parks include plazas, squares, street corners, vacant lots, schoolyards and church-related facilities, small sitting areas, and a variety of other spaces. Some of these are located on medians between heavily trafficked thoroughfares; some are on tops of buildings; and some are located in places so hidden from public view that their existence is known only by some local residents. Unofficial parks at the local level may be intensively used, furthermore, even while officially designated ones are abandoned. This first type of park, the local park, is determined by use, not by officials. Within the type of park deemed local, we will study both unofficial and official ones.

The second type of park to be studied is a *neighborhood or community park*. (We shall use the terms neighborhood and community interchangeably when discussing parks.) Whereas the local park is nearby, perhaps within a block or two, the neighborhood park is farther away, perhaps six or eight blocks. Although most neighborhood parks are officially designated, not all of them are. In terms of usage, neighborhood parks may be vacant lots, churchyards and schoolyards, areas along nearby bodies of water, and abandoned piers and boat docks.

Finally, the third type of park to be studied is the *metropolitan park*. It is large in size and serves the entire settlement (city, borough, county, metropolitan area). In the early stages of urbanization, there may be large tracts of land that can serve as parks other than the officially designated ones. As urbanization intensifies, including the developing phase of suburbanization, only officially designated parks survive. Let us now turn to observe each type.

Local parks: Unofficial

Fifty-nine users of unofficial local parks in New York City were interviewed in the middle of a weekday afternoon: 24 males and 35 females. Not quite half (26) of our nonrandom sample was over 55 years of age; 17 were between 30 and 54; 9 were between 18 and 29; 3 were 13 to 17; and 4 were under 12. Although they were thus varied in age, with an overrepresentation among the older segment of the population, they were homogeneous with respect to race. Fifty-six of the 59 were white, and in this our sample was representative of the surrounding residential area.

The most important reason for selecting the site they used was its accessibility, they told us, and indeed, 31 of the 59 lived within three blocks of the benches where they were interviewed. Fifteen people lived within 3 to 6 blocks, 9 lived within 6 to 12 blocks, and four said they lived more than one mile away.

Why did they come? Twenty-eight came with someone with whom to sit and visit, and another 17 said they came to meet someone. A total of 45 therefore came to visit with someone. Three persons came with their pets. The ten who came alone without specific plans to meet a certain person added that they "would probably see someone they knew." As we visited with these interviewees, they remarked that "we're all neighbors here," and "we all know each other and if we don't, we soon will." Indeed, from our observations this appeared to be the case.

Why did they not do their visiting at home? we asked. Did they have a yard in which to visit? Twenty-four had a yard available yet two thirds of them used such places as where we interviewed them more than once a week. Fifty-one percent of those without private yards used the sitting area more than once a week, suggesting that the availability of private outdoor space in which to visit was not closely related to frequency of use of public space.

Did they only come here or did they use other parks? Thirty-three said they did regularly use other parks. When we analyzed the relationship between park use and age, we found it to be inverse. However, it was the variety of parks used that decreased with age, not the frequency of total use. "I used to go to the Botanical Gardens," one said, "but I'm too old to get there now so I just come here."

Finding these interviewees willing to talk with us as long as we wished, and enjoying what they called "the relaxing atmosphere" ourselves, we continued to try to understand what pleasure anyone could find in sitting near thousands of passing cars, visiting with each other above the roar of traffic. A member of the research team (Carol Kravitz) who lived in the area had told us of a nearby park, which was much quieter and even had some grass and flowers. We therefore asked, "Why don't you use that park over by the school?" "Oh, there's never anyone there," they graciously replied to what was obviously a dumb question to them.

In his study, William H. Whyte (1974) suggests that active and busy open spaces are safe places, and Jane Jacobs (1961) earlier made the same point with respect to streets. Whyte suggests:

> The best way to meet the problem of undesirables is to make spaces attractive to all kinds of desirable people. . . .
>
> . . . it is not so much that they [the undesirables] are present, but that other people are not. . . .
>
> Busy plazas, the record is clear, are safe plazas. The same is true with vandalism. It often mirrors what the builders and designers think of people.

While our data certainly confirm the foregoing observations, we think that the concern for safety perhaps has been overemphasized. For although our 59 interviewees were not unconcerned with their safety, they made it clear that they first came to be with other people, to visit with them, to watch them, and just for the pleasure of being in their midst. Safety may indeed flow from busy places, but it is the presence of people that draws others to the spot.

Asked how they would like this place to be improved, 29 suggested that more benches be added. Twenty-one suggested better upkeep, 13 more trees, grass, and flowers, and 10 thought the dogs should be curbed. Only one of the 59 thought more safety should be provided.

"Well, tell us how long you've been here and when you plan on leaving and we'll let you get back to important matters," we asked as our last question. The range of time spent in the areas where we interviewed varied, from 10 or 15 minutes to five hours, with a modal length between 75 minutes and three hours.

An official local park

The foregoing were all unofficial parks. To learn if the use of official local parks differed from unofficial ones, we (Gail Horowitz, 1974) talked to some users of Paley Park, which is located on East 53rd Street, between Fifth Avenue and Madison. Surrounded on all sides by tall buildings, and only 42 feet wide and about 100 feet deep, its 4,200 square feet (less than one tenth of an acre) has so captured the hearts of its users that their only complaint is "there should be more of them."

"I *love* it. I come here all the time to eat my lunch and just enjoy the sound of the waterfall" (which is located at the rear; its 20-foot height and its flow of 1,800 gallons of water per minute helps to muffle the sounds of the street).

"After a long morning of shopping, I look forward to stopping off at the park to rest, to eat. I don't know what I'd do without it."

"Don't publicize the park; it will bring too many people. *Just make more of them.*"

"It is small and cozy, that's what I like about it. So what if it's crowded. New Yorkers are used to crowds."

Crowded it was, constantly. The individual chairs and tables were fully occupied and immediately reoccupied whenever someone left.

Neighborhood parks

Two of the neighborhood parks studied were selected for reporting here. Washington Square Park is a good example of an intensively used park, serving a large and heterogeneous population. The population is large because this area of Manhattan has less park space than any other area, and this park alone constitutes almost half of that available (Sexton and Wallace, 1974). Were we to distinguish between a neighborhood and a community park, in fact, Washington Square would qualify as a community park since so many people use it.

The second example consists of a series of official and unofficial parks scattered along Manhattan's West Side. The major portion of this combined area is Riverside Park, which stretches from 72nd Street to 123rd Street. The entire area of our study begins at 23rd Street and ends at 162nd Street.

Washington Square Park   In the initial field observation of Washington Square Park, we simply listed all types of activities observed, enumerating 39 activities, including scavenging, stoning, and lovemaking, in addition to the more frequent sitting, reading, and conversing. Random observation was followed by selected time samples, in which the frequency of each activity was tabulated. Learning then that activities varied by time of day, we calculated percentages for activities, using as a base the total number of users present at that particular time. Nine activities were found to dominate during one period. They became the basis for activity profiles, and the profiles in turn provided the basis for proportional sampling by activity.

Seven of the nine selected activities, including sitting, conversing, reading, cycling, dog walking, jogging, and chess playing, represented primary usage. Such usage differed from cutting through the park to go somewhere else. This latter usage of the park was considered to be secondary.

Slides, videotape, and 8mm film were used as part of the study of Washington Square Park (Harrison, Wallace, and Sexton, 1975). Viewing these visual data, we were struck by the differences in the speed with which people went through the park. The favored pace was a leisurely stroll. Men held their hands behind their backs, their steps were short and slow, and they gazed up into the trees and off to the sides. Women walked slowly, also, and, as if to prolong their journey through the park, they zigzagged from one side of the path to the other. Contrary to the dominant pattern, there were those who "raced" through Washington Square Park, with long strides, quick steps, and eyes trained on the path. Did these differences stem from differences in people? Did strollers stroll outside the park, too, or was their pace slowed upon entry into the park?

We moved outside the park to observe the context within which the park existed. Outside we observed that the dominant pace was what we termed "the New York rush." People's heads were down, their eyes were trained to the ground, and their forward momentum was great. The pace of pedestrian traffic in New York, in fact, has been rated by one observer as the fastest in the world (Rensberger, 1976). While we did not time pedestrians outside the park, all observers agreed that most walked fast and that those who did not were in the way.

The same "New York rushers," however, shortened their step and slowed their pace almost with the first foot that landed in the park. The head and eyes went up, the shoulders went back, and not infrequently the person was observed to take a deep breath. What happened to them? Solotaroff, an author and contributor to the *New York Times Magazine,* expresses it this way (1976:13):

> The city is a kind of tunnel that connects my home to my office, and my psyche has become conditioned to operate in the streets much as it does in the subway—withdrawn, protective, distracted: the chronic paranoia of the middle class. . . . As usual in the park on Sunday, a neglected part of me has begun to thrive. I have stepped out of my particular niche . . . and become instead simply another New Yorker who has come to the park to let himself off his particular leash.

The relief from what he calls "paranoia" [we wouldn't] does not last long. For when we shifted our sociological eye to the end of the park as our "strollers" exited, yes, we did indeed observe the majority to do once again "the New York rush." However brief their relaxation may have been, we reasoned that it was important, because people went out of their way to walk through the park.

Having observed that "strolling" was frequently park-induced, we divided secondary users into "strollers" and those who just "cut through," and included both types in the sample of secondary users to be interviewed. Once outside Washington Square Park, the research team had observed another interesting park-related activity. Some people had been observed to walk around the sides of the park, from one corner to another, in order to avoid entering the park at all. Such park avoiders also had to be interviewed, we decided, along with the primary and secondary users. Finally, we thought there were probably some people who lived close to the park but never used it, and that such nonusers should also be interviewed.

One part of the research team then developed an interview schedule for each of the proposed samples, with some questions common to all and some specialized for a particular sample. The other part of the team continued observation, establishing activity profiles by time of day and by weekday or weekend. The total number of users, regardless of activity, was also enumerated by selected time samples.

Primary users.   Ninety primary users were interviewed. Interviewers were instructed to interview a certain number of joggers, sitters, readers, and so forth. The number of each type of primary user to be interviewed was determined by the proportion engaged in that activity, which were established in activity profiles drawn from field observation. Since we used quota sampling by activity, i.e., a fixed number of joggers, sitters, readers, and the like, we think the persons interviewed are fairly representative.

Field observation had indicated that more males than females use Washington Square Park, and our sample reflects this. Interviewers were not told to select subjects by sex but by activity; but in so doing they produced a sample of about the same proportions by sex as we had observed in the field, 60–40. The males interviewed were also more frequent users, two thirds of them using the park more than ten times per month, whereas only 40 percent of the females use the park that often. Male and female patterns of park usage did not differ by type of activity, however.

Two thirds of the primary users, whether male or female, are satisfied with the park and feel a "sense of community" with the other users. They told us: "Here I can talk to people even if I don't know them." "Everybody is friendly as we are all in our park." About two thirds of them also use other parks, Central Park being mentioned most often. Why? They told us they could do things in Central Park that were not possible or available in Washington Square, such as kite flying or baseball playing.

Those who were dissatisfied (yet continued to use the park), again whether male or female, wanted more police and related security measures. Second on their list was the wish to get rid of the "undesirables": the drug addicts, sex perverts, winos, and the like, as they referred to them. Some of those who expressed satisfaction with the park also stated that they would like to get rid of the undesirables.

Secondary users.   Secondary users, the reader will recall, are those who stroll through or who cut through the park on their way elsewhere. They differ from primary users in not sitting down, conversing, reading, or engaging in other primarily park behaviors. The two types of secondary users differ from each other in the speed at which they move through the park. Field observation had revealed more males than females in this category, and our sample reflects this in being two thirds male.

Half of the secondary users say they are satisfied with the park; half are not. Nevertheless, 70 percent of them use the park nearly every day (to walk through), and almost half of the total return on weekends as primary users. Half say they feel no sense of community with other users.

Park avoiders.   To our surprise, even after additional field observation to confirm, males also are more frequently found among the park avoiders, and our sample reflects this, with 17 males and 13 females. While it may be that females avoid the park in less obvious ways than walking around its sides, an unobtrusive observer recorded slightly more males as park avoiders.

We began our interview, after introducing ourselves and securing permission, by asking: "Why are you avoiding the park?" Not one person denied that he or she was in fact avoiding it. Sixty percent told us that they avoid it all the time, whereas the others sometimes "cut through." In terms of frequency or regularity of avoidance, females' rates are somewhat higher (two thirds of the females avoid all the time, half the males do).

Half of these 30 park avoiders also avoid all other parks. Why? They answer: parks in general, and Washington Square Park in particular, are not safe places. Most park avoiders want more police in parks and other security improvements, such as better lighting. If such changes were made, they say, they would use this park and others. Until then, however, park avoidance will be part of their life style. The profile of our subjects makes it clear that for half of them the avoiding of Washington Square Park is but an instance of a larger park-avoidance pattern.

Nonusers.   The nonusers are those who live within two blocks of the park yet do not go to the park. To interview them we had to walk around the several adjacent blocks, try to recognize persons as both residents and nonpark users, then ask whether they lived nearby but did not use the park. We usually guessed wrong, and we had to approach over 100 people in order to secure 30 interviews. How representative they are we do not know. The fact that two thirds of them are female may not match the universe of all nonusers of parks.

As with park avoiding, nonuse of parks is general, not specific. That is, 60 percent of those who do not use Washington Square Park also do not use any other parks. Why not? Five said they felt "absolutely no need to frequent such places."

New York is the Big Apple, in part because its life is rarely boring. Thus even near the end of many interviews, our waning interest was revived by persons we dubbed "above parks people." "Young lady," one interviewer was addressed, "I should think people would be *much* better off spending their time in museums and theaters rather than romping around in places like parks."

Problems.   In addition to revealing the relationship between a park, those who live around it, and those who use it, the study of Washington Square Park also indicates that, while busy places may be sought by people, parks can also be too busy. Sixteen thousand persons use the Park on weekdays in the fall season, and some 19,000 use it on weekends, according to our conservative estimates. The area of Manhattan we have called the Village, whose boundaries are taken to be those of Planning District Number Two, has a population of about 80,000 persons and a total of 18.933 acres of park. With 8.626 acres, Washington Square Park constitutes almost half of the total park space available. The shortage of park space is reflected in what can only be described as the intensive overuse of Washington Square Park. Those who do use the park come from the surrounding area and from New York University. The composition of the park users more closely reflects the community in the evenings and on weekends, because NYU has few classes at those times.

Another theme running through the study is the negative impact of the so-called undesirables. When they take over the park at night, those unlike them leave. And when they are present during the day, they create much dissatisfaction. Therefore, to the homogeneity of race and class found among users can be added the homogeneity of behavior and appearance desired by the majority.

West Side parks   Along Manhattan's West Side near the Hudson River there are large and small parcels of land that are used as parks—including the formally designed Riverside Park. When Frederick Law Olmstead laid out Riverside Park, he designed a drive to carry vehicles along the edge of the city, with several places where vehicles could enter but not traverse the park. Ignoring Olmstead's plan, the city allowed a railroad to lay its tracks all along the West Side, through land being used as parks as well as that officially designated as such.

Robert Moses was the next to begin to turn the West Side neighborhood parks into traffic routes. In his 1934 project, Moses did improve the park by putting the railroad tracks underground. At the same time, however, he replaced the occasional trains on the two sets of tracks with continuous automobile traffic on four lanes of limited access and partially elevated expressways. Entrance and exit ramps, the expressway itself, and the local streets over which the West Side Highway is sometimes elevated, make it extremely difficult for West Siders to get to their parks.

Imagine trying to get to this West Side park, which is located at 23rd Street. "Thomas F. Smith Park . . . is bisected diagonally . . . by the main roadway elevated structure of the existing West Side Highway, and severed by the access ramps connecting the highway to 22nd Street" (West Side Highway Project, 1974). Or try to get to the Morton Street Pier, opened for public use in 1966 and used by several hundred people daily and an estimated 500 daily users on weekends. "Despite the rather sparse facilities, and the deteriorating conditions of the [pier], (hundreds) come to the pier mostly on foot or by bicycle, having to make their way beneath the existing West Side Highway, and across West Street-Twelfth Avenue between parked trucks and moving traffic" (West Side Highway Project, 1974).

Add to the problems of access the high noise levels (about 80 decibels, by our estimates), the air pollution, and the occasional accident that may bring an automobile careening into the park itself, and you begin to grasp the impact of the West Side Highway on West Side parks.

Park usage.   Aside from the incompatability of highway and parks, something which is obvious to nearly everyone but those who decide on highway routes, what else can we learn from this example of neighborhood parks? In his study of plaza usage, William H. Whyte (1974) states that his team counted users, determined the favorite places, and then spent months trying to explain why people sat where they did. "After three months of checking out various factors—such as sun angles, size of spaces, nearness to transit—we came to a spectacular conclusion: people sit most where there are places to sit."

Our study of parks parallels Whyte's conclusion. People *park* most where there are places to *park*. If there is only one sizable park, as with Washington Square Park, then it will be very intensively used. If there is a long strip of parks, park users will be more widely spaced. To Whyte's proposition, however, we add that people (some of them) will do almost anything to *park*. They will crawl under elevated structures, dart between parked trucks across busy streets, and be apparently oblivious to the roar of traffic as they *park*. Whatever purpose parks serve, from the behavior of their users we must conclude that parks are important to them.

Our calculations indicate that there are about 20,000 users of the West Side parks per weekend day, during the peak period of 11:00 A.M. to 4:00 P.M. We estimate weekday use to be one tenth the weekend use. For the spring season, we therefore estimate that approximately 50,000 people use the West Side parks each week.

On the basis of counts of automobiles within the park, we estimate that 98 percent of all park users arrive on foot or bicycle. The enumeration of major activities indicates that once in the park, 43 percent of the weekend park users were sitting and 32 percent were walking leisurely through the park. Cycling was the third most frequent activity, with 19 percent of the 2,805 persons enumerated being on bicycle. Loosely organized play, such as playing catch or frisbee, was the fourth most frequent activity, followed by 3 percent of the weekend park users who were walking their dogs. Interestingly, organized games such as baseball or basketball involved less than 1 percent of all park users, although they usually attracted a considerable number of spectators.

User satisfaction. One hundred park users were questioned regarding their satisfaction with the park. One fourth of these interviewees were black, one tenth were Puerto Rican, and one tenth Chinese, and the remainder were white. Fifty-five percent of the users interviewed stated they were satisfied with the park, 13 percent were neutral or ambivalent, and 32 percent were dissatisfied. When asked: "What should be done to this park to increase your satisfaction with it?" Sixty-eight percent mentioned items related to maintenance and repair. The numerous broken park benches, the uncut or absent grass, the broken and buried sidewalks, the damaged trees and deteriorating shrubs—all testify to the validity of such concerns.

While two thirds of the park users stressed the need for repair and general maintenance, only 21 percent mentioned the need for additional safety or safety-related measures. Since we lack data on park arrest and complaint figures, we do not know whether this low figure derives from the fact that crime is low, or from the fact that the maintenance problem is seen as being much worse.

At the time the survey was undertaken, a portion of the West Side Highway had been closed after a portion collapsed, and its future was then being debated. The opinions of the 100 users interviewed indicate their assessment of the highway's impact. Not one person favored its designation as an interstate highway or any other measure which would increase traffic. Fifty-five percent favored minor repair and resurfacing but many stressed this was only to get traffic off local roads (where it had been rerouted when the highway was closed). Forty-five percent would like to close down the highway entirely, some suggesting it could serve as a bicycle path.

Neighborhoods and their parks. The parks being analyzed border some 75 city blocks, parts of different neighborhoods, in Manhattan. The racial, ethnic, and social class composition of these neighborhoods is reflected in the parkland which they border. Thus, as observation moves from south to north, park users change from white, to Puerto Rican, back to white, and then to a mixture of black and Puerto Rican. Each neighborhood has its own park. Yet cyclists, joggers, and strollers easily move from one neighborhood's park to another's. The primary difference lies in who remains in a particular area. User activities change somewhat with the area, with black and especially Puerto Rican areas having more organized sports and more families present.

Metropolitan parks

The New York Botanical Gardens   This park is large, 260 acres, and perhaps more than our other examples it "looks like a park." That is, its 260 acres are almost exclusively woodlands, formal and informal gardens, lawns, trees and tree collections, and ponds.

This park was incorporated in 1891. After the first president of the park board, Cornelius Vanderbilt; the vice president, Andrew Carnegie; and the treasurer, J. P. Morgan, raised $250,000, then building and service programs were begun under an act of the state legislature and the initial 250 acres were increased to 400. Its library, greenhouses, conifer collections, and public education programs were soon recognized to be among the finest anywhere.

We will quickly pass over the 1937 loss of 140 acres—35 percent of the total park acreage—to Park Commissioner Robert Moses, who paved them over for "parkways" (express highways without trucks). The Gardens were designated a National Historic Landmark in 1967, and in 1978 major renovation was completed on its greenhouses.

One hundred and thirty users were interviewed on a Sunday afternoon in July of 1974, and an effort was made to count the total number of users. As for the latter effort the park proved too large, our energies insufficient, and our coordination over unknown terrain inadequate. Thus we have no remotely reliable data to report on total use. We can only safely say that with the two or three thousand who were probably in the park scattered over its 260 acres, it is the kind of park where one must look for people. Or, for those not doing research, it is a place to get away from people.

Seventy percent of the 130 persons interviewed were white, although the surrounding neighborhood is predominantly Hispanic and black. The difference in user and neighborhood racial composition (or "people" composition as we prefer to call it) stems from the metropolitan nature of the park. Metropolitan parks are special-purpose parks, containing perhaps a zoo or, as this one does, special gardens. Going to them is therefore typically a special event—a first trip or perhaps a yearly event.

The special nature of the park is reflected in our users, 46 percent of whom arrived by car (up from 2 percent in the other types of parks). Only 29 percent lived within six blocks, and 41 percent lived outside the community (including living in other cities and states, and there were three visitors from abroad). We did not observe anyone by himself or herself; 41 percent of the users interviewed were couples, and the others were in larger aggregations, usually families.

How did they like the park? Instead of repeating their many plaudits, to quote the student (Brad Wolff) who carried out this project would perhaps best illustrate what our interviewees told us: "The New York Botanical Gardens is one of the most beautiful, safest, and cleanest places in all of New York City."

COMMUNAL LIFE SYMBOLIZED

This series of studies documents the importance of parks to urbanites. Whether urban residents have private outdoor space, such as yards and patios, such private space does not fulfill the apparent need to be with others: to meet people there, to visit, to watch, and to be among others.

People meet each other in the park through casual conversations not sanctioned elsewhere. Whereas relationships are highly structured in the markets, at work, and in going to and fro, in the parks anyone can talk to anyone. However limited the contact, even though it remains confined to the park, such contact is important.

Users identify the parks they regularly use as "their" parks. As publicly owned and jointly occupied space, the park comes to symbolize their community or neighborhood. Parks change with changes in their user populations. Incursions that other uses make into parks also symbolize communal values. The sense of community is evident even in a people's protection of its parks. Parks thus become one arena for the creation, continuance, and revitalization of communal life. Neglected, abused, and vandalized, they testify to impoverished communal lives, just as the reverse indicates a strong communal sense.

In terms of human relationships, parks socialize each user into knowledge of who his or her "others" are. For in observing, casually conversing with, playing a game with, or perhaps jogging alongside another person, essential information about that "other" is conveyed. Without it, those strangers we see all the time even in our own community would remain distant. Urbanites do indeed live in a world of strangers, but knowledge about strangers makes a difference.

Besides, casual conversation or mutual involvement in a game sometimes leads to the development of more intimate relationships. As the justly famed *Regional Plan* (1929:24) phrased it: "In the process of this common [park] use, families naturally make new acquaintanceships, and later, some of these develop into more intimate social relations through mutual attraction."

Its homogeneity

Who are these others one meets in "our" park? For most, the "others" are remarkably like "self." About 75 blocks long and varying from the equivalent of one to the equivalent of several blocks wide, the linear strip of parkland on Manhattan's West Side changed according to the people adjacent that portion. This parallels Molotch's (1969:886) observation about Chicago's parks: "In those parks located in segregated areas (either all black or all white), participation was limited to [engaged in by] persons of the same race as the surrounding area. . . . almost all of South Shore's parks were racially segregated." From our earlier examination of residential differentiation we know that neighborhoods are usually homogeneous in ways in addition to race—by class and familism, for example—so we can expect park users also to reflect this and they do.

What happens when "peoples" who do not identify with each other are forced to share the same park was evident in Washington Square. With insufficient local and neighborhood park space, people had no choice but to use Washington Square Park. They could go to a metropolitan park, and they did mention Central Park most often, but it was distant. They did not use other neighborhood parks, like Union Square just six blocks away, because those parks "belonged" to someone else. ("Our" park is not yours unless you are one of "us." To bound is to exclude as well as include.)

Forced to share their local park with those whom they called "undesirable," users evidence a high degree of dissatisfaction. Although park use was intensive, high rates of dissatisfaction lessened use—lessened it among the desirable people, thus increasing the impact of the undesirables, and creating more dissatisfaction. Reversing history by tearing up the surrounding streets and putting in another park, as recommended by some, is part of the solution. Tearing down parking lots elsewhere to provide sufficient parks for all peoples is also in order. Acreage is important, as a gross measure, but the location and variety of space is far more critical.

Its recreation

The scant literature on parks mentions some other functions of parks. Parks serve as a contrast to the rest of the urban environment. The city is exciting, stimulating, filled with the purposive movement that has always attracted millions to it. Without contrast, though, even urbanity becomes stultifying. Without relief from the crowds, from the endless sights, sounds, and stimuli of any urban center, what was initially enervating becomes exhausting, then repetitious and boring. Parks provide relief.

All the senses need such contrasts. After being closed in visually by buildings, which grow taller every decade, the eyes need the contrast of distance, the magic and mystery of space, the relief of light-absorbing green surfaces.

All great cities inevitably have a roar of noise about them. Twenty-four hours a day the restless urban population is going somewhere: to work, to rest, to play, to eat, to recreate. While the newly arrived migrant may have difficulty sleeping, or even hearing anything but the roar of the city, the seasoned city dweller learns to block out the noise of the city. In giving him at least relative quiet, plus the sounds of children playing, people quietly conversing, and maybe even a bird singing, parks reawaken the auditory sense.

Parks also provide the fragrance of green, growing, and blooming plants, and the urban nose needs as much relief as the eyes and ears. To touch living things instead of stone and pavement, to feel like a part of the environment instead of being subjected to it, and to experience the life of nature are equally important individual needs served by city parks (Whitaker and Brown, 1971).

Traffic paths in the city are necessarily highly organized, controlled by complex traffic regulations. Their utilization depends upon their navigator's careful and constant attention, and mistakes are costly. Failure to be in the right-hand lane of the eight-lane Cross Bronx Expressway, and thus connect with the Henry Hudson Parkway, will cost nearly three hours in time to get back into Manhattan from New Jersey. Probably most residents of great cities can tell of the cost of mistakes in missing a subway stop, a connection to the elevated or the express train, or even one's own transit stop.

Parks provide for movement without such concerns. They give their users unrestricted pedestrian lanes, free from danger to life and limb by competing traffic, where attention can wander and the mind can focus on other things. For children such movement is essential to growth; for adults such freedom restores the ability to grow.

Living in the midst of a modern city puts every individual in contact with literally thousands of others. As I wrote this section from my study on the West Side of New York I looked out upon hundreds of windows, and more hundreds of persons passing on the streets below. On the IRT subway I took to work, I stood in the station with maybe 50 others, then rode on a train with several hundred more people. By the time I reached my office at New York University, I had come into contact with more than a thousand people—in the space of a single hour. And my experience was no different from many who live and work in dense urban areas; many of whom may, in fact, have contact with considerably more people—as does a friend of mine who is a subway-token seller.

Large parks allow for a kind of release from people. Within parks, citizens can rest and relax, not engage in social communication. If it is so wished, one can withdraw into oneself. Such withdrawal is a necessary component of social life, for without periods spent alone, in privacy, the energy necessary for sociability becomes drained, and interaction becomes forced.

Spatial release is also provided the urbanite by urban parks. Most city dwellers live in apartments, high off the ground, in closed-in and cavelike environments. Under such conditions, the experience of large space is salubrious for mental and physical health—much needed by inhabitants of the city.

Recreation is literally re-creation, and to engage in such creation is a vital part of everyone's life. Whether young or old, rich or poor, everyone needs to play, to participate with others for the sheer pleasure of it.

Through play, each learns more about the self, others, and the environment. Parks provide opportunities for play.

The number of children in a family is smaller in the city than elsewhere, and the proportion of households without children is larger. Often pets come partially to fill the resulting vacuum. Parks provide the space animals must have to exercise, to be healthy, and thus serve a valuable need for them as well as their owners. While the conflict between dog owners and those who dislike dogs sometimes threatens to disrupt the city parks, the answer here as elsewhere is the creation of sufficient space to satisfy all.

The pressures of the city are such that its inhabitants sometimes feel compelled to escape it. Parks therefore serve as valuable safety valves for the pressure of urban living. Cheaper than building highways or transit lines to take people out of the city, parks also help take the burden off adjacent resort areas.

Parks also filter and reduce noise and dirt, help cool the surrounding area, integrate areas and communities, and may increase property values. Parks come in many sizes and shapes, and serve an even wider array of uses. Numerous parks of a wide variety are essential for urban life.

SUMMARY

The urbanite is in public when he or she can be observed by strangers. Urban life today is lived in large part in public. Whether working, walking, riding, eating, drinking, dancing, worshipping, or engaging in many other activities, often the urbanite is in the presence of others whom he or she does not know.

People must eat, and, under some circumstances, they must eat in public. Many people must work, and their work places, too, are public. Likewise when they ride a bus or drive a car, go to the movies or attend school, like it or not they are in public. To study the urbanite in public we chose a place where he or she goes voluntarily—the public parks. In these lands, which have been set aside to be held in common and used by all, the urbanite was observed at play.

The data indicate that distance-accessibility, size, and intensity of use are the three most important criteria in evaluating parks. When parks are too far away, people will create their own. This is seen in small visiting areas, medians between traffic lanes, and in the "hangouts" of youth. Park authorities would better serve their publics by providing relevant facilities and services in some of these unofficial parks.

Small visiting areas are intensively used. People say they go to them with others, to meet others, and to be with others. The presence of others also makes these parks safe, and therefore some authorities have seen safety as the motivation for congregation. We saw people to be the primary attraction and safety not an unimportant by-product.

Neighborhood parks are farther away from the average urbanite than small visiting areas, and they are larger in size. The intensity of use of neighborhood and community parks depends upon what is their availability. Since parks are important to them, urbanites will intensively use even already overcrowded and poorly maintained park space. When asked, they will complain, but their dissatisfaction only marginally lessens their use of parks.

Park users will not use local parks outside what they define as their own neighborhood because they are said to belong to others. Indeed, when the linear strip of parks along New York's West Side was examined, the composition of park users changed as the adjoining neighborhoods changed. People did pass through, just as strollers were found to do through Washington Square Park, but the primary users of a park usually lived nearby.

Metropolitan parks, the third type, are quite different from local or neighborhood-community parks. To travel to them the average urbanite must go miles, probably between five and ten miles if not farther. Trips to such parks are infrequent, made on special occasions. Serving the entire population of the metropolitan area, these parks are not identified with the populations that immediately surround them, nor do the nearby inhabitants claim these parks as their own. Metropolitan parks are "ours" only as we mean belonging to all people who live in the settlement.

Metropolitan parks are large and are less intensively used than smaller parks. Such parks may therefore provide places where a person may escape from others—where the urbanite who spends so much time in public may be alone.

Whether local, neighborhood, or metropolitan—or one of the other types we did not have time to study (county, state, regional, national)—parks are important to urban people. As Solotaroff (1976) expresses it: ". . . the first days of spring are so piercingly tender in New York—more so than anywhere else because they come after such a prolonged lack of contact with the natural world."

Using the topic as a verb, people will park if they must create their own; they will park if they must dash across busy streets and then sit in the middle of its traffic; they will park regardless of the obstacles which planners (sic) create and in spite of the low priority given to parks in city hall. Their determination to park, however, does not mean they do not appreciate assistance in doing so, especially from those pledged to represent and to serve them.

Left to himself or herself, the urbanite meets and associates with like others in local and neighborhood parks, and travels with his or her own to metropolitan parks. Peoplehood is seen in residential differentiation and now in parks as well.

STUDY QUESTIONS ─────────────────────────────────

    1.   Where are the unofficial parks in your community?

    2.   How do local, neighborhood, and metropolitan parks differ?

    3.   Why are parks important to urbanites?

SUGGESTED READING ─────────────────────────────────

Whitaker, Ben, and Browne, Kenneth. *Parks for People* (New York: Schocken Books, 1971).

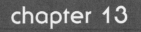

chapter 13

THE URBANITE IN PRIVATE

U.S. Department of Housing and Urban Development

PRIVACY DEFINED

The word *private,* as used herein, means "being kept or removed from public view or knowledge." Whereas the urbanite in public could be observed by strangers, the urbanite in private can be observed by no one or by only a small group of persons. To have privacy is to be withdrawn from the society of others or from public interest.

PRIVATE NEIGHBORHOODS

All neighborhoods are not equally private. To enter some neighborhoods, one must be admitted by a security guard. Entry of a newcomer into other neighborhoods may lead a resident to ask, "May I help you?"—a socially acceptable way of asking the entrant to justify his or her presence. Other neighborhoods, by contrast, may be entered at will and without challenge. The foregoing are all variations in the degree of privacy of neighborhoods, however, for all of them are closed to the public, at least to some degree.

DEFINING NEIGHBORHOODS AND NEIGHBORS

What is a neighborhood and who are one's neighbors? The variety of answers given to these two questions by urbanologists are based on the use of the criteria of (1) symbolic identification and (2) areal delineation. By symbolic criteria a neighborhood and one's neighbors are the area and the people an informant specifies. The resulting area may be small or large, and "neighbors" by this criterion may be scattered throughout the defined area. In contrast, when physical area is used as the basis of a definition, one's neighbors are all the people who reside in a specified area, whether this is a single street, a block, or a larger unit.

Understanding this difference in approach helps us to reconcile some of the differences reported in neighborhood life. Bell and Boat (1956), studying male residents in four San Francisco census tracts, found that nearly half were never involved in neighboring. This finding supports a common assumption: "Neighbors, signifying intimate association, have been replaced by nigh-dwellers, this designating adjacent residences coupled with anonymity" (Hallenbeck, 1951:536). Smith, Form, and Stone (1954), by contrast, reported much higher levels of neighboring when they asked such questions as: "How well do you think the people in the neighborhood know each other?" Bell and Boat used the census tract, whereas the definition of neighborhood was symbolic for Smith, Form, and Stone (1954). The differences in neighboring they report may stem from their different definitions. Both definitions have their value. The essential point is that the urban studies student, in interpreting research findings, needs to be aware of such differences in definition.

Keller (1968) points out a further difference in definition, this one in terms of the conception of who is a neighbor. Is a neighbor one whom one greets when meeting outside the home, from whom one borrows a tool or the traditional "cup of sugar," but not one who is counted among one's friends or close friends? Is neighboring a special role and relationship, distinct from the role and relationship of friend and friendship?

In the small rural community, where those who live nearby are one's kin and where kin work together, a separate role of neighbor does not arise. Likewise in a closely knit "urban village," such as a ghetto or enclave, the importance of sharing peoplehood may far transcent and absorb any relationship based on residential proximity. Therefore, in those parts of the urban settlement where one's spatial proximates are not one's kin, work associates, friends, or perhaps "people," the role and relationship of neighbor arises. Our neighbor is that person to whom we are related by proximity and not necessarily in any other way. We say "not necessarily" to recognize that many urbanites do live near their kin, work associates, and friends, but spatial proximity in the urban environment does not guarantee these relationships.

We have observed that people reside where they do because of their social class, their stage in the family and life cycle, and other characteristics not necessarily related to the proximity of kin, work associates, or friends. How then do people relate to those who live next door with whom they most likely share only spatial proximity? "Carefully," we would answer in a word.

In a more comprehensive treatment of the topic of urban neighborhoods, Suzanne Keller (1968:20–21) points out that people who jointly occupy space over time develop shared expectations. What they expect, however, varies. In one neighborhood people may expect "that neighbors respond unhesitatingly to requests for tools, money, food, or advice." In a second neighborhood, by contrast, "beyond polite greetings, people are expected to keep to themselves, to mind their own business, to stay out of other people's affairs, and neither to give nor ask for favors."

Good neighbors, say the Useems and Gibson (1960), are friendly but not friends. From our studies, plus Keller's, we say instead that whether neighbors are friends, are friendly, or are relative strangers depends upon the values of the people residing there. Therefore a "good neighbor is not necessarily a friendly or a nice person but one who conforms to the standards of the neighbor role common consent acknowledges" (Keller, 1968:21).

THE KNOWLEDGE OF NEIGHBORS

Although there is thus no universally shared set of expectations for a neighbor, Keller points out that there are several common elements. First of all, without any direct communication, neighbors know a great deal about each other. Beginning with the (perhaps discreet) observation of what is unloaded from the van, automobile, or other conveyance, neighbors learn something about who is moving in. Through continuing observation of arrival and departure routines, those visiting and those staying, parties given or not given, and dwellings maintained or neglected, neighbors learn about each other.

The information gained through spatial proximity induces certain tensions in the development of friendly relations. In contrast to neighbors, communication with friends may be selective in frequency, duration, and content. Whether or not one sees one's friends depends on mutual agreement. Neighbors, however, are mutually seen and observed regardless of the wishes of either. To allow neighbors to become friends means, therefore, to intensify communication by combining the roles of friend and neighbor. One's friend learns information as one's neighbor and one's neighbor learns those things communicated only to a friend.

The more intimate the relationship the more likely we are to excuse or ignore actions we would consider intolerable from those less intimate (Coser, 1956). Husbands and wives thus overlook many things which would end other relationships. The price paid, however, is that once conflict erupts among intimates it is more severe. Thus aggravated assault typically takes place among casual acquaintances and friends, while murder is more often committed by the victim's spouse (Wallace and Canals, 1963).

In the present context, the merger of the roles of friend and neighbor reduces the frequency of conflict but raises its severity when it erupts. And once conflict erupts, although friendships may end through words and other symbolic actions, relationships based on spatial proximity end only by someone's relocation. The two roles thus potentially conflict with each other, and neighbors, being well aware of such difficulties, relate to each other with care—carefully.

How carefully one must relate depends upon the ease with which one can move out of the neighborhood. Departures from small communities being most difficult, "not surprisingly, then, it is in these communities that definitions of the neighbor role and the rules regulating conduct among neighbors are most clear-cut, rigid, proscribed, and formalized" (Keller, 1968:23). Departures are also more difficult from ghettos, enclaves, and clusters, and here, too, what is expected by and from neighbors is more rigidly defined.

Where the escape from undesirable neighbors, including those who were once friends, is more easily accomplished, the pattern of neighborly expectations will be more diffuse. And under conditions where abject poverty, brutal authority, or perhaps complete passivity reigns, nothing or everything may be expected of a neighbor—another way of saying there is no neighbor role.

The role of neighbor as a person "spatially but not necessarily spiritually close" is thus one common element. As a second element, Keller (1968:25) notes, "the neighbor relation is usually, at least, in part collectively defined and has wider social implications than does friendship, which is generally a private and personal affair." A third and final common element in the role of neighbor is that it is more limited and less intimate than that of friend.

In summary, neighbors are those persons who are spatially close, whose relationships to one another are in part collectively defined, and whose relations are more limited and less intimate than those with friends.

TYPES OF NEIGHBORHOODS

The list of ways in which neighborhoods differ is much longer than the ways in which neighboring relationships have elements in common. It is convenient to array types of neighborhoods according to the component that classification describes. Consider a few of the ways in which neighborhoods have been described by population (P): according to social class (a society neighborhood, a working-class neighborhood); by ethnicity (a German or Greek neighborhood); by life style (a gay or swinging neighborhood); by religion (a Catholic neighborhood, a Jewish neighborhood); or perhaps according to the virtues of the people (a decent neighborhood, a respectable neighborhood) (Firey, 1945; Fried, 1965).

Neighborhoods have also been classified according to their organization (O): an integral neighborhood (Warren, 1975); a neighborhood bounded by personal ties (Seeley, 1959); a parochial neighborhood (Warren, 1969); a defended neighborhood (Suttles, 1968); an anomic neighborhood (Warren, 1976).

Because neighborhoods rarely have their own economies, the third of our components (E) is little used (except see Lowenthal, 1975); but the fourth, technology (T), has been: thus we have streetcar and automobile neighborhoods; brownstone, duplex, walk-up, and high-rise building neighborhoods (Warner, 1962). Finally, neighborhoods also are known in terms of symbolism (S): a stable city neighborhood, a stepping-stone neighborhood, a transitory neighborhood.

Research findings

Keller (1968) lists over 150 publications on neighborhoods and neighboring in her synthesis of those works relevant to physical planners. Caplow, Stryker, and Wallace (1964) cite perhaps 50 other studies that were not included by Keller. These two sources, furthermore, neglect a number of historical studies, such as R. D. McKenzie's (1921–22) classical series, as well as some published more recently (McGahan, 1972; Lee, 1968, 1973), and some done outside the United States (Peattie, 1968;

Perlman, 1976). These several hundred sources have much to say about neighborhood life, at its individual and collective levels.

Who are the people who live near one another? Parts Three and Four stress the many forces at work leading to residential differentiation. In terms of income, education, occupation, family status, ethnicity, life style, as well as some other variables, separate areas of the urban environment display high degrees of homogeneity. Therefore it follows that smaller areal units such as neighborhoods will also evidence a high degree of homogeneity.

In fact, the degree of homogeneity in neighborhoods will be even higher.[1] A specific neighborhood typically will contain not only just the wealthy, for example, but only the wealthy who have had their money for several generations, who are highly educated, who work in high executive positions, who are married and have children, who are native-born and white, and whose life style also conforms to that of their neighbors. A colleague's description of his neighbors provides another example: "We all earn between $22,000 and $34,000, have professional degrees and are employed in professional offices located 8.6 miles away; we are all native-born whites of immigrant parents from Germany; and we are all married and have 2.2 children." Although he was, of course, jesting about each having two tenths of a child in addition to two entire ones, his and others' neighbors are remarkably homogeneous.

How do these neighbors who are very alike relate to each other? In the first place, persons neighbor more with those who live closest to them. Timms (1971:11), among the many establishing the effect of propinquity, reports: "Women living within a radius of 100 yards of the respondent are more than ten times as likely to be chosen as friends as are those living more than 400 yards away." Furthermore, the lack of physical proximity has been determined to inhibit the development of close relationships. Thus persons living at the end of dead-end streets, those living in homes separated from their neighbors by trees, hills, or ravines, and neighbors physically isolated in other ways, have been found to be socially isolated as well (Festinger, 1952; Keller, 1968).

It is well to stress, as Gans (1967) does, that propinquity brings contact; but the development of contact into positive affect depends on social homogeneity. The next-door neighbor may be the first person we meet when we move in, but later we may find we prefer to neighbor with someone farther away. Only because neighborhoods are relatively homogeneous does propinquity make a difference. Finally, people are aware of the impact of proximity and choose their dwellings, in part, according to whether or not they wish to neighbor.

In summary, neighborhoods are typically homogeneous, propinquity

---

[1] In reviewing this literature earlier, the specific point was made that the smaller the areal definition, the higher is the homogeneity likely to be.

operates to bring proximates into contact, and sites are chosen in part according to whether or not people wish to become involved with others. The degree to which any given neighborhood is therefore anomic (without neighboring—Warren, 1969), or bounded by personal ties (Seeley, 1959), is strongly affected by the homogeneity of a population, their spatial relation to each other, and their own values and preferences.

Architectural design is held by Newman (1973) to be a powerful determinant of neighborhood life. Through analysis of the files of the New York Housing Authority, which contain records of 150,000 apartment units housing a total of 528,000 people, Newman was able to specity the four most important design elements that lead to what he terms "defensible space." Although Newman never focuses directly on neighboring but instead on the occurrence of crime as related to architectural design, neighbors who occupy defensible space may be presumed to have higher rates of neighboring than those occupying indefensible space. Newman suggests this in arguing that spatial design, for example, "allows residents to distinguish neighbor from intruder."

The design features that Newman mentions, and which are relevant to our study of neighboring, include boundaries that delimit public, semipublic, semiprivate, and private space. Each type of space reflects different degrees of influence or control by the users of that space. Private space is controlled by household members, semiprivate by proximate neighbors, semipublic by those who live in the building, and the public areas by officials, such as the police. When architectural design clearly specifies these four areas, the memberships of each level of community can control their space. Neighbors, for example, learn to recognize each other in semiprivate areas because, if properly designed, they are the only ones regularly using that space. Would-be intruders are therefore identified and challenged.

When design consists of seemingly endless high-rise apartment corridors, with many apartments off either side, the recognition of neighbors is inhibited, and this makes it difficult to differentiate intruder from resident. High rates of crime are therefore found in such indefensible space. As with proximity, it should be remembered that, although design may bring people together, whether their encounter eventually proves to be embracing or abrasive depends upon who they are.

Measuring neighborhood interaction

We already have discussed differences in what a neighbor should be. We now can focus on the symbolic interaction among neighbors, what is called neighborhood interaction. We begin with an examination of how neighborhood interaction has been measured. Perhaps not unexpectedly, we find that the "yardsticks" which have been used vary.

Smith, Stone, and Form (1954) developed a Neighborhood Social Inti-

macy Scale based on interviewees' responses to four questions, among
them: "How well do you think the people in the neighborhood know each
other?" If the response was "quite well" or "very well," it was placed in
the "Intimate" category. The neighborhood was judged "Intermediate"
in intimacy if the response was "fairly well," and it was rated "Non-
intimate" if the response was "not at all," or "not so well."

Using 12 questions that were asked of 733 women, Paul Wallin (1953)
scaled differences in neighboring according to mutual entertaining, bor-
rowing, and seeking and giving advice. Others (Lundberg and Steele,
1937) have asked people to name their "best friends" and then have
determined whether they were neighbors (Bott, 1957).

Caplow and Forman (1950) also developed a scale to measure neighboring. Their Neighborhood Interaction Scale has been used in three separate
studies (Caplow and Forman, 1950; Shimota, 1953; and Caplow, Stryker,
and Wallace, 1964). Their scale is the only one to measure independently
the neighboring relationship according to the assessment of both parties.
That is, Mrs. Jones is asked about her neighboring with Mrs. Smith, and
then Mrs. Smith is asked about her relationship to Mrs. Jones. Such
independent assessments improve the reliability and validity of the scale.

Neighboring is defined and scored on a scale ranging from zero to six in
the *Neighborhood Interaction Scale.* When the interviewee does not know
the neighbor's name or recognize him or her on the street, the scale value
is zero. When neighbors exchange greetings, as for example, "Good
morning," "Nice day isn't it," or "How are you today?" they are given a
scale value of one. Beyond the level of greeting, neighbors may stop and
talk with each other regularly (scale value of two if only one adult from
each family is involved, scale value of three if all adults are involved).
When neighboring relationships are limited to greeting and/or talking to
each other outside their dwellings, neighboring is said to be casual.

A relationship is closer, more intimate, according to Caplow and associates, when neighbors regularly borrow things from each other or regularly engage in common activities (scale values of four and five). And
neighbors are held to be even more intimate with each other when they
visit and entertain each other in their homes (scale value of six). Thus the
scale values increase as the neighbors move with each other from street to
doorstep to inside each other's houses.

Using this Neighborhood Interaction Scale, the author, along with
Theodore Caplow and Sheldon Stryker studied 25 neighborhoods in San
Juan, Puerto Rico. Each neighborhood was defined as 20 contiguous dwel-
ling units.

The researchers asked if neighboring increases with length of residence
in the neighborhood. Do persons who have lived in their dwelling for ten
or 20 years interact more than those who have lived there for just a few
years? Their data indicate that there is no relationship between length of
residence and the intensity of neighboring after people have lived in the

area for one year. During the first year's residence, neighboring does increase as persons become acquainted with their neighbors. After one year, however, the level of interaction with neighbors does not change. That is, if a subject neighbored with three others at the end of one year, their data indicate that person would neighbor with three others (not necessarily the same others) at the end of five or ten years.

Caplow, Stryker, and Wallace also report that there was no difference in neighborhood interaction among their subjects whether they lived in public or private housing, whether they owned or rented their dwellings, or whether the dwelling units were single or multifamily. The lack of a relationship between the foregoing sets of variables thus challenges some of the beliefs people have about neighboring. What variables, then, did have an impact on neighboring?

Neighboring

First, as we have observed, neighboring increases with proximity. Using the data from Caplow et al., a second generalization can be made: the intensity (higher-scale values) of neighboring increases with homogeneity.

Third, the intensity of neighborhood interaction increases with income, education, and occupational level; for example, the higher the income of the households in the neighborhood, the higher the levels of neighboring, and an inverse relationship was found between intensity of neighborhood interaction and the number of persons per room in the household. The lower the income or the more crowded the dwelling, the less the interaction with neighbors.

Neighboring increases with (1) proximity, (2) homogeneity, and (3) socioeconomic status, as we have seen. It also increases with the dependency status of the people involved. That is, both the very young and the very old are more spatially restricted and tend to form closer relationships with their neighbors. The traditional housewife who stays at home also tends to have higher rates of neighborhood interaction than those women who work outside the home.

There are studies which suggest that lower income populations are more dependent on the immediate area, the neighborhood, and that their neighborhood interaction is therefore higher than others who are less dependent on their neighbors. Using the term "spatial/social compression" to describe in part the dependence of blacks on their neighborhoods, Warren (1976) argues that such compression "is associated with significantly more central roles for such institutions as local neighborhoods and voluntary associations than in other populations."

The findings concerning dependency seem to contradict our earlier reported finding, that neighborhood interaction increases with socioeconomic status. The apparent contradiction is resolved when differences in the role of neighboring are taken into account. If being a "good" neighbor means entertaining neighbors in one's home, what we might therefore describe as "neighbors-as-friends" increases with socioeconomic status. There are, however, other roles which neighbors may play. These other roles may not increase with socioeconomic status.

THE IMPORTANCE OF NEIGHBORHOODS

There are different types of neighborhoods and different expectations of neighbors. These differences help explain the different needs which a neighborhood may satisfy.

The homogeneity of one's neighbors may help the urbanite to resist feeling alone and alienated in the vast and heterogeneous world outside. Jacobs (1961) pointed out how eyes on the street makes safe neighborhoods. When those eyes are also on each other's property, illegal entry is less likely to occur.

In addition to neighborhood social controls that protect insiders from outsiders, neighbors also exercise some control over each other's behavior. Neighbors learn each other's routines, and may investigate when the nonroutine appears. Neighbors may also be the first persons outside the family to learn of domestic conflicts, and to summon the authorities should the conflict become aggravated. In some neighborhoods, the neighbors themselves may serve as "the authorities" in the absence of the services of professional police (Peattie, 1968).

The neighborhood may be the organizational base for defining and resolving problems, such as a proposed highway or other new construction in the area, a flood or other natural disaster, or such problems as teenage drinking, drug traffickers, or a dangerous intersection.

In terms of economy, several investigators (Lowenthal, 1975; Warren, 1976) have observed a small-scale, local social economy of exchange. The goods and services reportedly exchanged are numerous, including not only "a cup of sugar" but tools, power equipment, and working on projects with each other. Lowenthal states that this social economy helps support a system for the distribution of goods and services. Warren adds that the system helps neighbors to survive temporary crises, such as loss of resources, and that it also helps them to maximize their resources through mutual support. For those most in need of this kind of economic assistance, as with many immigrants, the neighborhood may become a kind of way station.

For all, both insiders and outsiders, neighborhoods symbolize the individual and collective lives of their inhabitants. Those neighborhoods of expensive homes, manicured lawns and gardens, and winding streets symbolize the financial success of their inhabitants just as the tar-paper shacks once known as "Hoovervilles" symbolize failure. The neighborhood does provide the framework for considerable social behavior, in proportion to one's dependency. For children, the neighborhood is the locale of their lives. That this influence extends into young adulthood is evident from the fact that the frequency of marriage decreases as the distance between the two parties increases (Bossard, 1964). Consequently, as Beshers (1962) notes, families choose a neighborhood in part in terms of its potential mates for their children. Who the daughter marries depends on who the daughter meets, he concludes. The same, we presume, is true of sons.

The foregoing review makes it evident that neighbors are not necessarily one's intimates, nor are they always one's friends. They may simply be one's social and economic peers; they may be ones who help keep out a fast-food outlet; or they may be those from whom to borrow a chain saw or a snow thrower. In times of floods, fires, and other disasters, neighbors may even perform heroic deeds for each other. Such exchange and help-giving activities may continue for years without neighbors becoming friends.

To be "friends" does not mean to be "neighborly," and one's neighbors need not be friends. As Donald Warren (1976:232) puts it, although neighbors are not the source of intimate social contact, this "does not necessarily imply that such neighborhood-based contacts do not serve many important information, help giving, problem solving, and referral functions."

The Caplow-Forman scale must therefore be seen as but one definition of the role of neighbor, one we described as the friend-as-neighbor. This kind of neighboring increases with proximity, homogeneity, and social class. When we turn to other kinds of neighboring, other definitions of the role of neighbor, proximity and homogeneity continue to increase neighboring although social class may not. Thus even though nearby neighbors may not entertain each other in their homes, they are still more likely to borrow something from one another than from those living more distant. People are also more likely to borrow from neighbors most like themselves.

In terms of socioeconomic status, neighboring, when it includes activities beyond mutual visiting and entertaining, appears to decrease with status. The evidence stems from Keller's (1968:46) painstaking review. She relates the degree of neighboring (defined broadly) to (1) the number and kinds of crises, (2) the need for local social control, and (3) the degree to which neighboring is segmental. We add that all three are closely related to status.

Crises may be taken to include individual or neighborhood problems, and money does reduce their number and kind. With a chef and kitchen staff, one would be unlikely to need to borrow a cup of sugar, and even if borrowed the "neighboring" would most likely take place between the respective kitchen employees. The need for help, information, advice, or the many other things neighbors typically do for one another declines with increases in status. Thus both Keller's hypotheses about crises and the need for local social control can be incorporated into our framework, reversing the finding of a positive correlation of neighboring and socioeconomic status to a negative one: that is, neighboring when defined most broadly decreases as status increases.

Segmental refers to the degree to which neighbors are neighbors only. That is, when they are not also kin, or work, or recreational associates, persons in segmental relationships respond to segments of others. Keller notes that when neighboring is segmental it "will be a highly variable and unpredictable phenomenon."

The opposite of the segmental neighborhood is the neighborhood whose residents are also friends, work and recreational associates, schoolmates, and/or perhaps kin. Under these conditions, neighboring is highly patterned, widespread, and intense. What is true of the neighborhood is also true of the individual. To have a nonsegmental neighboring relationship means to have one's school and playmates as one's neighbors, as found among many children. For them, their neighbors do not occupy only the role known as "neighbor" but they also fill other roles. Neighboring therefore increases. To the extent, then, to which segmental relationships are linked to status, neighboring may be expected to decrease with status.

Taken as a whole, neighboring in this sense is greatest among the dependent and working classes and decreases as it moves up to the more self-sufficient and higher-status persons. Neighboring also increases with homogeneity and proximity.

NEIGHBORING AND URBANIZATION

Our study is of the process of urbanization, and we now therefore ask: how is neighboring related to urbanization? Not only should we know whether neighboring will increase or decrease with urbanization, but also we should know why.

The answer depends on the four factors just reviewed: proximity, homogeneity, dependency, and socioeconomic status. If we can trace their relationships to urbanization we should be able to predict the relationship of urbanization to neighboring.

Proximity

What we might call relative proximity does not change with urbanization. One's neighbors may be a half-mile away on the farm, a half-acre away in the suburb, or just across the hall in the city, yet neighboring still will be higher with those closer than with those farther away. In terms of absolute physical space, however, the same half-mile, which includes two families in the rural area, may include 500 in the suburb, and 1,000 in the innercity.

Homogeneity

Having two families with whom to associate in rural areas may make neighboring high regardless of how like or different they may be, simply because there is no choice (except isolation). As the pool of potential neighbors increases, the homogeneity of neighbors increases. Neighboring should increase with homogeneity. But as role segmentalization also increases with urbanization, gains in neighboring are offset by the segmentalization of the role of neighbor, which decreases neighboring and makes it more variable.

Dependency

Farm families are said to be more self-sufficient than those who reside in urban areas, and so they are, but only with respect to things physical. In the social sphere, farm families are far more dependent on each other. The urbanite can have a rich and varied social life without once speaking to his or her neighbors. He or she may work outside the neighborhood, marry outside, and pursue recreation at sites far distant from the neighborhood. To the extent that dependency decreases with urbanization, then we may expect neighboring to decrease.

If we compare children, who are generally dependent, in all places, the suburban child is probably more tied to his or her locale than is the urban counterpart. Suburban parents do seem to spend an inordinate amount of their time as chauffeurs, but even this dutiful effort underscores the suburban child's greater dependency. Bus, subway, train, bicycle, and the reliable foot all place the urban core child within range of hundreds of activities and facilities which, if available at all in suburban locations, are accessible only by automobile. And until one is 16, licensed, and has the use of the automobile, one remains dependent.

Socioeconomic status

Although we have seen that greater dependency does increase neighboring, it must be remembered that neighboring decreases as status increases. The tendency for the more dependent of the suburban population to neighbor more, may be offset by the tendency of higher status suburbanites to neighbor less.

SUMMARY

What is expected of a neighbor and what is the role of a neighbor vary highly in content. Generally we may say that the role itself decreases in extent, significance, and stability as settlement size increases. When neighboring is considered only in its mutual visiting and entertaining aspects, neighboring increases with socioeconomic status. Considered as a totality, however, neighboring decreases with socioeconomic status.

Neighboring increases with proximity and homogeneity. It finally increases with dependency.

STUDY QUESTIONS

1. Why and how do proximity, homogeneity, dependency, and socioeconomic status affect neighboring?
2. What do you consider a good neighbor? a bad neighbor? How does your stage in life and type of household affect your conception of a good and a bad neighbor?
3. Why does the role of neighbor only emerge in urban settlements?
4. How does neighboring change with urbanization?

SUGGESTED READINGS

Gans, Herbert J. *The Levittowners* (New York: Random House, 1967).

Keller, Suzanne. *The Urban Neighborhood* (New York: Random House, 1968).

Warren, Donald E. "The Functional Diversity of Urban Neighborhoods." *Urban Affairs Quarterly,* 12 (October 1976), pp. 88–98.

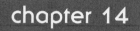

chapter 14

THE URBANITE AT HOME

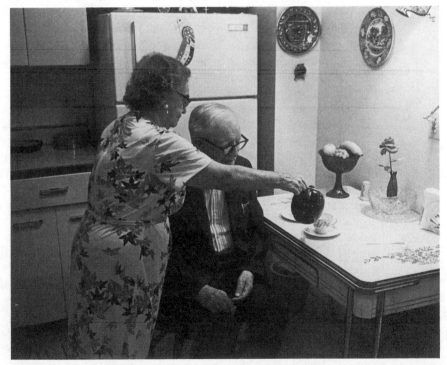

U. S. Department of Housing and Urban Development

267

THE COST OF HOUSING

The average urban dweller spends more on housing than on any other budget item. Between one fifth and one third of a household's total income is spent for housing. The high cost of housing is one indication of its importance to people. Changes in the cost of housing also reflect our values about it.

Examine one simple example: what is the price of a typical suburban ranch house—4 bedrooms, 2 baths, living room, separate dining room, fully equipped kitchen, and patio. There are a number of simple formulas to answer the question of price: number of square feet times construction cost per square foot in year built, plus inflation, interest rates, property taxes, and so forth. The price established by this calculation, however, could be as much as 100 percent off, depending upon the location of the house. Economics thus meets geography when we consider how the price of the same structure varies according to whether our hypothetical house is located on a 240-acre farm, a 2-acre suburban tract, or a lot 100 feet by 90 feet located in the innercity. The value of each location, furthermore, depends upon whether people are moving to or from the city or farm, whether the population is increasing or decreasing, whether household formation is up or down, and upon other demographic considerations.

What we thought was a simple question of "How much?" becomes even more complicated when we ask who now lives in the house. Are they black, white, Protestant, or perhaps Jewish? And how about their neighbors? Whether the answer is "black with black neighbors," "black with white neighbors," "white with black neighbors," or other variations vitally changes the price of a house.

Furthermore, a single detached dwelling may be worthless to people who wish to live communally, whereas it may be a priceless treasure for an overcrowded population seeking privacy. And if after establishing the economics, geography, demography, sociology, and psychology of the housing, we then ask about its past and are told its former occupants all died of a dread disease, we realize that history, too, makes a difference.

We could continue by pointing out that a house without services—without electricity, water, sewage systems, or garbage collection—would bear a different price than one with such services. We could go on and note the influence of the availability and cost of transportation, then analyze educational facilities, perhaps recreation, and other variables to learn that they, too, must be considered. And then we could discuss their many interrelationships—how psychology influences economics, how politics changes subsidies, how demography influences—but perhaps the multidimensional and interrelated nature of housing is now evident. Given the many ways in which housing varies, we must once again select a few examples for observation.

CONVENTIONAL STANDARD HOUSING

The goal of the United States 1937 Housing Act was to provide "decent, safe, and sanitary" housing for all. These three terms mean that the housing structure should be sound, capable of withstanding ordinary storms, and able to keep out inclement weather. Heating and lighting systems, whether gas, coal, oil, electricity, solar, or whatever, should not be fire hazards. Should a fire nevertheless start, the structure should have smoke and fire detection systems, fire extinguishers available, and easily accessible fire escapes. Finally, housing should have potable water, indoor toilets, and washing and bathing facilities. It should have adequate ventilation and light, and should be free from vermin.

The provision of decent, safe, and sanitary housing continues to be a widespread goal in spite of the difficulties in specifying when a house is or is not decent, safe, and sanitary. How much light or ventilation? How must heating and lighting systems be installed and maintained to be safe? Questions such as the foregoing underscore the difficulty of operationalizing goals. Some urbanologists (Gans, 1962) have also argued that the criteria for decent, safe, and sanitary classify some housing as substandard, which is not so considered by its occupants. Objective and subjective definitions also complicate the task of evaluating housing. Recognizing these problems, let us begin discussion with conventional standard housing.

Conventional housing consists of those residential units of permanent location and legally protected tenure that were constructed according to building codes existing at the time of construction; they constitute the official supply of housing. When conditions of occupancy change, as when squatters are given legal tenure, or when building codes and their definitions of standard housing change, as when mobile homes were reclassified as standard, the official housing stock also changes. Housing may deteriorate and become substandard, or a dilapidated unit may be renovated into a standard one, but all such changes take place according to the dictates of the standard that convention specifies.

Privacy

Housing is shelter but, were protection from the weather the only consideration, a single undivided structure would suffice. We expect our housing to provide us with something even more important than protection from the heat and cold, namely privacy. For without privacy, social life as we know it simply could not exist.

Privacy is "the state or condition of being withdrawn from the society of others." Withdrawal, however, may be effected or maintained by simply averting attention as well as by blocking others out by doors and walls.

Subway riders in New York, for example, secure and maintain their privacy by reading newspapers, being seemingly oblivious to the others around them. As many observers have noted, these "straphangers" are unresponsive to the others with whom they share transit space, unless an emergency or other unusual event intervenes. Even with family members who share dwelling space, privacy may be secured and maintained by social, not just spatial, withdrawal.

However strong the abilities of persons to isolate themselves while in the presence of others, the success of nonspatial social withdrawal depends upon others. Those who are co-present may prevent withdrawal in a wide variety of ways, including physical as well as verbal assault. The saxophone-playing blind person soliciting contributions on the subway car may force even those behind their newspapers to abandon, at least briefly, their withdrawal; children not yet socialized into the norms of the socio-spatial order may be similarly disruptive of others' efforts to withdraw. Therefore privacy may be said to be more secure when withdrawal is spatial, for spatial isolation always entails social withdrawal, while social withdrawal by itself can be interrupted by anyone co-present.

Withdrawal takes place according to the units of social organization legitimized by the society. Although many may think the individual to be universally legitimized, examination of some utopian communities indicates that this is not always so. Among some "hippy" communes of the 1960s, withdrawal by individuals or even couples was disapproved. According to the values of such groups, neither bedrooms nor bathrooms were private, and the person who insisted on such withdrawal was seen as at least unenlightened. Certain monasteries, cloisters, military bases, prisons, hospitals, and kibbutzim have also disallowed individual or, for that matter, couple and subgroup withdrawal, at times punishing those who violated such norms. Withdrawal by the individual, pair, or other grouping, as we have seen, depends on the values of the people.

Space and selfhood

Space of one's own is a value enshrined within American culture. The newborn infant should have a room of his or her own, most Americans feel. As Ernst and Schwartz (1962) observe in their work on privacy, during infancy the door remains open, "it shuts but is left ajar at prepuberty, and closes entirely—and perhaps even locks—at the pubertal and adolescent stages." As selfhood is gained, private space, when possible, is secured.

> The home tends to become the only or primary means of guarding any inviolability of the private self. . . . The Crestwooder may not know of the abstract distinction, but his behavior with regard to admitting people to his home tends to make important its function as the citadel of the private self. (Seeley et al., 1956:54)

Private space to which the individual may withdraw is the smallest unit that housing for Americans should include, and, while many may lack such private individual space, it remains a goal to which most strive. Only such emergencies as fire or a court-sanctioned search warrant may violate the boundaries with which Americans have surrounded their family dwellings.

Private space for the self and private space for one's spatial intimates, usually family, are two sets of boundaries contained within conventional standard housing.

> The behavior around doors, which control access from the outside world to all the areas of the house, is strongly differentiated. The back, or side door, exists for service deliveries. Honored guests are introduced into the house through a formal front entrance. Only a very intimate friend, usually a close neighbor, would think of entering through the side door, perhaps unannounced. . . .
>
> The same screening process goes on within the home. . . . The child . . . must learn at an early age the bathroom behavior which is fitting for family members and for guests. The door that was usually left open or ajar is, in the presence of the guest, locked. (Seeley, 1962:108, 117)

Invited guests should occupy space specifically set aside for them, American ideals also specify. The front parlor or living room, perhaps even a guest bedroom and bath, serve this type of relationship. Again, many households and families may lack such space, but such space is deemed highly desirable among Americans.

From individual space to the family-household area, to a place for their invited guests, and then to space that can be shared with neighbors is the progression of ever larger boundaries within the American ideal. Among examples of such space are local sidewalks, and perhaps streets, alleys, and courtyards, parks especially for toddlers, and sometimes swimming pools, clubhouses, parking lots, and refuse-collection centers. When all is as it should be, housing is located to provide such neighborhood private space.

Isolated, detached, with space on all sides, the typical suburban house best fits American and perhaps others' housing ideals. It is also by far the dominant type of housing in existence. Suburbanites—mother, father, and their children—all have their own private space. The family or recreation room provides family private space, and the living room typically functions to receive guests. Each space is separated by some transition to the next, affording maximum control of access.

The housing generally available in the suburbs, however organized, is the ideal, and other housing may be seen as less desirable. By sharing walls, to follow Michelson's (1970) lead, a duplex or garden apartment is considered less satisfactory. Three, four, or five story walk-up apartment buildings force their occupants to share walls, ceilings, floors, staircases, hallways, and the entrance to their building. In middle-class high-rise apartment buildings, the number of people with whom one shares such space increases greatly, making it even less desirable for privacy.

CONVENTIONAL SUBSTANDARD HOUSING

Prior to 1890 in the United States, there were few regulations concerning the construction and maintenance of housing (Hunter, 1965). While middle- and upper-class persons secured decent, safe, and sanitary housing through their greater economic resources, the working and welfare classes had to make do with whatever was built for them by those seeking profit, or perhaps by that which filtered down to them through conversion of units built for the higher classes.

The term *filtering* has been used for several different changes in housing, including changes in rents or prices, changes in the socioeconomic status of occupants, and increases in the intensity of usage through conversion. The process is always downward, however—a filtering down of housing from higher to lower classes. Terms such as *deconversion* are used for the upward changes brought about through renovation and rehabilitation (Grigsby, 1963).

Conditions of life in the substandard units at the turn of the century were so bad as to be almost beyond our conception today (Riis, 1898). Apartments without ventilation, light, water, heat, and other essentials were common. Disease, rodents, fire, and other dangers to life, including the collapse of entire buildings, were widespread. Such conditions, of course, were equally if not more typical of urban life in previous ages and countries. Substandard housing has been a regrettably universal feature of urban settlements from their beginnings.

The primary difference in today's substandard housing and previous such units is that, since the adoption of building codes and other regulations concerning housing, substandard units are formerly standard housing that has deteriorated and filtered down. The process of deterioration stems not only from the conversion of single-family dwellings to multifamily units, but also from less well understood processes whereby physically sound structures become substandard without conversion in use. Thus, for example, a portion of a government housing project in St. Louis called Pruitt-Igoe (Rainwater, 1970) had to be demolished less than a decade after it opened. Its deterioration makes evident the multidimensional nature of housing, for by physical criteria alone (construction, heating, lighting, indoor plumbing, and the like) it was not substandard housing.

Conventional substandard housing is typically overcrowded, with two, three, four, and more persons to a single room. In one such unit in Puerto Rico, the author interviewed a household of 26 persons residing in the same room. Under such conditions the maintenance of privacy is, of course, difficult if not simply impossible. The pursuit of such solitary, individual activities as reading or writing is inhibited, and each person is almost continuously subject to the moods and activities of co-residents (Wilner, 1962, 1963).

Security against even members of one's household is virtually nonexistent, resulting in the following human dangers, according to Rainwater (1966): "Violence to self and possessions, including assault, fighting and beating, rape, objects thrown or dropped, stealing, verbal hostility, shaming, and exploitation."

Beyond the dangers of other human beings, Rainwater (1966:29) also lists a series of nonhuman dangers for persons in substandard housing: "Rats and other vermin, poisons, fire and burning, freezing and cold, poor plumbing, dangerous electrical wiring, trash (broken glass, cans), insufficiently protected heights, other aspects of poorly designed or deteriorated structures (e.g., thin walls), and the cost of dwelling." The cost is not limited to physical damage in injury, illness, incapacity, or death. As Rainwater (1966:27) observes: "Because these potentialities and events are interpreted and take on symbolic significance, . . . inevitably there are also effects on their interpersonal relationships and on their moral conceptions of themselves and their worlds."

It is germane to observe here that many have assumed that people create slums. Their equally naive opponents have insisted that slums breed the problems their occupants have. From the perspective of symbolic ecology we know that all five ecological components are involved. Neither people alone nor houses, however substandard, create slums. Rather it takes a population, some, but not all, of whom have problems; who live in an organizational framework which brings them together socially and spatially; in an economy which creates housing for them by filtering; in a technological framework in which they are exposed to human and nonhuman dangers; all of which becomes identified as a slum; the symbolism of which leads outsiders to treat insiders in ways which stereotype slums and their inhabitants.

Behavior control

Within substandard housing, behavior control is high. For without the private space that permits minimum conformity to group values, surveillance is pervasive. In turn, a greater communality is produced, contributing to the lesser interaction with neighbors, which we have already observed. The large household by both its size and spatial compression becomes more self-sufficient socially.

Ernst and Schwartz (1962), following Simmel (1969), point out the need for privacy to maintain status distinctions. The lack of private spheres for the many persons in the slum households tends to reduce status distinctions on some levels. Entire communities that are organized on communal bases evidence fewer status distinctions (Mitchell, 1975).

The occasions for conflict are also increased. Whereas in the middle-class home such incidents are frequently resolved through spatial withdrawal, the limited space of the conventional substandard home contributes (among other factors) to the use of direct, physical punishment.

As a final consequence, spatial usage patterns evolve, with household members eating, bathing, and engaging in other activities, including sleeping, in shifts. According to the anthropologist Morgan (as cited by Mitchell, 1975), communal life may lead to the institutionalization of such shifts, whereby first the men eat, then the women and children. Included among such organizations of space usage may be shifts for husbands and wives to have sexual intercourse.

As the substandard dwelling is already overcrowded, friends and kin who visit find few, if any, neatly demarcated boundaries that set aside space for their use. Persons close in relationship to the members of the household eat, drink, and converse where space permits, becoming privy to whatever information may be evident in those places.

In an effort to capture badly needed additional space, semipublic and public space outside the dwelling is turned into extensions of the home. Hallways, staircases, door stoops, and the like are turned into places for the congregation of the household and its visitors, with children typically playing nearby. As this practice becomes institutionalized over time, the residential area may be called a *door-stoop neighborhood* (Friden, 1964).

Outsiders entering the home find no place for their reception. Conversations with priest, social worker, policeman, and any others are held in the hallway or perhaps on the street, subject to all the implied constraints of such, unless the outsiders become friends and close associates of the household and are invited in (or perhaps force their entry).

UNCONVENTIONAL DWELLINGS

Owning property—having a fixed place of residence—was required in the American colonies for one to be a citizen, to be able to vote. Although less stringently defined today, residency remains the basis for citizenship in the United States, with its specifics often excluding students, inmate populations, and persons without fixed residence. Educational opportunities, health and welfare benefits, even worship and death and burial rights, are often denied those without permanent residence; and credit, that bulwark of modern life, cannot be secured without proven long-term fixed residence. Social control is thus achieved partially through the spatial control which stems from a known permanent address (which must be legal, also; see Turner, 1968).

Those lacking permanent shelter are therefore feared and excoriated, in part because society has difficulty in controlling them. As early as A.D. 368, measures to control vagrancy were introduced in the British Isles, and in the some 1,600 years since then the Western countries have attempted to legislate vagrants out of existence (Ripton-Turner, 1887). Historically, such persons have been whipped, branded, enslaved, imprisoned, and hung. Even today the person with no permanent place of residence may be given a sentence of 90 days, all for the lack of an address. As one of the hoboes in the author's 1964 study of skid row aptly phrased it, "they say every man must have a bedroom."

Shelter for protection, including from the law, is therefore a prime requirement. Unconventional housing is thus first evaluated on the basis of its security against the police. Bittner (1967) observes that the police tolerate behavior on skid row that they do not permit elsewhere, including allowing persons to sleep on sidewalks and in doorways. Although the sidewalks of skid row may be safe from the police, outsiders as well as other skid rowers may beat up or at least rob persons sleeping out in the open, including stealing their shoes and clothes. Temporary shelter on sidewalks and doorways is therefore used only by the worst-off.

The homeless may also secure shelter in areas of high transiency, such as transportation depots. Since most people in these places are coming and going or waiting to do so throughout the day and night, temporary residence may be secured for a time. If one uses the correct props, newspapers, for example, and is dressed as if he or she could be going somewhere, detection may be prevented. Public libraries and reading rooms also fit into this category.

Homeless persons may also secure temporary shelter by appropriating what Duncan (1976) calls *marginal space*. Broadening his definition to include public and/or private places, we call marginal space that which is relatively inaccessible to police and citizen alike. Without easy surveillance, such areas as parks at night, warehouse districts, river fronts, abandoned buildings, and alleys may provide temporary shelter. Trash dumpsters, abandoned or unused housing, unguarded furnace rooms and cellars, rooftops, piers, and boxcars, and a variety of other space not sufficiently valuable to be patrolled, provide other places of temporary free housing. (Individuals may also build their own housing; see Turner, 1968a, 1969.)

In this housing for the lowest-status segment of our society, boundaries enclose very small amounts of space and are indistinct. Private space includes little more than the space bubble which surrounds the person; the semiprivate is also small, and public space includes nearly everyone.

Access, even to the person himself or herself, is maximal, because assailants can enter and do violence. Conditions of occupancy rest solely on possession, lasting until anyone stronger pushes the occupier out of that space. Security and privacy are therefore minimal, exposing the individual to wanton or legal invasion, making every act a public one. Without safe storage space, possessions must be reduced to what can be safely carried—in other words, to very little. Eating, bathing, washing, recreating, and all other human activities must also be done in public places.

Persons in conventional housing are assured of their identity in part by possessions from parents no longer alive and from friends now living elsewhere, or other reminders of the past which supports the present. The person who occupies temporary shelter lacks such reinforcements of identity, lacks the protection of privacy, and lacks any nonpublic aspect of life. The pressure to become what they are publicly treated as, namely bums, is therefore greater. Their lack of fixed location in space, their mobility, deprives them of sufficiently large and definite boundaries, allows access to their space by almost anyone, and produces insecurity in the occupancy of social as well as physical space. Their space is not their own nor is their identity; they live according to the dictates of others, unless they can mobilize counteroffensives.

Lest the reader think that such practices are only part of history, mention needs to be made of the "street people." These modern-day urban nomads arose in part with the beatniks of the early 1950s, and appear to have increased quite dramatically with the hippies of the 1960s. Although the bulk of both movements stemmed from the middle- and upper–middle-class segments of society, a portion of the hippie and beatnik populations either were unskilled or failed to acquire skills to enable them to move back into conventional society. Some may have also been disoriented by heavy and persistent drug usage. Baumohl and Miller (1974), who have studied these street people, found that they included about twice as many males as females, were usually between the ages of 15 and 29, almost uniformly displayed great hostility to their parents, and mostly had not had gainful employment for several years.

TYPES COMPARED

Each of the types we have observed constitutes someone's dwelling space. As dwelling space, the area is private, whomever may be its occupants. Even if one is sleeping on a door stoop or in a boxcar, others do not enter that space unless to expel or assault. That is, the space is mutually acknowledged to be private, with peaceable entry possible only upon the occupant's invitation.

The greatest danger to human life, however, continues to be other human beings. Without protective walls, the denizens of unconventional sleeping places are victimized, easily and often. Thus these places are inhabited by those with the least to lose—and often they do lose even the only pair of shoes or pants that they have. Unable as such people are to protect even themselves, their possessions fare still worse. They wear or carry what they have, perhaps three or four shirts and several coats, worn at the same time, summer and winter.

Under the foregoing conditions the boundaries of the self are limited, bounded only by the space bubble that surrounds the person. Furthermore, those personal boundaries are easily and frequently invaded. Occupants of unconventional housing have no co-residential group with which to affiliate. They are without spouses, siblings, buddies, families, households, or any other recognized groupings based on common residence. Sharing only the category into which others place them by virtue of their individual characteristics, they are not members of anything. Of the variety of names by which they are called—skid rowers, bums, street freaks—perhaps the most accurate is "homeless."

Housing is technological, but the distinction made between a house and a home underscores the far greater importance of its symbolic nature.

> Although Crestwooders attach great importance to the house as a vehicle for competitive display, they also call it "home." The terms "house" and "home" point up the fundamental differentiation between the technological item and its emotional connotations. . . .
> The Crestwooder, like his contemporaries, builds or buys a house; but he "makes" a home. He sells a house, it burns down, or it is broken into; but a home is "broken up." Adjectives like "happy" and "harmonious" go with home. One hears of an unhappy home; but a house is empty, or bleak, or noisy, or dirty, or gaudy. (Seeley et al., 1956:52)

The technological and economic dimensions of housing have so dominated official thinking that the symbolic aspect has been ignored. Defining the substandard in technological terms has caused symbolically highly valued housing to be torn down, regardless of human investment in it (Turner, 1972). And again using technical criteria, housing has been built which was standard in every way, only to be destroyed shortly thereafter because it was unfit for human life. A housing unit must first and foremost be seen as a home, as a dwelling place for one or more persons, and perhaps their co-residents; it must be examined as a creation of symbolic forces. Housing can then be built by shaping the technological and the economic to people.

Housing is property, but, as Gerson (1976) observes, property can only be defined in the last analysis as a form of relationship among people: specifically, the enforceable right to exclude or to be included. The enforceable right to exclude increases with socioeconomic class. Privacy also increases, and with it the boundaries of the individual self become larger.

The occupants of the substandard or the unconventional have difficulty in excluding both human and nonhuman threats. Residents of this type of housing have relatively little privacy but gain in co-residential solidarity. One result is that within such space, one is either accepted into the collectivity or expelled, there being no space set aside in which to receive outsiders as outsiders.

The right not to be excluded, the right to be included, should also be mentioned. "Family are those persons you cannot turn away from your door"—as Everett Hughes personally defined it for me—they have a right to be included. In this, too, the "homeless" differ in having no right to be included in any other's space.

The single detached house remains the ideal because it alone maximizes American ideals concerning space. It alone has separate, defined space for each individual, for the household as a unit, for the friends who are invited in, for guests, neighbors, and even the "parson" when he calls (Perrin, 1977). Should such housing therefore be the only type built?

In terms of housing subsidy, federal government policy has answered the preceeding question in the affirmative. By allowing the individual home owner to deduct interest payments and real estate taxes from the federal income tax, government policy subsidizes the home owner, reducing income taxes by about 17 percent, according to Sheton's 1978 figures. Those uninterested in purchasing or unable to purchase housing are penalized, in effect, since they are not subsidized. As Clawson (1971), among others, points out, single-family dwellings are typically built in suburban areas, so indirectly federal policy encourages suburban growth.

A second and more general policy also has favored the single detached house. As noted earlier, housing standards were nonexistent until the turn of this century, when housing reformers, such as Jacob Riis, awakened the public to the deplorable conditions of tenement life. Once standards were seen as necessary, the question became: to what standards should housing be built? Recognizing that local variations and changes over time are great, in general terms the answer to the question has been to set standards without considering whether people could afford the housing that had to be built according to them. How, then, was housing to be provided to those unable to pay? The answer has been: by filtering.

The theory developed that higher-income groups would pay for the new and more expensive housing that was constructed according to set standards; and as they later moved out of such housing, it would "filter" down to lower, and then to still lower income groups. Ratcliff (1976:322) describes filtering as "a result of decline in market value, i.e., in sales price or rent value." In this variously defined and hotly debated issue, Smith (1971:177) defines filtering as "a basic pattern of market behavior . . . a response to any change in conditions of supply or demand—in the number and types of households or in their incomes, in the physical quality of the stock . . . , or in construction of particular kinds of new units."

Among the many questions raised about "filtering" as a basic policy is whether the poor should have something besides the hand-me-down converted housing that is built for someone else, which, because of its decline in value, filters down to those unable to purchase new housing because of its high standards? Then we may ask when, if ever, housing will finally filter down to those living in poverty, such as many of the aged, and what its condition is likely to be by then?

At a more technical level, filtering assumes that housing units will become cheaper over time (Schorr, 1968), whereas through the 1970s, for example, this has not been the case. The degree of filtering furthermore accelerates or decelerates according to changes in migration, inflation, fertility, family size, household formation rates, and a variety of other factors.

Finally, and perhaps most basically, filtering does not work because it is based on the production of one type of housing, which a variety of users must convert and deconvert to make fit them—somewhat, at least. The suburban house is held as ideal by the majority, and it provides its occupants with high levels of satisfaction. Yet as many studies have indicated, suburban living is primarily for families pursuing familism. "For adults in anything but a fully functioning, economically secure family system, Levittown may be an invitation to trouble" (Poponoe, 1977). For the childless, the single-parent family, the widowed, divorced, or separated, for very young adults and the aged, suburban housing is far from ideal. Since those in need of different kinds of housing outnumber by three or four to one those finding satisfaction in suburban detached units perhaps it is time to diversify housing types and abandon filtering as basic policy in the process.

HOMES AWAY FROM HOME

Had we the space to analyze the many other public places we frequent as urbanites, what would we find? First, we would note that although we may work with thousands, even tens of thousands of others, we know but a small number of them. Our places of employment may be large, but we use only a small fraction of their total space. The same is true of the people and places where we eat, drink, make merry, or worship.

Earlier, we chose urban parks as our example of public places, observing that people there are free to go wherever they wish with whomever they choose. We learned that people in parks frequent the parks they call their own, and they do so with others whom they also call their own. In race, ethnicity, national origin, and life style, there is considerable homogeneity in the users of a specific park. When the desired homogeneity of people was not present, dissatisfaction with the park was high.

Suttles (1968:55) studied a wider variety of recreational establishments, including parks, social centers, a boys' club, and some church-related facilities. Here, too, he found that the ethnic groups established what we call "homes away from home" in their own areas. In each recreational establishment, users were homogeneous by ethnicity, as they were in their neighborhoods. Molotch (1969) made a further extension by including bars, taverns, drugstores, restaurants, barber shops, and other local public places. Once again the data indicate that the users of neighborhood facilities are homogeneous by peoples.

Territory

Realization that groups claim public space as their own has led to the recognition of territory: "the space which a person, as an individual, or as a member of a close-knit group (e.g., family, gang), in joint tenancy, claims as his/her or their own, and will 'defend'" (Parr, 1972:44). Territories are established both by individuals and by groups.

In classrooms where students may sit where they wish, particular seats are chosen and then used with such regularity that persons think of them as their own (Lipman, 1967). When they arrive late or for some other reason find "their" seat taken, a common reaction is to think: "What is he or she doing in my chair?" Bar stools, tables at restaurants, pews in church (Carr, 1979), seats on a bus and in other public places become privatized. Altman and Haythorn (1967) state that fixed positions (e.g., the left corner of the back of a classroom) become part of territory first, and then movable objects such as chairs become incorporated.

Territoriality structuring is one way in which urbanites conteract environmental stress (Altman and Haythorn, 1967). As incompatability between people increases, territoriality increases. The reverse is also true: as compatability increases, the boundaries marking off private territories become less important.

Urbanites live in a heterogeneous environment, and therefore territoriality is high (Lynch, 1977). In part, this is the psychological basis for the residential differentiation observed throughout urban settlements. Both devices are techniques to avoid and reduce aggression. Territory is defended when encroached upon, but in the vast majority of cases people acknowledge territorial claims.

Orbit

Territory is one kind of home away from home and orbit is another. An *orbit* is "the space through which an individual habitually roams" (Parr, 1972:88). The vast reaches of the urban environments are experienced only in small part by urbanites. Instead, people use the same routes to go to the same places, time and time again throughout lifetimes (Form and Stone, 1957).

Urbanites do move. As they change their marital status or employment, complete school, and age, they change their homes and their homes away from home. Upon arrival in the new location, the similar others around them begin to tell them where to go and, equally important, where not to go. This *locational socialization* (Lofland, 1973) quickly orients the newcomer, and after a brief period, usually less than a year, orbits and territories are established (Blaut and Stea, 1973).

SUMMARY

The urbanite is at home in the urban environment, for he or she bounds space according to relationship. There is a space bubble surrounding each person (Hall, 1966) and individual space in the home. Peaceable entry into such space is secured only by invitation. Family and/or household space is shared, and its members, too, have the right to include or exclude others.

Space for visitors is available in the ideal dwelling—areas apart from individual and family space. Outside the dwelling, on door stoops, by mailboxes, along fences, and at other places, neighbors communicate with each other. Strangers appearing in such areas may be challenged.

In such public places as parks, schoolrooms, churches (Carr, 1979), taverns, restaurants, and others, orbits and territories are staked out. The establishment of such homes away from home helps the individual urbanite live comfortably in a heterogeneous and vast settlement. For the individual, locational socialization forms a *mental map*. These maps, which each urbanite uses for orientation, helps him or her to travel safely through the urban environment and to survive in a world of strangers.

STUDY QUESTIONS

1. What is the difference between conventional standard and conventional substandard housing?
2. What is the relationship between space and selfhood?
3. What are homes away from homes?
4. Explain how the urbanite is able to live comfortably in a vast and heterogeneous environment.

SUGGESTED READINGS

Lofland, Lyn H. *A World of Strangers* (New York: Basic Books, 1973).

Warren, Roland L. *Perspectives on the American Community*. 2d ed. (Chicago: Rand McNally, 1973.)

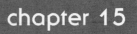

chapter 15

THE URBANITE IN PERSON

United Press International

ANTIURBANISM

There are few people so badly misunderstood as the urbanites. In the celebrated era of Chicago urbanology, Louis Wirth (1938) saw the urbanite as superficial, anonymous, and transitory. Wirth argued that the increase in the number of people with whom the urbanite comes into contact, the increased density of the population, and the heterogeneity of urban inhabitants lead to higher rates of "personal disorganization, mental breakdown, suicide, delinquency, crime, corruption, and disorder" (Wirth, 1938:18).

Wirth based his view of the urbanite on Simmel, and they are both used by Milgram (1970:1463), who sees the urbanite as suffering from *overload*—an "inability to process inputs from the environment because there are too many." Therefore the urbanite totally disregards the needs, interests, and demands of all those who are not useful to him or her, according to Milgram. He cites the case of Catherine Genovese—who "was stabbed repeatedly, over an extended period of time" while her neighbors (38 of whom admit they knew of the attack) took no action. For Milgram, this is just one example of urban "callousness." In Milgram's view the urbanite is deficient "even at the most superficial level of involvement"—the exercise of everyday civilities. "People bump into each other . . . do not apologize, knock over another person's packages. . . ."

So negative has the view of the urbanite become that some simply assume the evils of urbanism and limit their explanation to the source of the disorder they assume. Urbanites behave like rats, they at times argue, because they are overcrowded. Equating urban human beings and rats, a syndrome called "the behavioral sink" is used to explain the violence, the psychiatric disorders, the bisexuality, and the other conditions assumed to be urban in character.

These antiurban views are accepted, in part, because many Americans think antiurban (White, 1962; Schorske, 1968). They share a deep distrust of urban people and places. Asked to describe a New Yorker, or a person from Boston, New Orleans, Los Angeles, Dallas, or any other large city—many would be negative in their descriptions. Contrast this commonly negative image of the urbanite with what many imagine the person from the small town or rural area to be. American antiurbanism is also seen in that although three fourths of Americans live in urban places, the American ideal is the single-family dwelling of a small community (Perrin, 1978).

Herein we eschew antiurbanism (as we do obfuscation) for several basic reasons. First, antiurban theories do not explain how it is possible for people to live in cities. Instead, Wirth, Simmel, and the others like them tell us only how impossible it is to live in cities. Yet, if urban life is so impossible, how do people not only manage to survive it but even to find it attractive?

Rural-urban migration has been and continues to be universal—among all peoples, under all forms of government, and in all types of economies, whenever cities have existed. And once people have experienced urban life, they are forced back into the countryside only at gunpoint, as seen in Cambodia. Apparently, for the vast majority of humankind, cities represent if not our greatest work of art (Mumford, 1938, 1961) then at least our most attractive alternative.

Migration from rural to urban areas has been and continues to be attractive to hundreds of millions because urbanism offers a way of life they know to be better than that which preceeded it (Fisher, 1973). Commenting upon those who immigrated to urban settlements in the United States, Bell says: "the migrants were seeking 'the promised land' and to some extent many of them found it. A steady job; regular pay; a chance for economic advancement; some schools for their children; the right to a meaningful vote; clean clothes; decent food; Sundays off." (Bell, 1968:163). None of these choices existed in the rural world from which they came.

Second, the antiurbanists are factually wrong on many counts. Consider rates of violence. In the United States, where are rates of homicide the highest? Homicide is highest in Mississippi, the most rural of any state in the Union. Homicide is also higher in the South than in the North, although the North is more urban. Among nations of the world, England has a greater urban proportion of its population than Mexico, Italy, France, and many other countries, including the United States, yet England has a lower homicide rate than these countries.

The antiurbanists assume crowding is an urban phenomenon but, in fact, household crowding is higher in rural homes than in urban ones (Keyfitz, 1966). According to their theories, the population of Hong Kong would be expected to be the most violent, discourteous, rude, and overloaded in the world, followed by the populations of Asian cities, such as Tokyo, Peking, and Jakarta, but this is not the case. And finally, the antiurbanists are not even correct historically (McPherson, 1975). American urban centers have lower population densities today than in 1910, yet the antiurbanists argue that there is more crime, disorder, and overloading today.

Let us avoid antiurbanism as we seek to understand the urbanite. In doing so, we will be even pro-urban because we believe that people are pro-urban, Americans included. When asked, Americans do say that they would prefer living in a small community (Von Eckardt, 1978). Questioned further, however, they add that their ideal small community would be convenient to a big city.

People leave the innercity for the suburbs, they leave metropolitan areas for nonmetropolitan ones, and they relocate to thinly populated areas to form communes. This flexibility in location, however, is made possible by the spread of urbanization in the settlement form we have called the urban environment. If people had to give up what is urban in order to move farther out, we have no doubt that they would choose to remain where they could be urban. But of what does this thing called urban consist?

THE NATURE OF URBANIZATION

Given our empirically based rejection of antiurbanism, there are some measures of urbanization which we can reject outright. The disorganization-deviance perspective of urbanology has used rates of murder, assault, burglary, rape, other crime, and overcrowding as its essential definition of urbanization. Theorists of the personal breakdown-anomie persuasion have treated admissions to mental hospitals, suicide rates, and indications of malaise or despair as their evidence for the workings of the process of urbanization. On theoretical and empirical grounds, we reject these approaches.

Some of the many other at least potentially more neutral dimensions of urbanism that have been employed can be grouped according to the POETS acronym.

Population

Urbanization as a process involves an increase in the number of urban settlements in which population concentrates and a growth in the size of these concentrations. This *aggregation* of the population increases its size, density, and heterogeneity.

What impact does the increased size, density, and heterogeneity of the population have upon the urbanite? They multiply the number and nature of the interactions available—exponentially. Thus the urbanite has millions of others, nearby, with whom to carry on life's activities.

These millions of others are not an atomic sandpile of separate individuals (Kasarda and Janowitz, 1974), but are connected to each other in hierarchies of community. At home, the urbanite has the other members of his or her household, and those who visit the family. In the neighborhood, the urbanite has persons with whom to neighbor should he or she wish to do so. The urbanite has homes away from home, home territories in favorite bars, taverns, restaurants, parks, and other hangouts. And the urbanite has still other communities at work, at sports events, at school, at church, and at a wide variety of voluntary associations.

And at the top of the hierarchy is that large public within which one is anonymous. As Romains (1933:7:457) describes it:

> Anonymity is the great gift of every city. In London Jallez discovered a new, a heightened form of anonymity. He was not only unknown, but unnoticed too. . . . Utterly alone in the midst of a crowd, he felt, more than he had ever felt before, relieved of the pressure of identity.

Although anonymous people can turn into mobs, one negative feature of anonymity, the condition also has its positive aspects, as any person knows from experience. To be unknown and unnoticed, to be alone in the midst of a crowd is indeed the great gift of urban settlements. In these settings individuals can turn into their own selves with such concentration as to be unaware of others. Whether reading a newspaper on a subway or bus, or simply lost in thought, urbanites, when in the anonymous public, may be "utterly alone."

At other times and for other urbanites, being unknown and unnoticed provides opportunities for discrete observation—especially of those who are utterly alone. Here the heterogeneity of the urban population provides a *peoplescape* of endless fascination. The greater the city's size, the greater the heterogeneity of its population. In *world cities*, then, its inhabitants may see people from virtually every part of the world. (Even better, they can go to one of their restaurants.)

Looking from the windows of their apartments, riding transit vehicles, standing in the lines which also characterize urban settlements, and on many other occasions, urbanites spend hours observing those with whom they share their settlement's space. The fascination of observing endless variation in peoplescape is part of the attraction of the city. The experience of heterogeneous multitudes does not overload but stimulates; and when observation begins to bore, or perhaps when urbanites have other inclinations, interests, or needs, they simply pursue those while remaining in that same crowd—turning to read newspapers, to study homework, or perhaps to think how they are going to tell. . . .

Urbanites spend so much of their time in public that some urbanologists have characterized urban life as one filled with secondary contacts. Some have even thought that the secondary (service) contacts become substitutes for primary (personal) relations. For the vast majority of urbanites, such substitution is not the case. Family, household, and neighborhood remain important for urbanites, who simply add many secondary contacts to them (Stone, 1954; Williams, 1967; Bell, 1968:143; Smith, Stone, and Form, 1954).

Finally, the heterogeneity of the urban population also means that there are many extremes: the very short and the very tall; the very thin and the very fat; the very rich and the very poor; the least educated and the best educated; the most religious and the least religious; the most honest and the most dishonest. Extremes are also found, of course, in small towns and in rural areas. The difference that population size makes lies in urban forms of organization.

Organization

If a trait such as tallness (being over seven feet tall) is found in one tenth of 1 percent of a population, in a town of 10,000 there would be ten people (of both sexes of all adults) who were more than seven feet tall. In a city of 100,000 there would be 100, and with a population of 1 million there would be 1,000 very tall people. The difference that population size makes is that at some point there are enough people with a trait such as tallness to seek and to secure goods and services for their own kind. With a population of 8 million, New York City can (and does) have stores that sell clothing only to the very tall. Other shops sell tools for the left-handed, aids for the very fat, vehicles differentiated according to handicap, and an extensive variety of other highly specialized goods and services.

The same is true of interests and tastes. As the size of the city increases, the diversity of its establishments increases. The highly specialized organization of the city makes possible the satisfaction of every need, interest, taste, desire, or fancy. Given the excesses in which human beings have been known to indulge, great cities come to serve some very bizarre tastes.

Economy

Urban diversity includes the number and kinds of markets and they increase with population size. The markets of world cities are therefore stocked from every part of the world. Whatever the taste, style, period, country, quality, quantity, inspiration, or fetish—it is available. Do you need a broker for your yacht? A fortune teller? A masseuse to call at your home? A stone cut? A painting restored? Or just someone to talk to?

What is the impact of urban economy on individual urbanites? As the forms of organization, including the economic, diversify, so does the division of labor. In small towns there are barbers, but in great cities there are barbers, hair stylists, designers, and specialists in the razor cut, the shag cut, or the layer cut; there are scalp specialists, hair analysts, hair restorers, and those who specialize in hair transplants; there are those who train types of specialists, and others who educate the general practitioner; there are yet others who sell the tonics and tools, who make and advertise the goods, and those who invent new ones; and there are still others who manage the unions and associations, who lobby in legislatures, and who plan for the conventions of barbers. The heterogeneity of the city produces more heterogeneity, along with changing styles in goods and services.

Technology

The urban achievement we take so for granted today is dependent on an energy-expensive and complex technology. It was first the rails and then the roads on which urbanization flowed out into the countryside. And today the routes of technology—the telephone lines (Aronson, 1971) and television waves, the air traffic lanes, and the computer circuits—interconnect the populations of nations into national and international urban societies.

The impact of the technology component of urbanization upon urbanites is also evident in modern transportation and communications. To get the news, to learn about the important events, required access to the city's center until 150 years ago; it required access to a metropolitan newspaper until less than 50 years ago; but today not just news of, but observation of, many events comes into urbanites' own homes without travel anywhere. Through the mails, urbanites may shop in distant markets, read and perhaps write for distant publications, and support causes and organizations which are located far away. Through technology urbanization has spread, bringing many urban amenities to people in small settlements.

Jean Guillemin (1976:142), in her study of the urban tribal network of the Micmac Indians of the Northeast, observes how important automobiles are for them.

> The interpersonal network of most Micmac Indians is so dispersed that it requires travel from the Maritimes to Boston, from Boston to secondary centers and smaller groupings of Indians in Worcester, Springfield, Leominster, and Portland, and then travel back again up to the Provinces to insure frequent communication between its members.

The Micmac are but one small segment of the urban population for whom the automobile is crucial. Among many sources that could be cited documenting the dispersed nature of personal networks, Wellman (1972:96) reports that nearly nine tenths of his subjects' "intimates" lived in widely scattered parts of metropolitan Toronto and outside it. Robinson (1978) found that his subjects' associates lived about eight miles away, on the average. Finally, Warren (1976:22) reports that, in his study, the space encompassed by whites in their routine social interaction was 48 square miles and for blacks it was 13 square miles. Such interpersonal networks could not be maintained without modern technology.

Thus far we have argued that urbanization is a multidimensional, revolutionary, ecological process. We have added that the experience of it is universally attractive and irreversible for those who have had it. Through observation of the causes and consequences of urbanization—the subject matter of urbanology—we traced the interaction of population, organization, economy, and technology. But in attempting to apprehend the urbanite in person, perhaps it is in the component of symbolism that our essence of urbanization is to be found.

Symbolism

Urbanization is a process whereby rural people become urban and, over time, possibly urbane. Whereas the rural to urban transition is irreversible, except in catastrophes, to be urban is not necessarily to be urbane. To be urbane, Partridge (1958) tells us, originally meant to be "of a" or perhaps "of the" city. Over time, however, to be urbane came to mean "civilized, polished, refined, witty." Webster adds to be "civil, courteous, at ease in society, blandly polite, suave." How is it that urban living may produce urbane persons?

We have already reviewed the complex and richly diverse forms of organization that aggregations of populations make possible, and how those forms of organization are also dependent upon an energy-intensive technology, one which has created and distributed previously unknown wealth to millions. Ignoring for the moment the possible consequences of changes in any one of these four components, let us focus attention on the symbolism that structures their interdependency. Let us begin with the persons newly arrived to the urban life.

Anyone can be in a city; even the person who arrived just yesterday lives in it. The response of newcomers to the personal or unusual, whether southern belle looking for success or Texas tourist in ten-gallon hat, is likely to be urban, not urbane. "Did you see that?" he or she says while continuing to stare. To be urbane is to be civil, to exercise civil inattention—to ignore politely that which is in front of one's eyes.

The word "civil" stems from "civics," "civilized," and from the word "city" itself. To be civil is to attend very carefully to some things and to ignore, equally studiously, other things. The total life style of an urbane, and hence civil, person will be attended very carefully. Because the urbane person is urban, however, he or she while pursuing life will see many things which ought not be seen. Why ought not? Because the others who are doing them do not want them noticed.

Lovers may be spending their last few precious moments together; new friends may be absorbed in each other's perceptions; opera-goers returning home may still be caught up in the performance; perhaps a person has just lost his or her job; maybe a couple has just lost their child or a parent. No urban person can fail to see and hear things which reveal the lives of people as persons. The response to them, however, differentiates the merely urban from the urbane person.

Both the urban and the urbane person live in a plural society—but the urbane person knows it and lives in a way to preserve it. While the urbane person may be disdainful of anyone not like him or herself, the urbane person is tolerant in the sense of expecting differences and doing nothing to inhibit them. As Fisher (1976) puts it, he or she does not expect unanimity but "multinimity." (See also Fisher, 1973.)

To be urbane is to be refined, raised to a high degree of subtlety. Urbane persons express selves so subtly that only members of their own hierarchy of community, at whatever level, fully appreciate it. Because urbanologists have been overly occupied with measuring such phantoms as presumed overloads, it is writers like Bellow, Baldwin, Thompson, and a host of others that provide evidence of the endless tapestry of urban sophistication.

The urban person is, as we have documented, enculturated within numerous hierarchies of community. The urbane person, however, is aware that the existence of one's own communities is dependent upon the protection of others'. Their communities must be protected to preserve "our own."

Community preservation in the urban sense begins with the individual, extends to homes and to homes away from homes, and embraces neighborhood, section or area, settlement, region, nation, and planet. It involves not a reduction in the number of people with whom we interact, but an increase in the control of those who do.

People feel crowded, in our perspective, not when they are surrounded by and even packed together with their friends, but when they are close together with strangers (Sommer, 1969). Urbanites avoid unwanted contact with strangers by creating hierarchies of community to control their communication with them. At home and at homes away from home, urbanites live with those others with whom they assume some commonality. The assumption of commonality, along with other processes already described, creates social worlds of many types and sizes.

These urban responses to space are called territoriality. Territoriality is not inherited, it is not instinctual, but it is part of the symbolic nature of humankind—their values, beliefs, histories, peoplehoods. Territoriality is a technique to avoid and to regulate conflict and to reduce aggression (Mileski and Black, 1972).

Aggression is triggered by crowding when social worlds are invaded. Ask someone whose house has been robbed how he or she felt. A common reaction is to feel violated, personally touched by an unknown other. Subsequent security measures are taken only in part in an effort to prevent another such break-in. Locks, bolts, and alarm systems are also installed to counter the increased insecurity the invaded often experience.

In an urbane defense of the South, John S. Reed (1974) points to the anxiety levels raised by robberies and mugging, to say nothing of their other effects. Urbanity is not possible when one's own personal space is not secure. To the extent to which we seek to help urban persons become urbane we must protect that lowest level in the hierarchy of community—the individual. Invasions of personal space by total strangers are more common in the North than in the South, Reed continues, and therefore the North is more urban but less urbane. (Assault is also, of course, an invasion of personal space; but, as we have already observed from Simmel and Coser, and as Reed also points out, because aggravated assault is typically committed by one's friends, relatives, and other intimate space sharers, the threat of assault provokes less anxiety, especially of the diffuse variety.)

Protection of community must encompass the household, as Rainwater

(1966) among others has pointed out. How is it possible to be urbane when rats, rodents, fire, filth, and disorder are one's urban experience? Seeley (1956) says that one's home is one's citadel, at least among Crestwooders. While others may be less embattled, surely security in one's home is an essential precondition for urbanity.

The last two decades have witnessed a revival of neighborhoods. As a growing body of literature suggests (Gans, 1965; Anderson, 1966), the revival was necessary in large part because public actions had destroyed so much of neighborhood. Governmental slum clearance, urban renewal, highway construction, and other massive relocations temporarily uprooted millions from their hierarchies of community at the household and neighborhood level. Financial institutions further eroded these levels of communal life by red-lining, diverting resources to developers instead of home owners, and encouraging the "disposal" of homes instead of their recycling.

Forced to abandon not only a treasured dwelling with all its sentimental attachments, but also removed from easy contact with friends and neighbors of many years, such individuals, Marc Fried (1968) states, experience a type of grief. In our terms a citadel of private space, and the network of local relationships sustaining it, has indeed died, and the survivors mourn their loss.

When neighborhoods begin to deteriorate, those who lend money for housing may *red-line* the area. Companies such as savings and loan associations fear that further investment in deteriorating neighborhoods is not safe, that they will lose any money invested, and so they red-line the area. Residents of red-lined neighborhoods are unable to secure the funds necessary for periodic maintenance and repair. The consequence of red-lining therefore is to accelerate deterioration. Home owners may lose the money they had invested in their housing. They may also be unable to move since, again because of red-lining, no one can borrow the money to buy their houses, and so they are trapped in deteriorating housing.

Those in poverty include many aged persons who are trapped where they are. Their previous neighbors have moved away and been replaced by people with whom they assume no commonality. Secure space for them may be limited to their dwellings, which they feel are under seige. The invasions of their space by human and nonhuman sources is no less than life-threatening. Under such circumstances the inhabitants feel fortunate to survive. They certainly are unable to pursue urbanity.

There is a connection, we realize, between the protection of neighbors and the households within them, but how far should the protection extend? Whereas we may all agree that rape and robbery should be eliminated, what control should neighbors have in excluding whatever they may define as "undesirable?" Invasions of neighborhood space occur when anyone or anything considered "undesirable" attempts to move in. The "undesirable" may be a highway, a fast-food restaurant, a tavern, an actor, a musician, a black, a white, or any other of hundreds of things.

The distinction drawn between ghetto and enclave is relevant here. No one should be forced to live in a specific area because someone else defines that person as belonging to a certain people. People should have the choice, however, to live among those whom they define as their own. Within American experience, we noted that what we have defined as our own people has shifted from a religious to an ethnic base and that today life style is becoming increasingly important. The exception to the change is the relationship between blacks and whites.

> I have crossed many a frontier, have had my passport stamped, say, at the French-Swiss border, at the Swiss-Italian border . . . however dramatic the frontiers I have mentioned, the most dramatic, the most appalling, remains the invisible frontier which divides American towns, white from black. (Baldwin, 1968:144)

Urbane was defined as cultivated. To merge with a people because the circumstances of one's birth thrust it upon one, to define one's own as being "not one of them," or to force others into associations for which they care not, is all too frequently urban—but it is not urbane. Control, therefore, must be maximized over self in urbane society, but minimized over others.

The city was begun by people whose commonality consisted of sharing settlement space. Cities have become nation-states, whose citizens are most often defined as those who were born within that space. It is said of immigrants that they may become naturalized; that is, become invested with the privileges of a native-born subject. Urbanites share settlement space, and it is essential that they exercise that degree of control over it which begins with choice.

One way to understand a perspective is to ask what solutions it would effect. The antiurbanists, for example, would move people out of cities into small communities. Reducing the number of people with whom to interact, and lowering the density of the population, would also lower the heterogeneity of those encountered. According to antiurbanists, living in small, thinly settled, homogeneous, and self-contained utopias would end such problems as violence, despair, superficiality, and overload.

Our approach suggests that there are many advantages to size. Indeed, insufficient size may itself be a problem—in administration, governance, and planning, for example. The analyses of many of today's problems, as well as putting into practice their solutions, depend upon gaining sufficient size. The control of nuclear fuel and its wastes, for example, depends upon a worldwide community. The same is true with respect to resources such as water and air.

An increase in size does not necessarily increase population density, but it is doing so in most cities of the world today. Dense populations are far more energy-efficient than less-dense ones. One solution to the depletion of fossil fuels is to tear up some of the old highways and build houses on that land.

The very conditions producing urbanity multiply its spread. Population size encourages structural differentiation (Durkheim, 1933). The larger a settlement the larger its hinterland, and thus the larger the variety of groups for whom it is a central place. The more urban a place, therefore, the greater the number and the greater the intensity and diversity of its subcultures.

For the individuals involved, increases in the urban increase the probability that every individual will find the sort of social world in which he or she expands and feels at ease (Park, 1952:47). To the extent to which the individual finds those who bring his or her disposition to full and free expression, each becomes urbane.

Heterogeneity therefore is not the problem. The many homogeneous social worlds which heterogeneous people form and maintain do not constitute problems. On one hand we can say that problems arise from invasions of space which, on the other hand, stem from lack of control of space.

If the diagnosis of overcentralization is correct, the antidote is decentralization at all levels of community, decentralization through increases in participation. Our objective might be to restore to users of space a part in all decisions affecting its use—not only of one's own body, but one's home, neighborhood, community, region, nation, and world as well.

TO BE URBANE

The open and plural society that is the essence of urbanity weaves an endlessly varied urban fabric. The hierarchies of communities of hundreds of millions should be acted upon only with the full participation of those affected. No one person, group, neighborhood, or people can or should have exclusive control even over "their" locale; but use of their knowledge of the organization of their area would facilitate optimal change for the local and the wider community.

To be urbane is an ideal, we said. It is a goal in part achieved by sufficient control of space to create and sustain hierarchies of community. As the individuals who constitute those hierarchies live through their family, career, and life cycles, they change—and the space they organize changes. Multiplied by hundreds of millions, change comes to be perhaps the most fundamental trait of urbanity.

> By the diversity of its time structures, the city in part escapes the tyranny of a single present and the monotony of a future that consists in repeating only a single beat heard in the past. Through its complex orchestration of time and space no less than through the social division of labor, life in the city takes on the character of a symphony. (Mumford, 1938:4)

The process of urbanization is revolutionary as we have seen. That urban revolution with which we began in Chapter 1 is now seen to be a continuing one. It is a continuing and successful revolution to the extent to which its end product is the urbane.

About 100 years ago the movement called municipal reform arose to solve the problems of the then-emergent metropolis. Its goals included the elimination of representation by specific small locales—neighborhoods, wards, designated areas. At-large elections, political integration of formerly distinct municipalities, and other measures to centralize power would enable officials to better govern.

Municipal reform did better urban life. Integrated transit systems, safe water supplies, sanitation, and even financial accounting methods were among its results. When the same arguments were advanced at the national level, centralization of power there, too, achieved numerous beneficial results. Ought we therefore to consolidate power at yet higher levels as some urge us to do?

Past experience, the person who becomes urbane knows, is not necessarily the best guide for the future. The world changed with the creation of cities and change has become the hallmark of urban life ever since. In the 75 or so years since the urban environment began to emerge, change has so accelerated that we may suffer from future shock (Toffler, 1975). Or, being urbane, we may choose to work toward that future we would prefer.

> An urbane society may be contrasted not only with rustic, bucolic, agricultural, provincial, rural, or pastoral society but also with chaotic, fragmented, incoherent urban society. The rawness and harshness of industrial slums do not constitute urbaneness; nor do interactions marked by strong and continuous hostility, suspicion, and fear; nor an "impersonality" that treats persons as manipulable objects. There is detachment in urbanity but it is a detachment of civility and autonomy. (Williams, 1967)

In the urban world humankind makes itself; but in the world of the urbane the pursuit is self-conscious. In our view the choice is not between chaos at one extreme or some form of utopian primitivism at the other. Working toward an urbane society involves recognizing that strength lies in diversity. As members of an extremely heterogeneous society, the urbane make their choice, while preserving the right of others to make theirs. Given the millions now deprived of any choice through the centralization of power, how can yet additional power concentrations encourage urbanity?

Throughout our exhausting, if not exhaustive, study of the urban environment, scant attention has been given to urban problems. This neglect of the problems of the urban environment stems from their number and complexity. Adequate descriptions, analyses, and suggested solutions to today's problems require an entire text by itself. Herein we can only allude to one core set—those which stem from user's lack of participation in the control of the space(s) they inhabit.

To participate in the control of space requires choice, knowledge, conflict, accommodation, and compromise, within a context of self and other awareness which is based on meaningful communication. As participation increases, the number of choices, the knowledge involved, and the conflict or perhaps cooperation which participation necessitates goes up. The tasks for the urbane, and those who would be, are thus as highly variable as the urban fabric itself. And, given urbane heterogeneity, it is difficult to see how power concentrations would fail to undermine it.

The choices to be made do not include whether or not to be urban. From the thousands of years of experience with cities, and given today's rate of urbanization and urban growth, we know that the future is urban. The question is: will it be urbane?

STUDY QUESTIONS

1. Cite some examples of antiurbanism, including some from your own community.
2. Discuss the nature of urbanization in each of its components.
3. How do some urban problems arise through lack of control of space?
4. What does it mean to be urbane?

SUGGESTED READINGS

Becker, Howard S.   *Culture and Civility in San Francisco* (New Brunswick, N.J.: Transaction Books, 1971).

Sennett, Richard.   *The Uses of Disorder* (New York: Random House, 1970).

GLOSSARY

absorption final phase in suburbanization when the area is redeveloped from residential to commercial uses and absorbed into the core urban community

aggregation an increase in the number of urban settlements in which population concentrates and a growth in the size of these concentrations

annexation the incorporation by legal means of smaller communities into a larger central city

automobility the impact of the motor vehicle and the automobile and the highway industries on society

beachheaders initial migrants who serve as sources of information about their new location to those left behind

breaks in transportation places where goods are transferred from one vessel to another; for example, from a ship to a train

central business district (CBD) the center or core area of a metropolis, the location where access is/was the highest

central place a cluster of service functions located at the point most accessible to the maximum profit area

central place cities cities performing centralized services and functioning to coordinate goods and services

central place theory the theory that markets initially locate at or survive in central, transport, or special function sites according to their thresholds

chain migration movement among family or acquaintances started by one member of the group

citadel city a settlement enclosed by one or more rings of walls, with an inner wall enclosing a palace, temple, granary, or fortress

cluster an area wherein people are concentrated

community business centers   commercial enterprises, such as variety and clothing stores, bakeries, florists, post offices, and banks

compositionalists   theorists who stress the importance of the composition of population

concentration of a population   the relationship between the total number in the settlement and the number living in a specific location within the settlement

concentric zone theory   theory by Burgess showing the organization of the metropolis to be concentric with the socioeconomic status of the population increasing from the CBD outwards

conurbanation   a growing together of many metropolises

conventional housing   residential units of a permanent location constructed according to building codes of the time and legally protected in their tenure

crude birth and death rates   unrefined measures of the number per thousand population that do not take into account such factors as the age of the population or the proportion of females

cultural intensification   the process whereby the commonality of the group is strengthened within a social world formed within a spatial cluster

daily urban system   a measurement of the boundaries of a metropolitan area that includes areas surrounding the center if a certain percentage of the population commute to the core for work

deconcentration   a distribution of the population resulting in lowered densities overall

deconversion   change in residential units toward less-intensive usage

defended neighborhoods   neighborhoods withstanding the attempted invasion of a different people or land usage

definitive cities   walled settlements in which the POETS components were in interaction

demographic transition   a sharp drop in the death rates, with birth rates declining gradually, producing high levels of reproductive increase

developing phase of suburbanization   rapid uneven growth in an area, as when tract housing construction begins

dispersed urbanization   the spread of urban settlements throughout an area creating many urban communities

dominance   the hierarchical ordering of urban communities

door-stoop neighborhoods   neighborhoods where space outside of the dwelling, such as door-stoops, halls, and sidewalks, becomes an extension of the home

dormitory suburbs   an area surrounding the core of a metropolis that contains residences almost exclusively

economic determinists   theorists who stress the importance of economic variables (e.g., markets) on urbanization

economies of agglomeration   the economic advantages of the clustering of related and competing businesses

economy   the resources available to a society

enclave   an area in which a group of people predominate

ethclass   an ethnic grouping of primarily one economic class

ethnicity   a human collectivity based on an assumption of common origin—race, religion, national origin, or some combination of them; it is one basis for peoplehood

ethstyle   a distinctive ethnic life based on style rather than a single class

evolution   gradual change over a long period of time

exclusive occupation   the residence of one people in an area to the exclusion of any others

exurban   the outermost settlements from the core that have not been suburbanized

fertility rate   the rate of reproduction

filtering   a process of downward changes in housing

ghetto   an area which a people exclusively occupy

ghetto hypothesis   ''melting pot'' theory, where formerly diverse peoples become one and in doing so move from metropolitan core to periphery

hierarchy of business centers   the ordering of commercial activities by their thresholds and frequency of use, as specified by central place theory

highway-oriented commercial ribbons   strip development of businesses serving demands originating on the highways

imageability   the clarity with which an area can be apprehended

impersonally organized migration   migration organized by a recruiter or a company

incipient cities   the earliest walled settlements

index of centralization   measure designed to reflect degree to which suburbs differ from the core

index of segregation (or dissimilarity)   the measure of segregation used by urbanologists to indicate the percentage of two groups that would have to move to produce their complete integration—the scale value of 100 equals complete segregation and a value of zero equals complete integration

infill   development of land in suburbs missed in the development phase

in-migration   a stream of persons immigrating into one region or country

interactional density   the number of people using an area

interactionalists   theorists who stress the importance of symbolism in analyzing urbanization

invasion   the movement of a different group of people or land use into an area

isolated convenience stores   street-corner shops selling goods that are frequently purchased

local park   officially designated and unofficial small areas used as places to hang out, sit, visit, and so forth, which are located within several blocks of the users' homes

locational socialization   socialization of others, including children and newcomers, by being told where to go and where not to go in the area

marginal space   an area that is relatively inaccessible to the police and the citizens but not valuable enough to be patrolled

mature phase of suburbanization   phase characterized by a lower rate of growth, elimination of all rural land, and provision of many services to residents

megalopolis   a super city; a vast continuous urban settlement hundreds of miles wide and containing tens of millions of people

metro pattern   settlement pattern in which persons with minimal education are concentrated in the core, and larger than expected proportions of persons with higher educational standing are found in the suburbs

metropolis   a large urban settlement, with its core(s) dominating the surrounding area and the entire settlement dominating its hinterland

metropolitan parks   large areas set aside as special purpose parks for the entire settlement, including zoos and botanical gardens

mixed city and metropolitan pattern   pattern of development of a settlement characterized by an overrepresentation of persons at educational extremes within the core

mortality rate   the rate of death per thousand population

municipal reform   a movement to eliminate governmental corruption and to improve metropolitan government

negative exponential density distribution (n.e.d.d.)   the systematic decline from the center of the city of the average residential density of a population

neighborhood business centers   clusters of smaller businesses, such as grocery stores, drugstores, laundries and cleaners, barber and beauty shops, and small restaurants

Neighborhood Interactional Scale   a measure of the neighboring relationship according to both parties involved

neighborhood or community park   encompassing larger areas than local parks, neighborhood parks are usually officially designated areas held in common for joint occupancy

net increase   increase of population in an area from all sources, i.e., reproduction and migration

new city   an entirely new settlement established as a whole and intended to be relatively autonomous

new community   a settlement established as a small part of a settlement and less autonomous than a town or city

new town   a settlement established as part of a larger settlement

node   the center, also used to establish the boundaries of a region by nodal orientation

old city pattern   pattern of a settlement characterized by a large proportion of less-educated people residing in the suburbs

orbit   the space habitually utilized by an individual

organization   the block of variables in the social, political, geographic, and historical organization of society

organizationalists   theorists who state that the form of organization—historical, geographic, political, or social—is the most important factor to consider

out-migration   a stream of persons emigrating from one region or country

overload   an inability to process inputs from one's environment because there are too many

overurbanization   the condition when a population is growing faster than its economy is industrializing

people   a people are those who so call themselves and are so regarded by others

peoplehood   the society shared by a people

peoplescape   the experience of the people with whom one shares settlement space

place migration   movement wherein a specific destination is sought

population   a block of demographic variables including age, sex, and fertility

predominance   the proportion of one group relative to others in that area

primate or primary settlement   concentrated urban development in which one settlement grows at the expense of all others

private space   space being kept or removed from public view or knowledge

public space   places where a person can be observed by strangers, usually many

rate of urbanization   the change in the proportion of population living in urban and rural settlements

red-lining   designating an area as deteriorating and ineligible for loans by lending institutions, thus accelerating the deterioration

regional shopping centers   the cluster of department stores, music, hobby, toy, photo, and other shops

reproductive increase   the excess of births over deaths in a given population

residential density   the number of people living in an area

residential differentiation   the process of inclusion and exclusion in residential areas of people perceived to be similar or different

rurban area   the area around the bounds of a city containing unevenly developed rural and urban land

selective migration   the movement of a highly specified group of persons

sex ratio   the number of males per 100 females

social differentiation   the process of inclusion and exclusion of people perceived to be similar or different

spatial clustering   the grouping together of people who have some commonality

specialized function cities   cities geared to specialized functions, such as resorts, military headquarters, or religious centers or shrines

specialized functional areas   closely related businesses that cluster together, such as "automobile row"

sprawl   an uneven or low-density development of land

stage migration   successive movement until a final destination is reached

Standard Metropolitan Statistical Area (SMSA)   the population of one or more entire counties that contain a city or cities of at least 50,000 in population

suburban myth   the assumption that most suburbs were alike

succession   the phase when newcomers or new uses in an area come to predominate

symbolic ecology   the interdependence of the components of population, organization, economy, technology, and symbolism

symbolism the meaning given to space, time, and people because of the sentiments or values of a people

technological determinists theorists who stress the importance of technology in urban analysis

technology the tools and techniques of a society

territoriality a response to space in which people identify with a specific place and will defend it as if their own

territoriality structuring the organization of an area, with groups marking off their own territories

threshold point at which an area is able to support the entry of a business, i.e., the minimum volume of sales needed

tipping point the point at which the composition of an area quickly changes to favor the newcomers or new uses

transport cities cities providing for the transfer of goods from one vessel to another—from aircraft to land vehicles, for example

uniformity one criterion used to establish the boundaries of a region

urban arterial commercial developments businesses located on major traffic thoroughfares that serve the locality, for example, furniture and appliance stores, auto repair shops, and garden centers

urban environment a mosaic of interpersonal networks and social worlds, which may or may not share a common exclusive territory

urban field a mosaic of different forms and micro-environments that co-exist within a common communications framework

urban frontier currently the areas of the old urban heartland now experiencing deconversion and renovation

urban growth increase or decrease in the urban population

urban place settlements with 2,500 or more inhabitants

urban revolution the beginning and continuance of the process of urbanization

urbane a person who is considered to be refined, civil, and polite

Urbanism-Familism Scale a measure of urbanization using either fertility rates or female participation in the labor force, or both

urbanization a multidimensional, revolutionary, ecological process of becoming citylike

urbanized areas places that have a core population of at least 50,000 and the surrounding urbanized territories

velocity of migration the proportion of the migrants in a stream to the "home" population, multiplied by the proportion of the population in the destination area to the population of all potential areas of destination

wall, to to erect a boundary between those enclosed and those excluded

world cities cities at the top of the dominance order, with the world as their hinterlands

zone of transition the concentric ring surrounding the central business district, parts of which may be incorporated into the CBD

REFERENCES

Aaron, Henry J.
    1972 *Shelter and Subsidies* (Washington, D.C.: Brookings Institution).

Abrams, Philip, and McCulloch, Andrew
    1976 *Communes, Sociology and Society* (New York: Cambridge University Press).

Abu-Lughod, Janet
    1962 *India's Urban Future* (Berkeley: University of California Press).
    1964 "Urban-rural differences as a function of the demographic transition: Egyptian data and an analytical model." *American Journal of Sociology* 69:476–90.

Adams, Robert M.
    1960 "The origin of cities." *Scientific American* 203(September) 153–72.

Alihan, Milla A.
    1938 *Social Ecology: A Critical Analysis* (New York: Columbia University Press).

Alonso, William
    1971 "A theory of the urban land market." Larry S. Bourne, ed., pp. 154–59. *Internal Structure of the City* (New York: Oxford University Press).

Altman, Irwin, and Haythorn, W. W.
    1967 "The ecology of isolated groups." *Behavioral Science* 12:169–82.

Altshuler, Alan A.
    1970 *Community Control: The Black Demand for Participation in Large American Cities* (New York: Boffs-Merrill, Pegasus).

Anderson, E. N.
    1972 "Some Chinese methods of dealing with crowding." *Urban Studies* 1(Fall) 141–50.

Anderson, Martin
    1966   *The Federal Bulldozer* (Cambridge, Mass.: M.I.T. Press).

Andrew, Paul; Cristie, Malcolm; and Martin, Richard
    1972   "Squatter manifesto." *Ekistics* 34(August) 108–13.

Appleyard, Donald
    1973   "Notes on urban perception and knowledge." Roger M. Downs and
           David Stea, eds., *Image And Environment* (Chicago: Aldine).

Appleyard, Donald, and Lintell, Mark
    1972   "The environmental quality of city streets: The residents' viewpoint."
           Journal of the American Institute of Planners 38:84–101.

Ardsley, Robert
    1961   *African Genesis* (New York: Dell).

Aronson, Sidney
    1971   "The sociology of the telephone." *International Journal of Compara-
           tive Society* 12(September) 153–67.

Aronwitz, Stanley
    1970   "The dialectics of community control." *Social Policy* 1 (May–June)
           47–51.

Bacon, Edmund N.
    1967   *Design of Cities* (New York: Viking Press).

Baldassare, M.
    1975   "The effects of density on social behavior and attitudes." *American
           Behavioral Scientist* 18(July) 815–25.

Baldassare, M., and Fischer, C. S.
    1976   "The relevance of crowding experiments to urban studies." D. Stokes,
           ed., *Psychological Perspectives on Environment and Behavior* (New
           York: Macmillan, Plenum Press).

Baldwin, James
    1968   *Tell Me How Long The Train's Been Gone* (New York: Dial Press).

Baltzell, Digby
    1967   "Introduction to the 1967 edition." W. E. B. DuBois. *The Philadelphia
           Negro* (New York: Schocken Books; first published 1899).

Banfield, Edward C.
    1970   *The Unheavenly City Revisited* (Boston: Little, Brown).

Bangs, Herbert P., Jr., and Mahler, Stuart
    1970   "Users of local parks." *Journal of the American Institute of Planners*
           36:330–34.

Barclay, Thomas Swain
    1962   *The St. Louis Home Rule Charter of 1876* (Columbia: University of
           Missouri Press).

Barker, Roger G.
    1968   *Ecological Psychology* (Stanford, Cal.: Stanford University Press).

Barker, Roger G., and Wright, Herbert F.
    1954   *Midwest and Its Children* (Evanston, Ill.: Row, Peterson).

Baumohl, Jim, and Miller, Henry

1974   *Down and Out in Berkeley* (Berkeley, Cal.: City Community Affairs Committee).

Beale, Calvin L.
1975   "The revival of population growth in nonmetropolitan America." *Economic Development Division*. Economic Research Service, U.S. Department of Agriculture (June) No. ERS–605.

Becker, Howard S., ed.
1971   *Culture and Civility in San Francisco* (New Brunswick, N.J.: Transaction Books).

Bell, Wendell
1968   "The city, the suburb, and a theory of social choice." Scott Greer et al., eds., pp. 132–68. *The New Urbanization* (New York: St. Martin's Press).

Bell, Wendell, and Boat, Marion D.
1956–1957   "Urban neighborhood and informal social relations." *American Journal of Sociology* 62:391–98.

Bellow, Saul
1956   *Seize the Day* (New York: Fawcett World Library).

Bengough, W.
1895   "The Mulberry Bend Italian Colony." *Harper's Weekly* (June 29).

Berger, Bennett M.
1960   *Working-Class Suburb* (Berkeley: University of California Press).

Bernard, Jessie
1937   "An instrument for the measurement of neighborhood with experimental applications." *South Western Social Science Quarterly* 37:8–15.

Berry, Brian J. L.
1971   "General features of urban commercial structure." Larry S. Bourne, ed., pp. 361–67. *Internal Structure of the City* (New York: Oxford University Press).
1971   "Urban definitions beyond metropolis." Abbott L. Ferris, ed., pp. 151–57. *Research and the 1970 Census* (Oak Ridge, Tenn.: Southern Regional Demographic Group, Oak Ridge Associated Universities).

Berry, Brian J. L., and Pred, Allen
1961   *Central Place Studies: A Bibliography of Theory and Applications* (Philadelphia: Regional Science Research Institute).

Berry, Brian J. L., and Kasarda, John D.
1977   *Contemporary Urban Ecology* (New York: Macmillan).

Berry, Brian J. L., and Gillard, Quentin
1977   *The Changing Shape of Metropolitan America* (Cambridge, Mass.: Ballinger).

Berry, Brian J. L.; Goheen, Peter G.; and Goldstein, H.
1968   *Metropolitan Area Classification: A Review of Current Practice, Criticisms, and Proposed Alternatives* (Washington: U.S. Bureau of the Census, Working Paper No. 28).

Beshers, James M.
1961   *Urban Social Structure* (New York: Free Press).

Birch, David L.
  1970 *The Economic Future of City and Suburb* (New York: Committee for Economic Development, No. 30).

Bittner, Egon
  1967 "The police in skid row: a study of peace keeping." *American Sociological Review* 32:5(October) 701–6.

Blaut, James M., and Stea, David
  1973 "Some preliminary observations on spatial learning in school children." Roger M. Downs and David Stea, eds. *Image and Environment* (Chicago: Aldine).

Blecher, Earl M.
  1971 *Advocacy Planning for Urban Development* (New York: Praeger Publishers).

Blumberg, Leonard; Shipley, Thomas E.; and Shandler, Irving
  1973 *Skid Row and Its Alternatives* (Philadelphia: Temple University Press).

Blumenfeld, Hans
  1954 "The tidal wave of metropolitan expansion." *Journal of the American Institute of Planners* (Winter) 3–14.

Bogue, Donald J.
  1947 *The Structure of the Metropolitan Community: A Study of Dominance and Subdominance* (Ann Arbor: University of Michigan Press).
  1959 *The Population of the United States* (New York: Free Press).

Borchert, John R.
  1961 "The twin cities urbanized area: Past, present, future." *Geographical Review* 51:47–70.

Boskoff, Alvin
  1962 *The Sociology of Urban Regions* (New York: Appleton-Century-Crofts).

Bossard, James H., and Boll, Eleanor S.
  1968 *Family Situations* (New York: Greenwood Press).

Bott, Elizabeth
  1957 *Family and Social Networks* (London: Travistock Publications).

Bourne, Larry S., ed.
  1971 *Internal Structure of the City* (New York: Oxford University Press).

Bouvard, Marguerite
  1975 *The International Community Movement: Building a New Moral World* (Port Washington, N.Y.: Kennikat Press).

Boyce, Ronald R.
  1971 "The edge of the metropolis: The wave theory analog approach." Larry S. Bourne, ed., pp. 104–11. *Internal Structure of the City* (New York: Oxford University Press.

Bradley, Donald S.
  1977 "Neighborhood Transition: Middle-class Home Buying in an Inner-City Deteriorating Community." Chicago: paper presented to the ASA Meeting; unpublished.

Brazer, Harvey
   1962 "Some implications of metropolitanism." Gutherie Burkhead, ed. *Metropolitan Issues: Social, Governmental and Fiscal* (Syracuse, N.Y.: Maxwell Graduate School).

Breese, G., ed.
   1969 *The City in Newly Developing Countries* (Englewood Cliffs, N.J.: Prentice-Hall).

Bridenbaugh, Carl
   1938 *Cities in the Wilderness: The First Century of Urban Life in America, 1625–1742* (New York: Ronald Press).
   1955 *Cities in Revolt: Urban Life in America, 1743–1776* (New York: Alfred A. Knopf).

Briggs, Ronald
   1973 "Urban cognitive distance." Roger M. Downs and David Stea, eds. *Image and Environment* (Chicago: Aldine).

Browne, Kenneth, and Whitaker, Ben
   1971 *Parks are for People* (New York: Schocken Books).

Burgess, E. W.
   1925 "The growth of the city: An introduction to a research project." Robert E. Park et al., eds., pp. 47–62. *The City* (Chicago: University of Chicago Press).

Burnham, John C.
   1961 "The gasoline tax and the automobile revolution." *Mississippi Valley Historical Review* 48(December) 435–59.

Caditz, Judith
   1976 "Ethnic identification, interethnic conflict, and belief in integration." *Social Forces* (March) 632–45.

Calhoun, J.
   1962 "Population density and social pathology." *Scientific American* 206:139–48.

Caplow, Theodore; Stryker, Sheldon; and Wallace, Samuel E.
   1962 *The Urban Ambiance* (Totowa: Bedminster).

Caplow, Theodore, and Forman, Robert
   1950 "Neighborhood interaction in homogeneous community." *American Sociological Review* 15:357–66.

Caplow, Theodore; Lovald, Keith; and Wallace, Samuel E.
   1958 *A General Report on the Relocation of the Population of the Lower Loop* (Minneapolis: Minneapolis Housing Authority).

Carey, G. W.
   1972 "Density, crowding, stress, and the ghetto." *American Behavioral Scientist* (Spring) 495–509.

Carnaham, D.; Grove, W.; and Galle, O. R.
   1974 "Urbanization, population density and overcrowding." *Social Forces* 53(September) 62–72.

Caro, Robert A.
    1974   *The Power Broker: Robert Moses and the Fall of New York* (New York: Alfred A. Knopf).

Carr, Valerie
    1979   "The Micro-Ecology of A Church Worship Service." Paper presented to the Mid-South Sociological Association.

Cassel, J.
    1972   "Health consequences of population and crowding." *People and Buildings* (New York: Basic Books).

Cassidy, Neal
    1963   "Escape from the city." *Atlantic Monthly* (May).

Castells, Manuel
    1976   "Is there an urban sociology?" C. G. Pickvance, ed., pp. 33–59. *Urban Sociology: Critical Essays* (London: Tavistock Publications).

Cavan, Sherri
    1963   "Interaction in home territories." *Berkeley Journal of Sociology* pp. 17–32.

Chapin, F. Stuart, Jr.
    1954   "City planning: Adjusting people and place." Rupert B. Vance and Nicholas J. Demerath, eds. *The Urban South* (Chapel Hill: University of North Carolina Press).

Childe, V. Gordon
    1950   "The urban revolution." *Town Planning Review* 21:3–17.

Clark, Kenneth
    1965   *Dark Ghetto*. P. 81. (New York: Harper & Row).

Clark, Margaret
    1974   "Patterns of aging among the elderly poor of the inner-city." *Gerontologist* 11:1:58–66.

Clark, S. D.
    1966   *The Suburban Society* (Toronto: University of Toronto Press).

Clawson, Marion
    1971   *Suburban Land Conversion in the United States* (Baltimore, Md.: Johns Hopkins University Press).

Clelland, Donald A., and Form, William H.
    1964   "Economic dominants and community power, a comparative analysis." *American Journal of Sociology* 69(March) 511–21.

Cloward, Richard, and Pivin, Francis
    1967   "Black control of the central city: Heading it off by metropolitan government." *The New Republic* (September 30) 19–21.

Cole, William E.
    1958   *Urban Society* (Cambridge, Mass.: Riverside).

Cole, William E., and Harris, Diana
    1977   *The Elderly in America* (Boston: Allyn & Bacon).

Collins, Herbert, and Smith, Joseph
    1970   "Another look at socio-economic status distributions in urbanized areas." *Urban Affairs Quarterly* 5(June) 423–53.

Columbia Encyclopedia
    1963   3d ed. (New York: Columbia University).

Conzen, Kathleen Neils
    1976   *Immigrant Milwaukee* (Cambridge, Mass.: Harvard University Press).

Cooley, Charles H.
    1930   "The theory of transportation." Pp. 17–119. *Sociological Theory and Social Research* (New York: Henry Holt).

Cordasco, Francesco, and Bucchioni, Eugene
    1974   *The Italians: Social Backgrounds of an American Group* (Clifton, N.J.: August M. Kelley, Publishers).

Coser, Lewis
    1956   *The Social Functions of Conflict* (Glencoe, Ill.: Free Press).
    1974   *Greedy Institutions* (New York: Free Press).

Course Team
    1973   *The Built Environment* (Sussex, Eng.: Open University Press).
    1973a   *The Process of Urbanization* (Walton Hall, Bletchley, Bucks, Eng.: Open University Press).

Cressey, Paul
    1938   "Population succession in Chicago: 1898–1930." *American Journal of Sociology* 44(July) 59–69.

Curren, Donald
    1963   "The metropolitan problem from within." *National Tax Journal* 16:113–223.

Dahir, James
    1947   *The Neighborhood Unit Plan: Its Spread and Acceptance* (New York: Russell Sage Foundation).

Dahl, R. A.
    1972   *Democracy in the United States: Promises and Performances* (Chicago: Rand McNally).

Darwin, Charles Robert
    1936   *The Origin of the Species by Means of Natural Selection* (New York: Random House, Modern Library).

Dashefsky, Arnold, and Shapiro, Howard
    1974   *Ethnic Identification Among American Jews* (Lexington, Mass.: Lexington Books).

Davidoff, Paul
    1965   "Advocacy and pluralism in planning." *Journal of the American Institute of Planners* 31:331–37.

Davie, Maurice R.
    1937   "The pattern of urban growth." George P. Murdock, ed. *Studies in the Science of Society* (New Haven, Conn.: Yale University Press).

Davis, George A., and Donaldson, Fred O.
    1975   *Blacks in the United States: A Geographic Perspective* (Boston: Houghton Mifflin).

Davis, Kingsley
    1955   "The origin and growth of urbanization in the world." *American Journal of Sociology* 60(March) 430.

1968   "The urbanization of the human population." Sylvia F. Fava, ed., pp. 32–46. *Urbanism in World Perspective* (New York: Thomas Y. Crowell).

1972   *World Urbanization, 1950–1970* (Berkeley: University of California Press).

de Hostos, Adolfo
1948   *Ciudad Murada* (La Habana: Editorial Lex.).

De La Croix, Horst
1972   *Military Considerations in City Planning: Fortifications* (New York: George Braziller).

DeLong, Alton J.
1972   "The communication process: A generic model for man-environment relations." *Man-Environment Systems* 2(September) 263–305.

1976   "Coding the environment." *Psychic Factors in Design*. ASMER.

Demarath, Nicholas J., and Gilmore, Harlan W.
1954   "The ecoloty of southern cities." Rupert B. Vance and Nicholas J. Demarath, eds., pp. 135–64. *The Urban South* (Chapel Hill: University of North Carolina Press).

Detwyler, Thomas R., and Marcus, Melvin G.
1972   *Urbanization and Environment* (N. Scituate, Mass.: Duxbury).

Dinkel, Robert M.
1954   "Peopling the city: Fertility." Rupert B. Vance and Nicholas J. Demarath, eds., pp. 78–110. *The Urban South* (Chapel Hill: University of North Carolina Press).

DiPalma, Castiglione G. E.
1905   "Italian immigration in the United States 1901–1904." *American Journal of Sociology* 11(September) 183–206.

Dobriner, William, ed.
1958   *The Suburban Community* (New York: G. P. Putnam's Sons).

Douglas, Harlan P.
1925   *The Suburban Trend* (New York: Appleton).

Downs, Roger M., and Stea, David, eds.
1973   *Image and Environment* (Chicago: Aldine).

Drake, St. Clair, and Cayton, Horace
1962   *Black Metropolis* (New York: Harper & Row).

Dubois, W. E. B.
1967   *The Philadelphia Negro* (Philadelphia: University of Pennsylvania Press, 1899; republished by Schocken Books, 1967).

1968   *The Gift of Black Folk* (Boston: Stratford).

Duncan, Beverly, and Lieberson, Stanley
1970   *Metropolis and Region in Transition* (Beverly Hills, Cal.: Sage Publications).

Duncan Otis D.
1959   "Human ecology and population studies." P. Hauser and O. Duncan, eds. *The Study of Population* (Chicago: University of Chicago Press).

Duncan, Otis D., and Duncan, Beverly
    1955   "A methodological analysis of segregation indexes." *American Socio-logical Review* 20:210–17.
Duncan, Otis D., et al.
    1960   *Metropolis and Region* (Baltimore, Md.: Johns Hopkins University Press).
Duncan, Otis D., and Ogburn, W. F.
    1964   "City as a sociological variable." Donald J. Bogue and Ernest W. Burgess, eds. *Contributions to Urban Sociology* (Chicago: University of Chicago Press).
Duncan, Otis D.; Schuman, Howard; and Duncan, Beverly
    1973   *Change in a Metropolitan Community* (New York: Russell Sage Foundation).
Dumke, G.
    1940   "Early inter-urban transportation in the Los Angeles area." *Southern California Historical Quarterly* (September) 131–49.
Engles, Frederick, and Marx, Karl
    1975   *Collected Works* (New York: International Publishers).
Epstein, David G.
    1973   *Brasilia: Plan and Reality* (Berkeley: University of California Press).
Erasmus, Charles J.
    1977   *In Search of the Common Good: Utopian Experiments Past and Future* (New York: Free Press).
Ernst, Morris L., and Schwartz, Alan U.
    1962   *Privacy: The Right to be Let Alone* (New York: Macmillan).
Etzioni, Amitai
    1959   "The ghetto—a re-evaluation." *Social Forces* 37(March) 255–62.
Etzkowitz, Henry, and Schaflander, Gerald M.
    1969   *Ghetto Crisis* (Boston: Little, Brown).
Fainstein, Susan S., and Fainstein, Norman I.
    1971   "City planning and political values." *Urban Affairs Quarterly* 6(March) 341–62.
Farley, Reynolds; Schuman, Howard; Bianchi, Suzanne; Colosanto, Diane; and Hatchett, Shirley
    1977   "Chocolate City, Vanilla Suburbs: Will the Trend Toward Racially Separate Communities Continue?" Chicago: paper delivered for the 1977 ASA Meetings; unpublished.
Fava, Sylvia F.
    1968   ed. *Urbanism of World Perspective* (New York: Thomas Y. Crowell).
    1974   "Blacks in American new towns: problem and prospects." *Sociological Symposium* 12(Fall) 111–29.
    1975   "Beyond suburbia." *The Annals of the American Academy of Political and Social Science* 422(November) 11–24.
Fein, Leonard J.
    1971   *The Ecology of the Public Schools: An Inquiry into Community Control* (New York: Bobbs-Merrill, Pegasus).

Felipe, Nancy Jo, and Sommer, Robert
    1966   "Invasions of personal space." *Social Problems* pp. 206–14.

Fellman, Gordon, and Brandt, Barbara
    1973   *The Deceived Majority* (New Brunswick, N.J.: Transaction Books).

Festinger, Leon; Schachter, Stanley; and Back, Kurt
    1950   *Social Pressures in Informal Groups* (New York: Harper & Bros.)

Fink, James J.
    1975   *The Car Culture* (Cambridge, Mass.: M.I.T. Press).

Firey, Walter
    1945   "Sentiment and symbolism as ecological variables." *American Sociological Review* 10:137–46.
    1946   "Ecological considerations in planning for urban fringes." *American Sociological Review* 11(August) 411–21.
    1947   *Land Use in Central Boston* (Cambridge, Mass.: Harvard University Press).

Fischer, C. S.
    1971   "A research note on urbanism and tolerance." *American Journal of Sociology* 76(March) 847–56.
    1972   "Urbanism as a way of life: A review and an agenda." *Sociological Methods and Research* 1(November) 187–242.
    1973   "Urban malaise." *Social Forces* 52(December) 231–35.
    1975   "Toward a subcultural theory of urbanism." *American Journal of Sociology* 80(May) 1319–41.
    1975a   "The myth of 'territoriality' in van der Berghe's 'Bringing Beasts Back In.' " *American Sociological Review* 40(October) 674–76.
    1976   *The Urban Experience* (New York: Harcourt Brace Janovich).

Fisher, Joseph L.
    1971   "Environmental quality and urban living." Larry S. Bourne, ed., pp. 483–89. *Internal Structure of the City* (New York: Oxford University Press).

Foley, Donald L.
    1952   "The daily movement of population into central business districts." *American Sociological Review* 17:5:538–43.

Ford, Richard G.
    1950   "Population succession in Chicago." *American Journal of Sociology* 56:2:156–60.

Ford, Thomas R., ed.
    1962   *The Southern Appalachian Region* (Lexington: University Press of Kentucky).

Form, William H.
    1954   "The place of social structure in the determination of land use: some implications for a theory of urban ecology." *Social Forces* 32:4(May) 317–23.

Form, William H.; Smith, Joel; Stone, Gregory P.; and Cowhig, James
    1954   "The compatability of alternative approaches to the delimitation of urban subareas." *American Sociological Review* 19:4:434–40.

Form, William H., and Stone, Gregory P.
    1957   "Urbanism, anonymity, and status symbolism." *American Journal of Sociology* 62(May) 504–14.
Forman, Robert E.
    1971   *Black Ghettos, White Ghettos and Slums* (Englewood Cliffs, N.J.: Prentice-Hall).
Frazier, E. Franklin
    1937   "Negro Harlem: An ecological study." *American Journal of Sociology* 43:1:78–88.
Freeman, Linton C., and Sunshine, Morris H.
    1970   *Patterns of Residential Segregation* (Cambridge, Mass.: Schenkman Publishing).
Friden, Bernard J.
    1964   *The Future of Neighborhoods* (Cambridge, Mass.: M.I.T. Press).
Fried, Mark
    1963   "Grieving for a lost home." Leonard Duhl, ed., pp. 151–71. *The Urban Condition* (New York: Basic Books).
Friedman, J., and Miller, J.
    1965   "The urban field." *Journal of the American Institute of Planners* 31(November) 312–20.
Gale, Stephen, and Moore, Eric G., eds.
    1975   *The Manipulated City* (Chicago: Maaroufa Press).
Galle, O. R.; Gove, W. R.; and McPherson, J. M.
    1970   "Population density and pathology: What are the relationships for man?" *Science* 176:23–30.
Gallup Poll
    1977   July 8.
Gans, Herbert J.
    1962   *The Urban Villagers* (Glencoe, Ill.: Free Press).
    1965   "The failure of urban renewal: A critique and some proposals." *Commentary* 39(April) 29–37.
    1967   *The Levittowners* (New York: Random House).
    1968   "Urbanism and suburbanism as ways of life: A re-evaluation of definitions." Sylvia F. Fava, ed., pp. 63–81. *Urbanism in World Perspective* (New York: Thomas Y. Crowell).
    1974   "Gans on Granovetter's 'Strength of Weak Ties.'" *American Journal of Sociology* 80:2(June) 328–39.
Geddes, Patrick
    1915   *Cities in Evolution* (London: Williams & Norgate).
Gerson, Elihu M.
    1974   "Commitment Management and Urban Morphology." Paper submitted to the American Sociological Association.
Gillis, A. P.
    1974   "Population density and social pathology: The case of building type, social allowance, and juvenile delinquency." *Social Forces* 53(December) 306–14.

Gilmore, H. W.
  1944 "The old New Orleans and the new: A case for ecology." *American Sociological Review* 9:2:385–94.
  1953 *Transportation and the Growth of Cities* (Glencoe, Ill.: Free Press).

Ginsberg, Yona
  1975 *Jews in a Changing Neighborhood* (New York: Free Press).

Gist, Noel P., and Fava, Sylvia
  1974 *Urban Society* (New York: Thomas Y. Crowell).

Glaab, Charles N., and Brown, Theodore A.
  1968 "The emergence of metropolis." Sylvia F. Fava, ed., pp. 17–28. *Urbanism in World Perspective* (New York: Thomas Y. Crowell).

Goering, John M.
  1978 "Neighborhood tipping and racial transition: A review of social science evidence." *Journal of the American Institute of Planners* 44:1(January) 68–77.

Gordon, M. M.
  1964 *Assimilation in American Life* (New York: Oxford University Press).

Gottman, Jean
  1964 *Megalopolis* (Cambridge, Mass.: M.I.T. Press).

Gould, Peter, and White, Rodney
  1974 *Mental Maps* (Middlesex, Eng.: Penguin).

Granovetter, Mark S.
  1973 "The strength of weak ties." *American Journal of Sociology* 38:6(May) 1360–79.

Green, Constance McLaughlin
  1965 *The Rise of Urban America* (New York: Harper & Row).

Greer, Scott
  1962 *The Emerging City* (Glencoe, Ill.: Free Press).
  1963 *Metropolitics* (New York: John Wiley & Sons).
  1972 *The Urbane View* (London: Oxford University Press).

Greer, Scott, and Greer, Ann L.
  1974 "Introduction." *Neighborhood and Ghetto* (New York: Basic Books).

Greer, Scott; McElrath, Dennis L.; Minar, David W.; and Orleans, Peter, eds.
  1968 *The New Urbanization* (New York: St. Martin's Press).

Greer, Scott, and Orleans, Peter
  1968 "The mass society and the parapolitical structure." Scott Greer et al., eds., pp. 201–21. *The New Urbanization* (New York: St. Martin's Press).

Grigsby, William G.
  1963 *Housing Markets and Public Policy* (Philadelphia: University of Pennsylvania Press).

Grindley, William C.
  1972 "Owner-builders: Survivors with a future." John F. C. Turner and Robert Fichter, eds., pp. 3–21. *Freedom to Build* (New York: Macmillan).

Guillemin, Jeanne
    1975 *Urban Renegades* (New York: Columbia University Press).
Hadden, J. K.; Masotti, L. H.; and Larson, C. J.
    1971 *Metropolis in Crisis* (Itasca, Ill.: F. E. Peacock Publishers).
Halebsky, Sandor, ed.
    1973 *The Sociology of the City* (New York: Scribners).
Hall, Edward T.
    1966 *The Hidden Dimension* (New York: Doubleday).
Hall, Peter
    1966 *The World Cities* (New York: McGraw-Hill).
Handlin, Oscar
    1962 *The Newcomers* (New York: Doubleday, Anchor Books).
    1973 *The Uprooted* (Boston: Little, Brown).
Hanna, W. J., and Hanna, J. L.
    1971 *Urban Dynamics in Black Africa* (Chicago: Aldine-Atherton).
Hannerz, Ulf.
    1969 *Soulside* (New York: Columbia University Press).
Hansen, W. G.
    1959 "How accessibility shapes land use." *Journal of the American Institute
          of Planners* 25:72–76.
Harris, Chauncey D.
    1943 "A functional classification of cities in the United States." *Geograph-
          ical Review* 33(January) 86–99.
Harris, C. D., and Ullman, E. L.
    1942 "The nature of cities." *Annals of the American Academy of Political
          and Social Science* 242:7–17.
Harrison, Jerry; Sexton, Patricia; and Wallace, Samuel E.
    1975 "Public space in the urban environment: A visual study." Midwest
          Sociological Society (presentation made April 10, 12).
Harvey, Brian, and Hallett, John D.
    1977 *Environment and Society* (Cambridge, Mass.: M.I.T. Press).
Harvey, David
    1973 *Social Justice and the City* (Baltimore, Md.: Johns Hopkins University
          Press).
    1975 "Class-monopoly rent, finance capital and the urban revolution."
          Stephen Gale and Eric G. Moore, eds. *The Manipulated City* (Chicago:
          Maaroufa Press).
Harwood, Edwin
    1969 "Urbanism as a way of negro life." McCord, William; Howard, John;
          Friedberg, Bernard; and Harwood, Edwin, eds. *Life Styles in the Black
          Ghetto* (New York: W. W. Norton).
Hawley, Amos H.
    1951 "Metropolitan population and municipal government expenditure in
          central cities." *Journal of Social Issues* 7:107.

Helm, June
    1962   "The ecological approach in anthropology." *American Journal of Sociology* 67:6(May) 630–39.

Hiller, E. T.
    1941   "The community as a social group." *American Sociological Review* 6(April) 185–97.

Hilton, George W., and Due, John F.
    1960   *The Electric Interurban Railways in America* (Stanford, Cal.: Stanford University Press).

Hirsch, Warner, et al.
    1971   *Fiscal Pressures on the Central City* (New York: Praeger Publishers).

Hitt, Homer L.
    1954   "Peopling the city: Migration." Rupert B. Vance and Nicholas J. Demerath, eds., pp. 49–60. *The Urban South* (Chapel Hill: University of North Carolina Press).

Holmes, Urban Tigner, Jr.
    1952   *Daily Living in the Twelfth Century* (Marison: University of Wisconsin Press).

Horowitz, Gail
    1974   "Paley Park." New York: New York University; unpublished paper.

Hosken, Fran P.
    1972   *The Language of Cities* (Cambridge, Mass.: Schenkman Publishing).

Houriet, Robert
    1971   *Getting Back Together* (New York: Avon Books).

Housing and Urban Development, U.S. Department of, (HUD)
    1968   *Tomorrow's Transportation—New Systems for the Urban Future* (Office of Metropolitan Development, Urban Transportation Administration, Washington, D.C.).
    1968a   *Housing Surveys: Parts 1 and 2.* "Occupants of new housing units and mobile homes and the housing supply." (Washington, D.C.: Government Printing Office).

Hoyt, Homer
    1933   *One Hundred Years of Land Values in Chicago* (Chicago: University of Chicago Press).
    1939   *The Structure and Growth of Residential Neighborhoods in American Cities* (Washington, D.C.: Federal Housing Administration).
    1943   "The structure of American cities in the Post-War era." *American Journal of Sociology* 48(January) 475–81.

Hughes, Everett C.
    1936   "The ecological aspect of institutions." *American Sociological Review* 1:2:180–92.
    1943   *French Canada in Transition* (Chicago: University of Chicago Press).
    1971   "The gleichschaltung of the German statistical yearbook." Pp. 516–24. *The Sociological Eye* (Chicago: Aldine).

Hughes, Helen MacGill
    1970   *Cities and City Life* (Boston: Allyn & Bacon).

Humphreys, Laud
   1970   *Tearoom Trade: Impersonal Sex in Public Places* (Chicago: Aldine).

Hunter, Albert
   1971   "The ecology of Chicago: Persistence and change, 1930–1960." *American Journal of Sociology* 77(November) 425–44.
   1974   *Symbolic Communities* (Chicago: University of Chicago Press).

Hurd, Richard M.
   1903   *Principles of City Land Values* (New York: Record and Guide).

Jacobs, Jane
   1961   *The Death and Life of Great American Cities* (New York: Random House).

Janowitz, M.
   1967   *The Community Press in an Urban Setting* (Chicago: University of Chicago Press).

Jaret, Charles
   1977   "Recent Patterns of Chicago Jewish Residential Mobility." Chicago: paper presented to the 1977 ASA Meetings; unpublished.

Jefferson, Mark
   1939   "The law of the primate city." *The Geographical Review* 29:226–32.

Johnston, Norman J.
   1968   "The caste and class of the urban and historic Philadelphia." Sylvia F. Fava, ed., pp. 233–49. *Urbanism in World Perspective* (New York: Thomas Y. Crowell).

Jonassen, Christen T.
   1954   "Cultural variables in the ecology of an ethnic group." *American Sociological Review* 19:37–59.

Kaiser, Edward J.
   1976   *Residential Mobility in New Communities* (Cambridge, Mass.: Ballinger Publishing). Copyright © 1976 by The University of North Carolina.

Kanter, Rosabeth Moss
   1972   *Commitment and Community: Communes and Utopias in Sociological Perspective* (Cambridge, Mass.: Harvard University Press).

Kantrowitz, Nathan
   1973   *Ethnic and Racial Segregation in the New York Metropolis* (New York: Praeger Publishers).

Karp, David; Stone, Gregory P.; and Yoels, William
   1977   *Being Urban* (New York: D. C. Heath).

Kasarda, John D.
   1972   "The impact of suburban population growth on central city service functions." *Social Forces* 50:3 (March) 384–95.
   1972a   "The theory of ecological expansion." *Social Forces* 51(December) 166–75.

Kasarda, John D., and Janowitz, M.
   1974   "Community attachment in mass society." *American Sociological Review* 39(June) 328–39.

Katzman, David M.
    1975 *Before the Ghetto: Black Detroit in the Nineteenth Century* (Urbana: University of Illinois Press).
Kaufman, Harold F.
    1974 "Toward an interactional conception of community." *Social Forces* 38 (October) 8–17.
Keats, John
    1956 *The Crack in the Picture Window* (New York: Ballantine Books).
Keller, Suzanne
    1968 *The Urban Neighborhood* (New York: Random House).
Kenngott, George Frederick
    1912 *Record of a City: Social Survey of Lowell* (New York: Macmillan).
Kepes, Gyorgy
    1961 "Notes on expression and communication in the cityscape." *Daedalus* 90:1:147–65.
Kephart, William M.
    1976 *Extraordinary Groups: The Sociology of Unconventional Life Styles* (New York: St. Martin's Press).
Kerouac, Jack
    1958 *The Subterraneans* (New York: Avon Books).
Keyfitz, Nathan
    1966 "Population density and the style of life." *Bioscience* 16(December) 868–73.
Kie, Woo Sik
    1967 "Suburban population and its implications for core city finances." *Land Economics* 42(May) 202–11.
Kirkland, Edward Chase
    1948 *Men Cities and Transportation* (New York: Russell & Russell).
Kotler, Milton
    1969 *Neighborhood Government; the Local Foundations of Political Life* (Indianapolis: Bobbs-Merrill).
Kusmer, Kenneth L.
    1976 *A Ghetto Takes Shape: Black Cleveland, 1870–1930* (Urbana: University of Illinois Press).
LaGory, Ward M. R., and Juravich, T.
    1977 "The Age Segregation Process in American Cities." Chicago: paper presented to the ASA Meetings; unpublished.
Lampl, Paul
    1968 *Cities and Planning in the Ancient Near East* (New York: George Braziller).
Lavender, Abraham D., ed.
    1977 *A Coat of Many Colors: Jewish Subcommunities in the United States* (Westport, Conn.: Greenwood Press).
Lee, Terrence
    1968 "Urban neighborhood as a socio-spatial schema." *Human Relations* 21:2(Spring) 241–67.

Levine, Martin P.
    1977 "Gay Ghetto." Chicago: paper presented to the ASA Meetings.
Lewis, Oscar
    1965 "Further observation on the folk-urban continuum and urbanization
          with special reference to Mexico City." P. H. Hauser and Leo
          Schnore, *The Study of Urbanization* (New York: John Wiley & Sons).
Lipman, Alan
    1967 "Chairs as territory." *New Society* 9:564–69.
Little, Kenneth
    1968 "The migrant and the urban community." Sylvia Fava, ed., pp. 313–
          22. *Urbanism in World Perspective* (New York: Thomas Y. Crowell).
Liwak, Eugene
    1959 "The use of extended family groups." *Social Problems* 7(Winter)
          177–87.
Lofland, John
    1968 "The youth ghetto." *Journal of Higher Education*, pp. 121–43.
Lofland, Lyn H.
    1973 *A World of Strangers* (New York: Basic Books).
Long, Norton E.
    1968 "The local community as an ecology of games." *American Journal of
          Sociology* (November 1958) 251–61. In Scott Greer et al., eds., p. 241.
          The New Urbanization (New York: St. Martin's Press).
    1968a "Citizenship or consumership in metropolitan areas." Scott Greer et
          al., eds., pp. 367–75. *The New Urbanization* (New York: St. Martin's
          Press).
Loprecto, Joseph
    1970 *The Italian Americans* (New York: Random House).
Lorenz, Konrad
    1966 *On Aggression*. Trans. by M. K. Wilson. New York: Bantam Books).
Love, Edmund G.
    1957 *Subways Are For Sleeping* (New York: Harcourt, Brace & World).
Lowenthal, Martin D.
    1975 "The social economy in urban working-class communities." *The So-
          cial Economy of Cities* 9:447–69.
Lundberg, George A., and Steele, E.
    1937 "Social attraction patterns in a village." *Sociometry* 1:18–26.
Lynch, Kevin
    1960 *The Image of the City* (Cambridge, Mass.: M.I.T. Press).
    1976 *Managing the Sense of a Region*. P. 258. (Cambridge, Mass.: M.I.T.
          Press).
    1977 *Growing Up in Cities* (Cambridge, Mass.: M.I.T. Press).
MacAdams, Robert
    1968 "The natural history of urbanism." *Fitness of Man's Environment*
          (Washington: Smithsonian Institution Press).
MacDonald, John Stuart, and MacDonald, Leatrice
    1964 "Chain migration, ethnic neighborhood formation, and social net-
          works." *Milbank Memorial Fund Quarterly* 42:82–97.

Mackie, J. D.
  1964   *A History of Scotland* (Middlesex, Eng.: Penguin).

Manning, Russ
  1978   "The Overton Park controversy." *The Tennessee Conservationist* 44:1
         (Jan./Feb.) 15–17.

Mathews, Hilary
  1974   "A Small Area With Benches." New York: Queens College; unpub-
         lished paper.

Mayer, Harold, and Wade, Richard C.
  1969   *Chicago: Growth of a Metropolis* (Chicago: University of Chicago
         Press). Copyright © 1969 by The University of Chicago Press.

McCaffrey, Lawrence J.
  1976   *The Irish Diaspora in America* (Bloomington: Indiana University
         Press).

McCord, William; Howard, John; Friedberg, Bernard; and Harwood, Edwin
  1969   *Life Styles in the Black Ghetto* (New York: W. W. Norton).

McGahan, P.
  1972   "The neighbor role and neighboring in a highly urban area." *Sociolog-
         ical Quarterly* 13(Summer) 397–408.

McKelvey, Blake
  1963   *The Urbanization of America, 1860–1915* (New Brunswick, N.J.: Rut-
         gers University Press).
  1968   *The Emergence of Metropolitan America, 1915–1966* (New Brunswick,
         N.J.: Rutgers University Press).

McKenzie, R. D.
  1921   "The neighborhood: A study of local life in the city of Columbus,
         Ohio."
  1922   *American Journal of Sociology*, in five installments: 27:2:145–68;
         27:3:344–63; 27:4:486–509; 5:588–610; and 6:780–99.
  1923   *Neighborhood* (Chicago: University of Chicago Press).
  1925   "The ecological approach to the study of the human community."
         Robert E. Park, E. W. Burgess, and R. D. McKenzie, eds. *The City*
         (Chicago: University of Chicago Press).
  1926   "Movement and the ability to live." *Proceedings of the Institute of
         International Relations* pp. 175–80.
  1926a   "The scope of human ecology." *Publications of the American Socio-
         logical Society* 20:141–54.

McKinney, John C., and Thompson, Edgar T., eds.
  1965   *The South in Continuity and Change* (Durham, N.C.: Duke University
         Press).

McLuhan, Marshall
  1962   *The Gutenberg Galexy* (Toronto: University of Toronto Press).

McNeill, William Hardy
  1976   *Plagues and People* (Garden City, N.Y.: Doubleday, Anchor Books).

McPherson, J. M.
  1975   "Population density and social pathology: A reexamination." *Socio-
         logical Symposium* 14(Fall) 77–92.

Meadows, P.
    1973   "The idea of community in the city." M. I. Urofsky, ed., pp. 1–22. *Perspectives on Urban America* (Garden City, N.Y.: Doubleday, Anchor Books).

Meier, Richard L.
    1962   *A Communications Theory of Urban Growth* (Cambridge, Mass.: M.I.T. Press).

Melville, Keith
    1972   *Communes in the Counter Culture: Origins, Theories, and Styles of Life* (New York: William Morrow).

Menzler, F. A. A.
    1952   "An estimate of the daytime population of London." *Journal of the Town Planning Institute* 38(March) 116–20.

Mertins, Herman, Jr.
    1972   *National Transportation Policy in Transition* (London: D. C. Heath Ltd.).

Merton, Robert K.
    1957   *Social Theory and Social Structure* (Glencoe, Ill.: Free Press).

Michelson, William
    1970   *Man and His Urban Environment* (Reading, Mass.: Addison-Wesley).

Mileski, Maureen, and Black, Donald J.
    1972   "The social organization of homosexuality." *Urban Life and Culture* 1 (July) 187–201.

Milgram, Stanley
    1970   "The experience of living in cities." *Science* 167(March 13) 1461–68.

Molotch, Harvey
    1969   "Racial integration in a transition community." *American Sociological Review* 34:4:878–93.

Morris, R. N., and Mogey, John
    1965   *The Sociology of Housing* (London: Routledge & Kegan Paul).

Morris, Richard B.
    1953   *Encyclopedia of American History* (New York: Harper & Bros.).

Moses, Leon N., and Williamson, Harold F., Jr.
    1968   "The location of economic activity in cities." Scott Greer et al., eds., pp. 113–31. *The New Urbanization* (New York: St. Martin's Press).

Mumford, Lewis
    1938   *The Culture of Cities* (New York: Harcourt, Brace & World).
    1961   *The City in History* (New York: Harcourt, Brace & World).

Muth, Richard F.
    1969   *Cities and Housing: The Spatial Pattern of Urban Residential Land Use* (Chicago: University of Chicago Press).
    1975   *Urban Economic Problems* (New York: Harper & Row).

Nelson, Katheryn
    1978   "Black Suburbs and White Cities?" William E. Cole Lecture Series, University of Tennessee.

New York Times
    1886   July 8.
    1934   May 28, pp. 1, 2.
    1935   May 12, p. 35.
           June 13, p. 3.
    1936   January 19, p. 10.
           February 29, p. 17.
           September 7, p. 26.
           September 11, p. 28.
           September 13, p. 10.
           September 14, pp. 20, 29.
    1964   July 12, letters column.
    1964   September 21, p. 1.
    1964   October 28, p. 1.
    1969   July 17, p. 61.
    1975   May 17.

Newling, Bruce E.
    1971   "The spatial variation of urban population densities." Larry S. Bourne, ed., pp. 329–37. *Internal Structure of the City* (New York: Oxford University Press).

Newman, Oscar
    1973   *Defensible Space* (New York: Macmillan).
    1973a *Defensible Space: Crime Prevention Through Urban Design* (New York: Macmillan, Collier Books).

Ogburn, William F.
    1951   "Population, private ownership, technology, and the standard of living." *American Journal of Sociology* 56(January) 314–19.

Ogburn, William F., and Duncan, Otis D.
    1964   "City size as a sociological variable." Ernest W. Burgess and Donald J. Bogue, eds. *Contributions to Urban Sociology* (Chicago: University of Chicago Press).

Ophuls, William
    1977   *Ecology and the Politics of Scarcity* (San Francisco: W. H. Freeman).

Orwell, George
    1949   *Nineteen Eighty-Four* (New York: Harcourt, Brace & World).

Osofsky, Gilbert
    1966   *Harlem: The Making of a Ghetto; 1890–1930* (New York: Harper & Row).

Pahl, R. E.
    1968   "A perspective on urban sociology." R. E. Pahl, ed., pp. 3–44. *Readings in Urban Sociology* (New York: Pergaman Press).

Palen, John, and Schnore, Leo F.
    1965   "Color composition and city-suburban status differences: A replication and extension." *Land Economics* 41(February) 87–91.

Park, Robert E.
    1926   "The concept of position in sociology." *Publications of the American Sociological Society* 20(July) 1–14.

1929 "Urbanization as measured by newspaper circulation." *American Journal of Sociology* 35:1:60–79.

1934 "Introduction." Charles S. Johnson, ed. *Shadow of the Plantation* (Chicago: University of Chicago Press).

1936 "Human ecology." *American Journal of Sociology* 42(July) 1–15.

1936a "Succession, an ecological concept." *American Sociological Review* 1:2:171–79.

1938 "Reflections on communication and culture." *American Journal of Sociology* 44(September) 187–205.

1939 "Symbiosis and socialization: A frame of reference for the study of society." *American Journal of Sociology* 45:1–25.

1952 *Human Communities* (Glencoe, Ill.: Free Press).

1967 "The city: Suggestions for the investigation of human behavior in the urban environment." Robert E. Park, Ernest W. Burgess, and Roderick D. McKenzie. *The City* (Chicago: University of Chicago Press; published in 1925, republished in 1967).

Park, Robert E.; Burgess, Ernest W.; and McKenzie, Roderick D.
1967 *The City* (Chicago: University of Chicago Press; originally published in 1925).

Park, Robert E., and Miller, H. M.
1921 *Old World Traits Transplanted* (New York: Drake Publishers).

Partridge, Eric
1959 *Origins: A Short Etymological Dictionary of Modern English* (New York: Macmillan) 2d ed.

Peattie, Lisa Redfield
1968 *The View from the Barrio* (Ann Arbor: University of Michigan Press).

Perlman, Janice E.
1976 *The Myth of Marginality* (Berkeley: University of California Press).

Perrin, Constance
1977 *Everything in Its Place* (Princeton, N.J.: Princeton University Press).

Pettigrew, Thomas F.
1973 "Attitudes on race and housing: A social-psychological view." Amos H. Hawley and Vincent P. Rock, eds. *Segregation in Residential Areas* (Washington: National Academy of Sciences).

Pilcher, W. W.
1972 *The Portland Longshoremen: A Dispersed Urban Community* (New York: Holt, Rinehart and Winston).

Pinkerton, James R.
1969 "City-suburban residential patterns by social class: A review of literature." *Urban Affairs Quarterly* 4:509–19.

Pirenne, Henri
1956 *Medieval Cities*. Trans. by Frank Halsey (Garden City, N.Y.: Doubleday, Anchor Books, 1956, 1925).

Plato
1966 *The Republic* (Cambridge, Eng.: Cambridge University Press).

Poponoe, David
1977 *The Suburban Environment* (Chicago: University of Chicago Press).

Porteous, J. Douglas
1977 *Environment and Behavior* (Reading, Mass.: Addison-Wesley).

Pred, Allan R.
1971 "The intrametropolitan location of American manufacturing." Larry S. Bourne, ed., pp. 380–90. *Internal Structure of the City* (New York: Oxford University Press).

Pred, Allan R., and Berry, Brian
1965 *Central Place Studies: A Bibliography of Theory and Applications* (Philadelphia: Regional Science Research Institute).

Quinn, James A.
1940 "The Burgess zonal hypothesis and its critics." *American Sociological Review* 5:2:210–18.
1940a "Human ecology and interactional ecology." *American Sociological Review* 5:5:713–22.

Rabinovitz, Francine F., and Lamare, James
1971 "After suburbia, what?—the new communities movement in Los Angeles." Werner Z. Hirsch, ed., pp. 169–206. *Los Angeles: Viability and Prospects for Metropolitan Leadership* (New York: Praeger Publishers).

Rainwater, Lee
1966 "Fear and the house-as-haven in the lower class." *Journal of the American Institute of Planners* 32(January) 23–31.
1970 *Behind Ghetto Walls* (Chicago: Aldine).

Ratcliff, John
1976 *Land Policy* (London: Hutchinson).

Reed, John S.
1972 *The Enduring South* (Chapel Hill: University of North Carolina Press).
1974 "Summertime and the Livin' Is Easy: The Quality of Life in the South." *University of North Carolina Newsletter* 59:4(December 1974) 1–4.

Regional Survey of New York and Its Environs
(New York: Regional Plan, in eight volumes, 1927–1929).

Reissman, Leonard
1954 *The Urban Process* (New York: Free Press).

Rensberger, Boyce
1976 "Big city quickstep." *Daily Beacon* 13:25 (March 5) 1.

Riesman, David; Glazer, Nathan; and Denney, Reuel
1955 *The Lonely Crowd* (New York: Doubleday).

Riis, J.
1898 *Out of Mulberry Street; Stories of Tenement Life in New York City* (New York: The Century).

Ripton-Turner, C. J.
1887 *A History of Vagrants and Vagrancy and Beggars and Begging* (London: Chapman and Hall).

Roberts, Ron
1971 *The New Communes: Coming Together in America* (Englewood Cliffs, N.J.: Prentice-Hall).

Robinson, Walter W.
1978   *The Usefulness of the Urban Ambiance as a Descriptive, Explanatory, and Predictive Variable of Geographic and Social Mobility.* Knoxville: University of Tennessee, Ph.D. dissertation; unpublished.

Rogler, Lloyd H.
1972   *Migrant in the city: The Life of a Puerto Rican Action Group* (New York: Basic Books).

Romains, Jules
1933   *Men of Good Will* (New York: Alfred A. Knopf).

Rose, Stephen M.
1972   *The Betrayal of the Poor: The Transformation of Community Action* (Cambridge, Mass.: Schenkman Publishing).

Roskolenko, Harry
1971   "America the thief." Thomas C. Wheeler, ed., pp. 151–78. *The Immigrant Experience* (New York: Dial Press).

Sachar, Leon Abram
1964   *A History of the Jews.* 5th ed. (New York: Alfred A. Knopf).

Schlichting, Kurt C.
1975   *Urban-Suburban Ecology.* New York: New York University; unpublished Ph.D. thesis.

Schnore, Leo F.
1958   "Social morphology and human ecology." *American Journal of Sociology* 63:620–34.
1961   "The myth of human ecology." *Sociological Inquiry* 31:2:128–49.
1963   "The socio-economic status of cities and suburbs." *American Sociological Review* 28:1(February) 76–85.
1964   "Urban structure and suburban selectivity." *Demography* 1:164–76.
1967   "Measuring city-suburban status differences." *Urban Affairs Quarterly* 3(September) 95–108.
1972   *Class and Race in Cities and Suburbs* (Chicago: Rand McNally, Markham).

Schorr, Alvin L.
1968   "How the poor are housed in the United States." Sylvia F. Fava, ed., pp. 474–85. *Urbanism in World Perspective* (New York: Thomas Y. Crowell).

Schorske, Carl E.
1968   "The idea of the city in European thought: Voltaire to Spengler." Sylvia F. Fava, ed., pp. 409–25. *Urbanism in World Perspective* (New York: Thomas Y. Crowell).

Seeley, John R.
1959   "The slum: Its nature, use and users." *Journal of the American Institute of Planners* 25:1(February) 7–14.

Seeley, John R.; Sim, Alexander R.; and Loosley, Elizabeth W.
1956   *Crestwood Heights* (New York: John Wiley & Sons).

Sennett, Richard
1970   *The Uses of Disorder* (New York: Random House, Vintage Books).

326   References

Sexton, Patricia, and Wallace, Samuel E.
    1974 *Washington Square Park.* New York: New York University, Department of Sociology; mimeographed.
Shevky, Eshref, and Bell, Wendell
    1955 *Social Area Analysis* (Stanford, Cal.: Stanford University Press).
Shevky, Eshref, and Williams, Marilyn
    1949 *The Social Areas of Los Angeles* (Berkeley: University of California Press).
Shibutani, Tamotsu, and Kwan, Kian M.
    1965 *Ethnic Stratification: A Comparative Approach* (New York: Macmillan).
Shideler, Ernest H.
    1927 "The Chain Store: A Study of the Ecological Organization of a Modern City." Chicago: University of Chicago; Ph.D. dissertation.
Shimota, Kenneth L.
    1953 *A Literal Replication of a Sociometric Study of Informal Social Participation in a Homogeneous Community.* Minneapolis: University of Minnesota; unpublished M.A. thesis.
Shurtleff, Nathaniel B.
    1871 *A Topographical and Historical Description of Boston* (Boston: City Council).
Simmel, Georg
    1969 *The Sociology of Georg Simmel.* Ed. and trans. by Kurt Wolff (New York: Free Press).
Sjoberg, Gideon
    1960 *The Preindustrial City* (New York: Free Press).
Smailes, A. E.
    1947 "The analysis and delimination of urban fields." *Geography* 32:151–61.
Smith, Joel; Form, William H.; and Stone, Gregory P.
    1954 "Local intimacy in a middle-sized city." *American Journal of Sociology* 60:4:276–84.
Smith, Wallace F.
    1971 *Housing: The Social and Economic Elements* (Berkeley: University of California Press).
    1971a "Filtering and neighborhood change." Larry S. Bourne, ed., pp. 170–79. *Internal Structure of the City* (New York: Oxford University Press).
Solotaroff, Theodore
    1976 "Alive and together in the park." *New York Times Magazine,* June 13.
Sommer, Robert
    1969 *Personal Space: The Behavioral Basis of Design* (Englewood Cliffs, N.J.: Prentice-Hall).
Sommer, Robert, and Becker, D.
    1971 "Room density and user satisfaction." *Environment and Behavior* 3(December) 412–17.

Spectorsky, A. C.
    1955   *The Exurbanites* (Philadelphia: J. B. Lippincott).

Steffens, Lincoln
    1931   *Autobiography of Lincoln Steffens* (New York: Harcourt, Brace & World).

Stone, Gregory P.
    1954   "City shoppers and urban identification: Observations on the social psychology of city life." *American Journal of Sociology* 59:2:36–45.

Stone, Gregory P., and Form, William H.
    1957   "The local community clothing market: A study of the psychological contents of shopping." *Technical Bulletin 262* (East Lansing: Michigan State University; reprint).

Stouffer, Samuel A.
    1940   "Intervening opportunities: A theory relating mobility and distance." *American Sociological Review* 5:6:845–67.
    1960   "Intervening opportunities and competing migrants." *Journal of Social Science* 2:1:1–26.

Strauss, Anselm
    1961   *Images of the American City* (New York: Free Press).

Sullenger, T. Earl
    1956   *Sociology of Urbanization: A Study in Rurban Society* (Ann Arbor, Mich.: Braun-Brumfield).

Suttles, Gerald
    1968   *The Social Order of the Slum* (Chicago: University of Chicago Press).
    1972   *The Social Construction of Communities* (Chicago: University of Chicago Press).

Taaffe, Edward J.
    1962   "The urban hierarchy: An air passenger definition." *Economic Geography* 38:1–14.

Taeuber, Alma, and Taeuber, Karl
    1964   "White migration and socio-economic difference between cities and suburbs." *American Sociological Review* 69(March) 718–29.

Taeuber, Conrad
    1976   "Metropolitan America." William E. Cole Lecture Series, University of Tennessee.

Taeuber, Karl, and Taeuber, Alma
    1965   *Negroes in Cities: Residential Segregation and Neighborhood Change* (Chicago: Aldine).

Taylor, Graham Romeyn
    1915   *Satellite Cities: A Study of Industrial Suburbs* (New York and London: D. Appleton and Company).

Theodorson, George A., ed.
    1961   *Studies in Human Ecology* (Evanston, Ill.: Row, Peterson).

Thernstrom, Stephen, and Sennett, Richard, eds.
    1969   *Nineteenth-Century Cities: Essays in the New Urban History* (New Haven, Conn.: Yale University Press).

Thompson, Edgar T.
  1965 "The south in old and new contexts." John C. McKinney and Edgar T. Thompson, eds., pp. 451–80. *The South in Continuity and Change* (Durham, N.C.: Duke University Press).
  1975 *Plantation Societies, Race Relations, and the South* (Durham, N.C.: Duke University Press).

Timms, Duncan
  1971 *The Urban Mosaic: Towards a Theory of Residential Differentiation* (Cambridge, Eng.: Cambridge University Press).

Tisdale, Hope
  1942 "The process of urbanization." *Social Forces* 20:311–16.

Torres-Balbus, Leopoldo
  1954 *Resumen Del Urbanismo En Espana* (Madrid: Graficos Uguina).

Turner, J. F. C.
  1968 "The squatter settlement: An architecture that works." *Architectural Design* 38:8.
  1968a "Housing priorities, settlement patterns, and urban development in modernizing countries." *Journal of the American Institute of Planners* 34:6(November).
  1969 "Uncontrolled urban settlement: Problems and policies." *International Social Development Review* 1. New York: United Nations.

Turner, John F. C., and Fichter, Robert
  1972 *Freedom to Build* (New York: Macmillan).

Ullman, Edward
  1941 "A theory of location for cities." *American Journal of Sociology* 46:6:853–64.
  1954 "Geography as spatial interaction." *Annals of the Association of American Geographers* 44:283–84.

Vance, Rupert B., and Demerath, Nicholas J., eds.
  1954 *The Urban South* (Chapel Hill: University of North Carolina Press).

Vayda, Andrew P.
  1969 "An ecological approach in cultural anthropology." *Bucknell Review* 17:359:112–19.

Vernon, Raymond
  1962 *The Myth and Reality of Our Urban Problems* (Cambridge, Mass.: M.I.T. and Harvard).

Von Eckardt, Wolf
  1964 *The Challenge of Megalopolis* (New York: Macmillan).
  1978 *Back to the Drawing Board: Planning Livable Cities* (New York: Simon & Schuster).

Wade, Richard C.
  1968 "The transformation of slavery in the cities." Sylvia F. Fava, ed., pp. 334–50. *Urbanism in World Perspective* (New York: Thomas Y. Crowell).

Wallace, Samuel E.
  1964 *Skid Row and Its Inhabitants* (New York: Bureau of Applied Social Research, Columbia University).

1968   *Skid Row as a Way of Life* (Totowa: Bedminster, 1965; and New York: Harper & Row, 1968).

Wallace, Samuel E., and Canals, Jose
1963   "Aspectos socio-juridicos de un estudio de actos de violencia." *Revista de Ciencias Sociales* 7:2:103–13.

Wallace, Samuel E., and Caplow, Theodore
1961   "Ecologia social de la zona de San Juan." *Revista de Ciencias Sociales* 5:3:327–38.

Wallace, Samuel E., and Harrison, Jerry N.
1974   *Reading Guide to the Urban Environment* (Knoxville, Tenn.: Slide Tape Research System).

Wallace, Samuel E.; Harrison, Jerry N.; and Nacarano, Joan
1974   *Little Italy: The Symbolic Ecology of an Ethnic Enclave* (Knoxville, Tenn.: Slide Tape Research System).

Wallin, Paul
1953   "A gutman scale for measuring women's neighborliness." *American Journal of Sociology* 59:241–46.

Ward, David
1971   "The emergence of central immigrant ghettoes in American cities: 1840–1920." Larry S. Bourne, ed., pp. 291–99. *The Internal Structure of the City* (New York: Oxford University Press).

Warner, Sam Bass, Jr.
1962   *Streetcar Suburbs* (Cambridge, Mass.: Harvard University Press).

Warren, Carol A. B.
1974   *Identity and Community in the Gay World* (New York: John Wiley & Sons).

Warren, Donald I.
1969   "Neighborhood structure and riot behavior in Detroit: Some exploratory findings." *Social Problems* 16:2(Spring) 464–84.
1975   *Black Neighborhoods* (Ann Arbor: University of Michigan Press).
1976   "The functional diversity of urban neighbrhoods." *Urban Affairs Quarterly* 12(October) 88–98.

Warren, Robert
1966   *Government in Metropolitan Regions* (Davis: University of California Press).

Warren, Roland L.
1973   *Perspectives on the American Community*. 2d ed. (Chicago: Rand McNally).

Webber, Melvin M.
1968   "The post-city age." *Daedalus* 97:4:1093–99.
1971   "The post-city age." Larry S. Bourne, ed., pp. 496–501. *Internal Structure of the City* (New York: Oxford).

Weber, Adna
1963   *The Growth of Cities in the Nineteenth Century* (Ithaca, N.Y.: Cornell University Press; originally published in 1899).

Weber, Max
>   1958   *The City*. Trans. and ed. by Don Martindale and Gertrud Neuwirth. (Glencoe, Ill.: Free Press.)
>   1958a   *The Protestant Ethic and the Spirit of Capitalism*. Trans. by Talcott Parsons. (New York: Schribners.)
>   1974   *West Side Highway Project Draft Environmental Impact Statement Section 4(f) Re: Parks and Open Space* (New York: State Department of Transportation, March 15).

Wellman, Barry
>   1972   "Who needs neighborhoods?" Pp. 94–100. *The City: Attacking Modern Myths* (Toronto: McClelland & Stewart).

White, Morton, and White, Lucia
>   1962   *The Intellectual Versus the City* (Cambridge, Mass.: Harvard University Press and M.I.T. Press).

Whitehill, Walter Muir
>   1968   *Boston: A Topographical History* (Cambridge, Mass.: Harvard University Press).

Whyte, William H.
>   1974   "The best street life in the world: Why schmiozing, smooching, noshing, ogling are getting better all the time." *New York Magazine* (July 15):27–33.

Wilkinson, Kenneth P.
>   1970   "The community as a social field." *Social Forces* 48(March) 311–22.

Williams, Robin, Jr.
>   1964   *Strangers Next Door: Ethnic Relations in American Communities* (Englewood Cliffs, N.J.: Prentice-Hall).
>   1978   *Conflict and Accommodation* (Minneapolis: University of Minnesota Press).

Wilhelm, Sidney
>   1962   *Urban Zoning and Land Use Theory* (New York: Free Press).
>   1964   "The concept of the 'Ecological Complex': A critique." *American Journal of Economics and Sociology* 23:241–48.

Wilner, Daniel M.
>   1962   *The Housing Environment and Family Life* (Baltimore, Md.: Johns Hopkins University Press).

Wilner, Daniel M., and Walkley, Rosabelle Price
>   1963   "Effects of housing on health and performance." Leonard J. Duhl, ed., pp. 215–28. *The Urban Condition* (New York: Basic Books).

Winsborough, Hal H.
>   1963   "An ecological approach to the theory of suburbanization." *American Journal of Sociology* 68:5(March) 565–71.

Wirth, Louis
>   1928   *The Ghetto* (Chicago: University of Chicago Press).
>   1938   "Urbanism as a way of life." *American Journal of Sociology* 44(July) 3–24.
>   1964   "The ghetto." Albert J. Reiss, Jr., ed., pp. 84–98. *On Cities and Social Life* (Chicago: University of Chicago Press).

Wohl, Richard R., and Strauss, Anselm L.
  1958 "Symbolic representation and the urban milieu." *American Journal of Sociology* 63(May) 523–32.

Wolf, Brad
  1974 "Report on the users of the New York Botanical Gardens." Queens, New York City, Queens College, CUNY; unpublished paper.

Wolf, Eleanor P.
  1968 "The tipping in racially changing neighborhoods." Bernard J. Frieden and Robert Morris, eds., pp. 148–55. *Urban Planning and Social Policy* (New York: Basic Books).

Wood, A. A.
  1968 "The pedestrianization of traditional central areas." David Lewis, ed., pp. 182–93. *Urban Structure* (New York: Wiley-Interscience).

Wood, Arthur Evans
  1955 *Hamtramck—Then and Now: A Sociological Study of a Polish American Community* (New York: Bookman Associates).

Woodrow, Karen; Hastings, Donald W.; and Tu, Edward J.
  1978 "Rural-urban patterns of marriage, divorce and mortality: Tennessee, 1970." *Rural Sociology* (Spring) 70–86.

Yablonsky, Lewis
  1968 *The Hippie Trip* (New York: Bobbs-Merrill, Pegasus).

Zablocki, Benjamin
  1971 *The Joyful Community* (New York: Penguin Books).

Zinsser, Hans
  1935 *Rats, Lice & History* (Boston: Little, Brown).

Zorbaugh, Harvey W.
  1926 "The natural areas of the city." *Publications of the American Sociological Society* 20:188–97.

INDEX

*This book has been set VIP in 10 and 9 point
Times Roman, leaded 2 points. Part numbers and
titles are 30 and 24 point Serif Gothic Bold. Chapter numbers and titles are 18 point Serif Gothic
Bold. The size of the type page is 27 by 46½ picas.*